# RESEARCH HANDBOOK ON TRANSNATIONAL CORPORATIONS

# RESEARCH HANDBOOKS ON GLOBALISATION AND THE LAW

*Elgar Research Handbooks* are original reference works designed to provide a broad overview of research in a given field, while at the same time creating a forum for more challenging, critical examination of complex and often under-explored issues within that field.

Chapters by international contributors are specially commissioned by the editors, who carefully balance breadth and depth. Often widely cited, they present expert scholarly analysis and offer a vital reference point for advanced research. Taken as a whole they achieve a wide-ranging picture of the state-of-the-art.

The volumes in this series examine the legal dimensions of issues arising out of an increasingly globalized world. Edited by leading scholars in their respective fields, they explore notions of global justice and global development along with the complexities of international institutions and private actors operating on a global stage. Taking as their common thread the impact of globalisation on the world in which we live, they are unrivaled in their blend of critical, substantive analysis and synthesis of contemporary research.

Each *Handbook* stands alone as an invaluable source of reference for all scholars of globalisation. Whether used as an information resource on key topics or as a platform for advanced study, volumes in this series will become definitive scholarly reference works in the field.

Titles in this series include:

Research Handbook on Global Justice and International Economic Law
*Edited by John Linarelli*

Handbook on the Law of Cultural Heritage and International Trade
*Edited by James A. R. Nafziger and Robert Kirkwood Paterson*

Research Handbook on Political Economy and Law
*Edited by Ugo Mattei and John Haskell*

Research Handbook on Global Administrative Law
*Edited by Sabino Cassese*

Research Handbook on Transnational Corporations
*Edited by Alice de Jonge and Roman Tomasic*

# Research Handbook on Transnational Corporations

*Edited by*

## Alice de Jonge

*Department of Business Law and Taxation, Monash Business School, Monash University, Australia*

## Roman Tomasic

*School of Law and Business School, University of South Australia and Visiting Professor of Company Law at the Durham Law School, UK*

RESEARCH HANDBOOKS ON GLOBALISATION AND THE LAW

Edward Elgar
PUBLISHING

Cheltenham, UK • Northampton, MA, USA

Published by
Edward Elgar Publishing Limited
The Lypiatts
15 Lansdown Road
Cheltenham
Glos GL50 2JA
UK

Edward Elgar Publishing, Inc.
William Pratt House
9 Dewey Court
Northampton
Massachusetts 01060
USA


A catalogue record for this book
is available from the British Library

Library of Congress Control Number: 2016949949


This book is available electronically in the **Elgar**online
Law subject collection
DOI 10.4337/9781783476916

ISBN 978 1 78347 690 9 (cased)
ISBN 978 1 78347 691 6 (eBook)

Typeset by Servis Filmsetting Ltd, Stockport, Cheshire
Printed and bound in Great Britain by TJ International Ltd, Padstow

# Contents

PART II   TNC BEHAVIOR AND STRATEGY IN THE 21ST
CENTURY: INDUSTRY CASE STUDIES

PART III   TNC BEHAVIOUR AND STRATEGY IN THE
21ST CENTURY: COUNTRY CASE STUDIES

# Contributors

**Rachel J. Anderson** is a Professor of Law at the University of Nevada, Las Vegas, William S. Boyd School of Law. Her research focuses on international business, regulation, policy and human rights. Professor Anderson earned her Juris Doctor at the University of California, Berkeley, her MA (International Policy Studies) from Stanford University and her Zwischenpruefung (British and American Studies) from the Humboldt University of Berlin. She also worked on international development projects and business transactions at MVV Consulting GmbH in Berlin, Germany, and Skadden, Arps, Slate, Meagher & Flom (UK) LLP, respectively. Professor Anderson has published a book chapter on international trade and articles in reputed general and specialty law journals, as well as publications for legal practitioners. Her work is widely cited in law reviews, books and other publications. Professor Anderson is a Director of the American Society of Comparative Law, and a member of the Advisory Board of the Guinn Center for Policy Priorities and the investment committee of Nevada's evergreen venture capital program. She is the recipient of numerous honors and awards, including from several members of the US Congress, *Lawyers of Color Magazine*, *The National Jurist*, *pre-Law Magazine*, the Urban Chamber of Commerce, the Progressive Leadership Alliance of Nevada and the National Bar Association's Law Professors Division.

**Megan Bowman** is currently a Lecturer in the Dickson Poon School of Law at King's College London. She is also a climate finance consultant and qualified barrister and solicitor of the High Court of Australia and Supreme Court of Victoria with a PhD from the Australian National University, an LLM from McGill University, and a double degree in Arts and Law (with Honours) from Monash University. Dr. Bowman's research focuses on the intersections between commercial, financial and environmental regulation with emphasis on corporate actors in transnational contexts. She has presented on this work at Tsinghua and Cambridge Universities and also at Stanford and Harvard Law Schools. Her first book, *Banking on Climate Change: How Finance Actors and Transnational Regulatory Regimes Are Responding* (Wolters Kluwer, 2015), combines empirical and theoretical insights to inform best practice in regulating socially responsible finance and investment across key market economies and China. Dr. Bowman's teaching portfolios have included Commercial

Law, Finance for International Trade, Environmental Law, and Public International Law. She has taught previously in Australia and Canada and received a Vice Chancellor's Teaching Excellence Award.

**Larry Catá Backer** is the W. Richard and Mary Eshelman Faculty Scholar and Professor of Law and International Affairs at the Pennsylvania State University (BA Brandeis University; MPP Harvard University Kennedy School of Government; JD Columbia University). His research focuses on governance-related issues of globalization and the constitutional theories of public and private governance, with a focus on multinational corporations, production chains and the institutional frameworks where public and private law systems converge. He teaches courses in constitutional law, corporate law (including multinational corporations), transnational law, and international organizations. His publications include *Lawyers Making Meaning: The Semiotics of Law in Legal Education* (Springer, 2013), and *Signs in Law: A Source Book* (Springer, 2014) (both with Jan Broekman), casebooks, *Comparative Corporate Law* (Carolina Academic Press, 2002) and *Law and Religion: Cases, Materials and Readings* (West, 2015, with Frank S. Ravitch), an edited collection of essays, *Harmonizing Law in an Era of Globalization* (Carolina Academic Press, 2007) and a number of articles and contributions to published collections of essays. Shorter essays on various aspects of globalization and governance appear on his essay site, 'Law at the End of the Day', http://lcbackerblog.blogspot.com. His publications and other work are available on his personal website: http://www.backerinlaw.com/Site/ or through the Social Science Research Network: http://ssrn.com/author=259226.

**Anna Chou** earned a BA in Ethics, Economics, and Politics from Rutgers University in New Brunswick, New Jersey. This individualized course of study was designed with an emphasis on examining pressing issues with different perspectives, encouraging a holistic evaluation and effective decision-making relevant to the current world. Her research interests focus on corporate social responsibility, especially as related to the food industry, access and policy. Currently, she is a management consultant, working with health industry players in operations strategy and improvement. Originally from New Jersey, Anna now resides in southern California.

**Alice de Jonge** is a Senior Lecturer in law at Monash Business School, Monash University. Her post-graduate qualifications include an SJD and a Graduate Diploma in Asian Law from the University of Melbourne Law School, and a post-graduate certificate from Fudan University, Shanghai, China. She is the author of three books, including *Transnational Corporations and International Law: Accountability in the Global Business*

*Environment* (Edward Elgar, 2011), as well as various book chapters and journal articles. Alice lectures in the post-graduate subjects international law and policy and comparative Asian business law, and has taught in Singapore, South Africa and China.

**George Gilligan** is a Senior Research Fellow in the Centre for Corporate Law and Securities Regulation at the Melbourne Law School at the University of Melbourne. His post-graduate qualifications include a PhD and MPhil from the University of Cambridge and an MA from La Trobe University. He has taught at the University of Cambridge, Exeter University and Middlesex University in the United Kingdom, and La Trobe University, the University of Melbourne and Monash University in Australia. His research interests centre on: governance and regulatory theory and practice, especially in relation to the financial sector; white-collar crime; organized crime and corruption. He has published extensively in these areas and conducted numerous field research projects (which have included commissions from government agencies as well as competitive research grants), examining the praxis of regulation, resulting in numerous appearances as an expert witness before parliamentary committees.

**Deborah Gleeson** holds a Bachelor of Applied Science, a Graduate Diploma in Health Promotion, a Master of Public Health and a PhD in Health Policy. She is a Lecturer in Public Health in La Trobe University's School of Psychology and Public Health and an Associate of La Trobe University's Centre for Health Law and Society. Her primary research interest centres on the intersection between trade policy and public health. She convenes the Political Economy of Health Special Interest Group of the Public Health Association of Australia (PHAA) and represents PHAA on matters related to trade agreements. Her publications include over 20 peer-reviewed articles on trade and health, invited editorials in the *Medical Journal of Australia* and the *New Zealand Medical Journal*, many submissions to government departments and inquiries and over 30 opinion pieces published in Australian and international media outlets. A frequent media commentator, she has been interviewed on ABC Radio and quoted in the *New York Times*, the *Sydney Morning Herald* and the *Guardian*. She received a President's Award 2015 from the Public Health Association of Australia for public health leadership, engagement and commitment on the impact of international trade issues on health.

**Maria Alejandra Gonzalez-Perez** (PhD, MBS, Psy) is Full Professor of Management at Universidad EAFIT (Colombia). Maria Alejandra is the Vice-President of the Academy of International Business (AIB) (from 2015 until 2018), coordinator of the Colombian universities in the virtual institute of the United Nations Conference for Trade and Development (UNCTAD) (2009–present), and Editor-in-Chief of the business journal *AD-minister*. Prof. Gonzalez-Perez is the past Head of the Department of International Business (2009–2013) and former Director of the International Studies Research Group (2008–2013) at Universidad EAFIT (Colombia). Prior to her positions in Colombia, she worked as a researcher in various organisations such as the Centre for Innovation and Structural Change (CISC), Irish Chambers of Commerce, and the Economics of Social Policy Research Unit (ESPRU) in Ireland.

**Virginia Harper Ho** is a Professor of Law at the University of Kansas School of Law. Her recent scholarship has focused on shareholder activism, the boundaries and governance of transnational corporations and the intersections of corporate governance, legal compliance and sustainability in mainland China and the United States. Her work has been published by the *Journal of Corporation Law*, by leading international and comparative law journals, and by the University of California-Berkeley's Institute for East Asian Studies, among others. She received her JD, *cum laude*, from Harvard Law School and spent nearly a decade representing global companies in cross-border transactions and related compliance matters.

**Jodie A. Kirshner** is a research professor at New York University. Previously, she served as a technical advisor to the Bank for International Settlements and a visiting scholar and lecturer at Columbia Law School, teaching international bankruptcy law. Until 2014, she was on the law faculty at Cambridge University and also served as the deputy director of the Cambridge LLM program, the deputy director of the Cambridge Centre for Corporate and Commercial Law, and as a fellow of Peterhouse College, Cambridge. She is a senior research associate of the Cambridge Centre for Business Research, a fellow of the Columbia Center for Law and Economics, the Salzburg Global Seminar, and the Center for Law Economics and Finance in Washington, and has been a term member of the Council on Foreign Relations. Kirshner received her undergraduate degree from Harvard University, graduate degrees in law and in journalism from Columbia University, and studied in the UK as a Fulbright Scholar. Her book on international corporate bankruptcy law will be published by the University of Chicago Press in 2016.

**Diane Kraal** is a Senior Lecturer in tax law at the Monash Business School, Monash University, Australia. Her research areas include natural resource taxation.

Diane has worked in the financial services sector as the taxation manager with Australia's largest administrator of industry superannuation funds. Diane has also worked in the minerals resource sector with Conzinc Rio Tinto, Australia (CRA) Ltd.

In 2014 the National Research Institute of Papua New Guinea appointed Dr Kraal and Dr Craig Emerson (former Federal Minister with the Rudd and Gillard governments) to work on a petroleum and mining tax reform project, 'Analysis of Taxation Policies and Reforms Affecting Individuals and Businesses in PNG'. Tax reform in Papua New Guinea has the support of the International Monetary Fund (IMF). In 2015 Diane received a grant from the Government of Papua New Guinea to continue work on tax reform in the PNG mining sector, and the recommendations were included in the PNG Tax Review Committee's Final Report to Government. In 2015 Diane was awarded a Visiting Fellowship to the Australian National University to research about the impact of resource commodity prices on tax revenues. In 2016 Diane is visiting the extractive industry research team at the IMF, Washington DC.

**Liam Leonard** (BA; M Phil; PhD) is a researcher and international academic consultant based in University of California, Los Angeles USA. He is also an Adjunct Professor at West Virginia University, USA. Previously, Liam has been Chair of the Criminology Association of Ireland and a former Member Secretary and President of the Sociology Association of Ireland. He lectures in Sociology and Criminology.

Dr. Leonard was the senior academic and primary instructor on the award-winning Custodial Care Program, which trained over 1,000 recruits in a humane approach to prison and corrections for the Irish Prison Service. The author/editor of over 20 books and numerous journal articles, he is Senior Editor of the Ecopolitics Books Series, the Advances in Sustainability and Environmental Justice Book Series (both with Emerald UK) and founding editor of the *CRIMSOC Journal of Social Criminology*. Dr. Leonard has edited the 2011 Irish issue of the *Prison Journal*, as well as special issues of *Environmental Politics* and the *Irish Journal of Sociology*. Dr. Leonard was awarded the Sage Publishing Research Excellence Award in New York as well as the NAIRTL Research and Teaching Award in 2012, and he has over 12 years' experience as an academic and lecturer in the National University of Ireland and the Irish Institute of Technology sectors. He has given papers at the European Sociology Association, European Criminology Association, the Academy of Criminal Justice Sciences, the European Group for Crime and Deviance and the Irish Sociology and Irish Criminology Conferences. Dr. Leonard sits on the editorial boards of several academic journals, including the *Prison Journal* and the *Journal of Criminal Psychology*.

**Ruth Lopert** (BMed, MMedSc, FAFPHM) is a public health physician and pharmacoeconomist, and is currently an adjunct professor in the

Department of Health Policy and Management in the Milken Institute School of Public Health, and Adjunct Professor of Clinical Research and Leadership in the School of Medicine and Health Sciences at George Washington University in Washington DC. A 2006–2007 Commonwealth Fund Harkness Fellow, she was the Principal Medical Adviser in the Australian drug regulatory agency, the Therapeutic Goods Administration (TGA) from 2008 to 2011, and in 2005–2006 established and directed the Pharmaceutical Policy Taskforce in the federal Department of Health. In 2003–2004 she was primary negotiator of the pharmaceutical provisions of the Australia–US Free Trade Agreement. She has worked as a consultant in pharmaceutical policy in several low- and middle-income countries for the World Bank and NICE-International and is the author of over 40 peer-reviewed journal articles and book chapters, in major journals such as the *Lancet, Health Policy, Health Affairs* and *Milbank Quarterly.* Her research interests include comparative health policy; pharmaceutical policy and pricing; health technology assessment (HTA); therapeutics regulation; intellectual property (IP); and issues at the intersections of trade, IP, and access to care.

**Erik Monasterio** (MB ChB, FRANZCP) is a Consultant in Forensic Psychiatry and Clinical Director, with the Canterbury District Health Board's Regional Forensic Service, and Senior Clinical Lecturer in psychological medicine, University of Otago, Christchurch. Dr Monasterio has research interests and publications in personality characteristics, accidents and physiologic stress responses of extreme athletes, off-label use of antipsychotic medications, impact of trade agreements on access and equity in healthcare and health policy. He is also a founding member of Doctors for the Protection of Health in Trade Agreements ('Drs for Healthy Trade'), a New Zealand network of doctors and other health professionals committed to ensuring that trade agreements do not compromise effective and equitable health policy.

**Pat Neuwelt** (PhD, FNZCPHM, FRNZCGP) is a Senior Lecturer in public health and health systems at the University of Auckland. Pat's clinical experience includes general practice (in both Canada and New Zealand), palliative care and public health medicine. Her research focuses on addressing inequities in access to primary care in New Zealand and, more recently, on the health implications of international trade agreements. She was a co-author on the Feb/15 'international call' on the TPPA and health in *The Lancet* and has published on the potential implications of the TPPA for access to medicines. She is a founding member of Doctors for the Protection of Health in Trade Agreements ('Drs for Healthy Trade'), a New Zealand network of doctors and other health professionals committed to ensuring that trade agreements do not compromise effective and equitable health policy. She is a co-author of the Policy on Trade and Health of the Public Health Association of New Zealand.

**Justin O'Brien** is a specialist in the dynamics of financial regulation, with particular reference to capital market governance. He is the author of a trilogy of books on regulatory politics: *Wall Street on Trial* (2003), *Redesigning Financial Regulation* (2007) and *Engineering a Financial Bloodbath* (2009). He has recently published a political biography of the founder of capital market regulation in the United States, *The Triumph, Tragedy and Lost Legacy of James M. Landis: A Life on Fire* (2014). Professor O'Brien holds visiting positions at the Edmond J. Safra Center for Ethics at Harvard University and UNSW Law in Sydney. He is a former recipient of the prestigious Australian Research Council Future Fellowship, a four-year research only position.

**Roman Tomasic** is a Professor of Law at the University of South Australia Business School and a Visiting Professor of Company Law at the Durham Law School in the UK. He holds doctorates in law and in sociology and has published widely in the areas of corporate law and regulation. He also has a scholarly interest in comparative corporate law and in the use of empirical methods in the study of large corporate groups and corporate law. In recent times, he has written on the limits of legal regulation of international financial markets. He has undertaken major empirical studies of listed companies in Australia and China and is currently looking at the globalisation of Chinese companies and the governance of Chinese companies in Australia.

**Andreas Rühmkorf** is a Lecturer in Commercial Law at the University of Sheffield (UK). He completed his Law Degree at the Westfälische Wilhelms-Universität in Münster, Germany and obtained his PhD Degree in Law from the University of Sheffield in 2013. Andreas sat for his Second State Exam in law at North Rhine Westphalia, Germany, and was admitted to practice as a German lawyer (*Rechtsanwalt*) in 2007.

Andreas' research focuses on the legal aspects of Corporate Social Responsibility (CSR), responsible supply chains as well as corporate governance and company law. At the University of Sheffield, Andreas teaches both at undergraduate (LLB) and postgraduate (LLM) level in, *inter alia*, the areas of corporate law, comparative corporate governance, E-Commerce law and internet privacy. He has also been a visiting lecturer in company law at the Westfälische Wilhelms-Universität, Münster since 2012.

Andreas is the author of the monograph *Corporate Social Responsibility, Private Law and Global Supply Chains*, published by Edward Elgar

Publishing in June 2015. He has published several articles and chapters in his areas of research interest and he has also been a contributing editor of the loose-leaf commentary D. McClean et al. (eds), Shawcross and Beaumont on Air Law (LexisNexis), an international commentary on aviation law which is updated twice a year, since 2013.

**Manuel Wörsdörfer** is currently a research fellow (*Privatdozent*) at the Cluster of Excellence 'The Formation of Normative Orders' and associate member of the Centre for Business Ethics at Goethe University, Frankfurt. He has also been working as a visiting research fellow at Beijing University, Carnegie Mellon University, the University of Pittsburgh, the University of Toronto and York University.

Manuel's research interests in business ethics include business and human rights, political CSR, corporate citizenship and governance, multi-stakeholder CSR-initiatives and sustainable finance. In his habilitation thesis, he analyzed the Equator Principles, a voluntary and soft law CSR-initiative in the project finance sector, from a business and human rights perspective.

Most of Manuel's research has been presented at prestigious international conferences, such as the annual conferences of the Australasian Business Ethics Network, the European Business Ethics Network and the Society for Business Ethics, and has been published in peer-reviewed journals, such as *Business and Society Review*, *European Journal of the History of Economic Thought*, *Journal of Business Ethics Education*, *Journal of the History of Economic Thought*, *OEconomia*, *Philosophy of Management*, *Transnational Legal Theory* and *Journal for Business, Economics and Ethics*.

# Table of cases

# Table of legislation

## AGREEMENTS, CONVENTIONS AND TREATIES

## LEGISLATION

# DOCUMENTS FROM INTERNATIONAL ORGANISATIONS AND INSTITUTIONS

# Introduction: understanding transnational corporations in the 21st century
*Alice de Jonge and Roman Tomasic*

The past few decades have seen an acceleration in the globalisation of the international economy. This process has been assisted by advances in communications technology and reductions in transportation costs for globally oriented actors. Many actors have played a part in this process, among which Transnational Corporations (TNCs) have come to reflect the changes associated with globalisation more than ever before in view of their growing power, size and number.

This deepening global process has not developed without some perceived problems calling for global solutions. These include global climate change, population movements and environmental disasters. A further problem that affects TNCs relates to the regulation of the global economy and the fashioning of appropriate rules and institutions to further this goal. In an era of legal or regulatory pluralism, we have seen many new norms and institutions emerge to deal with 'market failures'.

Global corporations operate both within and between nation states. This can lead to major regulatory problems, as was seen during and following the Global Financial Crisis when large international financial institutions, such as Lehman Brothers, collapsed; creating problems for national legal systems. As Mervyn King, the former governor of the Bank of England, reminded us, many large corporate groups, such as global banks, are 'global in life, but national in death' as the world searched for appropriate insolvency and corporate rescue mechanisms. Creating and maintaining regulatory structures and rules to deal with the problems created by TNC remains a major challenge.

In this book, global corporate concerns are called 'Transnational Corporations' because their operations are not only *multi*-national – spanning and impacting on *multiple* states – but also affect the *relations between* and across those states, as well as impacting on global phenomena *transcending* state boundaries.

The lives of 21st century citizens are often more influenced by the activities of, and decisions made by, TNCs than they are by national governments. Yet TNCs are not exposed to the same democratic controls that seek to align governments with the wishes of national populations.

This is hardly surprising as corporations are artificial legal persons where control lies in the hands of narrower groups of persons. Despite the advances in accounting practices and market disclosure requirements imposed upon listed companies, it is also the case that TNC decision-making is rarely exposed to the same standards of transparency and public scrutiny that often apply to government decision-making.

There is therefore a greater need than ever before to understand the nature of the modern TNC, its operations and its influence; and to understand the different ways in which TNCs are being rendered more responsive. The ultimate question, of course, is the extent to which, when dealing with global problems, TNCs can be relied upon to solve problems, rather than merely being seen as part of the problem. Understanding TNCs in their interactions with other global actors on the global stage is therefore an important aim for 21st century researchers, and one which this volume is aimed at facilitating.

In line with these aims, the first and longest Part of this volume features seven chapters exploring global aspects of the TNC. Chapter 1 begins by outlining the changing nature of the TNC – including how globalisation has changed the traditional corporation and how the TNC has helped to shape patterns of globalisation. In Chapter 2, Rachel Anderson provides a clear-headed analysis of the different theoretical approaches that have been developed by scholars writing about the modern TNC. It is an important chapter that provides a systematic theoretical framework for understanding other chapters in this volume.

In Chapter 3, Larry Catá Backer takes us back again to the inevitably political nature of the modern TNC. The fact that TNCs are forced to negotiate with national, and often sub-national, governments within the local territory of the relevant host state is only one part of this inevitability. The ways in which TNCs are politically active in international forums is another part. At both national and international levels, TNCs are forced to encounter, and engage with, other political actors – most notably the NGOs that seek to influence national and international policy agendas but also including international organisations, including UN, multinational and regional organisations such as the various development banks, trade-agreement groupings, aid agencies and regional organisations. Catá Backer's chapter provides a sophisticated understanding of the evolving ecologies of relationship among TNCs, governments, other political actors and civil society groups. He paints a complex picture of overlapping relationships of shared and conflicting interests. He also takes an important step forward towards developing a new meta-theory for future analyses of these relationships.

Chapters 4 and 5 provide case studies of two global regulatory systems formed through the coming together of TNCs, governments, international organisations and NGOs. Maria Alejandra Gonzalez-Perez and Liam Leonard examine the history, evolution and current operation of the Global Compact's governance structures – beginning as an initiative launched by UN Secretary-General Kofi Annan in 2000. Manuel Wörsdörfer then takes us into the world of an important private sector initiative – the finance industry's Equator Principles for project financing. In both cases, UN and other multinational organisations have played an important part in influencing the eventual shape of governance structures, and in both cases the involvement of the private sector was – and remains – crucial to its viability and successful operation.

When is a TNC not a TNC? When it's a global supply chain? For there are now many different types of global supply chains – some clearly identifiable as corporate groups, others less easily identified with a single corporate name. In his 1988 book *The Rise of the Network Society*, Manuel Castels pointed to the rise of the network society and the network enterprise. Since that time, the complexity of global supply chain arrangements has only increased. In this context, the chapters by Jodie Kirshner and Andreas Rühmkorf examining different forms of corporate globalisation are both timely and relevant in the 21st century. Kirshner examines both the motives and the means of corporate global expansion. She notes that limited liability has made expansion through separately incorporated subsidiaries attractive for companies, such that many have developed into vast corporate groups with multiple layers of subsidiaries under the control of holding companies. Such structures, however, form only part, albeit an important part, of the sophisticated global sourcing strategies developed by TNCs, usually aimed at minimising production costs. The many different types of relationships that now exist between TNCs and their many foreign suppliers present major challenges for attributing accountability, responsibility and liability when human rights violations occur. It is these challenges, and the various strategies designed to address them, that form the focus of Rühmkorf's chapter on global supply chains.

Part II of this volume then takes the reader into the practical realities of the theoretical constructs outlined in Part I. In particular, it contains two detailed industry case studies examining the political and economic motivations of corporate decision-making and behaviour. The first of these explores strategies used by pharmaceutical industry TNCs and their industry associations to advance their economic interests through trade and investment agreements, with a particular focus on the proposed Trans Pacific Partnership (TPP) Agreement. As the implications of how TPP terms are implemented gradually become clearer, the chapter by Deborah Gleeson et al. provides valuable background material and insights for those seeking to safeguard equitable access to medicines for all.

In a somewhat more optimistic vein, Anna Chou's chapter examines initiatives in the consumer electronics industry aimed at building human rights due diligence into the minerals sourcing supply-chain. Case studies such as these serve to ignite a conversation and provoke further critical thinking. Chou's evaluation of the ways in which CSR theory has been applied in practice through Samsung's business strategy introduces readers to the tradeoffs involved in CSR strategies. It demonstrates that key values can conflict with each other, inviting readers to contemplate different facets of the decision-making and judgement process. Chou's chapter neatly illustrates the daily realities of the theoretical dilemmas discussed by Kirshner and Rühmkorf in Part I of this volume.

The country studies in Part III of this volume examine different aspects of the fluid and complex relationships formed between TNCs and nation states. China is, perhaps, the country where such relationships have been formed on the greatest scale, and with the greatest degree of fluidity and complexity. While there already exists an extensive literature examining the foreign TNC experience in its engagement with China as a host country, Megan Bowman et al. provide a new perspective on China and the modern TNC by tracing the history and current experience of Chinese outward direct investment using state-controlled TNCs as tools for achieving strategic purposes beyond short-term business profits.

The growing influence of Chinese TNCs in the global economy makes the question of accountability when it comes to state-controlled corporate vehicles of particular importance. Virginia Harper Ho's chapter on the role of disclosure obligations as a source of accountability for Chinese TNCs is therefore both timely and relevant. In particular, Harper Ho's exploration of the Chinese experience demonstrates the advantages of disclosure-based regimes as a source of accountability for TNCs even in institutional contexts that limit the effectiveness of external monitoring and traditional regulatory tools.

TNC accountability also features as a theme in Roman Tomasic's chapter examining negotiations between government and TNCs in relation to Australia's proposed minerals resource rent tax. That chapter returns to an emerging 21st century theme highlighted in de Jonge's chapter on the changing nature of the TNC – the desire and the need of governments worldwide to improve transparency, monitoring and accountability of TNCs in regards to their financial transactions and the fulfilment of taxation obligations and undertakings. Not surprisingly, TNCs have pushed back against state-led initiatives to combat tax base erosion and profit shifting, and this pushback has had – and continues to have – significant political and economic implications, both nationally and internationally. Tomasic's chapter brings to life the nature of the politics involved in state–TNC interactions when it comes to major policy changes affecting, or potentially affecting, TNC profits. The final chapter, by Diane Kraal, also illustrates starkly the real-life, long-term and historical implications of TNC power and influence when it comes to national policy decision-making. Important questions raised by both chapters include whether, when and how it is possible to ensure that TNCs involvement in national and international policy debates works to further the public good, rather than simply private gain.

# PART I

# THE GLOBAL CONTEXT

# 1. The evolving nature of the transnational corporation in the 21st century
### Alice de Jonge

## INTRODUCTION

Two key events held in 2015 revealed just how significantly the nature and role of corporations as members of global society have developed and changed over the past 70 years.[1] In particular, global business, in the form of the transnational corporation (TNC), is no longer seen as operating outside of the rules of international relations; now they are seen as forming an integral part of global society. The first event was the 20–21 May Business and Climate Summit.[2] Held 200 days before the UN Climate Change Conference in Paris (COP21), the Business and Climate Summit provided a unique forum for business and government leaders to engage in dialogue on the future of global climate change strategies. The second event was the Fourth Annual United Nations Forum on Business and Human Rights held in Geneva 16–18 November, during which a prominent guest list of stakeholder representatives from business, government and civil society engaged in dialogue on the future of human rights in a world where TNCs can have just as much, if not more, impact on human rights as governments can.

This chapter seeks, first, to examine briefly the history of the modern TNC since the founding of the United Nations in 1945, and, second, to chart the gradual evolution of regulatory norms aimed at shaping TNC behavior – norms which have taken shape at corporate level, at industry sector level, at national level and in international forums. Finally, this chapter highlights three recent developments with important implications for the future direction of the TNC in global society: (1) the drafting of a new instrument on TNCs and human rights, (2) the move towards taxation accountability for TNCs indicated in the Organisation for Economic Co-operation and Development (OECD)'s Base Erosion

---

[1]  For details, see: <http://www.ohchr.org/EN/Issues/Business/Forum/Pages/2015/forumBHR.aspx>. See also para. 12 of UN Human Rights Council 17/4 (UN Doc. A/HRC/RES/17/4 (6 July 2011).

[2]  For details, see: <http://www.businessclimatesummit.com/about/>.

and Profit Sharing (BEPS) initiatives, and (3) the 'carving out' of areas of national policy, including environment and health, to protect them from challenge under the Investor–State Dispute Settlement (ISDS) provisions of the recently agreed Trans-Pacific Partnership (TPP).

## THE EVOLVING NATURE OF THE TNC

As national economies have become more open under the guidance of International Monetary Fund (IMF) and World Bank-led trade and investment guidelines (the so-called Washington Consensus), so also have firms adapted their behavior to benefit from the new world order. It has become much easier to shift assets of all kinds (financial, human, physical) across national borders, and companies, along with their shareholders, have taken full advantage of this increased flexibility. Intra-firm trade has accelerated, and cross-border direct and portfolio investments have mushroomed.[3] In certain industrial sectors – including pharmaceuticals, semiconductors, telecommunications, accounting and financial services – cross-border mergers and acquisitions, strategic alliances and international redeployment of corporate resources suggest a qualitative change in the nature of transnational corporate behavior.[4]

The first notable feature of the qualitative change affecting corporations at the global level relates to sheer size and weight. Global corporations now have revenues that rival the entire GDP of many countries. Of the 100 largest economies, 50 are global corporations while 49 are countries. The combined sales of the world's top 200 corporations account for over a quarter of world GDP. Sheer economic weight means that TNCs can and do exert a great deal of influence over decision makers and over peoples' lives generally. This influence is compounded by close connections and communities of interest linking TNCs to each other.

A 2011 study conducted by complex systems theorists at the Swiss Federal Institute of Technology in Zurich combined the mathematics used to model natural systems with comprehensive corporate data to map ownership among the world's TNCs.[5] The authors' analysis of the

---

[3]   OECD, *Action Plan on Base Erosion and Profit Shifting* (OECD Publishing, 2013) <http://dx.doi.org/10.1787/9789264202719-en> Chapter 1.

[4]   (n 3).

[5]   Stephania Vitali, James B. Glattfelder and Stefano Battison, 'The network of Global Corporate Control' (2011) <http://arxiv.org/pdf/1107.5728.pdf>. For discussion, see Hugh Compston, 'The Network of Global Corporate Control: Implications for Public Policy' (2013) 15 *Business and Politics* 357.

relationships of control among 43,000 TNCs identified a relatively small group of companies, around 300, mainly banks and mutual funds, holding controlling interests in the majority of the world's corporate assets.

The Swiss Federal Institute study complements other recent studies which have also (though less comprehensively) examined changing patterns of corporate ownership in the United States and elsewhere. Armour and Gordon, for example, noted that ownership patterns in the United Kingdom and the United States have changed – and converged – quite dramatically over the past decades.[6] The US stock market, previously notable for its widely dispersed ownership pattern, in the 21st century has shifted so that institutional investors are now the dominant owners of US stocks. Similar change has occurred in the UK, but this time the change has been away from the cohesive, clubby domestic institutions of 1980s London towards a much more eclectic and international mix of passive funds, activist investors, private equity and sovereign wealth funds – very similar to, indeed often the same as, those which dominate the US market.[7] The number of TNCs from developing nations has also grown, and a large proportion of these are State-owned. The UNCTAD *World Investment Report 2014* noted that there were around 550 State-owned TNCs, from both developed and developing countries, in 2013, with more than 15,000 foreign affiliates and foreign assets of over $2 trillion. Although their number constituted less than 1 per cent of all TNCs, State-owned TNCs accounted for around 11 per cent of global FDI flows in 2013, making them FDI heavyweights compared with their privately owned counterparts,[8] though this trend has since declined.[9]

Along with changing patterns of ownership have come changing patterns of doing business. In particular, the formation of flexible and mobile global supply chains has now become a key aspect of success for some of the world's largest global corporations. What this has enabled, however, is the ability of firms to distance themselves from the least desirable, messier aspects of doing business – such as dealing with disappointed

---

[6]   John Armour, 'The Berle-Means Corporation in the 21st Century', public lecture delivered at the University of Leicester, 21 May 2010. John Armour and Jeffrey N. Gordon, 'The Berle-Means Corporation in the 21st Century' (2008) working paper <http://www.law.upenn.edu>.

[7]   Ibid, and see Gerald F. Davis, 'The Twilight of the Berle and Means Corporation' (2011) 34 *Seattle University Law Review* 1121.

[8]   UNCTAD, World Investment Report 2014: Investing in the SDGs: An action plan, ix, xvii–xvii, 20–21.

[9]   UNCTAD, World Investment Report 2015: Reforming international investment governance.

or injured farmers, miners, workers or local communities – while retaining within the global brand name the most desirable aspects of doing business. Greater flexibility of capital and business relationships has also enabled the separation of taxable income from the activities that generate it, to the advantage of corporate profits and to the overall disadvantage of national tax-funded spending.[10]

At national level there has been a rethink of what the growing power and influence of corporations means for local company law regimes. A series of major corporate collapses and financial crises in Asia (1997–1998) and globally (2001, 2008) has ensured that governments now take much more seriously the need for good corporate governance. Moreover, good corporate governance is now being defined much more broadly to include social and environmental aims.

### The Socially Responsible Corporation

Globalization has had a number of implications for legal reasoning about the nature of the corporation at national level. First, global economic integration has facilitated, and been facilitated by, increasingly harmonized understandings about the nature of the corporation as a shared enterprise. A number of scholars have examined differences between the Anglo–US understanding of the corporation as an owners' (shareholders') enterprise, on the one hand, and the continental European–German model of the corporation as a 'stakeholder' enterprise, on the other.[11] Over the past few decades, however, there has been a convergence of these two models, with company law in common law systems becoming more attuned to the interests of non-shareholder stakeholder groups, while company law in civil law systems has become more open to assertions of shareholder rights and powers.[12]

These shifts have occurred in a number of different ways. First, common law systems have increasingly become open to interpreting the directors' duty to make decisions 'in the best interests of the company' broadly to allow for stakeholder concerns. In 2006, the UK Companies Act was

---

[10]    OECD (n 3).

[11]    Louis W. Pauly and Simon Reich, 'National structures and multinational corporate behavior: Enduring differences in the age of globalization' (1997) 51(1) *International Organization* 1. See also Michael Spisto, 'Stakeholder interests in corporate governance: Is a new model of governance a change for the better for South Africa: Part 1' (2005) 18 *Australian Journal of Corporate Law* 129.

[12]    Christine A. Mallin (ed.), *Handbook on International Corporate Governance* (Edward Elgar, 2006).

specifically amended to provide that, when considering what would be 'most likely to promote the success of the company' a director should have regard, *inter alia*, to:

(a)　the likely consequences of any decision in the long term;
(b)　the interests of the company's employees,
(c)　the need to foster the company's business relationships with suppliers, customers and others,
(d)　the impact of the company's operations on the community and the environment,
(e)　the desirability of the company maintaining a reputation for high standards of business conduct.[13]

The UK government has also confirmed that pension fund trustees are not prohibited from considering social, environmental and ethical issues in their investment decisions, provided they act in the fund's best interests. Similarly, the Australian Parliamentary Joint Committee on Corporations and Financial Services has also stated that the Australian Corporations Act of 2001 'permits directors to have regard for the interests of stakeholders other than shareholders'.

As well as new understandings of what 'good' corporate governance encompasses, new understandings of what constitutes a 'viable' and 'worthwhile' enterprise are also emerging and being recognized as having legal validity. Social enterprises and Benefit or 'B' Corporations have now been recognized in a number of American, South American and European jurisdictions. In other cases, the law, as is not uncommon, still lags behind some of the more advanced and 'disruptive' technological innovations and enterprise forms, most noticeably in the case of the sharing economy. While these newer and more innovative enterprise formats remain, as yet, local variations on the traditional corporation, and so are beyond the scope of a volume on TNCs, their implications for the future of TNCs are unknown and could well be transformative.

Within civil law jurisdictions, including those in continental Europe, Japan and, to a lesser extent, mainland China, internationalization has

---

[13]　Companies Act (2006) UK, section 172. For discussion, see Igor Filatotchev, Howard Gospel and Gregory Jackson, 'Key Drivers of "Good" Corporate Governance and the Appropriateness of UK Policy Responses' (January 2007) Final Report to the Department of Trade and Industry <http://ssrn.com/abstract=961369>. See also Amita Chohan, 'Is Section 172 of the Companies Act 2006 Capable of Delivering for all Stakeholders?' <http://ssrn.com/abstract=2139528>.

been combined with deregulation and greater shareholder orientation –
and a shift away from network-oriented governance practices to more
market-oriented practices.[14] In the Netherlands, for example, an increasing number of foreign professional investors, an expanding shareholder
base and pressures exercised by institutional investors to limit the use
of anti-takeover devices, have all led to a shift in power in favor of
shareholders.[15] A new Law on Large Companies, which came into effect
on 1 January 2013, allows large Dutch companies to choose either a
one-tier or two-tier corporate structure, abolishing the previously compulsory requirement for all companies to have a supervisory board in
addition to a management board, and thereby rendering Dutch corporate structures much more familiar to Anglo–US investors.[16] Large
Dutch companies listed internationally in London or New York have
long been able to escape stakeholder requirements of Dutch law and
began to abolish stakeholder institutions such as the works council,
a civil-law institution designed to give employees a voice in company
decision-making.[17]

In addition to new thinking about corporate accountability, in many
nations there has also been a re-think of corporate liability, both criminal
and civil, associated with evolving notions of corporate responsibility.

### New Thinking about Corporate Criminal Liability

The concept of criminal liability and its application to corporations has
been a particular focus of reform, as states have examined whether – and
how – corporations can be held liable for wrongful conduct. Many countries,
including Brazil, Bulgaria, Luxembourg and the Slovak Republic, still do
not recognize any form of corporate criminal liability. Other countries,
including Germany, Greece, Hungary, Mexico and Sweden, while not
providing for criminal liability, nevertheless have in place regimes whereby

---

[14]    Jeffrey N. Gordon and Mark J. Roe (eds), *Convergence and Persistence in Corporate Governance* (Cambridge University Press, 2004). See also Cagman Palmer, 'Has the Worldwide Convergence on the Anglo-American Style Shareholder Model of Corporate Law Yet Been Assured?' (2011) 11 *Opticon1826* 1.

[15]    Steven Schult and Henk Arnold Sijnja, Allen & Overy LLP, Netherlands <http://globalcorporategovernance.com/n_europe/217_223.htm>.

[16]    Baker & McKenzie, 'Doing Business in the Netherlands 2015' <http://www.bakermckenzie.com/en/insight/publications/2015/03/doing-business-in-the-netherlands-2015/>.

[17]    R.H. van het Kaar, 'The Dutch System of Enterprise-level Participation', *SEEurope Country Report*, November 2004.

administrative penalties may be imposed on corporations for the criminal acts of certain employees.[18]

Traditionally, countries where criminal liability does extend to corporations have adopted a 'derivative' liability approach, whereby the corporation is held liable for the acts of one or more individual offenders. Under the vicarious liability or *respondeat superior* approach, used in US federal criminal law and in South Africa, the offenses of individual employees or agents are imputed to the corporation where the offense was committed in the course of their duties and intended, at least in part, to benefit the corporation. Another variant is the 'identification' model found in the United Kingdom and other British Commonwealth nations. Under this model, the offenses of individual senior officers and employees are imputed to the corporation on the basis that the state of mind of these senior officers and employees is that of the corporation. An expanded version of this approach, found primarily in continental Europe, retains the focus on the actions of high-level officers and employees, but also incorporates a duty of supervision, although whether that duty is owed by the corporation or its officers individually varies from country to country.[19]

More recently, experts have adopted a more sophisticated, alternative understanding of corporate criminal liability, focused on the acts or omissions of the corporation itself. Under this model, rather than the corporation being liable for the acts of individual offenders, a corporation is liable because its 'culture', policies, practices, management or other characteristics encouraged or permitted the commission of the offense. Australia is a prime example of this 'organizational liability' approach.[20]

**Extra-territorial and Transnational Accountability of TNCs**

As noted above, globalization has resulted in a shift from country-specific operating models to global models of corporate operation, based on matrix management and integrated supply chains. Governments have been forced to recognize the challenges these shifts represent to national legal systems. If corporations can simply evade the coverage of national laws by shifting

---

[18]   '"Corporate Culture" as a Basis for the Criminal Liability of Corporations' (February 2008) Report prepared by Allens Arthur Robinson for the United Nations Special Representative of the Secretary-General on Human Rights and Business.

[19]   (n 18).

[20]   (n 18). See Part 2.5 of the Australian Commonwealth Criminal Code. See also art 102(2) of the Swiss Penal Code.

the relevant component of their existence to a different jurisdiction,[21] then national governments must either seek to expand the coverage of national laws through extra-territorial legislation, and/or they must cooperate with other nations in creating transnational regulatory frameworks that operate without regard to national boundaries. Both of these things have occurred.

## Extra-territorial Civil Liability

The US Alien Tort Claims Act (1789) (ATCA) is possibly the most well-known example of extra-territorial legislation used by plaintiffs in claims against TNCs. The ATCA essentially gives US federal courts juris-diction over claims by aliens (foreign nationals) for torts committed in violation of the law of nations.[22]

By 2010, the ATCA had resulted in only three jury trials in cases involv-ing TNCs, resulting in two verdicts for the defendants,[23] plus one in favour of the plaintiffs.[24] But these were just part of a series of legal decisions raising expectations that the ATCA could provide an avenue through which foreign plaintiffs could seek relief against TNCs. Until September 2010, when, in a 2–1 decision, the US Court of Appeals for the Second Circuit held that corporations cannot be held liable for violations of (customary) international law, essentially on the grounds that international law does not recognize corporate liability.

Although the plaintiffs were granted review of the Second Circuit's decision,[25] the appeal was not successful. In 2013, the US Supreme Court

---

[21]   For discussion of examples, see Robin F. Hansen, 'Multinational Enterprise Pursuit of Minimized Liability: Law, International Business Theory and the Prestige Oil Spill' (2008) 26 *Berkeley Journal of International Law* 410 <http://scholarship.law.berkeley.edu/bjil/vol26/iss2/4>.

[22]   28 US Code para 1350, provides that 'The district courts shall have original jurisdiction of any civil action by an alien for a tort only, committed in violation of the law of nations or a treaty of the United States.'

[23]   *Bowoto v. Chevron* No. 3: 99-cv-02506 (ND Cal) 1 December 2008; *Estate of Rodriguez v. Drummond* No. cv-03-be-0575 (ND Ala) 26 July 2007.

[24]   *Nayeem Mehtab Chowdhury Chowdhury et al. v. WorldTel Bangladesh Holding Ltd and Amjad Hossain Khan* (2009) 1:08-cv-01659-bmc (US District Court for the Eastern District of New York, King County) August 2009. Another dispute involving Unocal and plaintiff claims, arising from Unocal pipeline opera-tions in Myanmar, was settled in March 2005 for an undisclosed sum.

[25]   *Kiobel v. Royal Dutch Petroleum Co.*, 132 S. Ct. 1738 (2012) (order directing re-argument on the question [w]hether and under what circumstances the Alien Tort Statute 28 U.S.C. 1350, allows courts to recognize a cause of action for viola-tions of the law of nations occurring within the territory of a sovereign other than the United States).

held that the presumption against extraterritoriality applies to claims under the ATCA and that nothing in the ATCA rebuts that presumption.[26] At least for the time being, therefore, the ATCA remains closed to claims against TNCs.

### International Enterprise Liability (Multinational Group Liability)

Within the context of civil liability, the international enterprise liability approach recognizes that when a parent and its subsidiaries are part of an economically integrated enterprise, there is, in effect, a single corporate actor – the multinational group. In doing so, this model of liability allows courts to overcome the fiction of the 'corporate veil' that deems each separately incorporated subsidiary as a separate legal person, so that liability is imposed on the parent firm for the conduct of the group. At least in common law jurisdictions, however, there are as yet only limited signs that the concept of international enterprise liability is being accepted.[27] In Canada, the international enterprise liability approach has been recognized in contaminated-sites legislation.[28] In the United States, the milestone cases of *Kiobel v. Royal Dutch Petroleum Co.* and *Daimler AG v. Bauman*[29] appear to have closed off many jurisdictional avenues for holding TNCs accountable. At the same time, however, they have given rise to new thinking, and new approaches to TNC liability for abuses committed by subsidiaries abroad are being explored – including approaches which seek to 'pierce the corporate veil' using arguments akin to international enterprise liability.[30] The fact remains, however, that the current legal landscape

---

[26]　*Kiobel v. Royal Dutch Petroleum Co.*, 569 US (2013). For discussion, see Anthony J. Colangelo, 'The Alien Tort Statute and the Law of Nations in Kiobel and Beyond' (2013) 44 *Georgetown Journal of International Law* 1329.

[27]　See Draft Code of Private International Law, Argentina (1985) 24 ILM 269, article 10. For discussion, see Sarah Joseph, *Corporations and Transnational Human Rights Litigation* (Hart Publishing, 2004) chapter 3.

[28]　'Submission to the Canadian Democracy and Corporate Accountability Commission' (17 June 2001) Aurora Institute <http://www.aurora.ca/docs/AccountabilityCommSubmission.pdf>.

[29]　134 S. Ct. 746 (2014). Daimler essentially held that a corporation is only 'at home' – and therefore subject to general jurisdiction – in, at most, two places: its state of incorporation and its principal place of business.

[30]　For discussion of the doctrinal pressures on alternative bases of jurisdiction to fill the void left by Daimler, see Tanya J. Monestier, 'Where is Home Depot "At Home"?: *Daimler v Bauman* and the End of Doing Business Jurisdiction' (2014) 66 *Hastings Law Journal* 233. See also Ma Ji, 'Multinational Enterprises' Liability for the Acts of their Offshore Subsidiaries: The Aftermath of *Kiobel* and *Daimler*' (2015) 23 *Michigan State International Law Review* 397.

which frames TNC activities facilitates strategies, including outsourcing and the operation of the corporate veil, which serve to minimize or exclude legal liability exposure in the event of claims.[31]

### Extra-territorial Legislation against Corruption, Money Laundering and Terrorist Financing

Possibly the most successful examples of an internationally coordinated network of legislation targeting TNCs (and individuals) acting illegally is in the (mostly) criminal law area of combating corruption, money-laundering and terrorist financing. The UN Convention Against Corruption (CAC) entered into force in December 2005 and obliges member nations to take anti-corruption measures in the public and private sectors, including measures against bribery of foreign officials, trading in influence and the concealment and laundering of the proceeds of crime.

The US Foreign Corrupt Practices Act (FCPA) of 1977 is the most widely enforced anti-corruption law. It was the first to introduce corporate liability and extraterritoriality for corruption offenses. Following the US precedent and the coming into force of the CAC, the UK Bribery Act of 2010 established company liability for corrupt acts committed by persons acting on behalf of the company anywhere in the world. The Act prohibits both bribery of public officials and business-to-business bribery. Article 13.3 of Russia's Federal Anti-Corruption Law No. 273 requires companies operating in the country to implement anti-corruption compliance programmes containing specific anti-corruption measures. By April 2015, there were 177 Parties to the UN CAC, making it one of the most widely ratified of all UN Conventions.[32] Its significance here is that the network of anti-corruption legislation and mutual obligations to assist in anti-corruption enforcement measures established under the convention is something that no TNC can ignore.

The 1988 United Nations Convention against the Illicit Traffic in Narcotic Drugs and Psychotropic Substances was the first international convention to criminalize money-laundering by organizations, including TNCs. In 2005, the scope of the money-laundering offense was widened by the UN Convention Against Transnational Organized Crime, which

---

[31]    For discussion, see Robin F. Hansen, 'Multinational Enterprise Pursuit of Minimized Liability: Law, International Business Theory and the Prestige Oil Spill' (2008) 26 *Berkeley Journal of International Law* 410.

[32]    For details, see <http://www.unodc.org/unodc/en/treaties/CAC/signatories. html>. For details of country-level legislation against corruption, see the Business Anti-Corruption Portal <http://www.business-anti-corruption.com/>.

states that the offense applies to the proceeds of all serious crime, not just drug trafficking. The International Convention for the Suppression of the Financing of Terrorism came into force in April 2002 and requires member states to take measures to prevent their financial systems from being used by persons planning or engaged in terrorist activities. The Convention is supported by UN Security Council Resolution 1373 and the United Nations Global Counter-Terrorism Strategy adopted in 2006.[33] Each of these international law initiatives has resulted in the passing of domestic criminal law legislation in jurisdictions around the world with extra-territorial impacts.

### The SRSG's 'Extraterritoriality Matrix'

In nearly all cases of litigation against TNCs with transnational cross-border implications, plaintiffs have faced one or more of a number of barriers to success. Most of these barriers are based on principles of private international law which establish limits to the exercise of state jurisdiction recognized by courts around the world. These principles include:

- The principle of *forum non conveniens*, which seeks to direct legal actions to the most appropriate forum;
- The principle of sovereign immunity;
- The act of state doctrine which prevents a court from inquiring into the legitimacy of a public act by a recognized foreign sovereign within that sovereign's own territory;
- The political act doctrine which, in a similar fashion to the act of state doctrine, prevents courts from investigating acts or omissions in foreign lands where doing so would have political implications;
- The doctrine of international comity, which has been defined as 'the recognition which one nation allows within its territory to the legislative, executive or judicial acts of another nation'.[34]

The importance ascribed in international relations to the concepts of sovereign equality, territorial integrity and non-interference (the idea that no state should be interfering, through the instrument of legislation, with the right of another state to determine the legal standards applying within its own boundaries) means that extra-territorial legislation is often controversial. The potential for diplomatic, legal, economic and other

---

[33]   Adopted on 8 September 2006 in the form of a Resolution (A/RES/60/288) and a Plan of Action.

[34]   *Hilton v. Guyot*, 159 US 113, 164 (1895).

tensions mitigates against the introduction of extraterritorial legislation and threatens its effectiveness when it is enacted. This is much less likely to occur where an international framework for such legislation, such as the CAC, exists. Recognizing the need for an agreed set of principles on the legitimacy, usefulness and acceptability of extra-territorial legislation, the Special Representative of the Secretary-General on Business and Human Rights (SRSG) has developed a matrix for assessment of extra-territorial initiatives.

In August 2010, the SRSG presented his third report on the implementation of his mandate to operationalize the 'Protect, Respect and Remedy' Framework for Business and Human Rights adopted by the UN Human Rights Council in 2008. Part III of the August 2010 report discusses the issue of extra-territoriality in the business and human rights context. While recognizing that extra-territorial legislation has often been controversial, the report also recognizes that global movements of goods, capital and people, and the global impacts of transnational corruption, climate change, bio-diversity depletion and terrorism have increased the potential for overlapping and/or conflicting jurisdictional claims. States have also recognized that effective regulation over local actors and events sometimes requires legislation that extends beyond national boundaries.

States have made use of domestic measures with extra-territorial implications to help influence the behavior of private actors abroad without the direct use of extra-territorial jurisdiction. Examples include asking locally incorporated parent companies to take certain steps in relation to the management of foreign subsidiaries. Other methods involve the use of reporting obligations, import or export controls, and taking steps to monitor and reduce risks associated with projects requiring export assistance. These measures can be highly influential in relation to private foreign conduct. They also often seem to attract less controversy than assertions of direct extra-territorial jurisdiction, presumably because they focus on acts or persons at home.

In addition, states are increasingly prepared to use direct extra-territorial jurisdiction in relation to criminal activity such as terrorism, money laundering, corruption and grave human-rights breaches. Often such legislation depends on the nationality of the perpetrator to justify the exercise of the enacting state's jurisdictions. In competition law and securities law, states have made more extensive jurisdictional claims over foreign companies and conduct, sometimes extending beyond 'territorial' or 'nationality' based claims to jurisdictional validity and based on previously contested legal theories (such as the 'passive personality' principle) or the universality principle when it comes to internationally recognized crimes.

The reactions of states – both to domestic measures with extra-territorial implications and to direct extra-territorial jurisdiction over private actors or activities abroad – depend greatly on regulatory motives and modes, and on

*Table 1.1    The SRSG's 'Extraterritoriality' Matrix*

|  | Public policies relating to TNCs | Regulation | Enforcement actions |
| --- | --- | --- | --- |
| Domestic measures with extra-territorial implications applicable to TNCs | Examples: corporate social responsibility policies relating to overseas subsidiaries; public procurement policies. | Examples: company laws; stock-exchange listing rules and guidelines; import-export regulations and controls. | Adjudicating alleged breaches of domestic legislation. Enforcing executive and judicial decisions against domestically located assets. |
| Direct extra-territorial jurisdiction over TNC actors or activities | Export-credit agency criteria: monitoring of overseas projects requiring financial assistance. Provision of consular support to overseas branches/ subsidiaries. | Anti-corruption and anti-money laundering legislation with extra-territorial application. Anti-terrorism, drug-trafficking and other criminal-law legislation with overseas application. | Not accepted Requires assistance from local agencies in the overseas jurisdiction of enforcement. |

the potential for inter-state regulatory conflicts. To facilitate a more nuanced discussion of extra-territoriality, the SRSG has constructed a heuristic 'extra-territoriality matrix' with two rows and three columns. The matrix shows that extra-territoriality is not a binary matter, but encompasses a wide range of possible regulatory actions, not all of which are equally likely to trigger objections. The matrix begins with two rows, representing a distinction between (a) domestic measures with extra-territorial implications; and (b) direct extra-territorial jurisdiction over actors or activities abroad. Its three columns represent a range of regulatory approaches, from policy based to regulation and enforcement actions. It seems that policy based or 'principles based' and 'outcomes oriented' regulation is less problematic for TNCs and their home states than more prescriptive legislation.[35]

---

[35]    Jennifer A. Zerk, 'Extraterritorial Jurisdiction: Lessons for the Business and Human Rights Sphere from Six Regulatory Areas' (June 2010) Corporate Social Responsibility Initiative Working Paper No. 59.

Much of recent debate about the use of direct extra-territorial jurisdiction, and its implications for state sovereignty, has focused on its use in the antitrust (competition law) field. Certainly the use of direct extra-territorial jurisdiction here, especially where based on the 'effects doctrine', has contributed to inter-state tensions. While there now appears to be greater acceptance of this jurisdictional basis, problems remain, including inconsistent standards between states, which can create compliance challenges and uncertainties for companies. On the other hand, states have exhibited greater consistency and cooperation regarding conduct that they can agree is pernicious or immoral, such as participation in illegal cartels, highlighting the importance of international dialogue and soft law standards in building greater convergence of standards and approaches. When it comes to extra-territorial regulation, concerns about certainty, legitimacy, efficiency and competitiveness are nearly always expressed in relation to unilateral rather than collective actions. For business, as for states, extra-territorial measures remain much more acceptable and effective if they are based upon collective measures, and it is to such measures that this chapter now turns.

## BRINGING TNCs INTO THE GLOBAL ACCOUNTABILITY SPHERE

Globally, a number of multinational efforts have been made to build regulatory structures designed to guide TNC behavior and, to a lesser extent, to render TNCs accountable for breaches of accepted standards. Some of these multinational regimes are limited to TNCs, while others (like the Global Compact) extend their coverage to other (business and non-business) organizations as well. These measures are similar to state regulatory measures based on internationally agreed standards, such as the CAC, but different in that they rely upon TNC action, rather than government action, for their implementation and effectiveness. As with voluntary codes at corporate, sector and national levels, such efforts have typically brought about meaningful results only to the extent that the relevant regime establishes standards which are measured, monitored and (rarely) enforced.

### Measuring: The Global Reporting Initiative

The lack of global standards for measuring and reporting on the environmental and other impacts of TNC activities has long been a weakness in global systems of TNC accountability. The Global Reporting Initiative (GRI) goes some way to remedying this weakness by establishing a comprehensive reporting framework for all business organizations. The GRI, first established in 1998, was formally inaugurated as a United Nations Environment Programme (UNEP) collaborating organization in 2002, the same year that the Sustainable Reporting Guidelines were unveiled at the World Summit on Sustainable Development in Johannesburg. The Sustainability Reporting Guidelines, now in their 4th generation (G4),[36] are supported by Sector Guidance principles applicable to different industry sectors, and other resources all aimed at facilitating greater transparency and accountability. As more and more jurisdictions work to strengthen and expand their corporate reporting requirements, the GRI is increasingly being used as a reference point. For example, all companies listed on the Johannesburg Stock Exchange have been required to report in accordance with the GRI Guidelines since 2003. Use of the GRI Guidelines is also promoted through cooperative engagement with other multinational initiatives including the OECD's Guidelines for Multinational Enterprises and the Global Compact. For most companies, though, subscribing to the GRI Guidelines remains entirely voluntary, and there is no independent body able to monitor, compare and verify reports that are issued by TNC. Nor is there any independent tribunal to which those aggrieved or harmed by TNC activities can have recourse.

**The UN Draft Code for TNCs and the ILO Tripartite Declaration: Neither Measuring Nor Reporting?**

The 1970s was the era of the 'new international economic order' and saw a number of initiatives aimed at bringing TNCs into the international legal order. A Commission on Transnational Corporations established by the UN Economic and Social Council in 1974 was charged with developing a multinational code of conduct for TNCs, and it produced a number of draft codes over the next two decades before the process was abandoned in 1994. Although never finalized as a legal instrument, the experience of drafting a Code of Conduct for TNCs has normative value and provides a valuable store of experience for current and future international lawyers to draw upon. It is particularly valuable for the lessons it teaches about the pitfalls of attempting to set binding legal rules and boundaries in the broad and ill-defined area of TNC responsibility.

---

[36]   GRI Sustainability Reporting Standards, G4. For Discussion, see 'Linking G4 and the UN Guiding Principles: Comply with the UN Guiding Principles on Business and Human Rights through G4 Reporting' (GRI, 2014).

The 1970s also saw the emergence of the International Labour Organisation's Tripartite Declaration of Principles concerning Multinational Enterprises and Social Policy (MNE Declaration). The MNE Declaration is a voluntary set of principles regarding employment and labor relations adopted by the ILO Governing Body in 1977. It has a lesser legal status than ILO Conventions adopted by the ILO Annual Conference, and its wording reflects its voluntary nature. While 'requests for interpretation' of Tripartite Declaration are specifically provided for, there is no dispute resolution mechanism as such built into the Declaration. A main achievement of the MNE Declaration was to generate a follow-up mechanism that asks governments, workers' and employers' organizations to respond at regular intervals to a survey questionnaire investigating aspects of national implementation of MNE Declaration principles. Unfortunately, response rates have not been high, amounting to less than 50 per cent of total ILO country membership, and when results of the regular survey are published, they are made anonymous, such that breaches of the principles by MNEs cannot be attributed.

Following a review of the follow-up mechanism of the MNE Declaration begun in 2010, the universal periodic survey has been replaced by a greater emphasis on promotional activities, capacity building and consultation, and the compilation of relevant data from different countries into a web portal known as the ILO Knowledge Information Gateway.[37]

### Reporting with (a Limited Degree of) Accountability: The Global Compact

Formally launched in 2000, the Global Compact allows not just TNCs and business organizations, but also public sector bodies, cities, academic institutions, NGOs and labor organizations, to sign up to a set of ten universally accepted principles in the areas of human rights, labor standards, the environment and, since early 2005, anti-corruption. The ten principles are drawn from four of the most widely ratified international legal instruments:

- the Universal Declaration of Human Rights;
- the International Labour Organisation's Declaration on Fundamental Principles and Rights at Work;

---

[37]   ILO Governing Body, 320th Session, Geneva, 13–27 March 2014, Tenth item on the Agenda: Implementation strategy for the follow-up mechanism of and promotional activities on the Tripartite Declaration of Principles concerning Multinational Enterprises and Social Policy (MNE Declaration), ILO Doc. GB.320/POL/10 (14 February 2014).

- the Rio Declaration on Environment and Development; and
- the United Nations Convention Against Corruption.

By November 2015, the Global Compact had grown to include over 12,000 signatories, including around 8,000 business participants. In November 2015, business participants included 3,447 companies with active participant (communicating) status. One of the most important commitments that a participant makes when joining the Global Compact is to submit annually a Communication on Progress (COP) using reporting indicators such as the GRI Guidelines. So far as TNCs are concerned, the COP must be placed on the UN Global Compact website and shared widely with company stakeholders. Failure to submit an annual COP results in a change in the participant's status from 'Active' to 'Non-Communicating'. Participants who do not communicate progress for two years in a row are delisted. As of November 2015, 2,063 companies were recorded as having 'Delisted' status on the Global Compact website.

The COP public reporting requirement was introduced in 2005 as one of a number of new 'Integrity Measures' developed in response to criticisms of the Compact as 'toothless' – allowing companies to associate themselves with a 'feel-good' UN initiative with no need to change their operations on the ground at all. Other measures introduced in 2005 included strict rules on the use of UN and Global Compact logos and a new complaints mechanism. Section 4 of the 2005 Integrity Measures creates a dialogue process for handling 'credible allegations of systematic or egregious abuse of the Global Compact's overall aims and principles by a participating organization'. The purpose of the dialogue is to 'assist participants in aligning their actions with the commitments they have undertaken with regard to the Global Compact principles'. If the participating company concerned refuses to engage in dialogue on the matter within two months of first being contacted by the Global Compact Office in regard to a credible allegation, it may be regarded as 'non-communicating' and identified as such on the Global Compact website until dialogue commences. If as a result of the dialogue process and based on a review of the nature of the matter submitted and the responses by the participating company, the continued listing of the participating company on the Global Compact website 'is considered to be detrimental to the reputation and integrity of the Global Compact, the Global Compact Office reserves the right to remove that company from the list of participants and to so indicate on the Global Compact website'.

An important achievement of the Global Compact is to facilitate dialogue and exchange between the language of human rights and the language of business management. The Global Compact's *Guide for Integrating Human Rights into Business Management*, for example, presents human rights protection in management-friendly language, rather than the language of international law. Other guidance material includes the Good Practice Notes developed in areas as diverse as 'Setting up a Multi-Stakeholder Panel as a Tool for Effective Stakeholder Dialogue', and, 'How Business Can Encourage Governments to Fulfil their Human Rights Obligations'.

The proportion of all TNCs that have signed up to be Global Compact participants remains low at less than 10 per cent. Country-wise, the highest number of actively communicating corporate participants comes from France (368 active corporate participants as of November 2015). Japan (164), Germany (144), the United States (123), Sweden (104) and the United Kingdom (90) each had around the same number of national companies actively participating in the Global Compact in November 2015.

**A Limited Network of Accountability: The OECD Guidelines for Multinational Enterprises**

The 1970s also saw the drafting by the OECD of its first set of Guidelines for Multinational Companies (1976). These have been developed, strengthened and updated on five occasions since 1976. The latest version of the Guidelines dates from May 2011[38] and describes itself as a set of 'recommendations jointly addressed by governments to multinational enterprises'. While 'Observance of the Guidelines by enterprises is voluntary and not legally enforceable', the Guidelines do serve as a statement of the standards expected by adhering home nations of their corporations operating abroad in areas such as employment and industrial relations, human rights, environment, information disclosure, combatting bribery, consumer interests, competition and taxation.

Since 2000, the OECD Guidelines have incorporated and been supported by a unique implementation mechanism of National Contact Points (NCPs) – agencies established by adhering governments to promote and implement the guidelines. By 2015, there were national contact points established in each of the 35 OECD nations, mostly located within national ministries or departmental bureaus. As part of their role in assisting enterprises and their stakeholders with further implementation of the Guidelines, the NCPs receive and consider complaints (known as 'specific instances') lodged against any corporation operating within the national

---

[38]   *OECD Guidelines for Multinational Enterprises* (OECD Publishing, 2011) <http://dx.doi.org/10.1787/9789264115415-en>.

jurisdiction of that NCP. The NCP's role upon receiving a specific instance is to investigate and, if necessary, provide a mediation and conciliation platform for resolving practical issues that arise. Under the relevant procedural guidance, NCPs issue a statement and notify the OECD Investment Committee of the results of any specific instance they receive, while at the same time 'protecting sensitive business and other information'. By 2015, approximately 330 specific instances had been considered by country NCPs, more than half relating to employment and industrial relations matters. In 2013 the Investment Committee established a Working Party on Responsible Business Conduct with a mandate to foster NCP functional equivalence across national differences, promote engagement with non-adhering countries, partner organisations and stakeholders, and to serve as a central point of information on the Guidelines.

**Towards a Shared Understanding of Social Responsibility: ISO and Other Standards Organizations**

The International Organization for Standardization (ISO) is an independent, non-governmental membership organization and the world's largest developer of voluntary International Standards. It essentially comprises a network of the national standards bodies of 162 ISO member countries. ISO standards include standards relating to occupational health and safety (ISO 45001), food safety (ISO 22000), sustainable events (ISO 20121) and environmental management systems (ISO 14000). By 2004, the ISO and its stakeholders had recognized the importance of, and the need to define, recognize and implement the roles and responsibilities of business in a social context. The ISO Working Group on Social Responsibility was established in 2004, and by 2009 its 91 member nations and 42 liaison organizations had developed a Draft International Guidance on Social Responsibility.

ISO 26000 Guidance on Social Responsibility was launched in 2010 following five years of negotiations among representatives from government, NGOs, industry, consumer groups and labor organizations around the world. Like the Global Compact before it, ISO 26000 is not limited to corporations, but is intended for use by public and private organizations of all types. ISO 26000 is not a formal ISO management system standard, and it is not intended for certification purposes. Rather, it comprises a consolidation of best practice social responsibility advice and guidance in seven core subject areas:

- Organizational governance;
- Human rights;
- Labor practices;

- The environment;
- Fair operating practices;
- Consumer issues; and
- Community involvement and development.

ISO 26000 is voluntary and is meant to complement and support, not supplant, other internationally recognized social responsibility standards. These include the SAI SA8000 standard for decent work.

In 1997, a multi-stakeholder NGO, Social Accountability International (SAI), was founded to develop the first globally recognized accreditation standard relating to socially responsible employment practices. The most recent version of SAI's SA8000 standard for decent work dates from 2014, and is the fourth issue of SA8000. It operates as a voluntary standard setting out the requirements to be met by organizations, including workplace conditions and effective management systems, at each specific worksite for which audited third-party certification is sought. The foundational elements of SA8000 2014 are based on internationally recognized human rights norms and key conventions of the ILO. The normative SA8000 certification audit reference documents are the SA800: 2014 Standard and the SA8000 Performance Indicator Annex which sets out the minimum performance expectations of an SA8000 certified organization. Additionally, the SA8000 Guidance Document facilitates compliance with the Standard by providing interpretations of SA8000, examples of how to implement its requirements and examples of methods for verifying compliance.

### Protect, Respect and Remedy: Towards a Globally Recognized Framework for Business and Human Rights

Attempts throughout the 1970s and 1980s to draft a globally recognized Code of Conduct for TNCs under the auspices of the UN Economic and Social Council (ECOSOC) failed, for reasons examined in depth elsewhere.[39] Attempts to obtain ECOSOC adoption of a 1990 Draft Code of Conduct for TNCs were abandoned by 1994. It was just over a decade later before the next serious attempt at UN level to explore the idea of a globally recognized set of human rights principles for TNCs was initiated in 2005, with the creation of a mandate for a Special Representative of the Secretary-General on the Issue of Human Rights

---

[39]    D. Kinley and J. Tadaki, 'From Talk to Walk: The Emergence of Human Rights Responsibilities for Corporations at International Law' (2004) 44(4) *Virginia Journal of International Law* 931–1023.

and Transnational Corporations and Other Business Organizations (the SRSG).

At its June 2008 session, the UN Human Rights Council was unanimous in welcoming the 'Protect, Respect and Remedy' framework for business and human rights, which was developed by the SRSG after widespread stakeholder consultations, and his mandate was extended for a second time to run until 2011. The SRSG's 'Protect, Respect and Remedy' framework is built around three basic principles: the state duty to protect human rights, the corporate responsibility to respect human rights and the need to build effective public and private avenues to access remedies for human rights harms.

States routinely provide support and assistance to their corporate nationals in their global trade and investment ventures. While states may not intend to allow corporate nationals to violate human rights in their extra-territorial operations, by their actions or omissions, states may facilitate or otherwise contribute to a situation in which such violations by a TNC occur. Extra-territorial activities of a TNC that violate international human rights law can give rise to state responsibility under customary international law if a relevant causal act or omission can be attributed to one or more states. Relevant customary international law principles have been codified in the International Law Commission's Articles on the Responsibility of States for Internationally Wrongful Acts. An act or omission of a TNC can be attributed to a state if the TNC is empowered by that state to exercise elements of public authority, and/or if the TNC acts on the 'instructions of, or under the direction or control of' the state. In addition, where a state, through aiding or assisting corporate activity, is complicit in the commission of an internationally wrongful act committed by another state or by the company itself, then the state will be internationally responsible.

So far as the corporate responsibility to respect human rights is concerned, the SRSG explains that in order to fulfill this responsibility not to infringe on the rights of others – to do no harm – corporations must engage in a process of 'due diligence'. For TNCs, human rights due diligence means first and foremost assessing the country context in which their activities take place and identifying any associated human rights challenges. Second, TNCs should consider what human rights impacts their own activities may have within the relevant country context within which they occur. The TNC should analyze the actual and potential impacts arising from its activities on employees, consumers, local communities and other affected groups. The production process, the products or services the company supplies, its labor and employment practices, the provision of security for personnel and assets, and the company's lobbying or political activities, all need to be scrutinized for their human rights impacts and adjusted if necessary to prevent human rights harms.

The third principle that TNCs should consider is whether they might contribute to human rights harms through the relationships connected to their activities, such as with state agencies, business partners, suppliers and other non-state actors. How far or how deep this consideration should go will depend on the circumstances. The aim is to ensure that the TNC does not become implicated in third-party harm through its relationships with these other parties. According to the SRSG, the possibility of complicity:

> can arise from a company's business activities, including the provision or con-tracting of goods, services and even non-business activities, such as lending equipment or vehicles. Therefore, a company needs to understand the track records of those entities with which it deals in order to assess whether it might contribute to or be associated with harm caused by entities with which it conducts, or is considering conducting, business or other activities.

Human rights due diligence thus involves both country-context risk assessment and supply-chain assessment. In terms of country-context risk assessment, the OECD has developed a Risk Awareness Tool for Multinational Enterprises in Weak Governance Zones, as well as a Due Diligence Guidance for Responsible Supply Chains of Minerals from Conflict-Affected and High-Risk Areas.

Outside of the minerals sector, TNCs have developed a number of approaches to address the many human rights gaps and challenges pre-sented by 21st century supply chain systems and arrangements. These include setting clear expectations with suppliers for responsible business conduct through codes of supplier conduct – currently the most common application of the MNE Guidelines to supply chain relationships.[40] Consequences for non-compliance with codes can vary significantly – from limited or no action taken by the TNC to requirements to participate in monitoring and remediation, to consequences with direct impact on the business relationship such as suspension of new orders or contract cancellation.

---

[40]   C. Sisco et al., 'Supply Chains and the OECD Guidelines for Multinational Enterprises' (2010) BSR discussion paper on responsible supply chain manage-ment. Presented at the 10th OECD Roundtable on Corporate Responsibility, OECD HQ, Paris, 30 June 2010.

# RECENT TRENDS: THE FUTURE OF TNCs IN GLOBAL SOCIETY

## A Legally Binding Global Framework for TNCs?

As the result of a September 2013 proposal bringing the issue of a 'legally binding framework to regulate the work of transnational corporations' back to the UN agenda, a vote was taken at the Human Rights Council on 26 June 2014. Two relevant resolutions were tabled at the 26th session of the Human Rights Council in Geneva in 2014. One, signed by Ecuador, South Africa, Bolivia, Cuba and Venezuela, and supported by 20 countries in a vote,[41] proposed the establishment of 'an open-ended intergovernmental working group with the mandate to elaborate an internationally legally binding instrument on Transnational Corporations and Other Business Enterprises with respect to human rights' (resolution 26/9). The other (resolution 26/22), drafted by Norway, supported by 44 co-sponsors, and adopted by consensus by all regions, does not support a binding legal instrument, but opts instead to continue the mandate of the UN Working Group on Business and Human Rights for another three years.[42] While including a request that the UN Working Group prepare a report considering, among other things, the benefits and limitations of legally binding instruments,[43] its main thrust is to reaffirm the normative content of the UN Guiding Principles on Business and Human Rights (UNGPs), focusing on improved domestic measures to implement the UNGPs, and improved access to remedies for victims of business-related abuses.

The first session of the open-ended intergovernmental working group took place from 6 to 10 July 2015 in Geneva and reflected the contentious nature of the debate between those who argue in support of

---

[41]   The vote was taken, and the resolution adopted, on 26 June 2014. Those in favor were Algeria, Benin, Burkina Faso, China, Congo, Cote d'Ivoire, Cuba, Ethiopia, India, Indonesia, Kazakhstan, Kenya, Morocco, Namibia, Pakistan, Philippines, Russia, South Africa, Venezuela, Vietnam. Countries which voted against were Austria, Czech Republic, Estonia, France, Germany, Ireland, Italy, Japan, Montenegro, South Korea, Romania, Macedonia, UK and USA. There were 13 abstentions (Argentina, Botswana, Brazil, Chile, Costa Rica, Gabon, Kuwait, Maldives, Mexico, Peru, Saudi Arabia, Sierra Leone, UAE).

[42]   For discussion, see Nicole R. Tuttle, 'Human Rights Council Resolutions 26/9 and 26/22: Towards Corporate Accountability?' *ASIL Insights* 3 September 2015 <https://www.asil.org/insights/volume/19/issue/20/human-rights-council-resolutions-269-and-2622-towards-corporate>.

[43]   Human Rights Council, 26th Session, Agenda item 3, draft resolution. UN Doc A/HRC/26/L.1 23 June 2014. Adopted by consensus on 27 June 2014.

binding mechanisms to address business and human rights, and those who prefer pursuing the more voluntaristic path laid out by the UN Guiding Principles on Business and Human Rights.[44] Those in favor of a binding instrument argue that the Guiding Principles, while widely accepted, have proven insufficient and have not provided accountability or real remedies for corporate abuses. Those against a binding instrument maintain that the Guiding Principles need more time and effort to fully develop their potential and that the pursuit of a treaty may obstruct this goal and become an excuse not to implement the Guiding Principles.[45]

Ultimately, it is likely to depend very largely on TNCs themselves, whether they pressure governments not to cooperate with any treaty-drafting process or whether, as in the case of the Global Compact, they become actively involved as participants. For unless TNCs themselves are actively involved in the drafting and 'maintenance' of a binding treaty, they are unlikely to either 'own' it or to recognize its legitimacy. So far, signs are that the Working Group set up to draft the treaty has yet to gain any convincing amount of support for its work from either governments or business. This does not necessarily mean that its work should cease, simply that energy should not be taken away from continued pursuit of the Guiding Principles. In other words, the debate should not be about a 'Guiding Principles' path versus a 'treaty path'.

One of the main reasons for the success of the Global Compact has been that businesses actively decide for themselves when and how to sign up, implement and further the Global Compact agenda. Engagement can be minimal or fully activist. While it can be argued that the Global Compact contains no mechanism through which victims of TNC human rights abuses can obtain remedies, its transparency mechanisms – in particular its regular reporting requirements – do provide for accountability. More important, the Global Compact continues to demonstrate a promising capacity for self-strengthening. The Global Compact Integrity Measures, including the introduction of public reporting requirements and a complaints mechanism, were added in 2005; largely in response to criticisms of the Compact as ineffective and toothless. If the complaints mechanisms could be built upon and strengthened to include access to remedies, then

---

[44] For discussion, see Olga Fernandez Sixto, 'Business and human rights: A study on the implications of the proposed binding treaty' (October 2015) (unpublished LLM thesis, University of Essex).

[45] For discussion, see Anita Ramasastry and Doug Cassei, 'White Paper: Options for a Treaty on Business and Human Rights' (2015) 6 (1) *Notre Dame Journal of International & Comparative Law* i–x, 1–50.

the Global Compact could become a key part of integrating TNCs (as well as other organizations) into the global regulatory order.

## Responsible Fulfilment of Taxation Obligations

Taxation is at the core of countries' sovereignty, but the interaction of domestic tax rules in some cases leads to gaps and frictions. The existing regime of domestic rules and over 3,800 bilateral double-taxation treaty regimes has, over time, developed weaknesses and gaps that create opportunities for base erosion and profit shifting (BEPS).[46] In particular, the spread of the digital economy has given rise to fundamental questions about how to determine residence and/or the jurisdiction where value creation occurs for tax assessment purposes. BEPS relates chiefly to instances where the interaction of different tax rules leads to double non-taxation or less than single taxation. It also relates to arrangements that achieve no or low taxation by shifting profits away from the jurisdiction where the activities creating those profits take place. No or low taxation is not *per se* a cause of concern, but it becomes so when it is associated with practices that artificially segregate taxable income from the activities that generate it.[47] The concern is that rapidly increasing amounts of income generated by an increasing number of cross-border transactions and a volume of cross-border activity may go untaxed.

In the changing international tax environment, countries have expressed concern about how international standards on which bilateral tax treaties are based allocate taxing rights between source and residence states.[48] At the urging of G20 finance ministers, the first version of an OECD action plan to address BEPS issues in a coordinated and comprehensive manner was issued in 2013. In October 2015, the OECD released its final BEPS Package. The Package includes reports on 15 'actions', ranging from countering harmful tax practices and treaty shopping to addressing transfer pricing, interest deductibility and transparency, to exploring the tax

---

[46] Itai Grinberg and Joost Pauwelyn, 'The Emergence of a New International Tax Regime: The OECD's Package on Base Erosion and Profit Shifting (BEPS)' *ASIL Insights* 28 October 2015 <https://www.asil.org/insights/volume/19/issue/24/emergence-new-international-tax-regime-oecd%E2%80%99s-package-base-erosion-and>.

[47] OECD, *Action Plan on Base Erosion and Profit Shifting* (OECD Publishing 2013) <http://dx.doi.org/10.1787/9789264202719-en>.

[48] Stephen E. Shay, J. Clifton Fleming and Robert J. Peroni, 'Designing a 21st Century Corporate Tax – An Advance U.S. Minimum Tax on Foreign Income and Other Measures to Protect the Base' (2015) 17 *Florida Tax Review* <http://ssrn.com/abstract=2651928>.

implications of the digital economy.[49] The end result of the BEPS Package should be an increase in the density of the global network of transparency, monitoring and accountability rules to which TNCs are subjected, at least in respect of their financial transactions.

The BEPS Package marks the first time that real progress has been made towards a multinational tax regime. Its successful approval by G20 leaders at a summit in Antalya, Turkey, on 15 November 2015 has been attributed to good political timing (following the global financial crisis and at a time when international tax issues were the focus of global political attention), and the voluntary, soft-law nature of (most of) the commitments involved.[50] The challenge will now be to expand consensus on BEPS measures beyond the 34 OECD and eight non-OECD members of the G20 and to establish a viable and enduring third-party dispute-resolution regime,[51] possibly by linking in to trade and investment-related dispute resolution mechanisms.

**Trade and Investment and Social Responsibility**

The Ruggie process found a lack of integration between regular government agencies with economic, commercial and trade mandates, and those with human rights mandates. Yet it identified considerable scope for trade and investment frameworks to become vectors for manifesting state duties to respect and protect human rights from adverse impacts by business actors. On the one hand, investor protection clauses, particularly investor-state dispute settlement clauses in bilateral and multilateral investment treaties, are seen to constrain host governments' abilities to regulate for social or environmental aims that potentially impact upon investor activities. Stabilization-clauses in investor–host-state agreements have a similar effect.

However, considerable precedent exists for using trade policy to promote governance improvements in partner states, though these have mostly been effective in regard to preventing reductions in labor rights. EU trade agreements, for example, have long contained human rights clauses enabling Brussels, in effect, to use trade-related actions to shape the political governance of emerging market and developing country partners. Since 1995, the

---

[49]   2015 BEPS Final Reports <http://www.oecd.org/ctp/beps-2015-final-reports.htm>.

[50]   Grinberg and Pauwelyn (n 45).

[51]   For discussion, see Grinberg and Pauwelyn (n 45), noting that Action 14 of the Package identifies mainly non-binding ways to make dispute resolution mechanisms under bilateral tax treaties (the so-called Mutual Agreement Procedure or MAP) more effective. But it falls short of imposing binding arbitration.

EU has required all trade agreements to contain provisions linking trade and other preferences to the fulfillment of human rights commitments in beneficiary countries. Under the EU's Generalized Scheme of Preferences (GSP) the EU offers developing states preferential access to the EU market subject to certain conditions. In addition to the core GSP tariff preferences, the EU also operates a system of positive conditionality: GSP+. Under GSP+, eligible states which commit themselves to key, universal obligations relating to human and labor rights, environment and good governance may apply for additional preferences. Under a third tier of the scheme, 'everything but arms', least-developed states (as defined by the UN) can benefit from free market access for all products, except for arms and ammunitions.

Much of the debate during recent negotiations over the TPP centered on how best to balance the free trade and investment-promoting economic aims of the treaty with the need to preserve state sovereignty in policy areas such as environmental protection and health. This balance was achieved through a number of carve-out provisions, ostensibly aimed at limiting the potential for TNCs to seek redress from host governments in the event of regulatory measures impacting on company profits. In reality, however, the wording of the relevant provisions in the TPP reflects a minimal compromise inserted to satisfy Australian demands that certain health measures, such as cigarette plain-packaging laws and the Pharmaceutical Benefits Scheme (PBS) could not be the subject of ISDS procedures.

TPP Article 9.15, titled 'Investment and Environmental, Health and other Regulatory Objectives', ostensibly seeks to ensure that 'Nothing in [Chapter 9] shall be construed to prevent a Party from adopting, maintaining or enforcing any measure otherwise consistent with this Chapter that it considers appropriate to ensure that investment activity in its territory is undertaken in a manner sensitive to environmental, health or other regulatory objectives'. Article 9.15 does not so much specifically allow TPP parties to enact environmental and/or health-related regulatory measures as it seeks to ensure that Chapter 9 itself is not used to limit the capacity of TPP Parties to enact such measures. Similarly, the wording of Article 9.16 in no way represents any sort of 'carve out' for 'Corporate Social Responsibility' measures that a TPP Party might seek to impose upon investors. Rather, its language expresses a sentiment without any legal effect at all:

> The Parties reaffirm the importance of each Party encouraging enterprises operating within its territory or subject to its jurisdiction to voluntarily incorporate into their internal policies those internationally recognised standards, guidelines and principles of corporate social responsibility that have been endorsed or are supported by that Party.

The whole effect is compounded by the wording in the TPP Annex which purports to list what are and are not understood to be measures amounting to 'expropriation' – wording which leaves so much leeway for different definitions as to be almost entirely meaningless:

> Non-discriminatory regulatory actions by a Party that are designed and applied to protect legitimate public welfare objectives, such as public health, safety and the environment, do not constitute indirect expropriations, except in rare circumstances.

This wording only protects from litigious attack public health and environment measures that are designed and applied for 'legitimate' public health, safety and/or environmental objectives; measures which even then, in 'rare circumstances' (which remain undefined), can still be deemed as an 'indirect expropriation'.

The only clear, hard-and-fast carve-out relates to tobacco control, which is explicitly and definitely removed from possible ISDS litigation – although governments *themselves* can still challenge other governments on tobacco, as part of inter-state dispute settlement provisions.

The TPP also compares poorly to the European Union's proposals to impose procedural and accountability discipline on ISDS in response to concerns expressed about ISDS provisions in draft treaties being negotiated by the EU. A 2015 EU concept paper notes a 'new approach' to the negotiation of ISDS in investment protection treaties, both in terms of substance (investment protection rules) and procedure (ISDS mechanism), found in the recent (2014) EU–Canada and EU–Singapore free trade agreements.[52] The new approach is reflected in a number of different provisions designed to preserve and protect the legitimate policy-making and associated regulatory space of states parties to the relevant FTA. These include:

- The preamble in the Canada–European Union Comprehensive Economic and Trade Agreement (CETA) which makes clear that the EU and Canada preserve their right to regulate and to achieve legitimate policy objectives, including public health, safety, environment, public morals and the promotion and protection of cultural diversity;[53]

---

[52]   European Commission, 'Concept Paper: Investment in TTIP and beyond – the path for reform. Enhancing the right to regulate and moving from current ad hoc arbitration towards an Investment Court' (May 2015) <http://trade.ec.europa.eu/doclib/docs/2015/may/tradoc_153408.PDF> (accessed 4 February 2016).

[53]   Canada–European Union Comprehensive Economic and Trade Agreement (CETA), text agreed as at August 2014, Published on 26 September 2014;

- A clear, precise and closed-text definition of 'fair and equitable treatment', designed to clarify the content of the standard without leaving unwelcome discretion to arbitrators. Similarly detailed language has been used to define what constitutes indirect expropriate, specifically excluding claims against public policy measures;[54]
- Preventing forum shopping by specifically prohibiting the making of an investment or business re-organization for the purpose of bringing a case against a host government (as is alleged Philip Morris did to bring its case against Australia). No other ISDS contains such a provision. Moreover, 'mailbox' companies are unable to bring cases to arbitration under the CETA. Only companies with real business operations in the territory of one of the Parties will be covered by the investment protection provisions;
- The CETA also incorporates the *UNCITRAL Rules on Transparency in Treaty-based Investor-State Arbitration*, which are designed to ensure full mandatory transparency of the arbitration process. All documents (submissions of the disputing parties, decisions of the tribunal) will be made publicly available. All hearings will be open to the public. Interested parties (NGOs, trade unions) will be able to make submissions;[55]
- Under CETA, the EU and Canada can issue binding interpretations on how its provisions are to be interpreted, and the ISDS tribunal is obliged to respect those interpretations. Governments, not tribunals, are thus given control over interpretation of the rules;[56]
- The CETA also includes a code of conduct for arbitrators, aimed at ensuring impartiality and high ethical and professional standards;[57]
- There is a fast-track system allowing for the speedy rejection of unfounded, frivolous or vexatious claims;[58]
- The CETA introduces a 'loser pays principle' meaning that investors who bring a case and lose pay for the entire legal costs of the proceedings;[59]

---

not in effect as of February 2016, <http://ec.europa.eu/trade/policy/in-focus/ceta/>.

[54]   CETA Section 4: Investment Protection. Article X.9 Treatment of Investors and of Covered Investments.

[55]   CETA, Article X.33: Transparency of Proceedings.

[56]   Declaration to Investment Chapter Article X.11 Paragraph 6.

[57]   CETA, Chapter 14. Rules of Procedure and Code of Conduct: Annex 1: Rules of Procedure for Arbitration.

[58]   CETA, Article X.29: Claims Manifestly Without Legal Merit; Article X.30: Claims Unfounded as a Matter of Law.

[59]   CETA, Chapter 10. Investment; Article X.36.

- Parties to the CETA have expressly agreed to work towards creating a future appeals mechanism aimed at ensuring consistency and predictability of the system;
- Also aimed at avoiding divergent verdicts and possible double compensation is the provision in the CETA which prohibits parallel proceedings so that investors are obliged to drop cases in national courts if they want to pursue ISDS.[60]

## CONCLUSION

Three themes running throughout this chapter characterize the evolution of the modern concept of corporate social responsibility, and thus of the modern TNC. These are: (1) an evolving understanding and acceptance of increased *transparency*; (2) an evolving understanding and (sometimes reluctant) acceptance of increased levels of *accountability*; and (3) a move towards greater acceptance of the need for TNCs to be involved in providing more effective *remedies* for individuals and groups harmed as the result of TNC behavior. These three themes form a constant motif throughout the concerns of an expanding network of stakeholders impacted by – and seeking to influence – TNC behavior, and throughout the various layers of an emerging global regulatory framework for TNCs. Transparency, accountability and access to effective remedies are also concerns at the forefront of recent developments in international tax negotiations and trade and investment treaty negotiations. These concerns reflect and demonstrate the public and social nature of the modern TNC in the 21st century.

---

[60]    CETA, Chapter 10. Investment; Article X.23: Proceedings under different international agreements. See also Chapter 14. Dispute Resolution, Article 14.3: Choice of Forum.

# 2. Theoretical approaches to global regulation of transnational corporations
## *Rachel J. Anderson*

## INTRODUCTION

Theoretical approaches to regulating Transnational Corporations ('TNC')[1] have blossomed as legal and other scholars continue to study the unique structure of TNCs since they were first theorized in the 1960s.[2] TNCs present challenges and opportunities for theoretical approaches to global regulation arising from, for example, their size, form, influence, public–private character and multi-jurisdictional nature. Their global presence and interconnectedness also create opportunities to advance a wide range of regulatory purposes, including goals related to development, rights and sustainability. Approaches to TNC regulation are embedded in broader legal theory as well as theoretical approaches from other disciplines. These approaches adapt and extend legal theory in ways that respond to the distinctive issues raised by TNCs. There are various ways to categorize theoretical approaches to TNC regulation. This chapter identifies six schools of thought: International Legal Theory, Corporate Social Responsibility Theory, Law and Economics Theory, New Governance Theory, Critical Legal Theory, and Law and Religion approaches.[3]

---

[1]  TNCs are networks of private economic entities operating simultaneously in multiple countries. UNCTAD, 'UNCTAD Training Manual on Statistics for FDI and the Operations of TNCs, Vol. II Statistics on the Operations of Transnational Corporations' (2009) 14; UNCTAD, 'Transnational Corporations Statistics' (2013) <http://unctad.org/en/Pages/DIAE/Transnational-Corporations-Statistics. aspx> (accessed 24 December 2015).

[2]  Stephen Hymer is credited with first theorizing TNCs in his 1960 doctoral dissertation. See Grazia Ietto-Gillies, 'The Theory of the Transnational Corporation at 50+' (2013) *Economic Thought: History, Philosophy, and Methodology* 2 <http:// etdiscussion.worldeconomicsassociation.org/wp-content/uploads/Theories-TNCs. pdf> (accessed 5 March 2016).

[3]  This chapter emphasizes selected aspects but is not intended to capture the full history or scope of the schools of thought identified and discussed in this chapter.

**Regulatory Challenges and Opportunities**

TNCs present a host of challenges for the creation and maintenance of international and global structures for their regulation. Some of these challenges stem from their form or influence. Others stem from the way TNCs straddle the public–private divide.

TNCs are networks of private economic entities operating simultaneously in multiple countries that may have multiple owners and that often generate and control massive amounts of wealth.[4] In the currently fragmented system of laws that govern TNCs, their multi-jurisdictional presence allows TNCs to evade national laws and escape market forces, for example, through transfer pricing in intra-company trade.[5] The possibility of multiple owners in varying ownership structures at multiple points in a TNC's network adds to the potential for regulatory complexity and arbitrage.

Operating in multiple countries and economic sectors subjects TNCs to multiple regulatory jurisdictions.[6] It also makes it possible for TNCs to engage in regulatory arbitrage.[7] TNCs' ability to influence the making of law and policy and to engage in regulatory arbitrage can have negative effects. These can be seen, for example, in the ways TNCs are able to seek out low-regulation environments and avoid enforcement of existing regulations resulting in employees' physical and economic harm due to poor working conditions, harms to the environment, and suppression of market competition.[8]

The complexity of TNC operations can make it hard to completely and accurately evaluate the potential and actual effects of TNCs in the world.[9]

---

    [4]    UNCTAD (n 1).
    [5]    See Jed Greer and Kavaljit Singh, 'A Brief History of Transnational Corporations' (2000) *Global Policy Forum* <https://www.globalpolicy.org/empire/47 068-a-brief-history-of-transnational-corporations.html> (accessed 24 December 2015).
    [6]    See Larry Catá Backer, 'From Moral Obligation to International Law: Disclosure Systems, Markets and the Regulation of Multinational Corporations' (2008) 39 *Georgetown Journal of International Law* 591, 619.
    [7]    Ietto-Gillies (n 2) 13 ('Nation-states are relevant because they are characterized by different regulatory regimes regarding (a) labour and social security systems; (b) fiscal systems; (c) currencies; (d) industrial policies including incentives to businesses; and (d) environmental and safety standards. The differences in these regulation regimes allow companies that can truly organize, manage and control their operations transnationally to arrange their activities as to benefit from these differences'.)
    [8]    Greer and Singh (n 5).
    [9]    See Małgorzata Jaworek and Marcin Kuzel, 'Transnational Corporations in the World Economy: Formation, Development and Present Position' (2015) 4 (1) *Copernican Journal of Finance and Accounting* 55, 58.

However, there are metrics that give an indication of TNCs' potential for influence individually and in the aggregate and, thus, the importance of regulations that shape and sanction the behavior of TNCs. The level of potential or actual control exercised within a TNC's network of companies is an important indicator of the level of coordination possible among the different entities that make up the TNC.[10] The number and location of TNCs' parent companies and foreign affiliates are indicators of the countries and jurisdictions in which TNCs might exercise influence. Total assets, revenue, profit, sales, exports of products and services, market capitalization, and foreign direct investment are indicators of the economic influence that TNCs could exercise individually and in the aggregate.[11] The number of people employed by TNCs is an indicator of the potential effects that TNCs can have around the world on working conditions, wealth generation and employees' and their dependents' economic status and physical welfare.[12] TNC spending on research and development suggests the level of TNC influence over innovation and 'the use of the world's knowledge, skills and technology'.[13]

As arbiters of massive amounts of wealth, TNCs have the potential to exercise significant influence, directly and indirectly, over all aspects of national and international life. TNCs can directly influence the making of international and national law and policy, for example, by employing government officials, participating on policy-making committees, providing information and drafting services to legislators and, in some cases, bribery.[14] TNCs can indirectly influence the making of international and national law and policy, for example, through lobbying or making campaign contributions.[15] This potential high level of access and influence increases the complexity of establishing a comprehensive regulatory framework as it can blur the lines between the regulators and the regulated.

The emergence of TNCs also creates regulatory opportunities. The massive number of people employed by TNCs around the world creates a regulatory one-stop shop for increasing economic security and quality of

---

[10]   Beth Stephens, 'The Amorality of Profit: Transnational Corporations and Human Rights' (2002) 20 *Berkeley Journal of International Law* 45, 47–48.

[11]   See Jaworek and Kuzel (n 9) 59, 67.

[12]   (n 9) 67.

[13]   (n 9) 65–66.

[14]   Raquel Alexander, Stephen W. Mazza and Susan Scholz, 'Measuring Rates of Return on Lobbying Expenditures: An Empirical Case Study of Tax Breaks for Multinational Corporations' (2009) 25 *Journal of Law and Policy* 401, 407–408.

[15]   Alexander, Mazza and Scholz (n 14); see also Jeffrey M. Berry, *The New Liberalism: The Rising Power of Citizen Groups* (Brookings Institution Press, 1999) 9–13.

life for people around the world. Targeted regulatory incentives for TNCs have the potential to encourage synergies that can advance widespread efficiency and plenty instead of a tragedy of the commons. Effective regulation of TNCs can encourage advancements through research and development that would have measurable benefits, for example, for human and enivonmental health on a global scale.

### Theoretical Approaches to TNCs

TNCs in their modern form are a relatively recent development and they present unique regulatory challenges and opportunities. In response to the emergence, growth, and expansion of TNCs, existing theories have been adapted and new theoretical directions are being explored.

Although modern TNCs first took shape in the 1900s, commerce and capital crossed borders prior to the emergence of nation states.[16] The precursors of TNCs date back to at least the late 14th century and include the Medici Bank (1397–1494), the East India Company (1600–1873), the Royal African Company (1672–1752) and the Hudson Bay Company (1670–present).[17] Over time, the movement of commerce and capital across borders has been regulated in a variety of ways. Religious doctrines guided the regulation of business, the rulers of communities and empires dictated the parameters of economic activity, and nation states established laws governing commerce within their borders. Catholicism, Judaism and Islam all have values and guidelines that have addressed the conduct of business and the role of economic activity in society since before the first TNCs were established.

Modern forms of TNCs did not emerge until the 19th century.[18] In 1960, Stephen Herbert Hymer proposed what is believed to be the first theory of TNCs, which Hymer referred to as international operations.[19] According to Hymer's theory, TNCs occur when there is interdependence in transnational markets, for example, international trade, combined with imperfect competition, a comparative advantage or other factors.[20] Hymer's 1960

---

[16]   John Dunning and Christos Pitelis, 'The Political Economy of Globalization – Revisiting Stephen Hymer 50 Years On' (2009) MPRA Paper No. 23184, 2.

[17]   Ietto-Gillies (n 2).

[18]   Rhys Jenkins, *Transnational Corporations and Uneven Development: The Internationalization of Capital and the Third World* (Routledge, 2013) 4.

[19]   See Ietto-Gillies (n 2), crediting Hymer with first theorizing transnational corporations.

[20]   Stephen Herbert Hymer, 'The International Operations of National Firms: A Study of Direct Foreign Investment' (1960) 91–95 (PhD diss. published posthumously by MIT Press, 1976).

insight regarding the analysis of TNCs still holds true today: the tools used to analyze TNCs are essentially the same as those used to analyze domestic corporations with the important difference that although the individual companies in a TNC are national, the operations of the TNC network are international.[21]

The emergence, expansion and increasing legal and financial complexity of TNCs have been accompanied by the development and evolution of a growing body of scholarship on their regulation. Within that body of scholarship, legal theories of TNC regulation span a wide range of approaches. Some of the approaches have developed out of legal theory, while others are interdisciplinary. The approaches are neither uniform in terms of their fundamental assumptions nor in terms of the issues they seek to address. Often they are complementary, and sometimes they are in direct opposition with one another.

Although the various theoretical approaches are in different stages of development, several schools of thought can be observed. This chapter identifies and discusses six schools of thought. These schools of thought vary in terms of the disciplines used, underlying assumptions, sources of law, key actors and goals of regulation. Many of these theoretical approaches began in the context of domestic regulation of corporations and were not applied in the international context until later.[22]

## INTERNATIONAL LEGAL THEORY APPROACHES

International Legal Theory approaches seek to determine the appropriate status of TNCs under international law and the rights, duties, and obligations that TNCs should have under international law. These approaches seek to answer questions related to spheres of authority, the applicability of direct or indirect regulation, the subjectivity of TNCs under international law, sources of law making and the source of the norms that apply to TNCs under international law. International Legal Theory approaches grapple with challenges to traditional spheres of authority

---

[21]  Hymer (n 20) 27–30.

[22]  Claire Moore Dickerson, 'Feminism and Human Rights' (2001) 22 *Women's Rights Law Reporter* 139, 141 ('Jonathan Macey was one of the first to use L&E language in an international law context'), citing Jonathan Macey, '"Chicken Wars As Prisoners" Dilemma: What's in a Game?' (1989) 64 *Notre Dame Law Review* 447, a review of John A.C. Conybeare, *Trade Wars: The Theory and Practice of International Commercial Rivalry* (Columbia UP, 1987).

under international law.[23] There are a wide range of International Legal Theory approaches to the regulation of TNCs and they include Public International Law and Interntional Legal Pluralism approaches.

For International Legal Theory, sources of law and key actors are central questions because of the absence of a central and supreme governmental structure with enforcement authority.[24] This is an issue that usually does not arise in a solely domestic regulatory context.

### Public International Law

Traditionally, the Public International Law Theory branch of International Legal Theory defined international law as made top down by and between nation-states and focused on nation-states as the subject of international law.[25] Under the Public International Law Theory approach, sources of law are generally in the form of treaties or customary international law.[26]

Over time, theories of Public International Law have expanded to include non-states as actors 'engag[ing] in international law activities'.[27] Some scholars posit that 'international law has already effectively recognized duties of corporations'[28] and that corporations have rights under international law.[29] They posit that since corporate rights and duties have already been accepted by states and other international actors, this can be expanded to include human rights and the corresponding attribution of rights and duties to corporations.[30] This approach takes existing understandings of liability under international law and transposes them onto TNCs.[31] It draws from theories of state responsibility and individual responsibility.[32]

---

[23]   Kevin T. Jackson, 'Rethinking Economic Governance: A Naturalistic Cosmopolitan Jurisprudence' (2013) 36 *Boston College International and Comparative Law Review* 39, 45.

[24]   Kelly Vinopal, 'Researching Public International Law', American Society of International Law, 5 (last updated 1 May 2015) <https://www.asil.org/sites/default/files/ERG_PUBLIC_INT.pdf>.

[25]   Vinopal (n 24).

[26]   International Court of Justice Statute, Article 38 <http://www.icj-cij.org/documents/index.php?p1=4> Carrie Menkel-Meadow, 'Why and How to Study "Transnational" Law' (2011) 1 (1) *U.C. Irvine Law Review* 101, 106.

[27]   Vinopal (n 24).

[28]   Steven R. Ratner, 'Corporations and Human Rights: A Theory of Legal Responsibility' (2001) 111 *Yale Law Journal* 443, 475.

[29]   Ratner (n 28).

[30]   (n 28).

[31]   (n 28).

[32]   (n 28).

**International Legal Pluralism**

International Legal Pluralism posits that international law is not solely made top-down through the consent of nation states.[33] Scholars argue that international law can also be made from the bottom up.[34] This section discusses Societal Constitutionalism Theory as an example of one of several International Legal Pluralism approaches.[35]

Societal Constitutionalism Theory, as the name suggests, has its roots in constitutional theory. It approaches constitutional theory through a lens informed by sociological methodology.[36] The core characteristics of Societal Constitutionalism Theory are: 'fracture, fluidity, permeability, and polycentricity'.[37] The Societal Constitutionalism Theory approach responds to the changes globalization has had on international lawmaking.[38] Under this approach, transnational legal fragmentation is a condition that makes possible the emergence of law made by non-state actors.[39] Scholars using a Societal Constitutionalism Theory approach theorize bottom-up effects of social movements as opposed to those of top-down global regimes.[40] This approach addresses the question of sources of international law.

Societal Constitutionalism scholars argue that Societal Constitutionalism is a legitimate form of law making because subjects of international law

---

[33] See generally, Gunther Teubner, 'Global Bukowina: Legal Pluralism in the World Society,' in Gunther Teubner (ed.), *Global Law Without a State* (Aldershot, 1997) 3.

[34] See generally, Janet Koven Levit, 'Bottom-Up International Lawmaking: Reflections on the New Haven School of International Law' (2007) 32 *Yale Journal of International Law* 393.

[35] See, e.g., Hari M. Osofsky, 'The Geography of Climate Change Litigation: Implications for Transnational Regulatory Governance' (2007) 83 *Washington University Law Quarterly* 1789, 1801.

[36] Gavin W. Anderson, 'Societal Constitutionalism, Social Movements, and Constitutionalism from Below' (2013) 20 *Indiana Journal of Global Legal Studies* 881, 885. See also Gunther Teubner, *Constitutional Fragments: Societal Constitutionalism and Globalization* (Oxford UP, 2012) and Gunther Teubner, 'Fragmented Foundations: Societal Constitutionalism Beyond the Nation State', in Petra Dobner and Martin Loughlin (eds), *The Twilight of Constitutionalism?* (Oxford UP, 2010) 327.

[37] Larry Catá Backer, 'Transnational Corporations' Outward Expression of Inward Self-Constitution: The Enforcement of Human Rights by Apple, Inc.' (2013) 20 *Indiana Journal of Global Legal Studies* 805, 873.

[38] Gavin W. Anderson, 'Societal Constitutionalism, Social Movements, and Constitutionalism from Below' (2013) 20 *Indiana Journal of Global Legal Studies* 881, 887.

[39] Backer (n 37) 810–813.

[40] Anderson (n 36) 883.

create law through their consent, the law is expressed, and it is effective.[41] Societal Constitutionalism varies from traditional positivism in international law because it does not view legal rules under international law as only being created by the consent of states but rather also by the consent of non-state actors.[42] Societal Constitutionalism approaches have been used to theorize international operations in several economic sectors, for example, intellectual property, international accounting, and forestry and fishery.[43]

Societal Constitutionalism Theory responds to a gap in traditional constitutionalism that omits the role of non-state actors. It has been described as 'establishing legitimate supreme authority for free and equal [people] engaged in a collective exercise of self-government'.[44] Others argue that the key constitutional question of the 20th century is 'the control of economic power'.[45] Societal constitutionalists argue that state-focused approaches overlook 'forms of sectoral private ordering in the world economy'.[46] Societal constitutions are either private or hybrid but not solely public.[47]

Traditional constitutionalism takes an approach that positions the public sphere and state actors as the sole bearers of legitimate constitutional authority.[48] However, some scholars have criticized traditional constitutionalism as being limited to protecting the private sector from the public sector without being able to protect the public sector from the private sector.[49] In contrast, Societal Constitutionalism posits that legitimate constitutional

---

[41]   (n 36) 885.

[42]   (n 36) 885. For a definition of positivism, see Adam Boczek Boleslaw, *International Law: A Dictionary* (Scarecrow Press, 2005) 23.

[43]   Gunther Teubner and Anna Beckers, 'Expanding Constitutionalism' (2013) 20 *Indiana Journal of Global Legal Studies* 523, 547; see also Dan Wielsch, 'Private Governance of Knowledge: Societally Crafted Intellectual Properties Regimes' (2013) 20 *Indiana Journal of Global Legal Studies* 907; Moritz Renner, 'Occupy the System! Societal Constitutionalism and Transnational Corporate Accounting' (2013) 20 *Indiana Journal of Global Legal Studies* 941; Saki Bailey and Ugo Mattei, 'Social Movements as Constituent Power: The Italian Struggle for the Commons' (2013) 20 *Indiana Journal of Global Legal Studies* 965; Florian Rödl, 'Fundamental Rights, Private Law, and Societal Constitution: On the Logic of the So-Called Horizontal Effect' (2013) 20 *Indiana Journal of Global Legal Studies* 1015.

[44]   Mattias Kumm, 'The Cosmopolitan Turn in Constitutionalism: An Integrated Conception of Public Law' (2013) 20 *Indiana Journal of Global Legal Studies* 605, 607.

[45]   Moritz Renner, 'Occupy the System! Societal Constitutionalism and Transnational Corporate Accounting' (2013) 20 *Indiana Journal of Global Legal Studies* 941.

[46]   Kumm (n 44) 626.

[47]   Rödl (n 43) 1015.

[48]   Kumm (n 44) 611.

[49]   Bailey and Mattei (n 43) 974–975, 979.

authority is located in both the public and the private spheres, and it focuses on the analysis of constitutional authority in the private sphere.[50]

The possibility of non-state actors as subjects of international law and the expansion of sources of law under a Societal Constitutionalism approach makes space in constitutional theory for TNCs.[51] Some scholars have theorized a community of TNCs made possible by globalization and that functions in governance gaps between national and international law.[52] This un-tethering of law making from geography creates the possibility of extra-territorial jurisdiction within which a 'self-referencing and autonomous regime of governance' can exist 'within a very narrow governance space'.[53] This has also been described as the emergence of informal jurisdictions.[54]

The characteristics of societal constitutionalism (fracture, fluidity and permeability) are also key factors that influence the behavior of TNCs and other non-state actors.[55] TNCs operate in governance spaces (fractures) between the jurisdictional authority of countries in which they operate, national and international law, requirements set by other TNCs, suppliers and third parties with which they interact, and gaps in international law itself.[56] TNCs' rules are impermanent (fluidity) and so, although structured, take different forms within an overarching framework. TNCs' rules change or fluctuate as needed when they interact with other systems of rules (permeability).[57] They are polycentric, which means that they present both the benefit of cooperation and the danger of collusion.[58]

Among other things, Societal Constitutionalism Theory makes it possible to identify moments when there is a potential for the development of bottom-up law making.[59] This theory posits that there are two prerequisites: 'sufficient pressure that calls for self-limitation' and 'internal self-reflection.'[60] Some international law scholars posit that corporate codes of conduct developed out of one such moment.[61] Pressure came from public

---

[50]  Kumm (n 44) 611.
[51]  Anderson (n 36) 885.
[52]  Backer (n 37) 810–813.
[53]  (n 37) 826–827.
[54]  Saskia Sassen, 'Visible Formalizations and Formally Invisible Facticities' (2013) 20 *Indiana Journal of Global Legal Studies* 3.
[55]  Backer (n 37) 873–874.
[56]  (n 37) 874.
[57]  (n 37) 874–875.
[58]  (n 37) 875–876.
[59]  Teubner and Beckers (n 43) 526.
[60]  (n 43) 527, 533.
[61]  (n 43) 526–527.

critiques of TNCs' operations, socially conscious investment and the proliferation of social and environmental standards in government procurement contracts.[62] Self-reflection took place as TNCs made choices about
how to make internal changes in response to external pressure.[63] Lastly,
some international law scholars argue that the effectiveness of Societal
Constitutionalism depends on the support of external constraints.[64] This
means that 'stabilization by a legal process' is a prerequisite for TNCs'
codes of conduct to become societal constitutions.[65]

## CORPORATE SOCIAL RESPONSIBILITY APPROACHES

One of the earliest theoretical approaches to corporate regulation remains
relevant today: Corporate Social Responsibility Theory. Early discussions
about Corporate Social Responsibility Theory began in the United States
in the late 1920s and they have continued through multiple iterations
into the present.[66] In the 1930s, scholars developed opposing theories of
Corporate Social Responsibility that became foundational positions that
have stood the test of time.[67] Although Corporate Social Responsibility
fell out of fashion in the mid-1930s, it returned to the fore in the mid-1950s
and received renewed attention in the 1990s in a new iteration.[68]

Corporate Social Responsibility Theory has its roots in philosophy
(ethics and morality) and philanthropy.[69] The goal of regulation under a
Corporate Social Responsibility Theory approach is to establish TNCs'

---

[62]   (n 43) 528.

[63]   (n 43) 534.

[64]   (n 43) 536.

[65]   (n 43) 537.

[66]   C.A. Harwell Wells, 'The Cycles of Corporate Social Responsibility: An
Historical Retrospective for the Twenty-First Century' (2002) 51 *University of
Kansas Law Review* 77, 83.

[67]   Rachel J. Anderson, 'Toward Global Corporate Citizenship: Reframing
Foreign Direct Investment Law' (2009) 18 *Michigan State International Law
Review* 1, 20; see Wells (n 66) 83; Adolf A. Berle and Gardiner C. Means, *The
Modern Corporation and Private Property* (1932) (rev. ed. 1967).

[68]   See Backer (n 6) 607; Douglas M. Branson, 'Corporate Social Responsibility
Redux' (2002) 76 *Tulane Law Review* 1207, 1216; Wells (n 66) 99.

[69]   See Antonio Vives, 'Corporate Social Responsibility: The Role of Law and
Markets and the Case of Developing Countries' (2008) 83 *Chicago–Kent Law
Review* 199, 200; Cheryl L. Wade, 'Corporate Governance as Corporate Social
Responsibility: Empathy and Race Discrimination' (2002) 76 *Tulane Law Review*
1461, 1466 ('distinguish[ing] the typical discussion of corporate social responsibility

responsibilities in relation to all of their stakeholders and to consider society's welfare.[70] This can be achieved by operation of law or through incentives that encourage TNCs to engage in practices that are not solely aimed at profit maximization but are intended to strengthen positive effects on stakeholders or ameliorate negative effects on stakeholders.[71] Regulation based on a Corporate Social Responsibility Theory approach draws from contract law, stakeholder choices, and soft law.[72] The Corporate Social Responsibility approach is often used to address problems related to, for example, the environment, human rights, and labor.

Corporate Social Responsibility Theory posits that TNCs are a network of companies that have obligations to all of the actors with whom they interact or who are impacted by their operations.[73] Scholars using a Corporate Social Responsibility approach have argued that these obligations and the justification for government intervention stem from a variety of sources. One argument is that TNCs should have legal obligations to stakeholders because they are similar to governments or public institutions.[74] This claim of a quasi-public nature is based on their size, effects, capital and influence.[75]

Many of the problems addressed by Corporate Social Responsibility Theory approaches in the transnational context stem from the ways that TNCs are different from domestic corporations and the limitations of state-based regulation. Laws tied to geographically limited jurisdictions may comprehensively regulate the activities of domestic corporations but may only partially regulate the activities of TNCs, which operate in multiple jurisdictions. Currently, national legal systems are unable to comprehensively regulate TNCs.[76] Scholars also have noted that gaps remain despite the overlapping mosaic of national and international law.[77]

---

that looks to businesses to achieve social good even when not required by law, from corporate responsibility that is required under the law').

[70] See Vives (n 69) 216.
[71] See Branson (n 68) 1215; see also Wade (n 69) 1466.
[72] Backer (n 6) 608.
[73] Backer (n 6) 607; Vives (n 69) 201 ('[M]ost people interpret these terms to mean that the corporation has a responsibility toward society, and that the corporation has a responsibility to do something about the problems that affect society; others interpret them to mean that the corporation must take responsibility for its own activities as they affect society.').
[74] Branson (n 68) 1212.
[75] Branson (n 68) 1212.
[76] Backer (n 6) 619.
[77] Rachel J. Anderson (n 67) 6, 13, 22.

Corporate Social Responsibility approaches seek to fill gaps in the law in addition to expanding TNCs' responsibility beyond the constraints of profit maximization.

Corporate Social Responsibility Theory differs from other theoretical approaches in significant ways. Unlike the Law and Economics approaches discussed below, Corporate Social Responsibility approaches do not view TNC actors as constrained to decisions and actions intended for profit maximization and, in fact, seek to promote goals that are not always related to short-term shareholder profit. Corporate Social Responsibility Theory differs from Public International Law Theory in that it does not assume that state actors are the only makers of laws and regulations.

Modern scholars using a Corporate Social Responsibility approach tend to prefer the stakeholder model to the shareholder primacy model of corporate governance. In modern iterations of Corporate Social Responsibility Theory, corporate governance often plays a significant role, and some scholars have suggested that modern Corporate Social Responsibility approaches are appropriately categorized as a subset of corporate governance theory.[78] Corporate Social Responsibility approaches in the transnational context include a combination of 'soft law' (norms, voluntary regulation or self-regulation) and 'hard law' (mandatory or enforceable regulation).[79]

There are several categories of Corporate Social Responsibility approaches including Progressive Corporate Law Theory, Global Corporate Citizenship Theory, Social Contract Theory, and Environmentalist Theory approaches. Corporate Social Responsibility approaches are an important part of the regulation of TNCs, in part because of the simultaneous overlapping regulatory jurisdictions, regulatory fragmentation, and prominence of international human rights law in the agendas of international institutions and non-governmental organizations. Some approaches, such as Progressive Corporate Law Theory and Social Contract Theory, apply to corporations generally, which includes TNCs. Others such as the Global Corporate Citizenship Theory and Environmentalist Theory approaches apply specifically to TNCs and corporations that are primarily domestic but engage in transnational economic activity.

---

[78]    Branson (n 68) 1217, 1225.
[79]    Michael Torrance, 'Persuasive Authority Beyond the State: A Theoretical Analysis of Transnational Corporate Social Responsibility Norms as Legal Reasons Within Positive Legal Systems' (2011) 12 *German Law Journal* 1573.

**Progressive Corporate Law**

Progressive Corporate Law Theory can be classified as a sub-category of Corporate Social Responsibility approaches although some scholars may view it as an independent category. It developed as a Corporate Social Responsibility response to the Law and Economics Contractarian approach that was prominent in the 1980s.[80] Progressive Corporate Law approaches gained traction in the late 1990s. Under Progressive Corporate Law approaches, the concentration and use of power by TNCs and other large corporations are core concerns, in addition to the moral and ethical obligations envisioned under a general Corporate Social Responsibility approach.[81] Many argue that the large corporations, like TNCs, have characteristics that distinguish them from mere 'aggregations of private property', which justifies additional social responsibilities.[82] Others go further and argue that the form, size and power of TNCs and other corporations demand operation in the public interest similar to a public institution.[83] Progressive Corporate Law approaches include mandatory legal requirements in addition to self-regulation, which is not a necessary characteristic of other forms of Corprate Social Responsibility Theory approaches.[84]

Progressive Corporate Law approaches do not accept the shareholder primacy model as a given, but instead make it the subject of critique.[85] Some scholars using a Progressive Corporate Law approach apply communitarianism whereby they view and analyze TNCs as a community rather than as a 'purely economic actor'.[86] Another subset of scholars using a Progressive Corporate Law approach argue for a stakeholder model in which TNCs and other corporations owe legal responsibilities to their stakeholders, including employees, consumers and the communities in locations in which they operate.[87]

---

[80]   Branson (n 68) 1217.
[81]   See Kellye Y. Testy, 'Capitalism and Freedom-for Whom?: Feminist Legal Theory and Progressive Corporate Law' (2004) *Law and Contemporary Problems* 87, 91.
[82]   Branson (n 68) 1212.
[83]   Testy (n 81) 92.
[84]   See Amiram Gill, 'Corporate Governance as Social Responsibility: A Research Agenda' (2008) 26 *Berkeley Journal of International Law* 452, 460.
[85]   Testy (n 81) 92.
[86]   Branson (n 68) 1217.
[87]   (n 68) 1215, 1217.

### Global Corporate Citizenship / Social Contract

Global Corporate Citizenship approaches and Corporate Citizenship approaches developed out of business and management theory and draw on political science theory.[88] Under Global Corporate Citizenship approaches, the rights and obligations of TNCs in society stem from the social contract that forms the basis of the relationship between a state and its citizens.[89] This is based on an argument that TNCs owe their existence to the rights and benefits granted by states and, therefore, may be subject to any regulations states choose to impose on them within their prescriptive jurisdiction.[90] As such, it is viewed as a voluntary relationship in which the TNC is bound to obey the law and to exercise its rights in light of other obligations that may be imposed by the state as part of that relationship.[91] Global Corporate Citizenship approaches require TNCs to act as stakeholders in society and to interact in an ethical manner with their stakeholders.[92]

### Environmentalist Approaches

Environmentalist Theory approaches focus on TNCs' obligations as they relate to the environment. A core tenant of Environmentalist Theory approaches is that economic growth should not be pursued at the cost of environmental protection and sustainability.[93] Some Environmentalist

---

[88]    See Rachel J. Anderson (n 67) 23.

[89]    See Stephen Bottomley, *The Constitutional Corporation: Rethinking Corporate Governance* (Ashgate, 2013) 44; see also Mugambi Laibuta, 'Multi-National Corporations in Human Rights Protection and the Role of the African Union' (2014) <http://papers.ssrn.com/sol3/papers.cfm?abstract_id=2477261>.

[90]    See, e.g., Susan J. Stabile, 'A Catholic Vision of the Corporation' (2005) 4 *Seattle Journal for Social Justice* 181, 195; Susan J. Stabile, 'Using Religion to Promote Corporate Responsibility' (2004) 39 *Wake Forest Law Review* 839, 898; David Millon, 'Theories of the Corporation' (1990) 1990 *Duke Law Journal* 201, 206; Susan J. Stabile, 'Freedom to Choose Unwisely: Congress' Misguided Decision to Leave 401(K) Plan Participants to Their Own Devices' (2002) 11 *Cornell Journal of Law and Public Policy* 361, 396; Steven M.H. Wallman, 'Team Production in Business Organizations: Understanding the Purpose of a Corporation: An Introduction' (1999) 24 *Journal of Corporation Law* 807; Martin E. Gold, 'Economic Development Projects: A Perspective' (1987) 19 *Urban Lawyer* 193.

[91]    See Bottomley (n 89) 44.

[92]    Rachel J. Anderson (n 67) 23.

[93]    Anthony D. Taibi, 'Racial Justice in the Age of Global Economy: Community Empowerment and Global Strategy' (1995) 44 *Duke Law Journal* 928, 973.

Theory approaches build on the general Corporate Social Responsibility Theory argument that certain corporations, like TNCs, are similar to public institutions and, therefore, should be regulated as such. They argue that some corporations should be classified as public trusts and, therefore, subject to greater oversight under public-trust regulations.[94] This would apply to corporations that meet certain criteria, for example, based on public protection, grant of a monopoly, market capitalization, gross revenue and shareholders.[95] Some scholars using Environmentalist Theory approaches have also suggested that TNCs might fit into this category.[96]

## LAW AND ECONOMICS APPROACHES

Law and Economics Theory approaches draw heavily on economic theory, in particular neoclassical economic theory (supply-side economics). Law and Economics approaches draw on property law, contract law, tort law and criminal law as sources of law.[97] These approaches can be traced back to the 1960s and their popularity expanded significantly during the 1980s.[98] The goal of regulation informed by Law and Economics Theory is to allocate and protect property rights and to enable the functioning of a market economy, both of which are generally viewed as short-term goals.[99] A functioning market economy is seen as one that is efficient, whereby efficiency is defined as the allocation of rights to the parties who 'would be willing to pay the most' for them.[100] Law and Economics Theory approaches are often used to address problems related to, for example, anti-trust and securities.

Under Law and Economics Theory approaches, TNCs are viewed as

---

[94] Herman F. Greene, 'Hot, Crowded, and Not-So-Flat: The Changing Climate for Corporations' (2009) 44 *Wake Forest Law Review* 799, 829.

[95] Greene (n 94).

[96] (n 94).

[97] Paul H. Rubin, 'Law and Economics' (2008) *The Concise Encyclopedia of Economics* <http://www.econlib.org/library/Enc/LawandEconomics.html> (accessed 29 December 2015).

[98] The Law and Economics Approach is also described by some as the Chicago and Post-Chicago Schools. See Robert D. Atkinson and David B. Audretsch, 'Economic Doctrines and Approaches to Antitrust' (2011) Indiana University-Bloomington: School of Public and Environmental Affairs Research Paper Series No. 2011–01–02, 4 <http://www.itif.org/files/2011-antitrust.pdf>; see also, e.g., Ronald H. Coase, 'The Problem of Social Cost' (1960) 3 *Journal of Law and Economics* 1; see also Branson (n 68) 1216.

[99] Atkinson and Audretsch (n 98); Rubin (n 97).

[100] Rubin (n 97).

primarily or solely economic actors. Law and Economics approaches assume the general efficiency of laws and markets.[101] They also assume that people are rational actors and responsive to incentives in a way that is proportional to potential penalties.[102] As a corollary, scholars using Law and Economics Theory preference market incentives over regulation and Law and Economics approaches focus on the allocation of rights and the use of incentives to influence behavior.[103] Law and Economics scholars argue for limited government intervention, for example, limited to enabling regulations or corrective regulations that simulate estimated market preferences.[104] In modern iterations of Law and Economics Theory, the Contractarian Theory of the firm is a core assumption. The Contractarian Theory approach is a sub-category of the Law and Economics Theory approach and posits that TNCs are 'private contractual arrangements' among owners and managers that are governed primarily by market forces.[105]

Law and Economics Theory approaches focus on TNCs' roles as economic actors, the role of markets, and the role of government in the market. Law and Economics scholars seek to address questions related to efficiency, competition, information asymmetries, distributional outcomes, fairness, property rights, risk allocation, the extent to which government should intervene in markets, and the intersection of micro- and macro-economics in the international context. Law and Economics Theory approaches tend to position regulation as a public intervention into a private sphere otherwise governed primarily by enabling laws.[106] Regulation is viewed as a market intervention, which requires a justification to explain the need for and form of government intervention.

Law and Economics Theory approaches differ from other theoretical approaches in significant ways. Unlike Corporate Social Responsibility Theory approaches, Law and Economics Theory approaches generally limit ethical responsibilities of managers to shareholders and do not recognize moral and ethical responsibilities for stakeholders who are not shareholders such as employees, customers, and surrounding communities. From the persepctive of a Law and Economics Theory approach, profit maximization for shareholders is paramount, and managers should only consider Corporate Social Responsibility measures if they contribute to the bottom line. Law and Economics Theory approaches tend to preference weak

---

[101]   (n 97).
[102]   (n 97).
[103]   (n 97).
[104]   (n 97).
[105]   Branson (n 68) 1217.
[106]   See, e.g., Atkinson and Audretsch (n 98); Rubin (n 99).

enforcement with limited exceptions.[107] Law and Economics approaches posit that law should be efficient.[108]

Scholars influenced by Law and Economics Theory approaches tend to view the goal of regulating TNCs as promoting economic efficiency in a system based on free market competition with secure property rights.[109] Some view the regulation of TNCs as a government intervention that is acceptable when needed to mitigate the effects of information asymmetry in the market or to promote social justice (often referred to as economic welfare in the economic literature).[110]

One critique of Law and Economics Theory approaches is that they assume that the common law system is efficient.[111] These characteristics may limit the applicability of Law and Economics Theory approaches in the international context, which does not have a shared common law system (judge-made law) and where many countries do not have a national common law system. Law and Economics Theory approaches have been critiqued from a Feminist Legal Theory perspective that argues that incorrect assumptions about equal bargaining power combined with a preference for minimal regulation result in a lack of protection for people who are 'economically vulnerable.'[112] Another feminist critique is that the Law and Economics approaches apply 'assumptions [that] protect the authority of those currently in power.'[113]

Differences in sub-categories of Law and Economics approaches are often linked to the differences between the economic doctrines with which they are affiliated.[114] There are several sub-categories, including the Public Interest Theory,[115] Regulatory Capture Theory, Shareholder Primacy Theory, Neo-Keynesian Theory, and Innovation Economics Theory. The Public Interest Theory approach argues that, when regulations repair market failures due to inefficiency or unfair outcomes, 'regulation increases

---

[107] Atkinson and Audretsch (n 98).
[108] Rubin (n 97).
[109] See, e.g., Richard A. Posner, *Economic Analysis of Law* (7th ed., Aspen Publishers, 2007) and Richard A. Posner and Francesco Parisi (eds.), *Law and Economics* (Edward Elgar, 1997).
[110] Posner 2007 (n 109); Posner 1997 (n 109).
[111] Rubin (n 97).
[112] Dickerson (n 22) 140.
[113] Dickerson (n 22).
[114] Atkinson and Audretsch (n 98).
[115] See, e.g., James C. Bonbright, *Principles of Public Utility Rates* (Public Utilities Reports, 1961), Kenneth Culp Davis, *Administrative Law Treatise* (West, 1958), and Henry J. Friendly, *The Federal Administrative Agencies: The Need for Better Definition of Standards* (Harvard UP, 1962).

social welfare'.[116] In contrast, the Regulatory Capture Theory approach sees regulation in the economy primarily as a response to pressure by interest groups attempting to maximize profits for their members.[117]

### Shareholder Primacy Theory

One of the dominant regulatory approaches today, the Shareholder Primacy Theory approach is a Corporate Governance approach.[118] It is a response to the separation of ownership and control in the governance structure of TNCs, a characteristic of corporations that was the focus of theoretical debates in the 1930s.[119] This supply-side approach positions the producers of goods and services as the central players in the economy. However, the discussions about ownership and control in the 1930s did not lead directly or immediately to Shareholder Primacy as a theoretical approach.[120]

The dominant aproach to corporate governance was based on Managerialism Theory in the United States from the mid-1930s until the 1970s.[121] This began to change as a governance model based on Shareholder Primacy Theory began to replace the one based on Managerialism and by the 1990s became the dominant theoretical approach to corporate regulation in the United States.[122] The model based on Shareholder Primacy Theory remains dominant in the United States and other countries although some scholars have begun to predict its decline.[123]

---

[116]   See Richard A. Posner, 'Theories of Economic Regulation' (1974) NBER Working Paper Series No. 1; see also Johan den Hertog, 'Review of Theories of Regulation' (2010) Utrecht School of Economics: Tjalling C. Koopmans Institute Discussion Paper Series No. 10–18, 2 <http://www.uu.nl/rebo/economie/discussionpapers>.

[117]   Posner (n 116).

[118]   Corporate Governance is 'a set of processes and structures for controlling and directing an organization.' Haslinda Abdullah and Benedict Valentine, 'Fundamental and Ethics Theories of Corporate Governance' (2009) *Middle Eastern Finance and Economics* 88.

[119]   Berle and Means (n 67) 6.

[120]   Lynn A. Stout, 'On the Rise of Shareholder Primacy, Signs of Its Fall, and the Return of Managerialism (in the Closet)' (2013) 36 *Seattle University Law Review* 1169, 1171–1173 (citing Michael C. Jensen and William H. Meckling, 'Theory of the Firm: Managerial Behavior, Agency Costs and Ownership Structure' [1976] 3 *Journal of Financial Economics* 305).

[121]   Stout (n 120) 1169, 1171–1173.

[122]   Stout (n 120) 1174, 1178.

[123]   Stout (n 120) 1178.

### Neo-Keynesian Theory

The Neo-Keynesian Theory approach is a demand-side economics approach and assumes that the demand for goods and services in the form of spending or investing by business, government, and consumers is the primary driver of economic growth.[124] As a corollary, scholars using Neo-Keynesian Theory tend to prefer government regulations that promote economic growth via increased consumption as a result of 'equitable distribution of income and wealth.'[125]

### Innovation Economics Theory

The Innovation Economics Theory approach is a production-efficiency orientation that assumes that innovation is the primary driver of growth.[126] As a corollary, the Innovation Economics Theory approach prioritizes regulation that benefits innovation even at the short-term expense of profit maximization or equitable distribution of wealth.[127] In addition, TNC regulation from an Innovation Economics Theory approach 'would be more open to seeing the benefits of inter-firm collaborative activity.'[128]

## NEW GOVERNANCE THEORY APPROACHES

New Governance Theory approaches bring together core elements of Corporate Social Responsibility Theory and Law and Economics Theory approaches, and scholars have argued that New Governance Theory approaches merge corporate governance and Corporate Social Responsibility approaches.[129] New Governance Theory approaches focus on the role of '[p]rivate forms of social regulation,' often in the form of self-regulation, operating in conjunction with state-centered regulation.[130]

---

[124]   Atkinson and Audretsch (n 98).
[125]   (n 98).
[126]   (n 98).
[127]   (n 98).
[128]   (n 98).
[129]   See, generally, Gill (n 84) 452.
[130]   Karen Bradshaw Schulz, 'New Governance and Industry Culture' (2013) 88 *Notre Dame Law Review* 2515 (citing Orly Lobel, 'The Paradox of Extralegal Activism: Critical Legal Consciousness and Transformative Politics' [2007] 120 *Harvard Law Review* 937, 983) and 2519 (citing Christine Parker, 'The Pluralization of Regulation' [2008] 9 *Theoretical Inquiries in Law* 349 and Joel Handler et al., 'A Roundtable on New Legal Realism, Microanalysis of Institutions, and the New

They are based on the assumption that states do not have the capacity to address the challenges presented by globalization and so, therefore, additional capacity is needed, which creates a need to involve non-state actors in regulation.[131] Scholars using New Governance Theory approaches study the regulations, the regulators and the institutional environments in which new governance emerges.[132] New Governance Theory approaches assign the state a role in the promotion of 'overall welfare and equity.'[133] New Governance Theory approaches emerged in the 1990s.[134]

New Governance Theory approaches have been described as a 'third way' situated on a continuum between state-centered regulation and market mechanisms.[135] Their emergence is viewed as a response to the failure of domestic and international actors 'to solve emerging problems.'[136] Private regulatory regimes are 'voluntary systems of rules developed, monitored, and enforced by non-state actors.'[137] Successful private regulatory regimes often have 'a strong similarity to government regulation operated by non-state actors.'[138]

New Governance Theory approaches are often presented as 'an alternative to command and control [theories of] regulation.'[139] Scholars argue that New Governance Theory allows the development of more flexible and participatory legal remedies.[140] There are many variations among scholars using New Governance Theory, but a common assumption is that a solely treaty-based, top-down model of global regulation has limitations that prevent it from fully addressing important challenges presented by modern globalization.[141]

---

Governance: Exploring Convergences and Differences' [2005] *Wisconsin Law Review* 479, 511).

[131]   John Gerard Ruggie, 'Global Governance and "New Governance Theory": Lessons from Business and Human Rights' (2014) 20 *Global Governance* 5, 8–9.

[132]   See Schulz (n 130) 2549.

[133]   Schulz (n 130) 2515–16 (citing Orly Lobel, 'The Paradox of Extralegal Activism: Critical Legal Consciousness and Transformative Politics' [2007] 120 *Harvard Law Review* 937, 983).

[134]   Ruggie (n 131) 5.

[135]   Schulz (n 130) 2519.

[136]   (n 130) 2549.

[137]   (n 130) 2548.

[138]   (n 130) 2548.

[139]   David M. Trubek and Louise G. Trubek, 'New Governance and Legal Regulation: Complementarity, Rivalry, and Transformation' (2007) Wisconsin Law School Legal Studies Research Paper No. 25 <https://media.law.wisc.edu/m/zyjnh/ssrn-id988065.pdf>.

[140]   Trubek and Trubek (n 139).

[141]   Ruggie (n 131) 8.

New Governance Theory approaches posit that private and self-regulation have been around for a long time and are more successful than state-centered or market mechanisms in some circumstances.[142] They straddle the line that previously was theorized as a clear and non-porous boundary between legally enforceable 'hard law' and 'soft law' comprising aspirations and norms that are not legally enforceable.[143] New Governance Theory approaches study the 'features' or potential effects of private and self-regulation.[144] Some scholars argue that the longevity of private regulation is positively influenced by '(1) strong, preexisting norms, (2) industry actors with a competitive advantage in setting rules, and (3) a robust market for public and private regulation.'[145] New Governance Theory approaches 'identif[y] a growing involvement of the private sector in shaping public policy and regulation.'[146]

Some New Governance theories seek to identify the contexts in which private and self-regulation emerges and flourishes.[147] Some New Governance Theory scholars suggest that this approach may be particularly suited to address certain types of sector-specific issues.[148] For example, some scholars argue that private regulation tends to be more successful in economic sectors in which there a small number of participants who are repeat players and who possess large amounts of information about other players.[149] New Governance Theory approaches posit that participants in a particular sector are often better suited to create regulations

---

[142]   Schulz (n 130) 2543.

[143]   See Gill (n 84) 463.

[144]   Schulz (n 130) 2539.

[145]   Schulz (n 130) 2550.

[146]   Gill (n 84) 464 (citing Lester M. Salamon, 'The New Governance and the Tools of Public Action: An Introduction' in Lester M. Salamon [ed.], *The Tools of Government: A Guide to the New Governance* (Oxford UP, 2002), 1–14.

[147]   See, e.g., Schulz (n 130); Lisa T. Alexander, 'Stakeholder Participation in New Governance: Lessons from Chicago's Public Housing Reform Experiment' (2009) 16 *Georgetown Journal on Poverty Law and Policy* 117; Julia Black, '"Paradoxes and Failures": New Governance Techniques and the Financial Crisis' (2012) 75 *Modern Law Review* 1037; Eric Tucker, 'Old Lessons for New Governance: Safety or Profit and the New Conventional Wisdom' (2012) Osgoode CLPE Research Paper No. 36/2012.

[148]   For example, 'the failure of traditional state governments to respond to the challenges of globalization and related environmental problems.' Schulz (n 130) 2520 (citing John Gerard Ruggie, 'Taking Embedded Liberalism Global: The Corporate Connection' in David Held and Mathias Koenig-Archibugi [eds.], *Taming Globalization* [Polity, 2003] 93, 95–97).

[149]   See, e.g., Schulz (n 130) 2540 (citing Douglass C. North, *Institutions, Institutional Change and Economic Performance* 12 [Cambridge UP, 1990]).

because of their industry-specific knowledge.[150] Rather than promoting the injection or overlay of a comprehensive system, New Governance Theory approaches call for individual 'building blocks' to be developed and integrated into existing regulatory structures.[151]

In addition, New Governance Theory approaches posit that private- and self-regulation are more effective when three factors that promote cooperation are present.[152] The first is that participants in the relevant economic sector value relationships ('relationship preservation').[153] The second is that there is an incentive to unify against a perceived external pressure or threat ('industry protection').[154] The third is that existing market participants have some preexisting form of common interaction (participation).[155]

Some scholars also posit that New Governance Theory approaches result in a regulatory structure that is situated between top-down and bottom-up approaches.[156] Others posit that New Governance Theory can create a benefit in the form of a 'market to regulate' in which regulatory competition drives the creation of regulation where there was none or better regulation that would exist without competition.[157]

New Governance Theory approaches have been critiqued for a lack of examples proving the benefits and effectiveness of private or self-regulation[158] and concerns that private or self-regulation will reduce the probability that more rigorous and enforceable regulations will be enacted.[159]

---

[150]   See, e.g., Schulz (n 130) 2543 (citing F.A. Hayek, 'The Use of Knowledge in Society' [1945] 35 *American Economic Review* 519, 524; Elinor Ostrom and Xavier Basurto, 'Crafting Analytical Tools to Study Institutional Change' [2011] 7 *Journal of Institutional Economics* 317, 319; and Mario J. Rizzo and Douglas Glenn Whitman, 'The Knowledge Problem of New Paternalism' [2009] 2009 *Brigham Young University Law Review* 905, 922–24).

[151]   Ruggie (n 131) 8.

[152]   See, e.g., Schulz (n 130) 2541.

[153]   See, e.g., Schulz (n 130) 2541.

[154]   See, e.g., Schulz (n 130) 2541 and 2545 (citing Peter Grajzl and Andrzej Baniak, 'Industry Self-Regulation, Subversion of Public Institutions, and Social Control of Torts' [2009] 29 *International Review of Law and Economics* 360, 363 and Saule T. Omarova, 'Wall Street as Community of Fate: Toward Financial Industry Self-Regulation' [2011] 159 *University of Pennsylvania Law Review* 411, 451).

[155]   See, e.g., Schulz (n 130) 2541.

[156]   See, e.g., Schulz (n 130) 2546.

[157]   See, e.g., Schulz (n 130) 2546 (citing Kenneth W. Abbott and Duncan Snidal, 'The Governance Triangle: Regulatory Standards Institutions and the Shadow of the Law' in Walter Mattli and Ngaire Woods [eds], *The Politics of Global Regulation* [Princeton UP, 2009] 44, 78).

[158]   Schulz (n 130) 2516 (citations omitted).

[159]   See, e.g., Schulz (n 130) 2546.

New Governance approaches also have been criticized as 'deregulation in disguise,' but others counter that these approaches reject deregulation.[160]

From a New Governance Theory approach perspective, TNCs present a special area of need. The lack of state capacity to comprehensively regulate TNCs stems from several factors, including the limitations of solely domestic regulation and the lack of international regulation coupled with the lack of some form of *respondeat superior* for separately incorporated subsidiaries.[161]

# CRITICAL LEGAL THEORY APPROACHES

Critical Legal Theory approaches call into question dominant theoretical doctrines and highlight ways that the claim to universality of these approaches is undermined by systemic exclusion and inequality. Critical Legal Theory approaches that have addressed issues in corporate law or the regulation of TNCs include Feminist Legal Theory, Critical Race Theory, and Third World Theory approaches.

## Feminist Legal Theory

Feminist Legal Theory approaches incorporate insights from multiple disciplines, including ethics, morality and political science.[162] Feminist Legal Theory approaches theorize gender and call into question assumptions of universality, objectivity and gender-neutrality that are present in many disciplines, including corporate and international law.[163] Feminist Legal Theory approaches focus on the 'use and distribution of power' and address issues related to social exclusion, vulnerability, and subordination.[164] Feminist Legal Theory approaches to corporate law began to develop in the 1980s and early 1990s following initial critiques of corporate law from a feminist perspective.[165]

---

[160]   Gill (n 84).

[161]   Ruggie (n 131) 9.

[162]   Martha Albertson Fineman, 'Feminist Legal Theory' (2005) 13 *American Journal of Gender, Social Policy, and Law* 13, 13–14.

[163]   Fineman (n 162) 14.

[164]   See Dickerson (n 22).

[165]   Testy (n 81) 94 (citing Kathleen A. Lahey and Sarah W. Salter, 'Corporate Law in Legal Theory and Legal Scholarship: From Classicism to Feminism' [1985] 23 *Osgoode Hall Law Journal* 543 and Theresa A. Gabaldon, 'The Lemonade Stand: Feminist and Other Reflections on the Limited Liability of Corporate Shareholders' [1992] 46 *Vanderbilt Law Review* 1387). Early feminist scholars

Core goals of Feminist Legal Theory are to improve women's lives and promote societal flourishing.[166] The goal of Feminist Legal Theory as it relates to regulation of corporations is to identify potential points of intervention where women and others have unequal power or are systemically subordinated.[167] Scholars using Feminist Legal Theory approaches have noted that TNC governance is often guided by assumptions of a gendered, specifically male, employee.[168] Regulations that are informed by Feminist Legal Theory approaches are developed with an explicit awareness of the effects on women and ways that regulation can reduce or mitigate negative effects of corporate actions on women. Feminist Legal Theory approaches are often applied to analyze problems related to human rights and labor.

Feminist Legal Theory approaches view corporations as comprised of and affecting a community of individuals who are all equally valuable as people.[169] Further, because they are equally valuable, their needs and interests should be given equal weight in corporate decision-making at the macro level.[170] In addition, valuing all community members' needs equally means that equal weight should be given to effects on others in individual decision-making.[171] Scholars applying Feminist Legal Theory approaches have argued that the regulation of TNCs 'should give transnational corporations an incentive to balance economic goals with socio-political goals.'[172]

---

applying feminist theory to business and corporate law include Ramona Paetzold and Ronnie Cohen. See, generally, Ramona Paetzold, 'Commentary: Feminism and Business Law: The Essential Interconnection' (1994) 31 *American Business Law Journal* 699 and Ronnie Cohen, 'Feminist Thought and Corporate Law: It's Time to Find Our Way Up From the Bottom (Line)' (1994) 2 *American University Journal of Gender, Social Policy and the Law* 1.

[166]   Testy (n 81) 95.

[167]   Testy (n 81) 94–95.

[168]   Rachel J. Anderson, 'Promoting Distributional Equality for Women: Some Thoughts on Gender and Global Corporate Citizenship in Foreign Direct Investment' (2010) 32 *Women's Rights Law Reporter* 1, 8 (citing Cynthia Enloe, *Bananas, Beaches and Bases: Making Feminist Sense of International Politics* 128 [Univ of California P, 2000] ['To clear the land and harvest the bananas they decided they needed a male workforce, sustained at a distance by women as prostitutes, mothers and wives.'])

[169]   See Barbara Ann White, 'Feminist Foundations for the Law of Business: One Law and Economics Scholar's Survey and (Re)view' (1999) 10 *UCLA Women's Law Journal* 39, 48.

[170]   White (n 169).

[171]   (n 169) 48.

[172]   Rachel J. Anderson (n 168) 19.

Core contributions of Feminist Legal Theory approaches include the feminist ethics of care and connectedness[173] and the perspective that the 'personal is political.'[174] The feminist ethic of care posits a fundamental equality that is based on a prioritization of 'concern for others.'[175] It presents an alternative set of criteria for decision-making that addresses a hierarchy embedded in the formal structures of traditional corporate governance. The 'personal is political' highlights the importance of addressing systemic oppression rather than focusing on its effects on one individual.[176]

Key contributions of Feminist Legal Theory approaches to corporate law include: inclusion of non-shareholder stakeholders in corporate decision-making, incorporation of concepts of care and connection into fiduciary duty law, identification of disproportionate harmful effects on women, and overburdening of women as a result of negative effects of corporations.[177] For example, scholars using Feminist Legal Theory approaches have argued that corporations should not prioritize profit maximization to the extent that it requires the externalization of risk to third parties because this violates the principles of care and connectedness.[178]

Feminist Legal Theory approaches posit that traditional theoretical approaches and the legal systems they justify are flawed if they assume neutrality and universality without incorporating an analysis of bias and inequality to determine whether these assumptions are accurate. Scholars using Feminist Legal Theory approaches have identified several potential areas of weakness in traditional approaches, including exclusion of women's experiences from analyses of purportedly universal international law,[179] gender bias in facially neutral rules,[180] omission of parties' unequal bargaining power in transactions from economic models,[181] and theoretically inconsistent application of public–private distinctions that

---

173 White (n 169) 48.
174 Testy (n 81) 107.
175 White (n 169) 45–46.
176 See Carol Hanisch, 'Introduction' in *The Personal is Political: The Women's Liberation Movement Classic with a New Explanatory Introduction* (2006) <http://www.carolhanisch.org/CHwritings/PIP.html>.
177 Testy (n 81) 95.
178 White (n 169) 85 (citing Theresa Gabaldon, 'The Lemonade Stand: Feminist and Other Reflections on the Limited Liability of Corporate Shareholders' [1992] 45 *Vanderbilt Law Review* 1387).
179 See Hilary Charlesworth, Christine Chinkin and Shelley Wright, 'Feminist Approaches to International Law' (1991) *American Journal of International Law* 626.
180 Charlesworth, Chinkin and Wright (n 179).
181 Dickerson (n 22).

appear to be based on gender bias.[182] Some scholars writing from a Feminist Legal Theory perspective have questioned theories that assume the goal of 'unlimited economic growth' as a norm and argued instead for an approach that includes 'the distribution of wealth and resources.'[183]

## Critical Race Theory

Critical Race Theory approaches incorporate insights from multiple disciplines and emerged in the 1970s.[184] Critical Race Theory approaches build on Critical Legal Studies and Radical Feminist Theory, as well as several others.[185] In the context of TNCs, scholars using a Critical Race Theory approach theorize race, racism and power and call into question assumptions of law's neutrality and objectivity. Scholars using a Critical Race Theory approach analyze issues related to oppression, privilege, distribution of wealth and access to resources.

The core goal of Critical Race Theory approaches is to end all oppression.[186] Critical Race Theory approaches posit that people who are on the receiving end of discrimination should inform public policy and law.[187] Further, some scholars who write from a Critical Race Theory perspective argue that markets should be restructured to function in ways that will result in procedural equality and substantive justice.[188] Some scholars have made calls for the incorporation of Critical Race Theory approaches into analyses of international law, for example, through engagement with economic and social rights on the international stage, deconstruction of claims of universalism and equality in human rights law, analysis of extra-governmental institutions such as TNCs that may negatively affect

---

[182]   See Dickerson (n 22) 143; White (n 169) 61 (citing Ronnie Cohen, 'Feminist Thought and Corporate Law: It's Time to Find Our Way Up From the Bottom [Line]' [1994] 2 *American University Journal of Gender, Social Policy and the Law* 1; and Shelley Wright, 'Women and the Global Economic Order: A Feminist Perspective' [1995] 10 *American University Journal of International Law and Policy* 861, 862).

[183]   Wright (n 182) 885.

[184]   Richard Delgado and Jean Stefancic, 'Introduction' in *Critical Race Theory: An Introduction* (NYU Press, 2012).

[185]   For a discussion of Critical Race Theory's relationship to other theoretical approaches and activist movements, see Delgado and Stefancic (n 184).

[186]   Daniel Solózano, 'Critical Race Theory, Racial and Gender Microaggressions, and the Experiences of Chicana and Chicano Scholars' (1998) *International Journal of Qualitative Studies in Education* 11, 121–136.

[187]   Regina F. Burch, 'Worldview Diversity in the Boardroom: A Law and Social Equity Rationale' (2011) 42 *Loyola University Chicago Law Journal* 585, 623.

[188]   Taibi (n 93) 983.

human rights, and engagement with international enforcement bodies and mechanisms.[189] Critical Race Theory approaches have been incorporated, although often not explicitly, into recent scholarship that addresses TNC regulation.

**Third World Theory**

Like other Critical Legal Theory approaches, Third World Theory incorporates insights from multiple disciplines, including history, political science, ethics and morality.[190] Third World Theory approaches take the position that law, markets and politics are interconnected.[191] They place an emphasis on substantive rights as opposed to formal or procedural rights.[192] As a corollary, Third World Theory critiques approaches that assume the formal equality of states under international law as ignoring the interconnectedness of law, economics and politics as well as the biases inherent in the international legal system.[193] Further, Third World Theory approaches argue that distinctions between public and private spheres are not relevant for addressing substantive issues, including 'the scope, type and structure of private interests and power' as well as the 'redistribution of power among different social groups.'[194]

Third World Theory approaches to TNC regulation are part of a

---

[189] Penelope E. Andrews, 'Making Room for Critical Race Theory in International Law: Some Practical Pointers' (2000) 45 *Villanova Law Review* 855, 881–882.

[190] See Seth Gordon, 'Indigenous Rights in Modern International Law from a Critical Third World Perspective' (2006–2007) *American Indian Law Review* 401, 414; see generally James Thuo Gathii, 'TWAIL: A Brief History of its Origins, its Decentralized Network, and a Tentative Bibliography' (2011) 3 (1) *Trade, Law and and Development* 26; see also Bhupinder S. Chimini, 'Third World Approaches to International Law: A Manifesto' (2006) 8 *International Community Law Review* 3, 4–7 for a discussion of the continuing relevance of the terminology 'third world.'

[191] See John D. Haskell, 'Trail-Ing Twail: Arguments and Blind Spots in Third World Approaches to International Law' (2014) 27 *Canadian Journal of Law and Jurisprudence* 383, 9–10; see also Zou Keyuan, *Chinese-Asean Relations and International Law* 26–27 (Elsevier, 2009) (crediting Mao Zedong with the development of 'the 'Three Worlds' doctrine in the early 1970s).

[192] See Haskell (n 191) 6.

[193] See Haskell (n 191) 6 and 13.

[194] See Haskell (n 191) 10 (citing James Thuo Gathii, 'Neoliberalism, Colonialism, and International Governance: Decentering the International Law of Governmental Legitimacy' (2000) 98 *Michigan Law Review* 1996, 2025 [quoting Kerry Rittich]; and Kerry Rittich, 'Recharacterizing Restructuring: Gender and Distribution in the Legal Structures of Market Reform' [SJD Thesis, Harvard Law School, 1998] 258).

broader body of scholarship on Third World Approaches to International Law (TWAIL), which emerged in the 1950s.[195] TWAIL emphasizes issues of 'morality, ethics, and justice' and an understanding of the interconnectedness of disciplines as necessary for an accurate analysis.[196] TWAIL scholars seek to analyze the role of international law in creating and maintaining a hierarchy of international norms and propose alternative structures for international governance.[197] The stated goal of TWAIL scholarship is to 'eradicate the conditions of underdevelopment in the Third World.'[198] A unifying characteristic of TWAIL scholarship is the repudiation of claims that international law is universal.[199]

From a TWAIL perspective, international law is inherently problematic because of its role in the subordination of the Third World, 'non-European peoples and societies' and most of the countries in the global south.[200] Some TWAIL scholars have argued that international law enables a hierarchy in which business and financial interests are treated as more important than people's political, cultural, or social interests.[201] For example, TWAIL scholars have critiqued international law for prioritizing the internationalization of property rights and the interests of transnational corporations while neglecting to establish corresponding transnational democratic structures and 'systems of representation and accountability.'[202]

Third World Theory approaches tend to view international law making through a decentralized lens that envisions a significant role for non-state actors.[203] They advocate for legal reform to promote regulation to protect and promote substantive rights and equity.[204] Some scholars writing from a Third World Theory approach identify a 'new imperialism' and argue that TNCs are one of four groups 'that primarily shape the current pattern of

---

[195]  See generally Makata Mutua, 'What is TWAIL?' (2000) *American Society of International Law Proceedings* 31, 31 (citation omitted) and Bhupinder S. Chimini, 'Towards a Radical Third World Approach to Contemporary International Law' (2002) 5 (2) *International Center for Comparative Law and Politics Review* <http://www.ibc.j.u-tokyo.ac.jp/pdf/Review5-2.pdf>.

[196]  Gordon (n 190) 414.

[197]  See Mutua (n 196) 31 (citation omitted).

[198]  See Gordon (n 190) 31 (citation omitted).

[199]  See Gordon (n 190) 31 and 33 (citations omitted).

[200]  See Gordon (n 190) 31 (citation omitted).

[201]  See Bhupinder S. Chimini, 'Third World Approaches to International Law: A Manifesto' (2006) 8 *International Community Law Review* 3, 8–9.

[202]  See Chimini (n 201) 8–10.

[203]  See John D. Haskell, 'Trail-ing Twail: Arguments and Blind Spots in Third World Approaches to International Law' (2014) 27 *Canadian Journal of Law and Jurisprudence* 383, 16.

[204]  See Haskell (n 203) 20.

economic and legal globalization.'[205] In this context, some scholars using a Third World Theory approach have argued that non-state actors, specifically 'an emerging transnationalist capitalist class . . ., which includes TNC executives and local affiliates, are shaping the regulation of TNCs.'[206]

Third World Theory approaches have been critiqued for a perceived lack of 'a wholistic critique' or normative proposals.[207] In response to this critique, some TWAIL scholars have proposed the redefinition of sovereignty to more fully incorporate concepts of peoples' soverign rights to expand the governance role of local communities in addition to, for example, the 'ruling elite.'[208]

Several different theoretical approaches have had varying levels of influence on Third World Theory approaches, including African, Maoist, Marxist, post-colonial and Soviet approaches.[209]

# RELIGIOUS APPROACHES

Many religions provide guidance regarding the nature, purpose, rights and responsibilities of corporations. As mentioned above, religious approaches to business regulation predate the emergence of TNCs as a business form. However, they include guidance that can and has been applied to TNCs. Most of the scholarship on religious approaches to TNCs focuses on Christian and Jewish approaches.[210] A smaller

---

[205] See Bhupinder S. Chimni, 'Capitalism, Imperialism, and International Law in the Twenty-First Century' (2012) 14 *Oregon Review of International Law* 17, 19.

[206] See Chimni (n 205).

[207] See Chimini (n 201) 3–4 (identifying reasons for these weaknesses, including hurdles facing TWAIL theorists such as '[t]he ideological domination of Northern academic institutions, the handful of critical third world international law scholars, the problems of doing research in the poor world, and the fragmentation of international legal studies') and Gordon (n 190) 412.

[208] See Chimini (n 201) 24.

[209] See Zou Keyuan, *Chinese-Asean Relations and International Law* (Elsevier, 2009) 26–27.

[210] Muhammad Adnan Khurshid, Abdulrahman Al-Aali, Ahmed Ali Soliman and Salmiah Mohammad Amin, 'Developing an Islamic Corporate Social Responsibilty Model (ICSR)' (2014) 24 *Competitiveness Review* 258, 259 (citing David Baron, *Moses on Management* (Pocket Books, 1999); Laurie Beth Jones, *Jesus, CEO: Using Ancient Wisdom for Visionary Leadership* (Hachette, 1995); Kam-hon Lee, Dennis P. McCann and MaryAnn Ching, 'Christ and Business Culture: A Study of Christian Executives in Hong Kong' (2003) 43 (1/2) *Journal of Business Ethics* 103–110; Moses L. Pava, *Business Ethics: A Jewish Perspective*

proportion of this body of scholarship focuses on Islamic approaches.[211] Islamic approaches tend to be an application of *Sharī'ah* law values, while Christian and Jewish approaches also provide more specific guidance.[212] In addition to the guidance provided by individual religions, the 1993 *Interfaith Declaration* also provides a multi-faith approach to corporate conduct.[213] Religious approaches view the environment as God-created and, therefore, often have specific guidelines related to conduct that affects the environment that stem from this perspective.[214] Although religious approaches are first and foremost intended to apply to members of that religion or actors in a market that is governed by the principles of that religion, the lines are permeable and have relevance beyond those bounds.

### Jewish Approach

Many religious scholars argue that under Jewish law corporations, including TNCs, should not be permitted to be legal persons because they are 'artificial persons.'[215] Jewish law differentiates between 'natural persons' and 'artificial persons.'[216] Jewish law only allows natural persons to have legal status.[217] Instead of granting TNCs and other corporations legal person status, the most common approach under Jewish law is to

---

(Ktav Publishing, 1997); Moses L. Pava, 'The Substance of Jewish Business Ethics' (1998) 17 (6) *Journal of Business Ethics* 603–617).

[211]   Khurshid, Al-Aali, Soliman and Amin (n 210) 259 (citing Rafik I. Beekun and Jamal A. Badawi, 'Balancing Ethical Responsibility Among Multiple Organizational Stakeholders: The Islamic Perspective' (2005) 60 (2) *Journal of Business Ethics* 131–145).

[212]   Khurshid, Al-Aali, Soliman and Amin (n 210) 261.

[213]   Parliament of the World's Religions, Interfaith Declaration (1993) <https://berkleycenter.georgetown.edu/publications/declaration-toward-a-global-ethic>; Khurshid, Al-Aali, Soliman and Amin (n 210) 259.

[214]   Khurshid, Al-Aali, Soliman and Amin (n 210) 262.

[215]   See, e.g., Byron L. Sherwin, *Jewish Ethics for the Twenty-First Century: Living in the Image of God* (Syracuse UP, 2000) 79–80; Steven H. Resnicoff, 'Jewish Law and Socially Responsible Corporate Conduct' (2006) 11(3) *Fordham Journal of Corporate and Financial Law* 691.

[216]   Sherwin (n 215) 79–80.

[217]   Sherwin (n 215) 79–80; cf. Resnicoff (n 215) 690 (claiming that '[a] strong argument can be made that Jewish law would regard corporations as legal entities because Jewish law seems to adopt the legal entity model in several contexts' (citing Michael J. Broyde and Steven H. Resnicoff, 'Jewish Law and Modern Business Structures: The Corporate Paradigm' [1997] 43 *Wayne Law Review* 1685, 1748–53).

view corporations as limited partnerships rather than a separate legal entity.[218]

Perspectives on TNCs under Jewish law make it possible to place expectations of moral and ethical conduct on the human partners who formed the corporation.[219] Rather than governing TNCs directly under Jewish law, TNCs' conduct is influenced from within by governing the individuals connected with the corporation, for example, the shareholders, directors, managers, and employees.[220] In addition, Jewish law exercises external influences on TNCs' conduct by 'authorizing and requiring communally imposed regulation.'[221] Jewish law (*Dina de-Malkhuta Dina*) preferences certain requirements under secular law when they require socially responsible behavior instead of profit maximization.[222] Jewish law also requires corporate conduct to be in accordance with 'established commercial customs' (*Minhag ha-Soharim*) and investors are assumed to have notice of relevant customs and to have given implicit consent.[223] Jewish law categorizes the theory of *caveat emptor* (buyer beware) as unacceptable.[224]

## Catholic Approaches

The Catholic Social Doctrine sets out the common good as a core value that 'involves recognition and advancement of the universal dignity of the human person.'[225] This sets limits on the pursuit of economic interests by placing them lower in priority than the 'promotion of human dignity.'[226] Catholic Social Doctrine prioritizes the promotion of the common good and articulates the view that 'businesses should be characterized by their capacity to serve the common good of society.'[227]

Corporations, including TNCs, are viewed as a community in which

---

218   Sherwin (n 215) 79–80; Steven H. Resnicoff (n 215) 691.
219   Sherwin (n 215) 79–80.
220   Resnicoff (n 215) 681, 694.
221   Resnicoff (n 215) 694.
222   Resnicoff (n 215) 693.
223   Resnicoff (n 215) 694.
224   Khurshid, Al-Aali, Soliman and Amin (n 210) 262.
225   Susan J. Stabile, 'A Catholic Vision of the Corporation' (2005) 4 *Seattle Journal for Social Justice* 181, 184 (citing the Pontifical Council for Justice and Peace, *Compendium of the Social Doctrine of the Church* [2004] 160).
226   Stabile (n 225) 186 (citing Pope Paul VI, *Populorum Progressio* [*On the Development of Peoples*] 240, 245 [1967]).
227   Stabile (n 225) 184 (quoting the Pontifical Council for Justice and Peace, *Compendium of the Social Doctrine of the Church* [2004] 338).

participants have obligations to each other and are evaluated based on their effects on human dignity and the societal community as a whole.[228] Contributing to the common good includes producing 'useful goods and services' and 'creating opportunities for meeting, cooperating, and the enhancement [of] the abilities of the people involved.'[229] More specifically, this means 'the active sharing of all in the administration and profits of these enterprises ... is to be promoted.'[230] Catholic approaches view private property as permanently encumbered by a 'social mortgage,' which means that even private property has an intrinsically social function.[231]

Catholic Social Teaching envisions limitations on economic competition to prevent the fraud and injustice that the Catholic approach expects would result from 'excessive focus on profits and competition.'[232] Profit maximization has been specifically critiqued from the perspective of the Catholic approach as undermining the common good.[233] Catholic Social Teaching expressly articulates the need for government regulation to encourage promotion of the common good and inhibit profit maximization and worker exploitation.[234]

---

[228]   Stabile (n 225) 185 (quoting National Conference of Catholic Bishops, 'Economic Justice for All, Pastoral Letter on Catholic Social Teaching and the US Economy' [1986] *A Pastoral Message*, ¶ 14).

[229]   Stabile (n 225) 185 (quoting National Conference of Catholic Bishops).

[230]   Stabile (n 225) 185 (quoting Pope Paul VI, *Gaudium et Spes* [*Pastoral Constitution on the Church in the Modern World*] 68 [1965]).

[231]   Stabile (n 225) 193 (quoting Pope John Paul VI, *Sollicitudo Rei Socialis* [*On Social Concern*], ¶ 42 [1987]).

[232]   Stabile (n 225) 191 (quoting Pius XI, *Quadragesimo Anno* (*After Forty Years*), ¶ 132–33 (1931).

[233]   Stabile (n 225) 191 (citing Pope John Paul II, *Laborem Exercens* [*On Human Work*], ¶ 17.1–17.4 [1981]; Pope John XXIII, *Mater et Magitra* [*On Christianity and Social Progress*], ¶ 38–40 [1961]; Gaudium et Spes, ¶ 68; Pope Paul VI, *Populorum Progressio* [*On the Development of the Peoples*], ¶ 22 [1967]; 'Ethics Comes Before Profit, Pope Tells Bankers' *Zenit Daily Dispatch*, 17 September 2004 <http://www.zenit.org> [ZE04091706]).

[234]   Stabile (n 225) 194 (citing Pope John XXIII, *Mater et Magitra* [*On Christianity and Social Progress*], ¶ 89–92 [1961]; Pope John Paul II, *Laborem Exercens* [*On Human Work*], ¶ 17 [1981]; John Paul II, *Centisimus Annus* [*Hundredth Year*], ¶ 35 [1981]; Robert A. Sirico, 'Subsidiarity, Society, and Entitlements: Understanding and Application' [1997] 11 *Notre Dame Journal of Law, Ethics and Public Policy* 549, 567; Susan J. Stabile, 'Subsidiarity and the Use of Faith-Based Organizations in the Fight Against Poverty' [2005] 2 *Villanova Journal of Catholic Social Thought* 313, 326–32).

**Islamic Approaches**

Islamic approaches are based on an assumption that there is an inherent integration of the public and private spheres because they are that way in the eyes of God.[235] This promotes a 'relatively holistic approach' to TNC regulation.[236] The theoretical framework provided by *Sharī'ah* law is believed to be static although flexibility in application is allowed.[237] *Sharī'ah* law views property rights as inherently paired with 'rules and ethical codes designed to protect the rights of society.'[238] Islamic approaches seem to reflect a stakeholder rather than a shareholder model of TNC regulation.[239] Islamic stakeholder models position the stakeholder-state as responsible for providing regulations and enforcement.[240]

The concept of vicegerency (*khalifah*) in *Sharī'ah* law positions TNCs and other businesses as groups of people who are agents responsible for management of both the shareholder's and society's economic resources.[241] *Sharī'ah* law includes formal law as well as norms and customs.[242] *Sharī'ah* law has three main components: belief and faith (*'aqīdah*), morality and ethics (*akhlāq*) and legal rules (*fiqh*) – all of which provide guidance regarding the operation of TNCs. This theory of trusteeship (*amanah*) requires managers to act 'in the best interests of owners' but does not permit profit-maximization 'at the expense of other stakeholders.'[243]

---

[235] Khurshid, Al-Aali, Soliman and Amin (n 210) 262.
[236] (n 210) 263.
[237] (n 210) 263.
[238] Asyraf Wajdi Dusuki, 'What Does Islam Say About Corporate Social Responsibility' (2008) *Review of Islamic Economics* 5, 14 (citing Zamir Iqbal and Abbas Mirakhor, 'Stakeholders Model of Governance in Islamic Economic System' presented in 2003 and later published as Zamir Iqbal and Abbas Mirakhor, 'Stakeholders Model of Governance in Islamic Economic System' [2004] 11[2] *Islamic Economic Studies* 43).
[239] Zulkifli Hasan, 'Corporate Governance: Western and Islamic Perspectives' (2009) 5(1) *International Review of Business Research Papers* 277, 285 (citing M. Umer Chapra and Habib Ahmed, *Corporate Governance in Islamic Financial Institutions* [Islamic Research and Training Institute 2002]).
[240] Hasan (n 329) 286.
[241] Dusuki (n 238) 17, 22.
[242] Dusuki (n 238) 5, 14.
[243] Khurshid, Al-Aali, Soliman and Amin (n 210) 262 (citing Rafik I. Beekun and Jamal A. Badawi, 'Balancing Ethical Responsibility Among Multiple Organizational Stakeholders: The Islamic Perspective' [2005] 60 [2] *Journal of Business Ethics* 131–145).

*Sharī'ah* law views God as 'the ultimate owner of all . . . resources.'[244] The relationship with God is viewed as a divine contract that also determines how corporate agents interact with others.[245] The corollary to this assumption is 'the belief that a company should be socially responsible regardless of the financial consequences.'[246] This includes 'how the firm treats its employees, whether or not it uses its resources in an environmentally sound way, and whether or not its products really make life better for those who use them.'[247] From the perspective of Islamic approaches, it would be contradictory to separate social responsibility from the role of the corporation.[248] This requirement for a God-conscious (*taqwā*) approach incorporates human dignity, free will, equality and rights, and trust and responsibility into this framework.[249]

Islamic law forbids profit making by certain means, including 'interest, bribery, gambling and games of chance, speculation, short weighing and short measuring and business negligence' as well as through practices that are illegal or unfair.[250] For example, Islamic approaches categorize the theory of *caveat emptor* (buyer beware) as unacceptable.[251]

## CONCLUSION

In the decades since the first theory of TNCs was proposed, theoretical approaches for their regulation have grown into a multifaceted although incomplete set of theories with which to analyze who, when, why, how, with what effects and for whom TNCs can or should be regulated. This chapter identified six schools of thought: International Legal Theory, Corporate Social Responsibility Theory, Law and Economics Theory, New Governance Theory, Critical Legal Theory, and Law and Religion approaches. There are other ways to classify these approaches and this is not intended to be a comprehensive or definitive list of all approaches.

---

[244]   Dusuki (n 238) 20.
[245]   Dusuki (n 238) 17.
[246]   Dusuki (n 238) 21.
[247]   Dusuki (n 238) 20.
[248]   Dusuki (n 238) 18.
[249]   Dusuki (n 238) 15–16.
[250]   Khurshid, Al-Aali, Soliman and Amin (n 210) 266.
[251]   Khurshid, Al-Aali, Soliman and Amin (n 210) 262.

This is a rapidly developing field of scholarship that is still in flux. The theoretical approaches discussed as part of these six schools of thought are not necessarily all compatible and they are not all necessarily mutually exclusive. In some cases, taking a comparative approach may reveal gaps or weaknesses in approaches that can be easily mitigated. In others it may call into question foundational assumptions. In still other cases, a comparative approach may reveal value differences that are difficult to reconcile. Table 2.1 gives an overview of the disciplines used, underlying assumptions, theoretical approaches to sources of law, key actors and goals of regulation.

As a body, these six schools of thought have the potential to inform the regulation of markets and market structures as well as the conduct of TNCs as well as actors in and with TNCs. They could shape the structure of markets (structural regulation) and the behavior of actors within those markets (conduct regulation). They could be used to explain and evaluate the effects of regulation and help project which regulations may be most appropriate for a specific context and goal.

Taken individually, each of these six schools of thought may only partially be able to explain or inform global regulation as it relates to TNCs' unique characteristics and the challenges and opportunities associated with TNCs. It may require the explanatory power of several or all of the theoretical approaches discussed above to develop a global regulatory structure that can manage entities with the size, form, influence, public–private character, and multi-jurisdictional nature of TNCs. It seems unlikely that one approach alone will have the explanatory power to inform global regulation that makes the most of the opportunities and overcomes the challenges associated with TNCs. As theoretical approaches continue to develop and expand, they may need to more clearly identify spheres of applicability or points of complimentarity. Either individually or in conjunction with some or all of the other approaches, these schools of thought have the potential to inform global regulation that targets or prioritizes one or more legal, economic or social policy objectives. These could include, for example, TNCs' regulatory compliance or arbitrage, beneficial or exploitative working conditions, promotion or suppression of market competition and wealth generation, environmental harm or protection and employees' and their dependents' physical safety and welfare.

From the perspective of world history, this is still a young field. It is also a very important but under-researched, although expanding, area of legal theory. There is still considerable room for ambitious scholars to shape the theories and to design the theoretical frameworks that will define global regulation of TNCs for years to come. There are many gaps,

Table 2.1   Overview of Theoretical Approaches to Global Regulation of Transnational Corporations

| Theoretical Approaches | Disciplines Used & Regulatory Focus | Key Actors & Sources of Law | Assumptions, Contributions & Critiques |
|---|---|---|---|
| **International Legal Theory Approaches** *Subcategories include:* Public International Law (PIL) / Human Rights (HR) International Legal Pluralism (ILP), e.g., Societal Constitutionalism (SC) and Law & Geography (L&G) | <u>Disciplines:</u> International Relations Natural Law (PIL / HR) Sociology (SC) Geography (ILP, e.g. Law & Geography) <u>Regulatory Focus:</u> Protect human rights (PIL) Protect environment (PIL) Establish universal rules (PIL) | <u>Key Actors:</u> States (PIL) Groups of non-state actors (SC) <u>Key Sources of Law:</u> Treaties & Customary Practices (PIL) Subjects of international law create law through their consent (PIL) | <u>Assumptions / Positivist Contributions:</u> International law is created by consent of state actors (PIL). Treaties are the most important form of international law (PIL). There is a clear line between hard law (enforceable) and soft law (not enforceable) (PIL). Regulatory fragmentation results in an environment in which non-state actors can make law (SC). Bottom-up approaches are a legitimate way to create law (SC, ILP). Overlapping regulatory authority can result in over- and under-regulation (ILP, e.g., L&G). Regulatory failures play an important role in negative effects on the environment (ILP, e.g., L&G). <u>Normative Contributions:</u> States should regulate other actors through national law (PIL). <u>Critiques:</u> Cannot be universally valid unless it includes women's experiences (Feminist) Perpetuates Western hegemony (TWAIL) |

| Corporate Social Responsibility (CSR) Approach | Disciplines: | Key Actors: | Assumptions / Positivist Contributions: |
|---|---|---|---|
| Subcategories include: | Philosophy (ethics and morality) | Corporations | Corporations are different in a way that justifies additional regulations (CSR). |
| Progressive Corporate Law (PCL) | Philanthropy | All categories of stakeholders | States are not the only makers of systems of social control (CSR). |
| Global Corporate Citizenship (GCC) / Corporate Citizenship (CC) | Business & Management (GCC / CC) | Regulators (Env.) | Current state-made legal systems are unable to comprehensively regulate TNCs (CSR). |
| Environmentalist (Env.) | Political Science (GCC / CC) | Key Sources of Law: | Corporations have responsibilities that go beyond making money (CSR). |
| | Regulatory Focus: | Soft law, contract law, stakeholder choices | Corporations are a community made up of shareholders, creditors, directors, managers, employees and maybe even customers (PCL: Communitarian). |
| | Regulate corporate governance (CSR) | Treaties & custom (PIL / Env.) | Corporate rights & obligations stem from social contract (GCC / CC). |
| | Regulate environment, human rights and labor (CSR) | | Regulation is necessary to ensure that corporations make environmentally friendly decisions (Env.). |
| | Regulate effects on environment (Env.) | | Some corporations have characteristics similar to public institutions and should be regulated as such (Env.). |

Normative Contributions:

Corporate leaders should bear responsibilities for non-shareholder stakeholders.

Corporations should be subject to regulations to promote environmental protection and sustainability.

Critiques:

Unrealistic, unfair burden on corporate shareholders & managers (L&E)

Corporations should bear responsibilities to the groups that make up the corporation-as-society (PCL).

*Table 2.1* (continued)

| Theoretical Approaches | Disciplines Used & Regulatory Focus | Key Actors & Sources of Law | Assumptions, Contributions & Critiques |
|---|---|---|---|
| **Law & Economics (L&E) Approach** <br> *Subcategories include:* <br> Shareholder Primacy (SP) <br> Regulatory Capture <br> Neo-Kenysian (NK) <br> Innovation Economics (IE) <br> Public Interest (PI) | Disciplines: <br> Neoclassical economics <br> Economics (Public Interest, Regulatory Capture, Neo-Kenysian, Innovation Economics) <br> Political Science / Public Administration (Regulatory Capture) <br> Science & Technology (IE) <br><br> Regulatory Focus: <br> Allocate and protect property rights (L&E) | Key Actors: <br> Producers of goods and services are central players (supply-side approach). <br> Neo-Kenysian: Purchasers and consumers of goods and services are central players (demand-side approach). <br><br> Key Sources of Law: <br> Use market incentives to influence behavior (L&E) | Assumptions / Positivist Contributions: <br> Corporations are primarily or solely economic actors (L&E). <br> Corporations belong to a private sphere (L&E). <br> Markets efficiently allocate rights and function best with limited government intervention (L&E). <br> Judge-made law is efficient (L&E). <br> People are rational actors who respond to incentives (L&E). <br> Demand for goods and services (consumption) is the primary driver of economic growth (NK). <br> Equitable distribution of income and wealth increases consumption (NK). <br> Innovation is the primary driver of economic growth (IE). <br> Normative Contributions: <br> Law should be efficient. <br> Law should enable markets. <br> Regulation's purpose is to correct market failure. <br> Corporations should be protected from government intervention. <br> Law should correct market failures (NK). <br> Regulations should promote equitable distribution of income and wealth (NK). <br> Law should preference innovation over short-term profit and equitable distribution of wealth (IE). |

| | | | |
|---|---|---|---|
| | Enable functioning of a market economy (L&E)<br>Maximize allocative efficiency (L&E)<br>Regulate markets, antitrust, and securities (L&E)<br>Increase social welfare (PI)<br>Promote innovation (IE) | | Critiques:<br>Focus on short-term goals overlooks long-term harm (CSR).<br>Inaccurate assumptions about bargaining power (FLT)<br>Omits consideration of economically vulnerable people and groups (FLT, CRT, TWAIL) |
| **New Governance Theory Approaches** | Disciplines:<br>Regulatory Theory<br>Regulatory Focus:<br>Fill gaps in regulation | Key Actors:<br>States<br>Groups of non-state actors<br>Key Sources of Law:<br>Some regulatory structures develop in a space between top-down and bottom-up approaches. | Assumptions / Positivist Contributions:<br>Domestic and international state actors are unable to comprehensively resolve challenges presented by globalization.<br>There is not a clear line between soft and hard law.<br>Private and self-regulation exist and have for a long time.<br>Industry participants are better suited to create regulations in certain circumstances.<br>Normative Contributions:<br>States should play a role in promoting overall welfare and equity.<br>Additional capacity should be developed among non-state actors.<br>Private regulatory schemes should be developed.<br>Individual building blocks should be developed and integrated into existing regulatory structures. |

*Table 2.1*  (continued)

| Theoretical Approaches | Disciplines Used & Regulatory Focus | Key Actors & Sources of Law | Assumptions, Contributions & Critiques |
|---|---|---|---|
| | | | Critiques:<br>Deregulation by another name<br>Lack of examples proving benefits and effectiveness of private or self-regulation<br>Self-regulation may inhibit creation of more rigorous and enforceable regulations |
| **Critical Legal Theory Approaches**<br>*Subcategories include:*<br>Feminist Legal Theory (FLT)<br>Critical Race Theory<br>Third World Approaches to International Law (TWAIL) | Disciplines:<br>Ethics and morality (FLT)<br>Political science (FLT)<br><br>Regulatory Focus:<br>Improve lives of women (FLT)<br>Enhance social flourishing (FLT)<br>Identify and eliminate disproportionate negative effects on women (FLT)<br>Regulate labor (FLT) | Key Actors:<br>Subordinated and vulnerable individuals and groups (FLT)<br>Exercisers of power (FLT)<br>States (TWAIL)<br>Non-state actors (TWAIL)<br><br>Key Sources of Law:<br>Ethic of care and connectedness (FLT) | Assumptions / Positivist Contributions<br>Distinction between public and private is artificial and the line between them is porous (FLT).<br>Parties to transactions often do not have equal bargaining power (FLT).<br>Women's experiences are excluded from some analyses of purportedly universal international law (FLT).<br>Gender bias is present in rules that appear neutral on their face (FLT).<br>Parties' with unequal bargaining power in transactions have been omitted from some economic models (FLT).<br>There are theoretically inconsistent divisions between what is classified as public or private that appear to be based on gender bias (FLT).<br>Law is neither neutral nor objective (CRT).<br>Markets alone will not eliminate racial discrimination (CRT).<br>Existence of antidiscrimination law alone will not eliminate racial discrimination (CRT). |

Racial and gender diversity will improve corporate decision-making because there is a unique voice of color (CRT).

Law, markets and politics are interconnected (TWAIL).

Distinctions between public and private are not relevant for addressing substantive issues (TWAIL).

<u>Normative Contributions:</u>

Concepts of care and connection should be incorporated into fiduciary duties (FLT).

Corporations should be responsive to needs of others (FLT).

Corporations should minimize negative effects on all stakeholder groups (FLT).

All community members' needs and interests should be given equal weight in corporate decision-making (FLT).

Equal weight should be given to the effects on others in individual decision-making (FLT).

Include non-shareholder stakeholders in corporate governance (FLT).

Corporations (as a state counterpart) should make decisions aimed at protecting the vulnerable (FLT).

Markets should be restructured to function in ways that will result in procedural equality and substantive justice (CRT).

Existing laws should be enforced (CRT).

Public policy and law should be informed by people on the receiving end of discrimination (CRT).

Enforcing antidiscrimination laws should be incorporated into corporate governance (CRT).

Law should be reformed to prioritize substantive rights over procedural rights (TWAIL).

<u>Critiques:</u>

Lack of normative proposals (TWAIL)

*Table 2.1* (continued)

| Theoretical Approaches | Disciplines Used & Regulatory Focus | Key Actors & Sources of Law | Assumptions, Contributions & Critiques |
|---|---|---|---|
| **Religious Approach** *Subcategories include:* Catholicism (C) Judaism (J) Islam (I) | <u>Disciplines:</u> Religious studies (C, J, I) <u>Regulatory Focus:</u> Advance the common good by recognizing and promoting universal human dignity (C). Align conduct of shareholders, directors, managers, and employees with Jewish ethics (J). | <u>Key Actors:</u> Catholics (C) Jewish persons connected with the corporation, e.g., shareholders, directors, managers and employees (J) Muslims (I) Participants in markets governed by Islamic law (I) <u>Key Sources of Law:</u> Catholic Social Doctrine (C) *Dina de-Malkhuta Dina* and *Minhag ha-Soharim* (J) *Shari'ah* law (I) | <u>Assumptions / Positivist Contributions:</u> Corporations are a community (C). Participants in corporations have obligations to each other (C). Private property is permanently encumbered by a social mortgage (C). Corporations are artificial persons and, as such, are prohibited from having legal status (J). Stakeholder-state is responsible for providing regulations and enforcement (I). Businesses are groups of people (agents) responsible for shareholders' and society's economic resources (I). Certain forms of profit-making are forbidden (I). <u>Normative Contributions:</u> Human dignity should be promoted over economic interests (C). Corporations should contribute to the common good (C). Competition should be limited to prevent fraud and injustice (C). Government regulations should limit profit maximization and worker exploitation (C). Corporate shareholders should behave morally and ethically (J). Socially responsible behavior should be preferred over profit maximization in some circumstances (J). Companies should prioritize social responsibility over financial effects (I). |

rough edges and open questions for more modest scholars to fill, refine and answer. This chapter simultaneously gives an overview of theoretical approaches to global regulation of TNCs and highlights the many gaps and inconsistencies in the field.

# 3. The evolving relationship between TNCs and political actors and governments

*Larry Catá Backer*[1]

## INTRODUCTION

This chapter examines one of the most interesting, and most elusive, areas of transnational corporations (TNC) regulation, and operation – the evolving relationships among the great stakeholders of TNC governance: political actors and governments. It is a dynamic and political topic, built on the slippery foundation of shifting definitions and agendas that has marked the lurch from the 1970s state-based internationalism[2] to the modern polycentric governance logics of economic globalization,[3] though one that still exhibits a substantial amount of national characteristics.[4]

The dynamic element of these relationships can serve as a conceptual starting point. At the start of the third quarter of the last century, the issue of any relationship among TNCs, political actors and government might have occupied very little conceptual space. For the most part, TNCs and non-governmental organizations (NGOs) tended to focus their interactions through the state, and politics. Direct popular mobilizations were just starting in the most developed states – the lettuce (and then grape) boycott led by Cesar Chavez, among the most remarkable and culturally important at the time[5] – but even these were centered around politics and

---

[1]  My great thanks to my research assistant Angelo Mancini (Penn State Law JD expected 2017) for his superlative work on this chapter.
[2]  *See, e.g.*, Tagi Sagafi-nejad, *The UN and Transnational Corporations: From Code of Conduct to Global Compact* (Indiana University Press, 2008) 41–88.
[3]  *See, e.g.*, John G. Ruggie, *Just Business: Multinational Corporations and Human Rights* (W.W. Norton, 2013).
[4]  *See, e.g.*, Dennis Paterson and Ari Afilalo, *The New Global Trading Order: The Evolving State and the Future of Trade* (Cambridge UP, 2008).
[5]  *See, e.g.*, United Farm Workers, History <http://ufw.org/_page.php?menu= research&inc=_page.php?menu=research&inc=history/01.html>; 'Farm Workers Press Lettuce Boycott,' *Harvard Crimson* (13 November 1970) <http://www. thecrimson.com/article/1970/11/13/farm-workers-press-lettuce-boycott-ppicketing/>.

law.[6] The same appeared true in the evolution of popular mobilization in developing states.[7] At the same time the political power of large global enterprises was being exposed in ways that suggested the extent of their power to affect the domestic political and legal orders of developing states.[8]

By the first decades of the 21st century, states appeared to have retreated from either a leading or centering role in the organization of relationships among non-state actors, governments and TNCs.[9] For the most part, states retreated because they were unable or unwilling to change even as economic globalization grounded in the increasing porousness of borders globalized politics and the operations of economic and political actors, producing governance gaps within which domestic legal orders could not reach and within which multi-state harmonization proved difficult.[10] The new center of state or public intervention appeared to have moved upward to international organizations, and then downward into some states (when willing) or outward into the non-state sector.[11] But public intervention no longer monopolized all governance space. Into the void, new transnational systems of self-referencing relationships suggested themselves[12] as critical actors realigned their relationships to create a new regulatory space within which each played a new and important role.[13] Where states once always set the structure of debate and served as the arbiter of rules, TNCs and NGOs began to amplify relationships that became at once both cooperative and adversarial and where they appeared to embrace both monitoring and rule

---

[6]  In the case of the lettuce boycott, the right of the United Farm Workers to unionize lettuce pickers in the Salinas Valley agricultural district of California.

[7]  S. Prakash Sethi, *Multinational Corporations and the Impact of Public Advocacy on Corporate Strategy: Nestle and the Infant Formula Controversy* (Kluwer Academic Publishers, 1994).

[8]  *See, e.g.*, Daniel Litvin, *Empires of Profit: Commerce, Conquest and Corporate Responsibility* (Texere, 2003).

[9]  *See, e.g.*, Susan Strange, *The Retreat of the State: The Diffusion of Power in the World Economy* (Cambridge UP, 1996).

[10]  Considered in some aspects in Robert O. Keohane, 'Global Governance and Democratic Accountability', in David Held and Mathias Koenig-Archibugi (eds), *Taming Globalization: Frontiers of Governance* (Polity Press, 2003) 130–157.

[11]  Discussed in Larry Catá Backer, 'The Structural Characteristics of Global Law for the 21st Century: Fracture, Fluidity, Permeability and Polycentricity' (2012) 17 (2) *Tilburg Law Review* 177–199.

[12]  Discussed in Larry Catá Backer, 'Economic Globalization and the Rise of Efficient Systems of Global Private Law Making: Wal-Mart as Global Legislator' (2007) 39 (4) *University of Connecticut Law Review* 1739–1784.

[13]  *See, e.g.*, Dorothea Bauer, *NGOs as Legitimate Partners of Corporations: A Political Conceptualization* (Springer, 2011).

making objectives.[14] And both were increasingly seen as political actors in both transnational and national space, no longer merely objects of state control but now also partners in governance.[15]

Within the emerging political space created through the realignments of power brought by economic globalization, TNCs, NGOs, states and public international organizations have developed a political ecology grounded in their inter-relationships that drives a dynamic political process beyond the state. The interactions of these actors suggest the richness of the ecology of TNC relationships with governments and NGOs, one in which each of the actors are sometimes locked in a series of adverse or cooperative relationships, and sometimes simultaneously in both. The object of the relationship is accountability on one side and risk management on the other.[16] The ideology of this ecology is not fixed and ranges from the notion that each of these actors must remain adverse if the 'system' is to produce welfare maximizing results, to notions that deep networks of collective action produce comprehensive systemic coherence.[17] Moreover, the role of each actor within this ecology also remains contested. The overall ideological framework within which these relations are framed also colors the view of these relationships. Three principal variations have proven of enduring importance as conceptual blinders which frame much of the academic, policy and political discourse: neoliberal, statist and production chain.[18]

Actors and ecology in motion suggest the spatial element of the relationships among the principal actors. But the temporal element is important as

---

[14]   *See, e.g.*, Mariëtte van Huijstee and Pieter Glasbergen, 'NGOs Moving Business: An Analysis of Contrasting Strategies' *Business Society* 11 May 2010, 591–618.

[15]   'Path breaking in the mid-1990s, strategic long-term collaborations among government, business, and civil society actors in the pursuit of common objectives are today a staple of the emerging global community.' William S. Reese, Cathryn L. Thorup and Timothy K. Gerson, *What Works in Public/Private Partnering: Building Alliances for Youth Development* (International Youth Foundation, 2002) 6.

[16]   *See, e.g.*, Matias Koenig-Archibugi, 'Transnational Corporations and Public Accountability' (2004) 32 (2) *Government and Opposition* 234–259.

[17]   Cf. Patti Rundall, 'Partnerships With TNCs – An Attempt to Compartmentalise Ethics?' and Anita Roddick, 'A Different Bottom Line' (2000) both part of World Vision UK Discussion Papers No. 10: 'Buy In or Sell Out? Understanding business-NGO partnerships' <http://archive.babymilkaction.org/pdfs/spinpdfs/appendices/buyinsellout.pdf>.

[18]   *See, e.g.*, Larry Catá Backer, 'Economic Globalization Ascendant: Four Perspectives on the Emerging Ideology of the State in the New Global Order' (2006) 17 (1) *Berkeley La Raza Law Journal* 141–168. Discussed at Part 2, infra.

well. The 1970s, the apex of state ideology, focused on domestic regulation. From the 1980s through the turn of the century was an age of deregulation and competition among states for positions within global production chains. This retreat from the normative project of regulation was filled by NGOs and international organizations, and to some extent by TNCs themselves, in multiple and complex systems that have come to dominate relations among these actors.[19] And indeed, this century is marked by a relationship between TNCs and political actors that underlines the extent to which TNCs now view as important the normative legitimacy of NGOs,[20] and to which NGOs view TNCs as sources and objects of governance power.[21] But it is marked by something else, especially outside of the Anglo-American world – the emergence of an increasingly influential view that TNCs, like state organs, have an obligation to realize social norms through their own operations.[22] In other words, that enterprises (and perhaps other political actors – governments and NGOs) have an obligation to act only in ways that are supportive of social norms.[23] Whether social norms might best be enforced through law remains highly contested.

This chapter, then, considers the nature of the relationships among TNCs, political actors and government, as a set of emerging ecologies of political economy. Each represents a distinct response to the transformation of the global legal, economic and political order in the face of globalization. Each exists autonomously and is evolving simultaneously, yet each is significantly interconnected within a polycentric governance order that lends overall structure without a centering position. The chapter starts with the conventional and traditional ecology of relationships, centered on the state. It then considers the three most distinctive forms of emerging relational ecologies that de-center the state. The first is based on the TNC as the centering element of the production chain order. The second

---

[19]   *See, e.g.*, Judith Richter, *Holding Corporations Accountable: Corporate Conduct, International Codes and Citizen Action* (Zed Books, 2001).

[20]   *See, e.g.*, Shelly L. Brickson, 'Organizational Identity Orientation: The Genesis of the Role of the Firm and Distinct Forms of Social Value' (2007) 32 *Academy of Management Review* 864 and discussed in Bauer (n 13).

[21]   *See, e.g.*, Larry Catá Backer, 'Multinational Corporations as Objects and Sources of Transnational Regulation' (2008) 14 *ILSA Journal of International & Comparative Law* 499–523.

[22]   See Peter Ulrich, *Integrative Economic Ethics: Foundations of a Civilized Market Economy* (James Fearns, trans., Cambridge UP, 2008) 269 et seq.

[23]   Cf. Jürgen Habermas, *The Theory of Communicative Action, Vol. II Lifeworld and System: A Critique of Functionalist Reason* (Thomas McCarthy, trans., Beacon Press, 1987); see also Habermas, *Vol. 1 Reason and the Rationalization of Society* (Thomas McCarthy, trans., Beacon Press, 1984).

is grounded on the emergence of non-state governance centers which assert order through certification, verification, and monitoring. The third posits the emergence of a multi-stakeholder autonomous and self-referencing system around production chains. The chapter briefly considers whether there is something like meta theory useful for the understanding of these otherwise disaggregated and scattered but intermeshed systems that have arisen around the state. The chapter ends with a brief suggestion of what may lie ahead.

## THE CONVENTIONAL ECOLOGY

The conventional ecology is built on a set of established premises that themselves are embedded in an ideology of politics that is still quite powerful. The starting point for any analysis of the TNC is society – whether to defend it or to seek to transform it into something more suited to the taste of the commentator or the institutions she may represent. This section considers first the ideologies around which relationships among TNCs, political and public actors are understood or theorized, and then the premises about the character of each of the principal actors. It then briefly describes the resulting ecology within which their interactions necessarily occur, constrained by the choice of disciplining ideology and premises.

### Westphalian Equality

The ideology around which relationships can be understood and constructed is based on certain fundamental notions of the state and the state system. Three principal approaches emerged by the last quarter of the 20th century, and all three are still with us.[24] The first is the most influential and describes the conceptual structure of contemporary globalization within or through the state system.[25] It posits a strong state system based on formal equality between states and the grounding notions that states are principally responsible for the creation of order and control within their territories, and that such order and control is exercised through the domestic legal order as interpreted by courts and enforced through the

---

[24]   The discussion that follows is largely drawn from Backer (n 18).

[25]   Robert W. Cox, 'A Perspective on Globalization' in James H. Mittelman (ed.), *Globalization: Critical Reflections* (Ipe Yearbook, 1996) 21–23. ('The dominance of economic forces was regarded as both necessary and beneficial. States and the interstate system would serve mainly to ensure the working of market logic . . . . [G]lobalization became an ideology.')

state's police power. But that internal control is balanced by the embrace of a global consensus on which norms are expected to be domesticated in states through law. Economic globalization represents one aspect of part of this system. States remain the central element of rule-making and enforcement, which are crafted in ways that are sensitive to local conditions, customs and tastes, but the basic principles from which rules are derived are developed elsewhere. This 'elsewhere' has been institutionalized within the organs of public and private international organizations – from regional human rights organizations to private standard-setting bodies.

This ideology produces systems of governance, justified on increasingly universal or absolute terms. This convergence then brings together the state, political actors and business in relationships shaped by an increased ability to participate in the development and implementation of the consensus norms around which state duty is understood. The internationalization of norm making, and the emergence of international organization within which these norms are made, creates a space for global private actors to participate. And that space then suggests the character of the relationships among states, civil society and business – at once cooperative and adversarial as they seek to influence the tone and direction of global consensus on norms, and thus on law-making in states, and behavior rules in the societal sphere.

> Systemic autonomy through convergence also tends to provide a basis for the autonomy of non-state actors, critical to the implementation of global systems of private activity. Rules governing merchants, for example, have become more independent from the commercial rules of particular states, especially with respect to transactions that cross borders.[26] Corporations that own themselves,[27] markets that are self-regulating within the bounds of transnational rules,[28] and non-state actors free of the constraints of regulation by a particular nation-state become more common and important.[29]

---

[26] *See, e.g.*, Michael T. Medwig, 'The New Law Merchant: Legal Rhetoric and Commercial Reality' (1993) 24 *Law and Policy in International Business* 589. ('Over the last century, merchants have slowly begun to extricate their commercial disputes from the tangled regulatory web of the national legal order.')

[27] See Katsuhito Iwai, 'Persons, Things and Corporations: The Corporate Personality Controversy and Comparative Corporate Governance' (1999) 47 *American Journal of Comparative Law* 583 (describing why under the form of capitalism adopted in Japan, corporations can effectively own themselves through the practice of cross ownership among a small number of corporations).

[28] The rise of international and transnational systems of dispute resolution, subject to their own rules, is a case in point. *See, e.g.*, Tim Ginsburg, 'The Culture of Arbitration' (2003) 36 *Vanderbilt Journal of Transnational Law* 1335.

[29] Backer (n 24).

This suggests that at its limits, these ideological foundations make plausible the notion that as the international systems become more developed and autonomous, the power relationships between states and international norm-making organizations will be reversed. 'The primary function of management of the traditional public realm . . . has gradually come to be . . . the maintaining of the conditions required for the well-being of the economy, including, above all, the legal conditions.'[30] As a consequence, the nature of the relationship among TNCs, state and political actors becomes political and economic, and the focus of that relationship is both on norm making and on influencing the political cultures that in turn influence the behavior of states and TNCs.

The 'official line' of many of the most developed states and of the international organization, global political actors and TNCs tends to revolve around variations of this liberal market and internationalizing political-economic ideology. It reaffirms the notion of horizontal equality among states and their central role in managing law systems, it internationalizes norm making through inter-governmental organizations which then provide an international platform within which TNCs and political actors can interact to produce both norms and cultural consensus which are then domesticated through further interactions among governments, political actors and TNCs. But this official line is contested by other actors.

**Economic Globalization**

The second ideological framework around which relationships among TNCs, political and public actors are understood or theorized considers the relationships built around economic globalization. It sees in these relationships both the affirmance and transformation of the current state system in which TNCs and global civil society are complicit.

Under this second view, the current system of globalization represents the culmination of the Westphalian state system of global governance, and globalization does not threaten that system of state-centered

---

[30]   Philip Allott, *The Health of Nations: Society and Law Beyond the State* 311–312 (Cambridge UP, 2002) 311–312. The full quote read thus: 'The primary function of management of the traditional public realm, where social power is exercised exclusively in the public interest, has gradually come to be, not the service of some common interest of well-being conceived in terms of general values (say, justice or solidarity or happiness or human flourishing), but the maintaining of the conditions required for the well-being of the economy, including, above all, the legal conditions.'

governance. Globalization, however, draws into sharper relief a natural distinction among nation-states. One group is made up of politically powerful and economically developed states. The other group consists of all other states. Globalization and legal internationalism serve as a cover through which the group of powerful states may project their power into the second group of states, which assume a role of legal and economic dependence. International organizations leverage state power and provide a veil of legitimacy – based on the premises of state equality and national sovereignty – for creating the sort of norm harmonizing consensus that is at the heart of liberal-markets based globalization.

The object is to use law and norm in the service of the interests of the more powerful states, especially to control resources and markets. To that end, the more powerful states will use a variety of indirect techniques of domination.[31] States may use agents for this purpose, including TNCs,[32] and NGOs, transnational private voluntary regulatory authorities, standard-setting bodies and the like. Under this ideological view, TNCs and private political organizations should be presumed to serve the interests of the states from which they originate or to which they owe allegiance. And it might follow that, to some extent, the differing agendas pursued by TNCs and political organizations reflect their efforts to influence the political and societal cultures of the most powerful states, which will then internationalize those norms and drive them down into similarly powerful states. The great battles to internationalize the US Alien Tort Claims Act and to use US courts to apply an internationalized version of US law provide an important case in point. Other areas of extra-territorial application of state rules have been suggested as necessary to solve transnational problems, which both

---

[31] For a discussion of the way the African Growth and Opportunity Act (AGOA) and the Cotonou Agreement worked in this way, see Patricia M. Lenagham, 'Trade Negotiations or Trade Capitulations: An African Experience' (2006) 17 *Berkeley La Raza Law Journal* 117 (arguing that power asymmetries between the developed states and African states raises suspicions that negotiation and implementation of these agreements fail to address African concerns by ensuring a passive role for the weaker states).

[32] For a discussion of the effect of an entity-based conception of corporations on the ordering of political communities, see Larry Catá Backer, 'Ideologies of Globalization and Sovereign Debt: Cuba and the IMF' (2006) 24 *Penn State International Law Review* 497 (discussing Fidel Castro Ruz, 'Una revolucion solo puede ser hija de la cultura y sus ideas, Discurso pronunciado por el Presidente del Consejo de Estado de la Républica de Cuba, Fidel Castro Ruz, en la Aula Magna de la Universidad Central de Venezuela', 3 Feb. 1999, <http://www.cuba.cu/gobierno/discursos/1999/esp/f030299e.html>).

internationalize and project the governing ideologies and interests of the most powerful states and their TNCs and civil society organizations.[33] The insight here is that (1) in contrast to the consensus liberal-market ideology, globalization serves the interests of states and (2) that powerful states, TNCs and globalized civil society tend to align in their relationships to create and impose norms and behavior structures downward through power-production chains. Just as the more powerful states assert power and influence over less powerful and less-developed states, so the largest TNCs and global civil society organizations tend to dominate the discourse within their respective spheres, and to serve the socio-cultural (and therefore) political agendas of the states from which they originate. In this version, the international system does not lose its focus on the political or on the importance of political communities, but it is more nakedly hierarchical and the hand and dynamics of state power are more apparent. Within these ideological presumptions, TNCs, political actors and governments build relationships that are based on state power and private power hierarchies, and though they may have adverse interests, the interests of the most powerful states, TNCs and civil society organs will tend to align against the interests of less-powerful business enterprises, civil society and states.

### Rule by Production Chain

The third structuring framework is a darker version of the second. It starts with the assumption that globalization is a necessary element in the sustainability of the power and wealth of the richest and most developed states. But in this variation, globalization represents a new form of imperium, one not grounded in the acquisition and control of territory, but rather in the acquisition and control of production chains. It starts from the fundamental premise that globalization is necessary as the principal means through which the otherwise unsustainable wealth production of the most powerful states, led by a single great hegemon is sustained.[34] In other words, the state system tends toward imperium, and the economic system can only be preserved by institutionalizing a production chain in which the poorest states and enterprises subsidize the consumption of the

---

[33]   Cf. Jonathan Turley, '"When in Rome": Multinational Misconduct and the Presumption Against Extraterritoriality' (1990) 84 *Northwestern University Law Review* 598.

[34]   With the rise of China and the European Union, perhaps three hegemons. Cf. George Lee, 'Rosa Luxemburg and the Impact of Imperialism' (1971) 81 *Economic Journal* 847.

wealthiest states. And thus the object of globalization – to institutionalize an efficient system designed to transfer the real costs of production from consumers in the richest states to those in the states in which overproduction occurs.

In effect, globalization masks an effective objective – convert the entire public sphere into a vast sphere of private activity – and a political objective that speaks of new forms of neocolonialism, to transform all nation-states into private property. If globalization transforms the state system into a special trade zone that benefits the hegemon and its allies, then all domestic production is to be eliminated in favor of an export model grounded in production specialization and overproduction. Production specialization eliminates state control over its labor markets. Overproduction amplifies the effects of production or labor specialization and is tied to cultures of consumerism. Universalizing cultures of consumption traps participants in the lower levels of production chains in their own subordination. The model produces a strong global zone under the control of the hegemon but otherwise produces state failure, which is to be ameliorated through charity (the loan regimes of international financial institutions), privatization and socialization. These are to be addressed not just by states but by efforts, coordinated or not, of TNCs and global civil society.

This ideological framework views TNCs, NGOs and other political actors, as serving the needs of the dominant states – as expressions of political authority manifested in economic activity. Within this ideological structure TNCs merge with the states whose interests they necessarily represent, and whose privileges are to be protected by states. To that effect international organizations – like the Organisation for Economic Co-operation and Development (OECD) and international financial institutions – are meant to leverage the power of developed states by internationalizing the system of control that serves their interests. And those interests do not just further hegemonic power but are the necessary elements to the stability of a system that is built on exploitation rather than on transactions for mutual benefits. Within this ideology, as well, TNCs serve states, and NGOs either serve to soften the inevitable exploitation at the heart of the global production process or might be fashioned into sites of resistance. States whose territories serve as the location of lower levels of production chains are bent to the interests of global production chains and the TNCs and social forces through which it is managed and made palatable. This is the conceptual foundation of developing states and of those societal forces, some of them globalized, that seek to oppose the dominant ideological foundation disparagingly referenced as the Washington Consensus or neoliberalism to suggest either the instrumentalism of the dominant ideology and its control by the United States.[35]

## From Structuring Framework to Perceptions of Ecology

If ideology provides the lens through which societal forces see and understand 'facts' and relationships; that is, if these ideologies provide the interpretive premises around which relationships among TNCs, political and public actors are understood or theorized, then the premises about the character of each of the principal actors can also only be understood as a function of the ideological lens through which they are identified. Still, there are sets of core characteristics that are supra-ideological and which are embedded in each of these approaches to the construction of the character of the inter-relations among these actors. Ideology, then, drives the premises that serve as a working organization of relationships among governments, political actors and TNCs by structuring the character, objectives and conception of each of these actors.

*The first touches on the state.* For the most part, the conventional ecology places the state at the apex of societal, economic, political (but not necessarily religious) spheres. It adheres to the premise that all states are equal and assert internal authority to the same extent. The state has a monopoly on law, which is assumed to be the most legitimate form of governance, authenticated by rule-of-law systems and the democratic processes through which law is produced and the state is operated. Both TNCs and NGOs look to the state to develop policy and norms, to enact laws on the basis thereof. Relations, thus, tend to be understood as a function of the role of the state in translating normative values to legal norms. Beyond that, all three stakeholders might be understood as working at aspects of mass mobilization. The object, again, is grounded on the premise of state centrality – managing popular opinion creates necessary leverage for effectuating legal change. The societal sphere is vibrant but, again, also based on developing a culture in which law is normalized through socialization. States also control those techniques of monitoring and assessment that drive behaviour, and both TNCs and NGOs shape their relationship to affect the aggregate of these techniques.

But states are also actors within the transnational sphere. As actors within international organizations they also serve as a centering element of the work of these organizations. The conventional ecology makes it

---

[35]    See, Larry Catá Backer 'Ideologies of Globalization and Sovereign Debt: Cuba and the IMF' (2006) 24 *Penn State International Law Review* 497–561.

self-evident that, as the UN Guiding Principles suggest, the state leverages national power through multilateral efforts, and that normative harmonization is the most advantageous road towards the closing of governance gaps that have been the greatest cause of the loss of national sovereignty in the face of global economic activity. To that end, states align within international organizations to enhance their collective influence, both on the crafting of internationalized norms and in the projection of those norms into all other states. Organizations like the OECD provide a clear example of the way that international organizations seek to set the agenda for policy through active engagement with non-members.[36] The World Bank and International Monetary Fund's engagement with developing states provides another example. In these cases, ideology provides the lenses through which these relationships are understood. Under the liberal market model they are understood as the leading edge of development and consensus that is socialized through consent-based imperatives of markets. Under the state dominance ideology, these are seen as instruments of the most developed states to ensure their dominance, the projection of their policies and interests through dominated international organizations, and the exploitative state ideology. To these distinct ends, both TNCs and civil society serve as instruments of the states from which they originate and from out of which their funds derive and supporters reside.

*The second touches on the TNC.* For the most part, the conventional ecology posited relationships with corporations or similar aggregations of capital, regulated and chartered by states or their political subdivisions. The issue traditionally centered on the theory of the corporation and its effect on the regulatory relationship between corporation and state.[37] And it centers on the culture of the business enterprise.[38] The question turned on the way that the distinct characteristics of the corporation operating beyond the sphere of national corporations could or ought to be regulated.[39]

---

[36] See, e.g., Morton Ougaard, 'A New Role for the OECD?: The "Enhanced Engagement" Strategy Toward Emerging Economies' in Dag Harald Claes and Carl Henrik Knutsen (eds), *Governing the Global Economy: Politics, Institutions, and Economic Development* (Routledge, 2011) 96–104.

[37] See, e.g., Janet Dine, *The Governance of Corporate Groups* (Cambridge UP, 2006).

[38] See, e.g., Tom MacMakin, *Bread and Butter: What a Bunch of Bakers Taught Me About Business and Happiness* (Macmillan, 2001).

[39] See, e.g., Seymour J. Rubin, 'Transnational Corporations: Supervision, Regulation, or What?' (1975) 1 *Maryland Journal of International Law* 1 <http://digitalcommons.law.umaryland.edu/mjil/vol1/iss1/5>.

To that end, a distinction was made between the *process* of production and the *institutionalization* of capital. The production process was viewed as either a transnational matter for international organizations to manage or a core function of the societal sphere. The institutionalization of capital was viewed as inherently national and political, touching on the structures through which national macroeconomic policies were to be reified and thus more jealously guarded as an aspect of state sovereignty. Process management issues became centered in the work of the OECD – the Guidelines for Multinational Enterprises, for example – and articulated through the imposition of societal norms crafted through public international organs and managed through non-binding facilitation by states. The same might be said of the UN Guiding Principles for Business and Human Rights within global regulatory networks. Institutional management was characterized as a function of corporate governance or as the subject of treaty – usually clusters of international agreements – bilateral and multilateral investment, commerce and friendship treaties, regional trade associations and the architecture of the World Trade Organization. Both process and institutionalized capital might also be affected by the policies and loan conditions of the great international financial institutions, whose conditional lending clauses, along with their socialization programs (technical assistance) would serve as sites within which TNCs, states and NGOs might negotiate norms then applied through loan work and its collateral structures.

These splits among process and institutionalization, between national and international organs, also tended to destabilize any consensus on the definition of TNCs themselves. That, in turn, has an important effect on the character of relations among TNCs, governments and civil society actors. If a TNC is understood in classical terms,[40] then one approaches the issues of relationship from the assumption that the TNC is a unitary actor and speaks with substantially one voice and out of the head office. One centers analysis, then, on issues of ownership and control relationships.[41] This is a view quite compatible with the three ideological frameworks, although each then approaches the consequences of this assumption of the character of TNCs in different ways. It constitutes the TNC either as an autonomous actor in markets or as an instrument of states either to advance state policy or as the mechanism for hegemonic

---

[40]   Cf. David K. Fieldhouse, 'The Multinational: A Critique of a Concept', in Alice Teichova, Maurice Lévy-Leboyer and Helga Nussbaum (eds), *Multinational Enterprise in Historical Perspective* (Cambridge UP, 1989) 9–14.

[41]   *See, e.g.*, Neil Hood and Stephen Young, *The Economics of the Multinational Enterprise* (Longman, 1979) 3.

sovereigns to exploit weaker states. And that, of course, changes the character of the relationship and interactions among TNCs and civil society and governments. But additionally, the ideological starting points also point to conceptual possibilities. TNCs are more likely to be understood as national enterprises with foreign operations under the state and exploitative ideologies than under the liberal markets ideology or as integrated management and control systems, like states. For governments and civil society, then, the object is to establish relationships with the controlling or managing center. And there is a draft toward the notion, inherently institutional in nature, that these organisms may be controlled by and through national law as factors in the production of national macroeconomic policy. The possibilities of diffuse organization – of networks and arrangements grounded in coordinated linkages – requires viewing TNCs as characterized by a process element – becomes harder to conceptualize within regimes organized around the premise of TNCs as inherently institutionalizations of capital.

Yet if a TNC is considered in process terms, as embedded within and a part of the processes of production to which it is directed, a very different set of relational consequences follow. Here the TNC cannot be understood as speaking with one voice – though all voices may sometimes speak in unison. The OECD definition provides a nice expression of this diffused model.[42] This idea of a TNC is more compatible with liberal-markets ideology and permits the expression of TNCs as processes that are market-based and subject to a diffused and multi-layered governance structure, both legal and societal. To some extent, this view is not anarchical in the sense that it supposes a centering element in the linked and coordinated systems that compromise a TNC enterprise. Yet a center does not suggest the sort of single point relationships that more classical definitions suggest. Rather, it fractures the TNC in terms of its engagement in relationships and opens the likelihood that such relationships will exist, with varying degrees of power and influence, at every level of the operation of the enterprise and among different actors. A process approach suggests that just as state power has fractured within regimes of economic globalization, so has the organizational unity of TNCs – at least with respect to its relations with civil society and states along its production chain.

*The third touches on the NGO.* Organized political actors represent both a transformation of mass politics and its internationalization from the last half of the 20th century – at least in its contemporary manifestation. The business of mass mobilization is organized along functional

---

[42]   *OECD Guidelines for Multinational Enterprises* (Paris, 2011).

lines, each organization representing a functionally distinct aggregation of like-minded individuals which have come together to advance their objectives, and for that purpose have developed an institutional organism that is self-referencing and autonomous. In a sense, civil society organs have begun to take on the characteristics of their coordinate partners in global norm making – states and TNCs. They also suffer the same challenges – their representational qualities, legitimacy, democratic deficits and authority.[43]

NGOs serve as a means to aggregate individual voices, performing mass mobilization in three distinct areas. First NGOs relate to both states and TNCs in the production of normative values. Like states and TNCs, they seek to influence or perhaps dominate the discourse through which policy is formulated. But they also seek to influence and form the particular policies and normative values of TNCs, especially in areas with governance gaps. Second, NGOs serve a source of expertise within their own area of specialization. To that end they augment the legitimacy of claims to influence in norm making. Third, NGOs serve a monitoring and enforcement function, often substituting for the state where state organs are less well developed or funded. NGOs provide the modern mechanism for organizing mass interests and for privatizing the executive function once reserved to the state. These are the organizations that hold states and TNCs accountable for compliance with their own policies and promises, as well as those organizations that advocate changes in the policies of both. They also seek to represent the masses whose interests they serve, at least in a narrow sense. It is to that end that civil society's relationship with TNCs and the state is often adversarial – even as they cooperate with both in the formulation of policy and its enactment as governance or law.[44]

Within the governance and policy spaces now opened in transnational space – that area of activity beyond the ability of any state to fully control and into which TNCs, international public and private organizations have entered to fill the void, NGO participation has become institutionalized, especially in the context of their formal relationships with governments (including international public organizations) and TNCs. The UN defines civil society as the 'third sector' of society, comprised of civil society and non-governmental organizations. According to the UN, partnerships

---

[43]   Discussed nicely in Bauer (n 13).
[44]   On the representational character of NGOs, especially in their relation to TNCs and government, see Larry Catá Backer, 'Fractured Territories and Abstracted Terrains: The Problem of Representation and Human Rights Governance Regimes Within and Beyond the State' (2016) 23 *Indiana Journal of Global Legal Studies* 61.

with civil society advance its ideals.[45] Moreover, the UN Office of the High Commissioner for Human Rights (OHCHR), in its *Handbook for Civil Society*, states that civil society actors 'share information; advocate and scrutinize implementation of human rights; report violations, assist victims of abuses; and campaign for the development of new human rights standards.'[46] The *Handbook* further recognizes that civil society actors are those 'individuals who voluntarily engage in forms of public participation and action around shared interests, purposes or values that are compatible with the goals of the [UN].'[47] Moreover, the *Handbook* describes the interconnected relationship between the OHCHR and civil society actors, providing some examples of how they interact. Civil society actors alert 'OHCHR to deteriorating human rights situations and emerging trends'; they provide 'information to OHCHR on human rights situations, developments and alleged abuses, locally and nationally'; they work in 'partnership with OHCHR on human rights seminars and workshops, human rights training programmes, and on national and regional projects to raise awareness of human rights'; and they work 'with OHCHR to promote the ratification of human rights treaties and their implementation'.[48]

The OECD reinforces its commitment to 'give a voice' to civil society stakeholders. The OECD maintains that 'stakeholders' views are factored into the OECD's work and OECD analyses are stronger when they include 'the perspectives of civil society.'[49] Furthermore, OECD engages with civil society through two core representative organs, a Business and Industry Advisory Committee to the OECD, and a Trade Union Advisory Committee.[50] The core engagement or relationship the OECD maintains with civil society is through co-operation with business and trade unions.[51]

---

[45]  *See, e.g.*, United Nations, 'Civil Society' <http://www.un.org/en/sections/resources/civil-society/index.html>.

[46]  *See, e.g.*, United Nations, Office of the High Commissioner for Human Rights, *Working with the United Nations Human Rights Programme: A Handbook for Civil Society* (United Nations, 2008) iii <available at http://www.ohchr.org/EN/AboutUs/CivilSociety/Pages/Handbook.aspx>.

[47]  See (n 46) vii.

[48]  See (n 46) 8.

[49]  *See, e.g.*, OECD, 'The OECD and Civil Society' <http://www.oecd.org/about/civil-society/the-oecd-and-civil-society.htm>.

[50]  Ibid. The OECD also notes that NGOO can participate in conferences and workshops. The Business and Industry Advisory Committee includes just under 3000 business experts and organizations. See <http://biac.org/quick-facts/>. The Trade Union Advisory Committee is an interface for labour unions with the OECD. See <http://www.tuac.org/en/public/index.phtml>.

[51]  OECD, 'The OECD and Civil Society', supra. n 49.

OECD further engages with other civil society actors such as NGOs, think tanks, academia and citizens through regular consultations, conferences and workshops, and the annual OECD forum.[52] Finally, the OECD claims that civil society actors' 'analytical work and consensus building' that takes place in OECD committees, working groups, and expert groups 'develop into government policies take place – and where civil society can have a real impact.'[53]

John Ruggie, in his influential work on regulating TNCs, describes the criticism others have made about the Guiding Principles and their inability to empower the participation of civil society.[54] Ruggie explains that during the drafting of the GPs, he held 'bilateral' meetings with NGOs and that civil society actors generally were the 'largest single number of participants in the multi-stakeholder consultations.'[55] Moreover, Ruggie concedes that civil society participation is crucial to the success of the GPs. However, Ruggie responds to criticisms that the GPs should have included a 'Fourth' pillar concerning civil society with standards for civil society actors by stating that such a pillar would have faced resistance from civil society.[56] In addition, Ruggie posits that he seriously doubts that this additional pillar would have survived the UN 'political process of getting the GPs approved[,]' describing such a proposed 'participation' pillar as a 'non-starter' for some stakeholders.[57] Ruggie fears that criticisms about how the GPs fail to engage civil society will potentially create a 'self-fulfilling prophecy' and instead invites those critics to shed further guidance 'on how such organizations can use and build on GPs.'[58] I have suggested that an institutional role for NGOs might center on both their expertise and representational character built around their areas of expertise. They might usefully assume a role of advocate as well as monitor of state and TNC compliance with legal and societal norms, even as they continue to help craft them and naturalize these emerging norms within society.[59]

---

[52]    Ibid.

[53]    Ibid.

[54]    *See, e.g.*, John Gerard Ruggie, 'Regulating Multinationals: The UN Guiding Principles, Civil Society, and International Legalization', in César Rodriguez-Garavito (ed.), *Business and Human Rights: Beyond the End of the Beginning* (forthcoming) <http://ssrn.com/abstract=2474236>.

[55]    *See, e.g.*, (n 54) 4.

[56]    *See, e.g.*, (n 54) 6.

[57]    *See, e.g.*, (n 54).

[58]    *See, e.g.*, (n 54).

[59]    See Larry Catá Backer, 'From Guiding Principles to Interpretive Organizations: Developing a Framework for Applying the UNGPs to Disputes

## THE EVOLVING ECOLOGIES OF RELATIONSHIP BETWEEN TNCs AND POLITICAL ACTORS AND GOVERNMENTS

The conventional ecology, and the ideologies and premises that both define and constrain it, has been challenged by the emerging realities of economic globalization and its effects on diffusing governance power. And, indeed, the conventional understanding of law, especially its connection with the actions of a duly constituted state, have been challenged as well.[60] Some analysts have suggested that perhaps some TNCs wield more power and influence than some nations. For example, some argue that the process of economic globalization has allowed some TNCs to gather more power and resources than the host nations in which TNCs operate.[61] In fact, in 1999, out of the top 100 economies, 51 were corporations.[62] Furthermore, the largest TNCs have become crucial players both in the world and 'the domestic jurisdictions in which they operate.'[63] Another empowerment tool TNCs have are bilateral investment treaties (BITs). BITs often allow TNCs to threaten legal action against host states whenever TNCs perceive that enforcement of a specific law would harm the company or expropriate some of its business.[64]

It is not surprising that efforts at regulating TNCs have gained momentum, especially through the UN Human Rights Council Working Group established in 2011, talks about a comprehensive treaty on business and human rights, and the latest UN Forum on Business and Human Rights. Some argue for a complete overhaul of how human rights accountability for TNCs must be organized. For example, Halpern argues that TNCs and other private non-state actors should be scrutinized under a more consci-

---

that Institutionalizes the Advocacy Role of Civil Society' in César Rodriguez-Garavito (ed.), *Business and Human Rights: Beyond the End of the Beginning* (forthcoming).

[60] Gralf-Peter Calliess and Peer Zumbansen, *Rough Consensus and Running Code: A Theory of Transnational Private Law* (Hart, 2010).

[61] *See, e.g.*, Iris Halpern, '"Tracing the Contours of Transnational Corporations" Human Rights Obligations in the Twenty-First Century' (2008) 14 *Buffalo Human Rights Law Review* 129, 144.

[62] See Sarah Anderson and John Cavanagh, *The Rise of Corporate Global Power* 6 (The Institute for Policy Studies, 2000) <http://www.ips-dc.org/downloads/Top200.pdf>; see also Halpern (n 61) 144–145.

[63] *See, e.g.*, Harri Kalimo and Tim Staal, '"Softness" in International Instruments: The Case of Transnational Corporations' (2014) 41 *Syracuse Journal of International Law and Commerce* 257, 263.

[64] *See, e.g.*, (n 63) 264.

entious human rights framework because the ability of TNCs to avoid any accountability for potential human rights violations has 'exponentially' increased.[65]

Moreover, others argue that the interaction between TNCs and the most economically advanced state actors has facilitated TNCs' ability to circumvent regulation or even avoid accountability for possible human rights violations.[66] A 'coalescence' of some of these governments and TNCs has led to agreements and the WTO framework that appears to advance the interests of TNCs.[67] Yet another way TNCs interact with the government of various hosts states is through direct or indirect actions that affect the political landscape of these host states.[68] TNCs may intervene in the political affairs of host nations (mostly in developing countries) through direct contributions to political campaigns, bribing local government officials or co-opting local elites.[69] A classic example of TNC involvement is the overthrow of Chile's democratically elected Marxist government of Salvador Allende.[70]

These challenges have revealed obstacles for governments, TNCs and civil society trying to interact in governance spaces. In regards to human rights accountability and international law, some argue that TNCs purposefully label themselves as bystanders in the field of international law.[71] When TNCs get involved, as they often do, with state actors who happen to commit human rights violations, TNCs claim that they cannot be held accountable because they were just bystanders and did not willingly participate in the alleged atrocities that may have been committed.[72] Amerson argues that this 'bystander' label is a proxy 'for the concept of the innocent bystander . . . [because] their role as an observer to the human rights atrocities was that of an impartial observer, at the scene by happenstance, and

---

[65]    *See, e.g.*, Halpern, *supra* note 61, at 146.

[66]    *See, e.g.*, Gbenga Bamodu, 'Managing Globalisation, UK Initiatives and a Nigerian Perspective' in Janet Dine and Andrew Fagan (eds), *Human Rights and Capitalism* (Edward Elgar, 2006) 145, 162; see also Halpern, *supra* note 61, at 144.

[67]    *See, e.g.*, Bamdu, 'Managing Globalisation', supra.

[68]    *See, e.g.*, Larry Catá Backer, 'Multinational Corporations, Transnational Law: The United Nations' Norms on the Responsibilities of Transnational Corporations as a Harbinger of Corporate Social Responsibility in International Law' (2006) 37 *Columbia Human Rights Law Review* 287, 312–313.

[69]    *See, e.g.*, Backer (n 68) 313.

[70]    *See, e.g.*, Backer (n 68).

[71]    *See, e.g.*, Jena Martin Amerson, 'What's in a Name? Transnational Corporations as Bystanders under International Law' (2011) 85 *St. John's Law Review* 1 (2011).

[72]    *See, e.g.*, Amerson (n 71) 5–6.

powerless to stop the tragedy that was happening on the ground.'[73] This 'bystander' label, Amerson argues, allows TNCs to escape liability because as 'bystanders' they cannot be held accountable for the human rights violation.[74]

Some argue that the TNCs' ability to escape regulatory control and 'to exert political pressures on decision makers' creates a legal void.[75] Kalimo and Staal define this legal void 'as a regulatory situation in which a TNC behavior, permitted in a host state, would have been in violation of the laws of the TNC home state or of international law.'[76] Kalimo and Staal further argue that although what they call 'hard law' has proved to be ineffective as a means of regulating TNCs, 'soft law' may fill the void left by hard law in governing TNCs.[77]

Lundan highlights one further interaction between TNCs and government actors.[78] Specifically, TNCs have been engaging in much more 'non-market interactions involving civil society and quasi-governmental institutions.'[79] Lundan further recognizes three types of engagement between TNCs and other institutions. These engagements were first recognized by Cantwell, Dunning, and Lundan.[80] These are (1) institutional avoidance, (2) institutional adaptation, and (3) coevolution.[81] Avoidance touches on TNC power to choose among different institutional environments.[82] Adaptation touches on institutional adaptation, TNCs 'adjusts its structure to better fit the environment.'[83] These efforts to adapt may include attempts to use political influence and even bribery.[84] Coevolution references the TNC's ability 'to effect change in the local formal and informal institutions.' For example, the TNC may engage

---

[73] See Amerson (n 71) at 5.

[74] See Amerson (n 71) at 47.

[75] *See, e.g.*, Kalimo and Staal (n 63) 264.

[76] See Kalimo and Staal (n 63).

[77] *See, e.g.*, Kalimo and Staal (n 63) at 521.

[78] *See, e.g.*, Sarianna M. Lundan, 'The Coevolution of Transnational Corporations and Institutions' (2011) 18 *Indiana Journal of Global Business Studies* 639.

[79] *See, e.g.*, Lundan (n 78) 643.

[80] *See, e.g.*, John A. Cantwell, John H. Dunning and Sarianna M. Lundan, 'An Evolutionary Approach to Understanding International Business Activity: The Co-evolution of MNEs and the Institutional Environment' (2010) 41 *Journal of International Business Studies* 567, 572–574.

[81] *See, e.g.*, Lundan (n 78) 649–50.

[82] *See, e.g.*, (n 78).

[83] *See, e.g.*, (n 78).

[84] *See, e.g.*, (n 78).

in 'political activities to advance specific kinds of regulation or market structure that give it an advantage over its competitors.'[85]

These currents have produced some substantial changes in the ecology of relationships among governments, TNCs and civil society. These changes reflect not merely the currents of contemporary debate. They also represent a reasoned response to the challenges that have been posed by the breakdown of the old power order, built around states and national control of macroeconomic policy, which has given way to more fluid and interconnected relations among economic and civil society actors within, between and through states, and whose interactions center around the normative framework for managing the conduct of global production chains over which TNCs assert a substantial measure of control. It is to a consideration of these changing ecologies that this chapter turns to here. In particular, three are considered. The first is based on the TNC as the centering element of production chain order. The second is grounded on the emergence of non-state governance centers which assert order through certification, verification and monitoring. The third posits the emergence of a multi-stakeholder autonomous and self-referencing system around TNC–NGO–Government relationships.

## The TNC as the Centering Element of the Production Chain

It has become common to speak about corporate self-constitution, not just in the domestic but also in the transnational sphere. Corporations have developed self-referencing governance regulatory orders based on their power to manage production chains across borders. These are usually built around corporate control or influence throughout global production chains. Usually governance is manifested through internal policies and contract terms in supplier codes of conduct and in the rules of inter-corporate operations.[86] These are particularly relevant with respect to their connection with the public interest and corporate communication among stakeholders.[87] Corporate self-constitution and the emergence of

---

[85]    *See, e.g.*, (n 78).

[86]    *See, e.g.*, Gunther Teubner, 'Self-Constitutionalizing TNCs?: On the Linkage of "Private" and "Public" Corporate Codes of Conduct' (2010) 18(2) *Indiana Journal of Global Legal Studies* 17–38.

[87]    *See, e.g.*, Victor Imanuel Nalle, 'The Corporate Constitutionalism Approaches in Formulation of CSR' (2015) 5 (1) *Indonesia Law Review* 1–13. Cf. Gunther Teubner, 'Societal Constitutionalism: Alternatives to State Centered Constitutional Theory' in Christian Joerges, Inge-Johanne Sand and Gunther Teubner (eds), *Constitutionalism and Transnational Governance* (Oxford UP, 2004)

corporate conduct governance codes have changed the character of TNC–NGO engagement. While both groups continue to work towards control of the discourse of corporate social responsibility, NGOs and TNCs now engage directly in formulating, monitoring and enforcing corporate codes of conduct through both formal and informal arrangements. Patti Rundall, policy director of the NGO Baby Milk Action, explained the difficulty:

> about the phenomenon of partnerships between the United Nations, not-for-profit non-governmental organisations [NGOs working in the public interest], and for-profit corporations [specifically transnational corporations or TNCs] which operate in many countries.

> The development of partnerships has arisen, oddly enough, from a growing awareness of the damaging impact that TNCs can have on development, public health and the environment. NGOs are now aware of the need to think globally, and many are looking for ways to encourage corporate responsibility. In turn, TNCs are aware that they can no longer pursue profit with scant regard for the wider community.[88]

The ecologies of these relations are highly contextual but involve both partnership and competition for governance discourse and consensus.[89] They highlight both the cooperation and completion that marks the relations among TNCs and NGOs as they work through the parameters of the governance of corporate behaviors within their production chains and internally with respect to their operations.

Walmart engages with NGOs in several ways and through several partnerships. For example, Walmart is a founding member of the Alliance for Bangladesh Worker Safety, which is a group composed of brands and retailers seeking to improve working conditions for those who are employed in the ready-made garment industry.[90] The Alliance's annual report from September 2015 states that it trained 1.2 million factory employees on basic fire safety.[91] Furthermore, through a partnership with the Coalition of Immokalee Workers and Florida tomato suppliers, Walmart joined the Fair Food Program. Walmart asserts that its collaboration helped expand the Fair Food program, committed Walmart to using suppliers who best

---

3–28; Stephen Bottomley, *The Constitutional Corporation: Rethinking Corporate Governance* (Routledge, 2007).

[88]   Rundall (n 17).

[89]   *See, e.g.*, Boaventura de Sousa Santos and César Rodriguez-Garavito, eds, *Law and Globalization From Below: Towards a Cosmopolitan Legality* (Cambridge UP, 2005).

[90]   *See, e.g.*, <http://corporate.walmart.com/sourcing/collaboration>.

[91]   See (n 90).

reflect the group's principles, and explored whether the group can expand its focus beyond tomatoes. Finally, again in the garment sector, Walmart has collaborated with the ILO and IFC's Better World Program, designed to improve factory working conditions in the garment sector.[92]

Siemens includes NGOs as a key stakeholder in their 2015 Sustainability report.[93] They claim that maintaining an 'intensive dialog' with their partners along the supply chain and NGOs is important to the enterprise.[94] Moreover, Siemens asserts that they require their suppliers to comply with the principles of their 'Code of Conduct for Siemens Suppliers and Third-Party Intermediaries,' which is based on the 10 principles of the UN Global Compact and reflects 'Siemens Business Conduct Guidelines.'[95] Siemens monitors its supply chain through 'sustainability self-assessments by suppliers, risk evaluations conducted by our purchasing departments, sustainability questions within supplier quality audits and sustainability audits by external auditors.'[96]

Nike interacts with NGOs to ensure standards are met. For example, reports by NGOs and other labor activists in the early 1990s claimed that four Indonesian plants owned by Nike's Korean suppliers were 'rife with exploitation, poor working conditions, and a range of human rights and labor abuses.'[97] Another example of the Nike–NGO relationship is the 1997 leak of an audit performed by Ernst and Young of one of Nike's Korean subcontractor's factory operating in Vietnam to the NGO Transnational Resource and Action Center (TRAC), which was later renamed CorpWatch.[98] This report led to backlash and condemnation from other NGOs because it revealed that these factories in Vietnam were being operated in violation of Nike's code of conduct.

Apple, much like Nike, has been criticized by NGOs. For example, Green America and China Labor Watch have called for a complete boycott of Apple's products because of alleged dangerous working conditions in plants operated by Apple's manufacturing partners in China.[99] Furthermore, the environmental NGO, Friends of the Earth, launched

---

[92]    See (n 90).

[93]    *See, e.g.*, Siemens, Sustainability Information 2015 8, <http://www.siemens.com/about/sustainability/pool/en/current-reporting/siemens_sustainability_information2015.pdf>.

[94]    *See, e.g.*, (n 93).

[95]    *See, e.g.*, (n 93) 18.

[96]    *See, e.g.*, (n 93).

[97]    *See, e.g.*, Richard M. Locke, 'The Promise and Perils of Globalization: The Case of Nike' (2002) MIT Working Papers Series 10.

[98]    *See, e.g.*, Locke (n 97).

[99]    See Damon Poeter, 'NGOs Call for Boycott of Apple Products Over

a campaign to press Apple to find alternate sources of tin because the NGO believes that Apple may be mining tin from the Indonesian island of Bangka.[100] Finally, NGOs' campaigns aimed at Apple's supply chain have forced the enterprise to 'start reporting on supplier responsibility.'[101]

Samsung has stated that it recognizes the importance of collaborating with NGOs to address alleged human rights violations in mineral mining in conflict zones in Africa and environmental degradation on Bangka Island.[102] Samsung claims that this collaboration is essential to finding 'effective measures to work toward responsible procurement of minerals in its supply chain.'[103] In response, Samsung 'plans to set up a monitoring system to track its suppliers' use of conflict minerals.' Also, the company has requested that its suppliers submit 'lists of the smelters in their supply chains to be shared with global CSR-related organizations,' such as the Business of a Better World (BSR). Moreover, like Apple, Samsung was affected by the Friends of the Earth's 'Make it Better' campaign which sought to bring attention to the environmental damage in Indonesia's Bangka Island caused tin mining.[104] As a result, Samsung promises to uphold its social responsibility and work with other electronic companies and NGOs 'to ensure responsible and ethical sourcing of minerals.'[105]

British department store Marks and Spencer (M&S) established a partnership with Greenpeace UK regarding the company's seafood supply chain. For example, in 1996 the enterprise adopted its Policy on Sustainable Sourcing of Fisheries Products. When Greenpeace issued a study of UK supermarkets entitled 'Recipe for Disaster,' it ranked M&S as number one based on their responsible seafood policy.[106] The

---

Worker Safety' *PC Magazine* 10 March 2014 <http://www.pcmag.com/article2/0,2817,2454796,00.asp>.

[100] *See, e.g.*, 'NGO Pushes Apple on Tin' *Chemical Watch* 1 May 2013 <http://chemicalwatch.com/14695/ngo-pushes-apple-on-tin>.

[101] *See, e.g.*, 'Five NGO Campaigns Targeting Big Brands' *Sustainability Consult* 8 January 2013 <http://sustainabilityconsult.blogspot.com/2013/01/five-ngo-campaigns-targeting-big-brands.html>; see also 'Supplier Responsibility at Apple' Apple Inc., <http://www.apple.com/supplierresponsibility>.

[102] *See, e.g.*, Samsung Electronics, Mineral Sourcing <http://www.samsung.com/us/aboutsamsung/sustainability/suppliers/conflictminerals/>.

[103] *See, e.g.*, (n 102).

[104] *See, e.g.*, (n 102).

[105] *See, e.g.*, (n 102).

[106] *See, e.g.*, 'Greenpeace, NGO – Retailer Partnership Case Study: Greenpeace and Marks & Spencer', Greenpeace.org <http://www.fmi.org/docs/sustainability/Greenpeace_and_Marks_and_Spencer_Partnership.pdf>.

partnership become so close that Greenpeace even adopted M&S's sustainable seafood tag line: 'Support the best, avoid the worst, help the rest improve!' Finally, Greenpeace claims that M&S has supported the NGOs campaign and has provided the NGO with key information about the seafood industry.[107]

### Non-state Governance through Certification, Verification and Monitoring

Corporate self-constitution presents one set of structures within which political actors, and TNCs arrange their relationships. Another is grounded on the privatization of corporate responsibility codes within NGOs that themselves serve to produce, monitor and certify compliance with codes of behaviors that are normative but not legally binding.[108] These bring NGO and TNC relations within a direct governance framework. But they can also affect the form and movement toward legalization in states.[109] They describe both closed circuits of governance in which NGOs provide the standards under which TNC operate, but also the means through which that conduct may be monitored and 'certified.' At the same time, it describes a system in which NGOs and TNCs vie for dominance in the construction of those principles through which such standards are developed and both interact with the state with respect to the possibility of the legalization of these 'soft' contractual consensus norms.[110]

Oxfam has been active in criticizing sports apparel companies for alleged violations of labor rights and suppression of union activity. For example, in 2006 Oxfam issued a report in which they 'publicized the degree to which some sports apparel companies have responded to trade union rights violations in their supply chains.'[111] The report calls out TNCs for not doing enough to 'ensure trade union rights throughout their supply

---

[107]   *See, e.g.*, (n 106).

[108]   *See, e.g.*, Errol Meidinger, 'Multi-Interest Self-Governance Through Global Product Certification Programmes' in Olaf Dilling, Martin Herberg and Gene Swinter (eds), *Responsible Business: Self Governance and Law in Transnational Economic Transactions* (Oxford UP, 2008) 259–291.

[109]   *See, e.g.*, Robert W. Hamilton, 'The Role of Non-Governmental Standards in the Development of Mandatory Federal Standards Affecting Safety and Health' (1978) 56 *Texas Law Review* 1329.

[110]   On legalization and its critique, *see, e.g.*, Larry Catá Backer, 'A Lex Mercatoria for Corporate Social Responsibility Codes without the State?: On the Regulatory Character of Private Corporate Codes' (2016) 23 *Indiana Journal of Global Legal Studies*.

[111]   *See, e.g.*, Kevin Kolben, 'Integrative Linkage: Combining Public and

chains.'[112] Oxfam specifically criticized Nike for the enterprise's actions in its Indonesian factory called PT Doson, where they claim that Nike cancelled an order with the factory once they found out that the factory had established a trade union.[113]

The Fair Labor Association (FLA) interacts with powerful TNCs, such as Apple and Nike. For example, one of the many ways that Nike seeks to enforce its Code of Conduct is through inspections from the FLA.[114] The FLA conducts periodic inspections every year on a sample of 5 per cent of Nike suppliers across the world. FLA certification and monitoring provide a similar degree of supervision of Apple. Apple joined the FLA in 2012, allowing the association to audit working conditions in Apple's supply chain.[115] During one of these audits, the FLA 'observed at least 50 issues related to the FLA Code and Chinese labor law, including in the following areas: health and safety, worker integration and communication, and wages and working hours[,]' in Foxconn, Apple's biggest final assembly supplier in China.[116]

Fair Trade USA, the leading fair-trade certifier in the United States, audits 'Fair Trade supply chains for manufacturers and importers to ensure that all products labeled as Fair Trade Certified comply with our standards.'[117] The Fair Trade Certification 'model is designed and audited to ensure equitable trade practices at every level of the supply chain.'[118] In order for companies to earn a license from Fair Trade USA, enterprises 'must buy from certified farms and organizations, pay Fair Trade prices and premiums and submit to rigorous supply chain audits.'[119] The

---

Private Regulatory Approaches in the Design of Trade and Labor Regimes' (2007) 48 *Harvard International Law Journal* 203, 232–233.

[112] *See, e.g.*, (n 111).

[113] *See, e.g.*, (n 111) at note 192.

[114] *See, e.g.*, Richard M. Locke, Fei Qin and Alberto Brause, 'Does Monitoring Improve Labor Standards? Lessons from Nike' (2007) 61 *Industrial and Labor Relations Rev.* 9 <http://eprints.lse.ac.uk/59405/1/Qin_etal_Does-monitoring-improve-labor-standards_2007.pdf>.

[115] *See, e.g.*, Larry Catá Backer, 'Realizing Socio-Economic Rights Under Emerging Global Regulatory Frameworks: The Potential Impact of Privatization and the Role of Companies in China and India' (2013) 45 *George Washington International Law Review* 615, 665–666.

[116] *See, e.g.*, (n 115) 666; see also, 'Supplier Responsibility at Apple' Apple Inc. <http://www.apple.com/supplierresponsibility>.

[117] *See, e.g.*, Fair Trade USA, Sell Products <http://fairtradeusa.org/certification/get-certified>.

[118] *See, e.g.*, Fair Trade USA, Certification & Your Business <http://fairtradeusa.org/certification>.

[119] *See, e.g.*, (n 118).

organization claims that this process 'entails a high level of transparency and traceability in their global supply chains.'[120]

The Forest Stewardship Council (FSC) offers two types of certification: Forest Management and Chain-of-Custody certification.[121] With both certifications, independent certifiers 'verify that all FSC-certified forests conform to the requirements contained within an FSC forest management standard.'[122] Moreover, with regards to supply chains through Chain-of-Custody certification, the FSC 'traces the path of products from forests through the supply chain, verifying that FSC-certified material is identified or kept separated from non-certified material throughout the chain.'[123]

Amnesty International (Amnesty) exposes corporate abuse in many different regions. Amnesty demands that TNCs be required by law to identify, prevent and address human rights abuses, that corporations be held accountable for abuses they commit, that people who have been affected by these abuses have access to justice and remedy, and that laws operate across borders to protect people's rights.[124] In an effort to accomplish these goals, they have 'exposed countless instances when corporations exploit weak and poorly enforced domestic regulation with devastating effect on people and communities.'[125] For example, in 2015 Amnesty released a report condemning the diamond trade in the Central African Republic.[126] Amnesty based their report on 'extensive desk research on the international diamond supply chain, including reviewing documents on the import and export of diamond[,]' as well as field research in four countries.[127] During these field research missions, Amnesty 'visited Dubai to investigate the

---

[120]   *See, e.g.*, (n 118).

[121]   *See, e.g.*, FSC United States, Become Certified <https://us.fsc.org/en-us/certification/become-certified>.

[122]   *See, e.g.*, (n 121).

[123]   *See, e.g.*, FSC United States, Chain-of-Custody Certification <https://us.fsc.org/en-us/certification/chain-of-custody-certification>.

[124]   *See, e.g.*, Amnesty International, Corporate Accountability <https://www.amnesty.org/en/what-we-do/corporate-accountability/>.

[125]   *See, e.g.*, (n 124). See also Amnesty International, India: '"When land is lost, do we eat coal?" Coal mining and violations of Adivasi rights in India' (13 July 2016) <https://www.amnesty.org/en/documents/asa20/4391/2016/en/>; Amnesty International, 'The Ugly Side of the Beautiful Game: Exploitation of migrant workers on a Qatar 2022 World Cup site' <https://www.amnesty.org/en/documents/mde22/3548/2016/en/>.

[126]   *See, e.g.*, Amnesty International, 'The Global Diamond Supply Chain and the Case of the Central African Republic' 2015 <https://www.amnesty.org/download/Documents/AFR1924942015ENGLISH.PDF>.

[127]   *See, e.g.*, (n 126).

way in which the UAE implements the Kimberley Process.'[128] Similarly, Amnesty also visited Belgium to investigate how Belgium implements the Kimberley Process, and this visit was 'facilitated by the Antwerp World Diamond Centre (AWDC), and researchers met with representatives from AWDC and the Ministry of Economic Affairs (which oversees Belgium's Diamond Office).'[129] Amnesty based its findings on these and other types of similar research and monitoring missions.

The Electronics Industry Citizenship Coalition (EICC) is composed of several electronic enterprises. It provides 'joint systematic responses to emerging CSR-related topics and issues in the electronics industry,' and establishes 'operating principles and guidelines, such as the EICC Code of Conduct and standards, etc.'[130] The 'EICC Code of Conduct is a set of standards on social, environmental and ethical issues in the electronics industry supply chain.'[131] EICC has collaborated with electronics enterprises such as Samsung; for example, Samsung has 'conducted an audit on the use of conflict minerals by its major suppliers both inside and outside of Korea using the EICC conflict minerals reporting template.'[132] Moreover, the EICC offers a variety of tools for TNCs to conform to the EICC's standards, such as audits, and many others.[133] The EICC states that these tools 'help members meet [EICC] standards and drive continuous improvement.'

### The Emergence of Multi-stakeholder Autonomous and Self-referencing Systems

Corporate self-governance and TNC–NGO certification systems focus on the relationships among TNCs and political actors. Simultaneously with the development of these systems are those, principally at the level of public international organizations, that have sought to adopt specific normative standards and, at least in the case of the OECD Guidelines for Multinational Enterprises,[134] to adopt rudimentary remedial systems.

---

[128]   *See, e.g.*, (n 126) 10.

[129]   *See, e.g.*, (n 126).

[130]   *See, e.g.*, Samsung Electronics, Mineral Sourcing (n 102).

[131]   *See, e.g.*, EICC, Code of Conduct <http://www.eiccoalition.org/standards/code-of-conduct/>.

[132]   *See, e.g.*, Samsung Electronics, Mineral Sourcing (n 102).

[133]   *See, e.g.*, EICC, Assessment, available at <http://www.eiccoalition.org/standards/assessment/>.

[134]   See Organisation for Economic Co-Operation and Development, *OECD Guidelines for Multinational Enterprises: 2011 Edition* (May 25, 2011) <http://

These, then, center a three-way relationship that is built around governance frameworks, but governance beyond the state and beyond law. These are standards addressed to states but applied to enterprises. These are standards that are not binding but which leave a large space for political actors to use them to develop consensus on corporate behaviors.

> The OECD system of principles for the management of corporate behavior beyond the domestic law of states creates a three-dimensional governance 'space' through networks of soft law systems developed by complex partnerships between states, international organizations that serve them and global actors, and the global actors that form the core of the regulatory community.[135]

> The clearest example is drawn from the recent work of the OECD's National Contact Point system for the enforcement of global soft law frameworks that radiate out from the OECD's Guidelines for Multinational Corporations.[136]

> These principles tie autonomous multinational regulatory systems to the law systems of states in which they operate, but at the same time, institutionalize a stateless space.[137]

The UN Guiding Principles for Business and Human Rights[138] provide a normative framework for the governance of enterprise behavior. It is grounded on the institutionalization of relations among states (through a

---

www.oecd.org/daf/internationalinvestment/guidelinesformultinationalenterprises/48004323.pdf>.

[135]   And thus seeks to rebut the early conceptual critique: '[S]oft law expresses a preference and not an obligation that states should act, or should refrain from acting, in a specified manner. The underlying assumption is that behavior, or forbearance from behavior, in accordance with this preference will be directly beneficial to states.' Joseph Gold, *Interpretation: The IMF and International Law* (Springer, 1996) 301. This governance space is sometimes understood as 'spaceless' in the sense that it moves governance beyond territory, and thus beyond the premises that constrain law making in the state system. *See, e.g.*, Larry Catá Backer, 'Transnational Corporate Constitutionalism: The Emergence of a Constitutional Order for Economic Enterprises' (10 April 2012) <http://ssrn.com/abstract=2038081>; Larry Catá Backer, 'On the Tension between Public and Private Governance in the Emerging Transnational Legal Order: State Ideology and Corporation in Polycentric Asymmetric Global Orders' (16 April 2012) <http://ssrn.com/abstract=2038103>.

[136]   See OECD Guidelines (n 134) 67–78.

[137]   Larry Catá Backer, 'Transnational Corporations' Outward Expression of Inward Self-Constitution: The Enforcement of Human Rights by Apple, Inc.' (2013) 20 *Indiana Journal of Global Legal Studies* 805–879.

[138]   U.N. *Guiding Principles for Business and Human Rights* (2011).

state duty to protect human rights), TNCs (through a corporate responsibility to respect human rights), and political actors (through remedial provisions). Professor Ruggie noted early in the process of Guidelines formulation:

> The 'protect, respect and remedy' framework lays the foundations for generating the necessary means to advance the business and human rights agenda. It spells out differentiated yet complementary roles and responsibilities for states and companies, and it includes the element of remedy for when things go wrong. It is systemic in character, meaning that the component parts are intended to support and reinforce one another, creating a dynamic process of cumulative progress – one that does not foreclose additional longer-term meaningful measures.[139]

A 2015 'Final Statement' of a National Contact Point (NCP) proceeding from Canada evidences the relational aspects of these multi-stakeholder public–private mechanisms.[140] The Canadian NCP announced that, although Canada would not embed the Guidelines into its domestic legal order directly, Canada would enforce an expectation that Canadian enterprises would promote Canadian values abroad, including the values in the Guidelines and that a 'Company's non-participation in the NCP process will be taken into consideration in any applications by the Company for enhanced advocacy support from the Trade Commissioner Service and/ or Export Development Canada (EDC) financial services, should they be made.'[141] But more importantly, the NCP process itself encourages a broad participation from political actors. These may use the quasi-remedial processes of NCP proceedings to frame their interactions with TNCs and states.[142] Thus the Guidelines provide a framework within which TNCs, governments and political actors can structure their relations within a

---

[139]   Special Representative of the Secretary-General on the Issue of Human Rights and Transnational Corporations and Other Business Enterprises, Opening Remarks on the Consultation on Operationalizing the Framework for Business and Human Rights, Business & Human Rights Resource Centre (5 October 2009) <http://www.business-humanrights.org/Links/Repository/105128>.

[140]   See, Final Statement on the Request for Review regarding the Operations of China Gold International Resources Corp. Ltd., at the Copper Polymetallic Mine at the Gyama Valley, Tibet Autonomous Region (8 April 2015) <http://www.international.gc.ca/trade-agreements-accords-commerciaux/ncp-pcn/statement-gyama-valley.aspx?lang=eng>.

[141]   (n 140).

[142]   See, 'Initial Assessment by the UK National Contact Point for the OECD Guidelines for Multinational Enterprises: Survival International and Vedanta Resources plc' (27 March 2009) <http://www.business-humanrights.org/Links/Repository/969215/jump>.

system that is governance-oriented but not law. As in other emerging forms of governance, relationships follow structures of governance. But critical to all governance are the simultaneously cooperative and adversarial relations between TNCs and political organizations.

## IS THERE A META-THEORY HERE?

Taken together the structures of the relationships among states, TNCs and NGOs appear to produce an ecology the purpose and effects of which are contested but from which certain generalizations may be extracted. The possibility of corporate self-constitution and NGO standard setting and governance suggests a set of parameters for inter-group relations that has systemic quality. The TNC stands at the center of the system.[143] These serve as system legislator through contracts that imposes a complex set of norms with social, cultural and political effects. These are enforced against its controlled groups – along production chains. Though they affect others those relationships and effects have societal but no legal effect. These standards themselves are also targeted to key outsider stakeholders for whom such codes may be important enough to affect their own conduct, the enterprise's investors and customers. While the standards are developed and implemented by the enterprise, they are usually constructed with input from elements of civil society – non-governmental organizations that have a policy or other interest in the subject of the standards. At the same time, the TNC expends much energy shaping consumer and investor opinion.

Non-governmental organizations help shape the standards that TNCs implement. They participate in the creation of standards actually developed by enterprises, and, perhaps most important, they serve as independent monitors of compliance with these standards. The work of many organizations mobilized in large and small scale campaigns against this practice contributed to the formation of a public opinion that made it desirable for an enterprise to adopt policies against the practice beyond a mere reliance on the will of the local government to actually enforce whatever sanctions that had been imposed there by law. But most importantly, non-governmental organizations are instrumental in monitoring compliance with the norms adopted by TNCs to govern the behavior of its suppliers and their subcontractors. And there is an economic aspect to the participation of non-governmental organizations as well.

---

[143]   This section is drawn largely from Backer (n 21).

Involvement in the efforts of TNCs to harmonize the regulation of their supplier chains through the imposition of labor, environmental and other norms, is a critical source of funds, motivating members and increasing membership in such organizations. TNC regulatory work is good for the business of non-governmental organizations.

Critical to the work of both the TNC and the non-governmental organization is the media. Newspapers, television, internet-based news and other information dissemination enterprises play a critical role in the development and enforcement of TNC-developed standards of conduct. The media serves principally to legitimate the work of both multinational actors legislating conduct over their networks of stakeholders or the monitoring work of non-governmental organizations. The media, then, serves as the critical vehicle for communication across stakeholder organizations and to consumers, investors, and governments. The media sometimes mediates conversations among these groups as well. This is good for business. Such a role inures to the benefit of the media as an industry in its own right. The media is the largest consumer of information on the globe. Information is a critical factor in the production of news – the product that makes money for the media. Corporate social responsibility targeted at consumers and investors, overseen by TNCs and monitored by non-governmental organizations are very good for the business of the production of news.

Like the citizens and residents of political states, consumers and investors play a critical yet passive role in the governance systems of TNCs. By their actions, consumers and investors (collectively) determine the efficacy of the actions of each stakeholder – consumption of the products and investment vehicles peddled by TNCs, support for the efforts of non-governmental organizations, readership of media. Consumers and investors are the object of the efforts of the other stakeholders in this system to get them to act on certain sets of beliefs. Control of the beliefs and desires of these groups – or the ability to express those beliefs and desires as policies, rules and conduct (and impose all of those on those in networks of control) – affects the shape and character of the 'desires' of TNCs (and their taste for things like social responsibility, good governance, environmental protection, long- or short-term strategic thinking and the like) and the extent of their willingness to legislate for their network of stakeholders. To a great extent, then, corporate regulation has moved from a foundation in efficiency to a focus on values and their elaboration in the action of economic actors.[144]

---

[144] See Larry Catá Backer, 'Values Economics and Theology: The Contribution of Catholic Social Thought and its Implications for Legal Regulatory Systems'

Like consumers and investors, government – both domestic and international public entities – plays a significant but passive role in the control of the social and economic relationships of TNCs and their suppliers. Government serves as a source of authentic memorialization of conduct norms. It is not necessarily the legal effect of these norms so much as their expression of communal values they express that count. As important, governmental pronouncements and actions, international and domestic declarations of policy or aspirational goals tend to set the parameters of the debate that produces beliefs in consumers and investors on which both governmental and non-governmental actors base their own responses. And lastly, government sometimes tends to follow the actions of its stakeholders.

But what of the objects of all of this activity – the business people operating supplier factories, or their subcontractors, the children and their families, and the local communities in which all of these activities occur? These groups tend to be objectified and muscled out of direct and primary engagement in governance and governance-related relationships among the privileged groups of stakeholders. Conditions are improved to better their condition. Business relationships are changed on the basis of values that might or might not be shared by local business. Yet there is little expectation that the objects of all these activities will actually participate actively in the formation and elaboration of standards and enforcement norms. All of those are imposed from outside the communities affected. Global power, in effect, is exercised on their behalf, but based on the sensibilities of consumers and investors in developed states. From the perspective of the global order, it seems that the people of the developed world continue to impose their beliefs on others. This time, it is for their own good and the moral betterment of those who impose their values, through their decisions to purchase goods or invest in financial instruments.[145] This remains the greatest challenge of the relations among TNCs, NGOs and governments – as they all each engage with each other there appears very little engagement by the objects of all of this activity. From the perspective of democratic legitimacy, the issue remains substantially unexplored.

Relations among TNCs, governments and political actors are functions of power – principally regulatory power. Shifts in regulatory power, in turn, are a function of the great changes in the regulatory sphere made

---

*Law at the End of the Day* 12 January 2008 <http://lcbackerblog.blogspot.com/2008/01/values-economics-and-theology.html> (accessed January 12, 2008).

[145]   Discussed in more detail in Larry Catá Backer, 'Fractured Territories and Abstracted Terrains: The Problem of Representation and Human Rights Governance Regimes Within and Beyond the State' (2016) 23(1) *Indiana Journal of Global Legal Studies* 61–94.

possible by the free movement of goods, capital, and investment made possible through globalization. The nature and extent of NGO engagement, of their relations with states and TNCs has changed as the scope of governance has expanded, as the role of international governmental organizations and TNC self-governance has grown. Relations are understood best as power relations. But these relations are a function of power sharing among the three within the sphere of governance. But societal power also shapes the structures and direction of relations among these actors. Here one understands power relations in terms of the influence of TNCs, states and NGOs to shape the discourse and expectations, the normative expectations, that serve as the foundations of governance. The relations among these actors have become, to some extent, a mirror for the engagement of the emerging manifestations of popular power in representative form. The battlegrounds – the space within which corporate social responsibility is managed beyond the state, for the state and through the state – define the spaces within which relations among these actors now serve in lieu of the traditional relations among state, demos and their normative political ideologies.

## CONCLUSION: WHAT MAY LIE AHEAD?

This chapter considered the nature of the relationships among TNCs, political actors and government as a set of emerging ecologies of political economy. The evolving relations among them represent a distinct response to the transformation of the global legal, economic and political order in the face of globalization. Each exists autonomously and is evolving simultaneously, yet each is significantly interconnected within a polycentric governance order that lends overall structure without a centering position. The chapter started with the conventional and traditional ecology of relationships, centered on the state. It then considered the three most distinctive forms of emerging relational ecologies that de-center the state. The first is based on the TNC as the centering element of production chain order. The second is grounded on the emergence of non-state governance centers which assert order through certification, verification, and monitoring. The third posits the emergence of a public–private multi-stakeholder autonomous and self-referencing system. The chapter then briefly considered the possibility that these structured relations suggest something like meta theory structuring that is disaggregated and scattered by intermeshed systems that have arisen around the state.

What lies ahead? Projecting outward in time it seems clear that the spaces for governance created through economic globalization have also produced substantial transformations in the nature, structures and frameworks within which the relationships among states, TNCs and political actors are understood and manifested. Though the state remains a critical actor, relationships no longer are networked exclusively through or for the object of inducing state action. TNCs and political organizations are as likely to engage in governance related interactions as both are to reach out to the state. And even in the context of public institutional communication, those interactions might as likely be made to or through international public bodies as they are to be directed to any single or group of states. Among these stakeholders, the nature of communications continues to be complex. To some extent cooperation mechanisms – tilted toward joint governance efforts – are likely to continue to grow. Yet because the interests of political actors and TNCs do not align, there will be instances of relations that are adversarial – from those touching on monitoring and assessing TNC conduct to projections of stakeholder power onto consumer and investor communities to seek to influence discourse (and consensus) on appropriate behavior rules. What is certain, though, is that the relationship among these actors will be central to the evolution of governance norms and structures applied increasingly to production chains across states well into this century.

# 4. The UN Global Compact

## Maria Alejandra Gonzalez-Perez
## and Liam Leonard

> The Global Compact asks companies to embrace universal principles and to partner with the United Nations. It has grown to become a critical platform for the UN to engage effectively with enlightened global business.
>
> – UN Secretary-General Ban Ki-moon (2007– 2016)[1]

## INTRODUCTION

The United Nations Global Compact has generated both success and criticism since its inception in 2000. The Global Compact has been criticised by some observers, who believe that the United Nations loses some of its independence through alliances with corporate entities. This chapter will discuss the significance of the Global Compact within a number of contexts. These contexts include an examination of the Global Compact's origins, key participants and its principal signatories. The details of the UN Global Compact Governance structures will be outlined to allow a better understanding of how the agency operates regionally and internationally. The extent of Global Compact members' engagement with corporate social responsibility, and related issues such as environmental protection, human rights and social issues, will be detailed, and the interaction between the UN and engaged participants, from both the business and non-business sectors, will also be outlined. This will be supplemented by an account of the Ten Principles which lie at the heart of this endeavour. Finally, the connectivity between the United Nations Global Compact and the global market will be discussed.

The introductory quote from UN Secretary-General Ban Ki-moon outlines the underlying concepts that shape the UN Global Compact (UNGC). Since its inception in July 2000, The Compact has provided a framework for businesses, labour groups, agencies, advocacy groups and the United Nations to work together to promote a more equitable world

---

[1]   United Nations Global Compact, 'What is the UN Global Compact' <http://www.unglobalcompact.org/> accessed January 2016.

for markets, employers and employees. The journey undertaken by UNGC participants can be understood from this quote by its former Executive Director Georg Kell:

> At the UN Global Compact launch in 2000, approximately 40 companies came together with a dozen labour and civil society leaders to commit to universal principles. Today, the Global Compact stands at 8,000 companies and 4,000 non-business signatories based in 150 countries, representing nearly every industry sector, size, and with equal representation from developed and developing countries. The idea and practice of responsible business has been rooted in all continents, and our 100 Local Networks are convening companies and acting on key issues at the ground level.[2]

At the heart of the Global Compact, we find the core value of 'global citizenship'. From a United Nations perspective, the idea of active global citizenship can be understood through the main priorities of the priorities of the Global Education First Initiative led by the UN Secretary-General. These priorities include the following:

- **Put Every Child in School**: education for all children by overcoming obstacles such as child labour, discrimination and financial barriers;
- **Quality of Learning**: overcoming barriers to learning such as language barriers, teacher shortages, lack of learning materials, family support and foundations for learning, and hunger and nutritional issues;
- **Global Citizenship**: dealing with issues such as outmoded educational systems and curricula, focusing on leadership, values and teaching skills, and promoting the common good in today's world.[3]

The UNGC provides an opportunity for business and agencies to support initiatives such as Global Citizenship Education (GCE). The creation of this form of global citizenship ethic lay at the heart of the Millennium Development Goals (MDG, 2008–2015) and remain fundamental to the Sustainable Development Goals (SDGs, 2016–2020). The UNGC provides a platform for participants to become part of transformative activities on a transnational level. Key activities include participation in programmes which allow business and agencies to help provide clean water, food and

---

[2]    Georg Kell, 'Foreword' in Maria Alejandra Gonzalez-Perez and Liam Leonard (eds), *The UN Global Compact: Fair Competition and Environmental and Labour Justice in International Markets* (Emerald Group Publishing, 2015).

[3]    Global Education First, 'Priority #3: Foster Global Citizenship', <http://www.globaleducationfirst.org/220.htm> accessed September 2014.

improved agricultural production and enhanced peace-building capacities. The 'Ten Principles' of the UN Global Compact provide participants with a humane and rights-based framework from which contributions may be developed (see below). These Principles will be explored in more detail later in the chapter. The 'Ten Principles of the UN Global Compact' are set out in the following manner:

The UN Global Compact asks companies to embrace, support and enact, within their sphere of influence, a set of core values in the areas of human rights, labour standards, the environment and anti-corruption.[4] These principles are derived from:

- The Universal Declaration of Human Rights
- The International Labour Organisation's Declaration on Fundamental Principles and Rights at Work
- The Rio Declaration on Environment and Development
- The United Nations Convention Against Corruption

Once these Principles were agreed upon, the UN Global Compact established its framework for governance. This governance must be transnational, dynamic and flexible in order to deal with rapidly changing issues, while maintaining an ethical set of core values. Global Compact Governance has a voluntary and network-based ethic, as outlined in the 2005 UN Global Compact governance review and updated in 2008. The governance review recommended a process whereby stakeholders could take ownership of projects, with reduced bureaucracy and increased corporate and agency participation and involvement. As a result of these initiatives, the Global Compact Donor Group was reconstituted as the 'Global Compact Government Group'.

## GLOBAL COMPACT GOVERNANCE

Global Compact Governance (GCG) is an overall framework designed to facilitate a series of tasks. These tasks include running entities such as the Global Compact Leaders Summit, Local GCG Networks, the Local Network Forum, the Global Compact Board and Office and the Global Compact Governance Group. The Leaders Summit meets every three years and brings together key stakeholders and participant executives.

---

[4] United Nations Global Compact, 'The Ten Principles' <https://www.unglobalcompact.org/what-is-gc/mission/principles> accessed September 2016.

*Table 4.1    The UN Global Compact Principles*

---

**Human Rights**
 1: Businesses should support and respect the protection of internationally
    proclaimed human rights; and
 2: make sure that they are not complicit in human rights abuses.
**Labour**
 3: Businesses should uphold the freedom of association and the effective
    recognition of the right to collective bargaining;
 4: the elimination of all forms of forced and compulsory labour;
 5: the effective abolition of child labour; and
 6: the elimination of discrimination in respect of employment and occupation.
**Environment**
 7: Businesses should support a precautionary approach to environmental
    challenges;
 8: undertake initiatives to promote greater environmental responsibility; and
 9: encourage the development and diffusion of environmentally friendly
    technologies.
**Anti-Corruption**
10: Businesses should work against corruption in all its forms, including
    extortion and bribery.

---

*Source:*    United Nations Global Compact, 'The Ten Principles' <https://www.
unglobalcompact.org/AboutTheGC/TheTenPrinciples/index.html> accessed January 2015.

The focus of the Leaders Summit is global citizenship. Participants discuss new initiatives and implementation. The Local Networks are regional groups within the Global Compact. They provide various cultural contexts and oversee regional growth and expansion. The Networks also assist corporations in devising best practices in relation to the Ten Principles. With over 100 Local Networks globally, opportunities to participate in projects are communicated via networks to participants, and also individual participants could design and implement initiatives, in which the local networks might play a co-ordinating role. Local Networks maintain local autonomy through self-governance; they nominate officials for election to the Global Compact Board and participate in the Local Networks Forum.

The Global Compact Board is the overall advisory body for stakeholders, with 31 members. It is comprised of four main groupings; the United Nations and representatives of Labour, Business and Civil Society. Key officials in the UN Global Compact such as the UN Secretary-General also participate in the Global Compact Board, alongside the Foundation Chair, the Investments Chair and the UNGC Office Director. The UNGC

Board seeks to implement initiatives with integrity, as they liaise with their constituent communities.[5]

The Global Compact Office provides management and expertise for the UNGC. The UNGC Office promotes new methods and best practices, provides leadership and oversees network development. The Office also maintains communications links across the UNGC, develops partnerships with other UN agencies, and plays a role in all of the activities of the Global Compact governance structures. The Global Compact Governance Group operates with the support of 13 UN member states (China, Colombia, Denmark, Finland, France, Germany, Italy, Norway, Spain, Sweden, Switzerland, the Netherlands and the United Kingdom) who provide funds for its existence. The United States does not participate in the UNGC as it was considered contrary to US foreign and economic policy under President George W. Bush.

The Global Compact Government Group develops Strategies and Work Plans for the UN Compact. These states also contribute to the UNGC Trust fund and UNGC Local Networks as well as supporting regional Global Compact initiatives. These states may also provide staff for UNGC Officers, events or further studies in this area. The Government Group reviews the progress of initiatives and maintains the efficiency and effectiveness in Global Compact processes.[6]

## GLOBAL COMPACT PARTICIPANTS

In response to the rise of neoliberal relationships between markets and societies (and increasing interactions between transnational corporations and non-governmental organisations), corporate citizenship, corporate governance and corporate social responsibility initiatives can be understood as attempts to engage transnational corporations with regional communities.[7] The UN Global Compact (UNGC) is an example

---

[5] United Nations Global Compact, 'The UN Global Compact Board' <https://www.unglobalcompact.org/about/governance/board/members> accessed September 2016.

[6] United Nations Global Compact, 'About Us' <http://www.unglobalcompact.org/> accessed January 2015.

[7] Débora Vargas Ferreira Costa, Delane Botelho and Marcos Paulo Do Couto Costa, 'Socially Responsible Attitude or Commercial Strategy: The Global Compact case' (2013) 9 *Organizações em context* 143. See also: Gerald D. Helleiner, 'Markets, Politics and Globalization: Can the Global Economy be Civilized?' (2001) 2 *Journal of Human Development* 27–46; Georg Kell and Gerald Ruggie, 'Global Markets and Social Legitimacy: The Case of the "Global

of evolving 'complex multilateralism on a global level'[8] and offers the possibilities of implementing global multi-stakeholder governance and corporate citizenship values.[9, 10]

It is currently the largest corporate citizenship international network, framework and voluntary mechanism joined (as of September 2016) by over 22,446 organisations of all types around the world, with two thirds having joined since 2010, as shown in Figures 4.1 and 4.2.

Business participation in the Global Compact by a firm requires a commitment at the highest managerial level to implement, promote and report on the UNGC Principles, and to contribute to the broad development objectives of the UNGC (Millennium Development Goals and 2030 sustainable development agenda). An explicit written commitment by the company's chief executive officer (or equivalent) supported by its governance body is required. Participating companies are asked to make a regular annual (often tax deductible) financial contribution to support the work of the UN Global Compact Office. For 2016, the minimum suggested annual contribution for organisations with annual sales below US$50 million was $250. This suggested contribution increases according to the annual sales/ revenue of participant companies.

The Global Compact is a voluntary initiative and therefore 'does not intend to either regulate or monitor participant activities.'[11] However, by launching the Global Compact, the UN inserted itself in the corporate responsibility

---

Compact"' (1999) 8 *Transnational Corporations* 101; Liam Leonard and Maria Alejandra Gonzalez-Perez, *International Business, Sustainability and Corporate social Responsibility* (Emerald Group Publishing, 2013); Andreas Rashe, Sandra Waddock and Malcolm McIntosh, 'The United Nations Global Compact: Retrospect and Prospect' (2013) 52 *Business Society* 6; Lissa Whitehouse, 'Corporate Social Responsibility, Corporate Citizenship and the Global Compact: A New Approach to Regulating Corporate Social Power?' (2013) 3 *Global Social Policy* 299.

[8]   Stefan Fritsch, 'The UN Global Compact and the Global Governance of Corporate Social Responsibility: Complex Multilateralism for a More Human Globalisation?' (2008) 22 *Global Society* 1.

[9]   Dorethée Baumann-Pauly and Andreas Georg Scherer, 'The Organizational Implementation of Corporate Citizenship: An Assessment Tool and its Application at UN Global Compact Participants' (2013) 117 *Journal of Business Ethics* 1.

[10]   Peter Utting, 'Multistakeholder Regulation of Business: Assessing the Pros and Cons' in Rob van Tulder, Alain Verbeke and Roger Strange (eds), *International Business and Sustainable Development* (Emerald Group Publishing, 2013).

[11]   Georg Kell, 'The Global Compact: Origins, Operations, Progress, Challenges' (2003) 11 *Journal of Corporate Citizenship* 35.

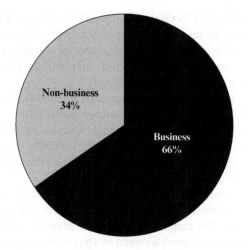

*Source:* United Nations Global Compact, 'Participants search' <https://www. unglobalcompact.org/participants/search> accessed May 2014.

*Figure 4.1 Global Compact signatories by organisation type, 2010–2014*

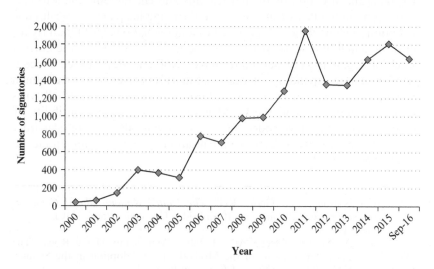

*Source:* United Nations Global Compact, 'Participants search' <https://www. unglobalcompact.org/what-is-gc/participants> accessed September 2016.

*Figure 4.2 Number of organisations per year that have signed the Global Compact, 2000–2016*

ground.[12] According to UN Global Compact's head Georg Kell (2000–2015), the growing strengths and weaknesses of the Global Compact participants demonstrate growth with 'continued relevance of the initiative's underlying idea, sustained institutional leadership support, governmental support (political back-up), and operational viability.'[13]

The reasons why companies participated in the Global Compact, and their perceived impact vary.[14] Companies participating in the UNGC receive both reputational and economic benefits in being part of the global initiative.[15] Some companies have indicated that participating in the UNGC could increase network opportunities and also improve corporate image.[16]

The Global Compact emerged in a context in which the international economic order (constructed after World War II) relied on an ideological consensus that the responsibility of the State in addressing national socio-economic needs, was challenged by the presence and power of global networks of production, consumption and finances in which international business and corporate actors have an active role to play in tackling socio-economic issues.[17]

On January 1999, then-UN Secretary-General Kofi Annan addressed the audience at the World Economic Forum (WEF) at Davos, Switzerland, engaging the attention of the participants and encouraging them to take action on the fragility of globalisation, the rising inequality in wealth distribution, the imbalances in governance and regulations for human rights, environmental and social issues, and the unsustainability of the current levels of degradation of natural resources. Kofi Annan proposed a reconnection among expanding international-markets players and core human values, suggesting that international business, governments, and all types of organisations around the world have a substantial responsibility of embracing new business models and social responsibility networks in order to reverse the negative effects of globalisation by giving a 'human face to the global market.'

---

[12]    Andreas Rashe and Georg Kell, *The United Nations Global Compact: Achievements, Trends and Challenges* (Cambridge University Press, 2010).

[13]    Kell (n 11).

[14]    Jorge A. Arevalo, Deepa Aravid, Silvia Ayuso and Merce Roca, 'The Global Compact: An Analysis of the Motivations of Adoption in the Spanish Context' (2013) 22 *Business Ethics: A European Review* 1.

[15]    Dilek Cerindamar and Kristoffer Husoy, 'Corporate Social Responsibility Practices and Environmentally Responsible Behaviour: The Case of the United Nations Global Compact' (2007) 76 *Journal of Business Ethics* 163.

[16]    Cerindamar and Husoy (n 15).

[17]    Kell and Ruggie (n 7).

At the WEF, Kofi Annan maintained that international businesses and multinational companies could use their economic power and high standards as models in their spheres of influence for leveraging principles of human rights, labour rights and environmental protection. As part of his speech, the Secretary-General suggested a role that the United Nations and its agencies could play in adopting this global challenge, specifically the Office of the High Commissioner for Human Rights (OHCHR), the International Labour Organisation (ILO) and the United Nations Environment Programme (UNEP). The International Chamber of Commerce on 5 July 1999 adopted a statement 'arguing for a stronger United Nations as the most sensible way forward, and pledged to work with United Nations agencies to implement the Global Compact at the corporate level.'[18] Business, governments and civil society organisations with different points of view on other issues united to overwhelmingly support the UN initiative, and the Global Compact was officially launched together with framework for action on July 2000 at the UN Headquarters in New York.[19]

By 2014, the Global Compact office is supported by seven bodies: (1) the United Nations Framework Convention on Climate Change, (2) Office of the High Commissioner for Human Rights, (3) International Labour Organisation, (4) United Nations Environment Programme, (5) United Nations Development Programme, (6) the United Nations Office for Drugs and Crime and (7) the United Nations Industrial Development Organisation.

Because of varying interests and social relations of power between the profit-driven MNEs and not-for-profit and cause-motivated organizations, perceptions of the Global Compact differ.[20] On one hand, the UNGC faced high-pitched criticisms and generated suspicion from non-governmental organisations, which warily regard the Global Compact as a possible opportunity for 'corporate criminals' to 'bluewash' their image 'by wrapping themselves in the flag of the United Nations.'[21] They fear that the UNGC may become part of a corporate-led, highly exclusionary

---

[18]   Kell and Ruggie (n 7).

[19]   Andreas Rashe and Georg Kell, *The United Nations Global Compact: Achievements, Trends and Challenges* (Cambridge University Press, 2010).

[20]   Susanne Soederberg, 'Taming corporations or Buttressing Market-led Eevelopment? A Critical Assessment of the Global Compact' (2007) 4 *Globalization* 500.

[21]   John Gerard Ruggie 'Global_governance.net: The Global Compact as a Learning Network' (2001) 7 *Global Governance* 371.

neoliberal strategy to legitimate MNEs' increasing social power.[22] On the other hand, those who support the UNGC might have unrealistic expectations.[23]

In some countries, governments have designed and implemented corporate social responsibility policies (and laws) based on Global Compact Principles. These policies help ensure that UNGC principles are complemented by domestic institutions and policies and, in practice, have also served as measures for promoting the international competitiveness of domestic businesses.[24]

## THE TEN PRINCIPLES

The UN Global Compact's intentional goal is that organisations embrace, support and promote a set of ten principles grouped into four areas: human rights, labour standards, the environment and anti-corruption. Their level of involvement reflects their capacity to promote these ten Principles in their spheres of influence. The UN Global Compact was initially launched with nine key Principles, but the tenth principle – anti-corruption – was added at the Global Compact Leaders Summit on June 2004.

### Human Rights

One of the most challenging areas of business sustainability is the respect and support for human rights. The human rights principles of the UN Global Compact are taken from the Universal Declaration of Human Rights (UDHR) that was originally adopted on 10 December 1948 and ratified in 1949 by the United Nations General Assembly in Paris. The UDHR consists of 30 articles and was directly inspired by the atrocities experienced during World War II, and this represented the first global consensus of 'Never Again', expressing the (individual and group) rights and

---

[22]  Soederberg (n 20).

[23]  Andreas Rashe, '"A Necessary Supplement" What the United Nations Global Compact is and is not' (2009) 48 *Business Society* 511. See also Ruggie (n 21); Sandra Waddock and Malcolm McIntosh, 'Business Unusual: Corporate Responsibility in a 2.9 World' (2011) 116 *Business and Society Review* 303; Olivier F. Williams, 'The UN Global Compact: The Challenge and the Promise' in Walther C. Zimmerli, Markus Holzinger and Klauss Richter (eds), *Corporate Ethics and Corporate Governance* (Springer International Publishing, 2007) 287.

[24]  Jette Steen Knudsen and Dana Brown, 'Why Governments Intervene: Exploring Mixed Motives for Public Policies on CSR' (2014) 30 *Public Policy and Administration* 51.

dignity that all human beings are inherently entitled to 'without distinction as to race, sex, language or religion'.[25] Despite the universal character of the UDHR, this Declaration has been criticized by some authors[26] for having a Western bias, for example by not including Islamic Shari'ah considerations. Also, Islam focuses on personal responsibility, and it does not admit corporations as legal persons, which could undermine the notion of corporate responsibility.[27] Nonetheless, since the doctrines of Islam offer an explicit codification of ethical standards and precise enforcement, it may be compatible with the UN Global Compact and with corporate social responsibility values.[28]

Traditionally human rights had only concerned States and were only addressed by international human rights instruments. However, since the announcement in 2011 of the Guiding Principles on Business and Human Rights by the Human Rights Council more companies (regardless of their size, location or industry) were confronted with the idea that they should address and adopt human rights frameworks in their commercial and production activities.

The first two principles of the Global Compact are:

1.   Businesses should support and respect the protection of internationally proclaimed human rights; and
2.   Make sure that they are not complicit in human rights abuses.

**Labour**

The UN Global Compact includes four labour principles, derived from the ILO Declaration on Fundamental Principles and Rights at Work. This Declaration was adopted in 1988 at the 86th International Labour Conference, and it states that 'all Members, even if they have not ratified the Conventions in question, have an obligation arising from the very fact of membership in the Organisation to respect, to promote and to realise, in good faith and in accordance with the Constitution, the principles concerning the fundamental rights which are subject of those Conventions.'

---

[25]   United Nations Charter, preamble and article 55.

[26]   David Little, John Kelsay and Adbulazis Sachadina, *Human Rights and the Conflicts of Cultures: Western and Islamic Perspective on Religious Liberty* (University of South Carolina Press, 1988).

[27]   Geoffrey Williams and John Zinkin, 'Islam and CSR: A Study of the Compatibility Between the Tenets of Islam and the UN Global Compact' (2009) 99 *Journal of Business Ethics* 519.

[28]   Williams and Zinkin (n 27).

This Declaration references eight core conventions, which cover collective freedom of association and collective bargaining, abolition of forced labour, effective abolition of labour by children before the end of compulsory school, and no workplace discrimination.[29, 30] The Declaration clearly states that these rights have universal coverage and apply to each worker in all States (regardless of the economic and social development level of the country). The four labour principles included in the Global Compact are:

3. Businesses should uphold the freedom of association and the effective recognition of the right to collective bargaining;
4. Eliminate all forms of forced and compulsory labour;
5. Abolish child labour; and
6. Eliminate discrimination in respect of employment and occupation.

### Environment

The UN Global Compact includes three environment principles that reflect corporate environmental responsibility. These principles are derived from the 1992 Rio Declaration on Environment and Development. The Rio Declaration consists of 27 principles to guide future international sustainable development. These environmental principles aim to address environmental challenges such as climate change, drinking water availability, pollution, ecosystems damages, waste production, deforestation, and land degradation, among others. These principles are:

7. Businesses should support a precautionary approach to environmental challenges;
8. Undertake initiatives to promote greater environmental responsibility; and
9. Encourage the development and diffusion of environmentally friendly technologies.

### Anti-Corruption

Controlling corruption and establishing and implementing sanctions for corrupt practices are often considered the sole domain of public authorities. But in the last decade civil society (including the private sector)

---

29   Equal Remuneration Convention, 1951, No 100.
30   Discrimination – Employment and Occupation – Convention, 1958, No 111.

has increased proactive measures to fight corruption.[31] The tenth Global Principle addresses one of the greatest world challenges. Corruption interferes with sustainable development, skews competition, obstructs economic growth, incurs severe legal penalties, affects reputations and undercuts liberal economic mechanisms. This principle was only included in 2004, and it derives from the United Nations Convention Against Corruption (UNCAC), which was the first legally binding international anti-corruption instrument. The UNCAC contains 71 Articles and requires all Member States to implement measures for preventing and criminalising corrupt acts. The Global Compact Working Group on the 10th Principle includes the UN Office on Drugs and Crime, Transparency International, the International Chamber of Commerce (ICC), the World Economic Forum Partnership Against Corruption Initiative (PACI) and the World Bank Institute (WBI).

10.   Businesses should work against corruption in all its forms, including extortion and bribery.

## SUPPLY CHAIN SUSTAINABILITY AND THE GLOBAL COMPACT

Sustainability of products depends to a large extent on the control producer companies can exercise over the sustainability attributes of their suppliers; the collaboration and engagement mechanisms companies can develop across their supply chain. To fulfil these aims, it is crucial to ensuring the credibility of sustainability claims through tracking human rights, environment, labour (including health and safety), and anti-corruption impacts of supplier activities. Traceability is the process of pinpointing and tracking the constituents of a product from raw material to completed good.[32] The UN Global Compact encourages companies to incorporate and promote material initiatives to integrate the ten principles into supply chain management systems. The Global Compact together with Business of a Better Word (BSR) launched in April 2014 the

---

[31]   François Vincke, 'Emerging Control of and Sanctions Against Corruption: The International Chamber of Commerce' in Stefano Manacorda, Francesco Centonze and Gabrio Forti (eds), *Preventing Corporate Corruption* (Springer International, 2014) 295.

[32]   United Nations Global Compact, 'A Guide to Traceability: A Practical Approach to Advance Sustainability in Global Supply Chains' <https://www.unglobalcompact.org/resources/791> accessed January 2015.

'Guide to traceability: A practical approach to advance sustainability in global supply chains'.[33, 34] With concrete lessons from different industries, different company sizes (large transnational corporations and small business) and types (for profit, governmental and NGOs), and located in different geographic regions, this guide aims to help companies and their stakeholders to understand, implement, develop and multiply traceability in their supply chain.

## FINANCIAL MARKETS AND THE GLOBAL COMPACT

Over the past decades, environmental, social and governance (ESG) considerations have increasingly attracted the attention of investors, activists and academics. Terms such as socially responsible investment (SRI), sustainable investment and ethical investment have been used since the 1990s and have only intensified following the global financial crisis. In June 2004, the UN Global Compact at the UN Headquarters in New York initiated meetings with a number of global stock exchanges and proposed the initiative 'Who Cares Wins' for encouraging investors and analysts to focus on ESG materiality and how these are related to climate change, anti-corruption, water and human rights.

Investors and financial analysts who take into consideration ESG criteria reject investment in industries and sector regarded unacceptable for ethical or moral reasons. Instead, they preference potential portfolio companies with good ESG performance and considered compatible with societal interests. As an example, the Equator Principles (EPs), which have been adopted by over 80 financial institutions, were proposed in 2013 to be a credit risk management framework for identifying, and managing social and environmental risks to support responsible risk decision-making.[35]

Also, in 2009, the United Nations Conference for Trade and Development (UNCTAD) together with the Principles for Responsible Investment (PRI) held meetings at the UN Headquarters in Geneva with stock exchanges, public policy officials, investors and financial information providers. This meeting resulted in a call for action by UNCTAD, Global

---

[33]    (n 32).

[34]    (n 32).

[35]    Equator Principles, 'About the Equator Principles' <http://www.equator-principles.com/index.php/about> accessed January 2015.

Compact and PRI motivated the UN initiative: The Sustainable Stock Exchanges (SSE). For the SEE, UNCTAD has developed voluntary technical assistance for stock exchanges and regulators (who have responsibility in the implementation of sustainability report initiatives).[36]

These initiatives create market-rewarded incentives for stock exchange listed transnational corporations to increment materiality in their ESG practices, and to be transparent when reporting progress towards the ten UNGC principles.

**Principles for Responsible Investment (PRI)**

Financial markets around the world have increasingly incorporated the Principles for Responsible Investment (PRI). These principles were launched at the New York Stock Exchange in April 2006 and are specially directed towards large institutional investors (e.g., pension funds). By May 2014, there were 1,258 signatories to the PRI. To become a voluntary signatory to the PRI, companies must demonstrate public commitment to responsible investment and ensure their interest in building more sustainable financial systems by committing to six principles. These principles are:

1. Incorporate ESG issues into investment analysis and the decision-making process.
2. Actively incorporate ESG issues into companies' ownership policies and practices.
3. Provide appropriate disclosure on ESG issues.
4. Accept and implement the PRI within the investment industry.
5. Work together to enhance effectiveness in implementing the Principles.
6. Report activities and progress towards implementing the Principles.

**Global Compact 100 (b)**

On September 2013, the UN Global Compact, in partnership with Sustainalytics, launched the Global Compact 100 (GC 100) Index, which is comprised of 100 companies which have demonstrated leadership and commitment to the UN Global Compact's ten principles and have also demonstrated financial health (steady base-line profitability). Sustainalytics is a research and analysis organisation created in Canada in 1992 to serve

---

[36] UNCTAD 'Best practice guidance for policymakers and stock exchanges on sustainability reporting initiatives. Note prepared by the UNCTAD secretariat' <http://unctad.org/meetings/en/SessionalDocuments/ciiisard67_en.pdf> accessed May 2014.

financial institutions and investors in providing ESG information to support sustainable investment decision-making. The UNGC 100 was released at the Global Compact Leaders Summit in 2013. During its first year (2013), the indexed companies averaged investment returns of 26.4 per cent (exceeding the global stock market).[37]

**Dow Jones Sustainability Index (DJSI)**

Another mechanism to integrate the Global Compact into the financial markets and which informs investors concerned with the sustainability performance of the companies in their portfolio is the Dow Jones Sustainability Index (DJSI). The DJSI was launched in 1999, as the first global sustainability benchmark. It comprises 2,500 large companies listed on the Dow Jones Global Total Stock Market Index that have exceptional sustainability standards, and therefore are a reference point for investors who are considering sustainability in their investment decisions. The Dow Jones Sustainability Index considers the financial, environmental and social performance of companies as well as sector-specific sustainability criteria. To be included in the index, companies are assessed based on their long-term performance in the mentioned dimensions (financial, environmental and social), and on the provision of longstanding sustainability plans to address this. The DJSI has a global index, as well as specific regional and country benchmarks in the Asia Pacific, Emerging Markets, North America, Australia, Eurozone 40 and the Nordic region. The indexing criteria are updated yearly, and companies included in the index are continuously monitored through a corporate sustainability assessment.

## GLOBAL COMPACT LOCAL NETWORKS (GCLNs)

The Global Compact can be understood as a 'Global Policy Network supporting ten universal principles in the areas of human rights, labour standards, environmental protection and anti-corruption.'[38] Since its beginning, the Global Compact has, rather than taking a regulatory approach,

---

[37]    United Nations Global Compact 'Global Compact 100' <http://www.unglobalcompact.org/Issues/financial_markets/global_compact_100.html> accessed January 2015.

[38]    Dirk Ulrich Gilbert and Michael Behnam, 'Trust and the United Nations Global Compact: A Network Theory Perspective' (2013) *52 Business and Society* 135.

adopted an explicit learning approach to encourage corporate change.[39] Local networks integrate domestic dimensions (cultural, economic, social and environmental) in their discussions and priorities.

According to the Global Compact, by 2012 there were 101 Local networks around the world. The Global Compact has established local networks in countries geographically distributed across all the continents. These networks were mostly established before 2005, with a few exceptions such as Australia (2009), Belgium (2009), Ecuador (2011), Republic of Korea (2007), Russia (2008), Viet Nam (2007), and the United States (2007). Local networks play a pivotal role in the governance of the Global Compact, and they have the participation of business (domestic and multinational operations operating locally) of all sizes, academic institutions, government entities and NGOs. Local network representatives meet together in the Annual Local Networks Forum chaired and coordinated by the Global Compact Office. Also, working in networks facilitates the progress and implementation of the ten principles in current and potential members, and according to Executive Director Kell, the initiatives and contributions of the local networks 'provide an important base to jump-start action and awareness on the ground.'[40]

Almost one-third of the organisations (business and non-business) that have signed the Global Compact are located in Europe, and this is followed by organisations in the Americas.

## GLOBAL COMPACT REPORTING INITIATIVES

### Communication on Progress and Communication on Engagement

Organisations that have signed the Global Compact commit to publicly report every year on their progress regarding the ten principles. This communication on progress (COP) ought to be disclosured to stakeholders (consumers, investors, employees, etc.), and it is a mechanism to be accountable and to demonstrate commitment to advance towards broader UN development goals. COPs also should be submitted and posted on the UN Global Compact's website, therefore building an increasing repository of corporate practices. Also, the Global Compact shares these COPs with financial markets through Bloomberg.

---

[39]   John Gerard Ruggie, 'The Theory and Practice of Learning Networks' (2002) 5 *Journal of Corporate Citizenship* 27.

[40]   Global Compact, Global Compact International Yearbook (Macondo, 2012).

Based on a self-assessment of the COP's content, these are classified into UNGC Learner, UNGC Active and UNGC Advanced. On October 2013, the Global Compact introduced a Communication of Engagement (COE) for non-business participant organisations. For non-business organisations the COE ought to be submitted every two years (instead of annually).

Organisations that fail to communicate their annual progress are first labelled as 'non-communicating' and then de-listed from the Global Compact after 24 months, and they are publicly exposed. By May 2014, almost 4,500 organisations from all sectors and from every continent had been expelled.

### Global Reporting Initiative (GRI)

The Global Reporting Initiative (GRI) is currently the most widely used voluntary corporate reporting framework for sustainability. In May 2010, at the Amsterdam Global Conference on Sustainability and Transparency, the UN Global Compact signed a partnership with GRI for aligning their initiatives to advance transparency and corporate responsibility through a joint encouragement to companies to increase their sustainability commitments. GRI's framework provides companies a structure for their annual Communication of Progress (COP), but also integrating other dimensions of sustainability, thereby enhancing the value of the COP. GRI was founded in 1997 in Boston, and it was pioneered by the Coalition for Environmentally Responsible Economics (CERES) and the Tellus Institute. The initial aim of GRI was to provide a multi-stakeholder accountability mechanism for companies' responsible environmental behaviour. This objective was amplified to other sustainability dimensions, including social, economic and governance issues. The first version of GRI was launched in 2000, then in 2002 the second-generation guidelines (known as G2) were presented at the World Summit on Sustainable Development in Johannesburg and embraced by the United Nations. In 2006, the third generation (G3) was launched, and it has a particular emphasis on strategic alliances with the UN Global Compact, the Organisation for Economic Co-operation and Development (OECD), the United Nations Environment Programme (UNEP), and the International Standards Office (ISO). G3 took into consideration the development of a consultancy process involving over 3,000 business and civil society experts. Furthermore, G3 proposed sector-specific guidelines and provided educational and training support to potential reporters. In 2011, G3.1 was proposed; it included guidance on reporting gender equity, community engagement and human rights performance.

In May 2013, the fourth generation of GRI Sustainability Reporting Guidelines (G4) was launched. In order to increase the possibilities for cross-organisational comparisons, G4 includes potentially transferable international metrics on sustainability. The specific difference of the G4 in relation with previous versions of the GRI is its emphasis on the importance of materiality. This implies that organisations, in order to achieve their organisational objectives and increase their impact on society, should focus their sustainability reports on those issues that are material to their business and their strategic stakeholders.

## PRINCIPLES FOR RESPONSIBLE MANAGEMENT EDUCATION (PRME)

The Global Compact acknowledges that in order to ensure a future generation of managers aware of sustainability and social responsibility issues, higher education institutions should be voluntarily involved, as they 'help shape the attitudes and behaviours of business leaders thought business education, research, management development programmes, training, and other pervasive, but less tangible, activities, such as the spread and advocacy of new values and ideas.'[41]

The PRME standards were first developed in 2007 by an international task force of deans from business schools in the United States, Latin America, the Middle East and Europe, and international academic institutions (Association to Advance Collegiate Schools of Business (AACSB), European Foundation for Management Development (EDMD), the Aspen Institute Business and Society Programme, European Academy of Business and Society (EABIS), Globally Responsible Leadership Initiative (GRLI), and Net Impact) together with the UN Global Compact supported the drafting of the final document. UN Secretary-General Ban Ki-moon hailed the initiative, declaring, 'The Principles for Responsible Management Education have the capacity to take the case for universal values and business into classrooms on every continent.'

PRME is a 'global UN-supported initiative whose mission is to inspire and champion responsible management education, research leadership globally.'[42] It consists of six Principles:

---

[41]  PRME, 'Principles for Responsible Management Education' <http://www.unprme.org> accessed May 2014.
[42]  (n 40).

1. Purpose: We will develop the capabilities of students to be future generators of sustainable value for business and society at large and to work for an inclusive and sustainable global economy.
2. Values: We will incorporate into our academic activities and curricula the values of global social responsibility as portrayed in international initiatives such as the United Nations Global Compact.
3. Method: We will create educational frameworks, materials, processes and environments that enable effective learning experiences for responsible leadership.
4. Research: We will engage in conceptual and empirical research that advances our understanding about the role, dynamics, and impact of corporations in the creation of sustainable social, environmental and economic value.
5. Partnership: We will interact with managers of business corporations to extend our knowledge of their challenges in meeting social and environmental responsibilities and to explore jointly effective approaches to meeting these challenges.
6. Dialogue: We will facilitate and support dialogue and debate among educators, business, government, consumers, media, civil society organizations and other interested groups and stakeholders on critical issues related to global social responsibility and sustainability.

By 2014, over 500 leading business schools from over 80 countries, including more than one-third of the *Financial Times'* top 100 business schools had become signatories to PRME.

## CONCLUSION

The importance of the UN Global Compact is understood through the successful corporate engagement with its initiatives. Bandi[43] describes this engagement as follows:

> In the last two decades the corporate sector has started to play a growing role in international development. The separation between business and the United Nations has become less significant. One expression of this evolution is the United Nations Global Compact.[44]

---

[43] Nina Bandi, 'United Nations Global Compact: Impact and its Critics', Covalence Analyst Papers, Geneva, 2007.
[44] (n 42).

Bandi goes on to outline some criticisms of the Global Compact, including the following:

- UN Global Compact would only provide a superficial contribution to development, but not touch the unequal structures of the system.
- It rather serves as a PR tool and helps to disguise the true goal of private enterprise, which is profit making. The UN serves thus as a 'bluewashing' tool.
- A main criticism concerning the non-binding character of membership. There is neither serious monitoring nor any kind of sanctions. In 2004 less than 60% surveyed reported taking any action in compliance with the ten principles.
- The Global Compact is also seen as a break with the traditional position of the UN on issues of economic policy.
- The UN had the role of an actor apart and operated a non-interventionist policy. With the direct involving of the UN in the corporate sector's activities, the UN would thus loose this privileged position, which contributed largely to the legitimacy it gained, also from developing countries.
- This might have contributed to deterioration in the UN's reputation and make the UN a less reliable partner for NGOs and other partners particularly in developing countries.
- The rapprochement would also bring up a new power relationship between the corporate sector and the UN that results in a weakening of the UN.[45]

These criticisms notwithstanding, the UN Global Compact can be seen as a success. This chapter outlined the significance of the Global Compact within a number of areas of operation. This included a discussion of the Global Compact's origins, key participants and its principal signatories. The chapter went on to outline the distinction in contributions between business and non-business participants in the UNGC. In addition, an understanding of the commitments of senior management to the Compact was presented to demonstrate the UNGC's government structures.

Moreover, the extent of Global Compact members' engagement with corporate social responsibility issues such as environmental protection, human rights and social issues was presented. In addition to presenting a discussion of the United Nation's role in developing the UN Compact, the interaction between the UN and key stakeholders from both business and

---

[45]   Bandi (n 42).

non-business sectors was outlined. An account of the 10 Principles was provided and discussed.

Ultimately, the significance of networks developed among the UN Global Compact and today's globalised markets and corporate entities, with the assistance of key member states, provides us with the best understanding of the Compact's potential for success in establishing global development projects based on integrity within a spirit of partnership and co-operation.

# 5. The Equator Principles and the 'Business and Human Rights Debate': hype or hope?

*Manuel Wörsdörfer*[1]

## 1. INTRODUCTION

The Equator Principles (EPs) are officially described as a voluntary and self-regulatory finance-industry benchmark in the project-finance sector. In particular, they are characterized as a 'credit-risk-management framework for determining, assessing, and managing socio-environmental risk in project-finance transactions.'[2] The EPs apply globally to four financial products: (1) Project finance with total project capital costs exceeding US$10 million, (2) project-finance advisory services, (3) project-related corporate loans and (4) bridge loans. The EPs are based on the International Finance Corporation's Performance Standards on Environmental and Social Sustainability (IFC PS) and the World Bank Group's Environmental, Health and Safety Guidelines. As of September 2016, the EPs have been adopted by 84 Equator Principles Financial Institutions (EPFIs) from 35 countries covering over 70 per cent of international project-finance debt in emerging markets.[3]

On 4 June 2013, the EP-Association (EPA) celebrated the formal launch of the third generation of the EPs (EPIII) and at the same time the tenth anniversary of the EPs. The two major innovations of EPIII are, first, the intended fight against global warming, that is, the most recent version of the EPs aimed at environmental stewardship and ecological sustainability mainly by evaluating less greenhouse gas-intensive technologies and procedures and by reducing $CO_2$-emissions during the design, construction and operation of the projects. The second innovation of EPIII is the inclusion and explicit reference to Ruggie's Protect, Respect and Remedy (PRR) framework which forms the basis of the UN Guiding Principles on Business and Human Rights (UNGP). The latest generation of the EPs

[1] The author would like to thank Alice de Jonge for her constructive comments. They helped to improve the chapter significantly. The usual caveats apply.
[2] Equator Principles Association website <http://www.equator-principles.com/> (all websites accessed 17 September 2016).
[3] (n 2).

strives for social sustainability which entails the respect of the rights of project-affected communities and other stakeholders such as Civil Society Organizations (CSOs) and NGOs. Projects financed 'under the EPs' require a stakeholder dialogue either in the form of 'Informed Consultation and Participation' or in the form of 'Free, Prior and Informed Consent' – given that indigenous peoples are affected by a particular project.

But what does the reference to the Ruggie-framework and the incorporation of the UNGP into the EP-framework imply? Which practical consequences follow from that link? Which institutional strengths and weaknesses do the EPs exhibit? This chapter reviews the recent 'Business and Human Rights' (BHR) debate and analyzes the EPs from business (ethics) and human rights perspectives. There is a substantial need for improving the EPs, especially, in terms of human rights protection and realization. In particular, the current 'human rights minimalism'[4] of the EPs – focusing solely on the negative duty to respect while neglecting positive duties to protect and realize human rights – needs to be overcome, e.g., by introducing (more) mandatory and legally binding elements into the EP-framework and by strengthening the governance-mechanisms of the EPs and its association. The chapter reviews potential reform steps that should be taken to 'harden' this soft law transnational governance regime and to move towards a positive and leverage-based CSR-concept.

The remainder of the chapter is structured as follows: Section 2 elaborates the main characteristics of the 'post-Westphalian' and transnational world order. It is this 'post-national constellation' which sets up the stage for the EPs as a voluntary and self-regulatory private governance initiative. Section 3 gives an overview of the key terminology of the BHR-debate, that is, it picks up the distinctions between negative and positive duties as well as 'influence as impact' versus 'influence as leverage'. Section 4 analyzes the EPs from a BHR-perspective. Here, the main institutional shortcomings of EPIII as a mainly negative and impact-based CSR-concept lacking adequate governance structures are revealed. Section 5 proposes reform steps which should be adopted to overcome the weaknesses of the EP-framework and to further strengthen EPIII in terms of human rights protection. The chapter argues that the EPA should integrate (more) mandatory and legally binding elements into the EP-framework and move towards a positive impact- *and* leverage-based CSR-concept. The chapter ends with a summary of the main findings.

---

[4]    Florian Wettstein, 'CSR and the Debate on Business and Human Rights' (2012) 22 *BEQ*, 739, 745.

## 2. BEYOND THE PUBLIC-PRIVATE DIVIDE: THE 'POSTNATIONAL CONSTELLATION'[5]

In recent years, a gradual transition from the traditional, nation-state based Westphalian setting towards a transnational 'post-Westphalian world order'[6] has occurred. This 'shift from *government* to [post-Westphalian] *governance*'[7] is characterized by the following features:

1. (Partial) disempowerment and erosion of the regulatory power of the nation-state;
2. Fragmentation of legal-political authority (coexistence of polycentric and hybrid governance regimes);
3. Existence of regulatory or governance gaps, in particular in transnational regulations;
4. Increasing ambiguity of borders and jurisdictions (deterritorialization);
5. Blurring of the separation between private and public spheres; and
6. Politicization of non-state actors.[8]

The global politico-economic arena is characterized by the coexistence and interplay of state and non-state, public and private actors, and the presence of intermediaries such as non-state agencies. Furthermore, different types of regulations exist side by side: National and international, nation-state and market-based, public and private, centralized and decentralized, mandatory and voluntary, formal and informal, hierarchical and non-hierarchical, hard- and soft-law regulations.[9] These hybrid and often

---

[5]  Jürgen Habermas, *The Postnational Constellation* (MIT Press, 2001); Andreas Scherer and Guido Palazzo, 'Globalization and CSR' in Andrew Crane et al. (eds), *The Oxford Handbook of CSR* (OUP, 2008); Florian Wettstein, 'For Better or For Worse' (2010) 20 *BEQ*, 275, 279ff; Dorothea Baur, *NGOs as Legitimate Partners of Corporations* (Springer, 2011).

[6]  Anthony McGrew, 'Globalization and Territorial Democracy' in Anthony McGrew (ed.), *The Transformation of Democracy* (Polity, 1997); David Held and Anthony McGrew, *Globalization/Anti-Globalization* (Polity, 2007); Stephen Kobrin, 'Private Political Authority and Public Responsibility' (2009) 19 *BEQ*, 349.

[7]  James Rosenau and Ernst-Otto Czempiel (eds), *Governance without Government* (Cambridge UP, 1992); Roderick Rhodes, 'The New Governance' (1996) 44 *Political Studies*, 652; Michel Foucault, *The Birth of Biopolitics* (Palgrave, 2008); John Conley and Cynthia Williams, 'Global Banks as Global Sustainability Regulators?' (2011) 33 *Law & Policy*, 542, 545.

[8]  Stephen Kobrin, 'Private Political Authority and Public Responsibility' (2009) 19 *BEQ*, 349.

[9]  Kernaghan Webb and Andrew Morrison, 'The Law and Voluntary Codes' in Kernaghan Webb (ed.), *Voluntary Codes* (Carleton, 2004), 106/115f; Kernaghan

de-territorialized public–private orderings overlap, intersect and collide with each other.[10] Zumbansen speaks in this regard of 'transnational legal pluralism' and 'polycentric governance regimes' as the new world order is occupied by a plurality of transnational governance systems and new forms of political–legal regulation 'above and beyond the nation-state'.[11] Transnational regulatory regimes are thus populated by a multitude of norm-making authorities. Public and private, state and non-state rule-producers and norm-creating actors engage and interact in the formulation, implementation and enforcement of (in)formal norms.[12]

This transition from a Westphalian to a post-Westphalian world order is accompanied by a fundamental transformation of the role of (hard) law as well as a transformation of the role of the nation-state: There is a shift in law-making from public mandate to private (voluntary) self-regulation and a transition from formal rule-creation in politically embedded state legal systems towards a system of specialized transnational law[13] regimes. Law outside the nation-state and within dispersed and fragmented spaces of norm-production, that is, 'post-regulatory' or 'reflexive law', transcends a nation-based understanding of law.[14]

Moreover, the state and other regulatory actors are undergoing dramatic changes with regards to their respective regulatory capacities, functions and instruments. The state is far from diminishing; there is no retreat, demise or death of the nation-state. Rather, the role of the state has changed – from the primary or exclusive author of binding norms to being one among a group of non-state actors involved in the norm-generation and enforcement process. Traditional, state-originating and formal processes of norm-production are transformed in favor of increasingly decentralized and denationalized processes of norm-setting by different

---

Webb, 'Voluntary Codes' in *Voluntary Codes*; Kernaghan Webb, 'From De-Responsibilization to Re-Responsibilization' (2012) <http://www.crsdd.uqam.ca/pages/docs/04-2012.pdf>.

[10]    Webb and Morrison (n 9), 100ff.

[11]    Peer Zumbansen, 'Transnational Legal Pluralism' (2010) 1 *TLT*, 141.

[12]    Peer Zumbansen, 'Globalization and the Law' (2004) 5 *GLJ*, 1499; 'Beyond Territoriality' (2005) 4(2005) Constitutionalism Web-Papers; 'Transnational Law' in Smits (ed.), *Encyclopedia of Comparative Law* (Elgar, 2006); 'Post-Regulatory Law' (2009) <www.mcgill.ca/files/legal-theory-workshop/PZumbansen_Post-Regulatory-Law.pdf>; 'Corporate Governance' (2010) 24/2010 *CLPE*; 'Neither "Public" nor "Private"' (2010) 22/2010 *CLPE*; Zumbansen (n 11).

[13]    Philip Jessup, *Transnational Law* (Yale UP, 1956).

[14]    Gunther Teubner, 'Substantive and Reflexive Elements in Modern Law' (1983) 17 *LSR*, 239; Teubner (ed.), *Global Law Without a State* (Dartmouth, 1997); Webb, *Voluntary Codes* (n 9), 383; Zumbansen (n 11–12).

norm-creators. This implies transnational, multi-level processes of norm-generation and enforcement and a fundamental contestation and erosion of the boundaries between state and non-state actors. The regulatory state is transformed into a moderating, enabling and supervising state[15] within a knowledge-based and globalized world economy-society.[16]

The role of non-state actors has also undergone fundamental transformations. In particular, Multinational Corporations (MNCs) gradually slip into the role of 'primary agents of global justice';[17] they are no longer mere addressees of the regulation, but they are also (co-) authors of the regulation. Moreover, MNCs act as de facto (quasi-) political actors,[18] rule-makers[19] and standard-setters, that is, they act in (quasi-) governmental roles,[20] acquire (quasi-) government-like powers and exercise (quasi-) government-like functions such as the provision of public goods.[21]

## 3.   THE 'BUSINESS AND HUMAN RIGHTS' DEBATE

Within the BHR-debate two distinctions play an important role, that is, the distinctions between negative versus positive duties and 'influence as impact' versus 'influence as leverage'. The following paragraphs give an overview of these keywords. The chapter applies these insights of the

---

[15]   Nicholas Deakin and Kieron Walsh, 'The Enabling State' (1996) 74 *Public Admin*. 33.

[16]   Zumbansen (n 11–12).

[17]   Onora O'Neill, 'Agents of Justice' (2001) 32 *Metaphilosophy*, 180; Melissa Lane, 'Autonomy as a Central Human Right' in Tom Campbell and Seumas Miller (eds), *Human Rights and the Moral Responsibilities of Corporate and Public Sector Organisations* (Kluwer, 2004), 148; Tom Sorrell, 'Business and Human Rights' in Campbell and Miller, *Human Rights and the Moral Responsibilities of Corporate and Public Sector Organisation* 134; Florian Wettstein, *Multinational Corporations and Global Justice* (Stanford Business Books, 2009).

[18]   Jeremy Moon et al., 'Can Corporations be Citizens?' (2005) 15 *BEQ*, 429; Andreas Scherer and Guido Palazzo, 'Toward a Political Conception of Corporate Responsibility' (2007) 32 *AMR*, 1096; Florian Wettstein, 'The Duty to Protect' (2010) 96 *JBE*, 33, 39ff; Scherer and Palazzo (n 5); Kobrin (n 6), 354.

[19]   Andreas Scherer et al., 'Global Rules and Private Actors' (2006) 16 *BEQ*, 505; Wettstein (n 5), 275.

[20]   Florian Wettstein, 'Beyond Voluntariness, Beyond CSR' (2009) 114 *BSR*, 125; Wettstein (n 17).

[21]   Dirk Matten and Andrew Crane, 'Corporate Citizenship' (2005) 30 *AMR*, 166; Andreas Scherer et al., 'Introduction to the Special Issue' (2009) 19 *BEQ*, 327; Andreas Scherer et al., 'The Business Firm as a Political Actor' (2014) 53 *Bus. & Society*, 143; Moon et al. (n 18); Scherer and Palazzo (n 18), 1098; Wettstein (n 17).

BHR-debate directly to the EPs and critically evaluates the EPs from a BHR-perspective.

### 3.1   Negative versus Positive Duties[22]

Human rights obligations can be divided into the negative duties to respect and the positive duties to protect and realize human rights:[23] Negative duties are often couched in terms of avoiding, preventing or minimizing. With regard to human rights, this implies that businesses should not infringe on the rights of others; they should 'do no harm' and refrain from violating human rights. The major negative duty they have is the responsibility to respect human rights and to obey the human rights laws in their daily operations; yet, they are not obliged to actively promote the protection of human rights.

Positive duties, to the contrary, are couched in terms of supporting, improving, fulfilling or contributing. They refer to the proactive realization, promotion and protection of human rights. These duties to protect and realize human rights are particularly expected from those institutions which are equipped with superior powers, capabilities and/or leverages.[24] They, thus, refer to state and non-state actors and in particular to MNCs which have unique capabilities and leverage-opportunities to protect and realize human rights.

### 3.2   Impact versus Leverage

The second relevant distinction within the BHR-debate is the one between 'influence as impact' and 'influence as leverage'.[25] Influence as impact refers to the effects and outcomes which are (in) directly caused by an institution's decisions and activities, while influence as leverage refers to an organization's ability to influence other organizations' decisions and activities through its business relationships.

---

[22]   Stepan Wood, 'Four Varieties of Social Responsibility' (2011) 07/04 *CLPE*; Stepan Wood, 'The Case for Leverage-Based Corporate Human Rights Responsibility' (2012) 22 *BEQ*, 63; Florian Wettstein and Sandra Waddock, 'Voluntary or Mandatory' (2005) 6 *zfwu*, 304, 314; Wettstein, 'Silence as Complicity' (2012) 22 *BEQ*, 37, 41ff; Wettstein (n 17), 290ff.

[23]   Henry Shue, *Basic Rights* (Princeton UP, 1980/1996), 52.

[24]   Kobrin (n 6); Wettstein (n 17); Wood, 'Four Varieties' (n 22); Wood, 'The Case' (n 22).

[25]   Wood, 'Four Varieties' (n 22).

The concept of 'Sphere of Influence' (SOI)[26] may illustrate the notion of influence as leverage: SOI assumes that the business relations of a company are organized in concentric circles, that is, 'a series of nested circles radiating outward from the organization's own workplace'.[27] The workplace of the company is in the center of this network of relationship. The other concentric circles are moving outward – seen from the workplace as the center – to the supply- and value-chain, the industry branch, the marketplace, the government and civil society. SOI assumes that the degree of influence of a company diminishes from one circle to the other and with increased distance from the center.[28]

### 3.3 Four Varieties of CSR

The combination of the two distinctions – negative versus positive duties and 'influence as impact' versus 'influence as leverage' – yields four varieties of influence-based CSR:[29]

1. *Negative impact-based responsibility*: A company has the obligation to avoid contributing to negative socio-environmental impacts in its operative business;
2. *Negative leverage-based responsibility*: A company has the duty to make use of its leverage, that is, its opportunities to influence business partners in their decision-making with the aim to avoid or minimize negative socio-environmental effects;
3. *Positive impact-based responsibility*: A company has the obligation to consciously and purposefully contribute to positive socio-ecological impacts;
4. *Positive leverage-based responsibility*: A company has the duty to make use of its leverage with the aim to increase or maximize positive socio-environmental effects among their business partners.

---

[26] John Ruggie, 'PRR' (2008) 3(2) *Innovations*, 189, 202ff; Ruggie, *Just Business* (Norton, 2013), ch. 3; Stepan Wood, 'The Meaning of "Sphere of Influence" in ISO 26000' in Adrian Henriques (ed.), *Understanding ISO 26000* (British Standards Institution, 2011).

[27] Wood, 'Four Varieties' (n 22), 3.

[28] (n 22).

[29] (n 22); Wood, 'The Case' (n 22).

### 3.4   Corporate Complicity

Corporate complicity in human rights abuses is defined as 'aiding or abetting' in the violation of human rights committed by a third-party actor such as host governments or suppliers and contractors in the corporation's value-chain.[30] A company acts as accomplices in human rights violations 'if it authorizes, tolerates, or knowingly ignores human rights abuses committed by an entity *associated with it*'.[31] Clapham/Jerbi and Wettstein distinguish four categories of corporate complicity in human rights violations:[32]

1.   *Direct* corporate complicity: the corporation directly and causally contributes to specific human rights violations;
2.   *Indirect* corporate complicity: the corporate activities support, in a general way, the ability of the perpetrator to carry out widespread and systematic human rights violations. Indirect complicity is usually divided into two sub-categories, namely beneficial and silent complicity;
3.   *Beneficial* complicity refers to a corporation which knowingly benefits from human rights abuses committed by a third party;
4.   *Silent* complicity refers to the refusal of a company to speak out and to make use of its leverage-opportunities to influence socio-political change.

There are several constitutive requirements which need to be fulfilled for an agent to be guilty of silent complicity: the omission and legitimization requirement, the criterion of influence and power; the criterion of absence of fear and coercion; the scale of human rights violations criterion.[33] Given that all these conditions are fulfilled, the corporation has a positive (moral) duty to speak out against the abuses of human rights, to help protecting victims of human rights violations[34] and to foster socio-political change in oppressive and authoritarian regimes.

---

[30]   Andrew Clapham and Scott Jerbi, 'Categories of Corporate Complicity' (2001) 24 *HICLR*, 339; Olivier de Schutter, 'The Challenge of Imposing Human Rights Norms on Corporate Actors' in Olivier de Schutter (ed.), *Transnational Corporations and Human Rights* (Hart, 2006), 13ff; Matthew Murphy and Jordi Vives, 'Perceptions of Justice' (2013) 116(4) *JBE*, 781, 794; Ruggie, *PRR* (n 26), 203ff; *Just Business* (n 26), ch. 3; Kobrin (n 6), 352ff.
[31]   Wettstein (n 22), 45.
[32]   Ines Tófalo, 'Overt and Hidden Accomplices' in de Schutter (n 30), 335; Wettstein (n 17), 295ff; (n 18), 36ff; (n 22), 40ff.
[33]   Wettstein (n 18), 37ff; (n 22), 40ff.
[34]   Lane (n 17).

In other words, (corporate) silence in cases of severe and systematic human rights violations is to be interpreted as moral support or encouragement for the perpetrator or at least as a sign of acquiescence. Not speaking out against the wrongdoings done to human beings equals the implicit approval and toleration of the wrongdoings by a potent agent. As such, silence is not morally neutral.[35] Due to the moral nature of human rights as universal moral norms or (hyper-) norms of global justice,[36] a positive duty to speak out exists (positive leverage based responsibility) – of which more later.

### 3.5 Equator Principles and Human Rights

The latest generation of the EPs (EPIII) consists of two pillars: ecological sustainability (fight against climate change) and the respect for human rights. With regards to human rights, EPIII explicitly acknowledges Ruggie's PRR-framework and the UNGP.[37] Additionally, the EPs indirectly[38] acknowledge the Universal Declaration of Human Rights, the International Covenants on Civil and Political Rights and on Economic, Social and Cultural Rights, the core ILO-conventions and the Declaration on the Rights of Indigenous Peoples.

Within the EP-framework, the respect for human rights is interlinked with the inclusion of project-affected communities, especially indigenous peoples, but also NGOs and CSOs in decision-making processes. Principle 5 of the EPs is designed to establish an ongoing and culturally appropriate stakeholder engagement, consultation, and participation process. Information has to be made readily and publicly available to the

---

[35] Wettstein (n 4), 756.

[36] Wettstein and Waddock (n 22), 309.

[37] Direct references to the Ruggie-framework can be found in the EP-preamble (EPA, 'The Equator Principles' (2013) <http://equator-principles.com/index.php/ep3/ep3>, 2); paragraph 3 of IFC PS 1 and paragraph 2 of IFC PS 7 (IFC, 'Performance Standards' [2012] <www.ifc.org/wps/wcm/connect/115482804a0255db96fbffd1a5d13d27/PS_English_2012_Full-Document.pdf?MOD=AJPERES>); IFC's Guidance Note 1 (IFC, 'Guidance Notes' [2012] <www.ifc.org/wps/wcm/connect/e280ef804a0256609709ffd1a5d13d27/GN_English_2012_Full-Document.pdf?MOD=AJPERES>, 15f); and in the Thun Group's working paper (Thun Group of Banks, 'UNGP' [2013] <www.csrandthelaw.com/wp-content/uploads/2013/10/thun_group_discussion_paper.pdf>).

[38] No direct references to these conventions can be found in the EPs themselves. Yet, the IFC's Guidance Notes 1, 2 and 7 contain several references to the aforementioned declarations (n 37). Since the EPs are based on the IFC PS the EPFIs are also bound by these conventions.

affected communities in their local languages. The disclosure of information should occur as early as possible in the assessment process – ideally within the planning stage and before construction commences – and on an ongoing basis. Project-affected communities must have the right to participate in decision-making. Their voices have to be heard, and the interests and needs of disadvantaged and vulnerable groups have to be taken into consideration. The whole stakeholder engagement process should be free from external manipulation, interference, coercion and intimidation. Projects with adverse impacts on aboriginal peoples require their 'Free, Prior and Informed Consent' (FPIC). This consent, however, does not create any veto rights nor does it require unanimity. Nevertheless, FPIC aims at reaching a consensus and the term 'consent' goes beyond the previous consultation and disclosure procedure.

Thus, the respect for human rights, together with environmental stewardship, is at the center of EPIII. It is remarkable – and in a way typical – that it took exactly ten years until the human rights terminology got introduced for the first time into the EP-framework. Only EPIII contains direct references to corporate human rights policy and corporate Human Rights Due Diligence (HRDD). As such, EPIII has to be regarded as a major step forward compared with EPII in terms of respect for human rights.

Yet, the current EP-version is in great need of improvement: The term 'human rights' is mainly mentioned in the preamble and the exhibit; HRDD is mentioned only once and with the addition 'may be appropriate',[39] while the terms 'human rights impact assessment' and 'human rights action plan' are lacking. Furthermore, EPIII refers only once to gender issues and women's rights (tellingly, in exhibit II), and there is no explicit and direct reference to the major human rights conventions and declarations (only the IFC PS refer to these).

Most important, a huge gap between theory and practice exists. In general, the EPs (and other extra-legal CSR-initiatives) are accused of being a PR-tool, a 'green-washing' instrument, an appeasement strategy or a 'paper tiger', that is, high-minded commitments on paper which fail to be enforced in practice. Indeed, when taking a closer look at the EPs, it becomes apparent that the governance mechanisms are fundamentally inadequate. Up to today, effective enforcement, monitoring and sanctioning mechanisms are missing (which will be discussed more below). Thus, it comes as no surprise that theory and practice fall apart. In practice, socio-environmental and human rights standards are (still) massively abused and undermined by the involved MNCs; e.g., EPFIs and their

---

[39]   EPA (n 37), 5.

clients (still) engage in (funding) 'dirty projects' or 'dodgy deals'; that is, projects which involve serious socio-environmental and human rights standards violations.[40]

### 3.6   The EPs' 'Human Rights Minimalism'

It has already been pointed out that the EPs explicitly acknowledge and refer to the Ruggie-framework. This framework states that the protection of human rights is the primary duty of nation-states (*state duty to protect*). In other words, nation-states are considered to be the main duty-bearers and trustees when it comes to human rights protection. According to Ruggie, international human rights laws apply primarily to state actors. Thus, any positive duty to protect and realize human rights is part of the domain of nation-states.

The baseline requirement for all companies in all contexts requires corporations to not infringe on the rights of others and to comply with the (human rights) legislation, that is, legal compliance.[41] Corporations, thus, mainly need to fulfill the negative duty to avoid causing or contributing to adverse human rights impacts (*corporate responsibility to respect*). All proactive and positive measures which aim at exercising leverage to protect and realize human rights and which go beyond this negative duty to respect human rights are regarded as an optional or voluntary matter of corporate philanthropy, not as a legal obligation.[42] Ruggie's PRR-framework with its state-sovereignty assumption, state-centrism and nation-state-based perspective is thus to be classified as a traditional Westphalian approach

---

[40]   Examples include the Baku-Tbilisi-Ceyhan oil-pipeline project; the Sakhalin II oil- and gas-project; the Galilee Basin and Abbott Point coal- and gas-project; the Orion Paper-Pulp Mill case in Uruguay; the Belo Monte Dam in the Brazilian Amazon; fracking, tar and oil sands mining in Canada; the Bristol Bay controversy in Alaska; the Keystone XL pipeline from Alberta, Canada, to the Gulf of Mexico; the Marlin and Fenix mining projects in Guatemala; and the Pascua Lama mining project in Argentina and Chile. The latter project is of particular importance since two Equator Banks (Ex-Im Bank and Export Development Canada) decided not to finance the project due to NGO-pressure and the clear violations of the EPs, including serious human rights violations committed against the Diaguita Indigenous community. In October 2013, Barrick Gold has decided to temporarily suspend construction activities at Pascua-Lama. This case illustrates that the EPs have the potential to make a difference on the ground; yet, most EPFIs do not make (sufficient) use of their leverage over their clients and the EPs still lack proper governance-mechanisms that could help to prevent these kind of 'dodgy deals'.

[41]   John Ruggie, 'Business and Human Rights' (2009) <http://www.refworld. org/docid/49faf98a2.html>; Ruggie, *Just Business* (n 26).

[42]   Ruggie, *PRR* (n 26); *Just Business* (n 26); (n 41).

(the political (and leverage-based) responsibilities of MNCs play only a minor role in here). By tendency, it can be labeled as a negative and impact-based CSR-concept, which means that the company's main responsibility is to avoid causing or contributing to human rights abuses and violations.[43] Ruggie himself is quite skeptical when it comes to the concepts of positive and/or leverage-based CSR[44] (this is one of the main reasons for his rejection of the UN-Norms and the SOI-concept).[45]

Since the EPs explicitly acknowledge and refer to the PRR-framework,[46] they can also be classified as a negative and impact-based CSR-concept, one which stands in contrast to a positive and leverage-based CSR-concept. Furthermore, since the EPs are built on Ruggie's framework, they also face similar points of criticism as the PRR-framework does (this is even more the case since the EPs fall in several regards behind the Ruggie-framework, e.g., in terms of the third pillar of the UNGP, that is, [non-] judicial remedy mechanisms).[47]

This chapter argues against the EPs' 'human rights minimalism', their state-centered perspective and bias towards corporate voluntarism.[48] It argues that a moral necessity to overcome this bias towards voluntariness

---

[43]   To be precise, the Ruggie framework consists of negative *and* positive duty elements. It thus holds an intermediate position between negative and positive CSR-concepts. The main reason for classifying it here as a negative (and impact-based) CSR-concept is twofold. First, the negative CSR-elements inside the Ruggie framework (clearly) outweigh the positive ones (cf. Ruggie's emphasis on *preventing* and *mitigating* adverse human rights impacts; *avoid* causing or contributing to negative human rights impacts; avoid infringing on the rights of others; legal compliance; etc.) (this, however, does not imply that positive CSR-elements are completely absent, to the contrary, think of Ruggie's discussion of [non-] judicial remediation of corporate-related harm as well as the HRDD requirements; the PRR-framework thus goes beyond the mere notion of 'doing no harm' and minimum legal obligations). Second, a major element of a positive and leverage-based CSR-concept is missing; that is, the notion of leverage: A detailed and qualitative examination of the leverage-based responsibilities of MNCs is lacking in Ruggie's recent book *Just Business* and in the UNGP (in here, only short references to companies ending their business relationships are included). Moreover, the UNGP refer to the term 'leverage' only a few times, exceptionally in paragraph 19b, while Ruggie's *Just Business* refers to it mainly in the context of nation-states, but not in the context of (multinational) corporations.

[44]   Wood, 'Four Varieties' (n 22); 'The Case' (n 22), 65ff.

[45]   Ruggie, *Just Business* (n 26), 16.

[46]   Cf. (n 37).

[47]   Wettstein (n 4), 758ff; (n 22), 41ff; Wood, 'Four Varieties' (n 22); 'The Case' (n 22); Kobrin (n 6), 352ff; Scherer and Palazzo (n 5 and 18); Scherer et al., 'Introduction' (n 21); *Business Firm* (n 21).

[48]   Wettstein (n 5, n 20).

exists: What is needed is an extension of direct, morally grounded and positive human rights obligations for corporations as well as a push towards (more) non-voluntary rules for state AND non-state actors.[49] In particular, two arguments speak in favor of moving towards (more) mandatory and legally-binding rules for MNCs ('hardening the soft law') and positive, impact- and leverage-based responsibilities:[50]

First, the EP-framework seems to view MNCs as private and apolitical entities as does the traditional Westphalian world view.[51] Yet, the political nature of human rights responsibilities in a post-Westphalian setting clashes with this perceived apolitical (private) nature of the corporation.[52] Recent research in the fields of political CSR and transnational legal theory have shown the gradual politicization of MNCs as well as the gradual shift in business–government–society relations.[53] Foucault[54] and other proponents of 'governmentality studies' speak of a 'post-regulatory model'[55] in which private (soft law) self-regulation is amending and complementing the traditional governmental (hard law) regulation. These new forms of (transnational) governance regimes come with a 'shift from government to governance', that is, various state and non-state actors form coalitions and public-private partnerships and the 'governmentality regulatory network' is emerging: The traditional top-down government regulation approach is weakened, governmental functions are outsourced towards non-state actors,[56] and a far-reaching diffusion of powers, rights and responsibilities occurs. New governance agents such as MNCs, NGOs and CSOs appear on the stage. They often transcend national boundaries and make use of market forces to achieve their socio-environmental goals.[57] These 'governance without government' regimes[58] are followed by a new division of labor associated with regulation between private and public actors (state, civil society and market sectors).

Especially, MNCs take over certain roles and functions previously

---

[49]   Wettstein and Waddock (n 22); Wettstein (n 5, n 20).
[50]   Wettstein and Waddock (n 22); Wettstein (n 5, n 20).
[51]   Stephen Kobrin, 'Private Political Authority and Public Responsibility' (2009) 19 *BEQ*, 349; (n 6), 352f.
[52]   Wettstein (n 4), 748.
[53]   Kobrin (n 6), 353ff, ch. 2–3.
[54]   Foucault (n 8).
[55]   Conley and Williams (n 8), 554.
[56]   Matthew Chan, 'What about Psychological Actors?' (2012) 13 *GLJ*, 1339, 1358.
[57]   Conley and Williams (n 8).
[58]   Rosenau and Czempiel (n 8).

ascribed to nation-states. This is particularly true regarding the 'protection, facilitation and enabling of citizen's rights'.[59] In terms of *social and cultural rights*, corporations function as providers; that is, they supply individuals with social services. In terms of *civil rights*, corporations function as enablers, in that they are able to capacitate or constrain citizen's civil rights. In terms of *political rights*, corporations fulfill a channeling role, that is, they function as an 'additional conduit for the exercise of individual's political rights'.[60] Thus, MNCs take a growing pivotal (quasi-) political role in granting and facilitating major rights linked to citizenship; they are major players in the arena of political rights.[61] In short, MNCs are not only *de facto* rule-makers, standard-setters and (co-) authors of regulations, they are also (quasi-) political actors that assume (quasi-) governmental roles and exercise (quasi-) government-like functions.

It is this heightened political status of MNCs which justifies and requires enlarged moral duties. Shifting powers must necessarily come with shifting moral responsibilities and obligations. Political authority and power should thus imply public responsibilities[62] and in particular a political or regulatory co-responsibility of MNCs.[63] The moral and political obligations entail more than doing no harm: MNCs must use their powers for the common good (e.g., in the sense of human rights protection). The 'argument of symmetry' states that powers, authorities and rights should imply duties, obligations and liabilities.[64] To put it differently: Leverage – understood here in terms of a company's size, scale of operations, profits, financial and human resources, strategic position in certain networks, privileged access to elites, etc.[65] – is equal to responsibility, and the more leverage, means the more responsibility. In other words, the larger the company, the larger the SOI is likely to be.[66]

Second, the EPs' human rights 'voluntarism' also clashes with the moral nature of human rights.[67] Human rights are considered fundamental moral rights or entitlements inherent to and constituent for all human beings (absolute and categorical character of human rights as moral rights).[68]

---

[59]    Matten and Crane (n 21), 11.
[60]    (n 21), 13f.
[61]    (n 21), 12.
[62]    Kobrin (n 6), 350.
[63]    Wettstein (n 5), 276; Scherer/Palazzo (n 18).
[64]    Kobrin (n 6), 350.
[65]    Wood, *The Case* (n 22), 77.
[66]    (n 22); Kobrin (n 6).
[67]    Wettstein (n 4), 748.
[68]    Wettstein (n 17), 284ff.

They, thus, refer to the principle of the fundamental moral equality and equal worth of all human beings as humans.[69] Furthermore, human rights flow from human dignity and they are rooted in it;[70] that is, they are essential for a self-determined, autonomous and dignified life in freedom. It is this moral nature of human rights and the fact that they are rooted in human dignity[71] which justifies their status as universal,[72] egalitarian, indivisible, inalienable, undeniable and unconditional moral rights. Human rights exist *a priori*, that is, antecedent to and independent of nation-states and legal laws: They have (partial) legal standing, as they find their expression in statutes and laws which are enacted by legislative and juridical authorities. They are embodied in national constitutions and statues and/or as part of proclamations by international institutions or political bodies, which is the legal dimension of human rights as juridical rights. Yet, human rights are not contingent on legal rights; they contain a claim to universal moral validity.[73] Thus, these kinds of moral obligations[74] outreach legal obligations.[75]

The status of human rights as moral rights rules out any form of moral arbitrariness, discretion and voluntariness (e.g., in the form of corporate charity or philanthropy). In other words: Human rights are not a matter of voluntary 'compliance'. Thus, (multinational) corporations have direct negative and positive moral obligations to unconditionally respect, protect AND realize human rights (these human rights responsibilities are independent of the legal requirements in the corporation's countries of operation).[76] Businesses are direct duty-bearers, and should thus be held directly liable for their (complicity in) human rights violations.[77] To put

---

[69] Björn Fasterling and Geert Demuijnck, 'Human Rights in the Void?' (2013) 116 *JBE*, 799, 801f; Wettstein (n 4, 5, 18, 20 and 22).

[70] Wettstein and Waddock (n 22), 312; Kobrin (n 6), 351; Stefan Gosepath, 'Zu Begründungen sozialer Menschenrechte' in Gosepath and Lohmann (eds), *Philosophie der Menschenrechte* (Suhrkamp, 1998/1999); Georg Lohmann, 'Menschenrechte zwischen Moral und Recht' in Gosepath and Lohmann (eds), *Philosophie der Menschenrechte* (Suhrkamp, 1998/1999).

[71] Gosepath (n 70).

[72] Wesley Cragg, 'Human Rights, Globalisation and the Modern Stakeholder Corporation' in Campbell and Miller (eds), *Human Rights and the Moral Responsibilities of Corporate and Public Sector Organisations* (Kluwer, 2004), 125; Wesley Cragg, 'Business and Human Rights' in Brenkert/Beauchamp (eds), *The Oxford Handbook of Business Ethics* (OUP, 2010/2012), 291/297; Wettstein (n 20), 145.

[73] Lane (n 17), 145.

[74] Sorrell (n 17), 134.

[75] Cragg, *Human Rights* (n 72), 124.

[76] Wettstein and Waddock (n 22), 313.

[77] Kobrin (n 6), 355.

it differently: States are not the exclusive and only bearers of positive human rights obligations. Corporations' (legal and) moral duties must go beyond 'do no harm' and they must do more than merely respect human rights.[78] Their scope of responsibility also includes a positive duty to protect and realize human rights, a universal duty[79] which has commonly been ascribed only to nation-states. Thus, due to their political authority and power (MNCs as (quasi-) political actors and de facto rule-makers and (co-) authors of regulations) and due to the moral nature of human rights, (multinational) corporations (including (EP)FIs) have positive and leverage-based responsibilities to fulfill; e.g., a duty to protect victims of human rights abuses, in particular when a humanitarian emergency occurs; a positive duty to speak out; a duty to promote human rights-compatible institutions in home and host countries; and a duty to foster politico-economic change (inside and outside the supply- and value-chain).

In summary, MNCs as (quasi-) political authorities bear political responsibilities and direct human rights obligations and they have duties to respect, protect AND realize human rights. The tripartite typology of human rights obligations[80] is thus valid for state and non-state actors, and companies have to fulfill negative and positive human rights duties.

The EPA is well advised to take the aforementioned critique seriously: What is needed from the BHR-perspective of this chapter is a push towards (more) mandatory and legally binding rules for businesses, particularly with respect to human rights protection.[81] Additionally, an impact- and leverage-based CSR-concept including positive human rights obligations for corporations and a corporate human rights activism and advocacy campaign[82] is needed. This comprehensive impact- and leverage-based CSR-concept shall aim at making use of one's leverage/organization's capacity to influence other parties' decisions and activities, especially those which are part of the supply- and value-chain. This chapter, thus, argues to move beyond the current BHR-status quo. The overall aim must be to overcome the EPs' (and other CSR-initiatives') bias towards voluntariness ('going beyond voluntariness') and to argue for a positive impact- and leverage-based CSR-concept. The human rights 'chapter' of the EPs (including the Thun Group's working paper) is a necessary step in the right direction, yet it does not go far enough. What is needed is a comprehensive, positive leverage-based CSR-concept, one which holds MNCs directly

---

[78]   Murphy and Vives (n 30), 785/793f.
[79]   Fasterling and Demuijnck (n 69).
[80]   Shue (n 23).
[81]   Wettstein and Waddock (n 22), 310.
[82]   Wettstein (n 18).

accountable for their actions and establishes positive human rights obligations for (multinational) corporations. In its current version, however, the
EPs are not readily equipped for a positive leverage-based CSR-conception.
Thus, the following section analyzes the various shortcomings of EPIII and
points out necessary reform steps that need to be implemented to (further)
strengthen the EP-framework (and to bring positive impacts and value creation, e.g., in the sense of a proper human rights protection).

## 4. A CRITICAL BUSINESS-ETHICAL EVALUATION OF THE EPS

It has already been pointed out that many EPFIs still engage in so-called
dodgy deals and that they fund 'dirty projects'. The reasons for these
ethically dubious deals and the apparent gap between theory and practice
have to be seen in the inadequate and ineffective governance mechanisms.
Among the main shortcomings and continued deficiencies of the latest
version of the EPs and (its association) are the lack of accountability
and liability, the existing exit-door strategies, the lack of monitoring and
screening, the lack of implementation and enforcement, and the lack of
sanctioning-mechanisms.

For example, the Disclaimer and the Governance Rules of the EPs[83]
state that the EPs do not create any rights or liabilities. As such, they
ensure that there are no mandatory obligations or direct punitive actions
that can arise from the EPs. The EP-framework is a legally non-binding
governance system which relies solely on voluntary self-regulation and
self-enforcement. Minimum entry requirements and absolute performance
standards are lacking. Furthermore, clear, verifiable metrics that are transparently and independently monitored are absent.[84] In short, no adequate
governance mechanism exists which could ensure external and internal
accountability and liability.

Moreover, lots of loopholes and grey areas exist which allow for circumventing the EPs in myriad ways. The EPs are vaguely, even ambiguously,
formulated, leaving enough discretionary leeway for diverging interpretations and exit-door strategies. The language used is often declaratory
rather than compulsory; some principles are conditional in nature, others

---

[83] EPA, 'Governance Rules' (2010/2013) <http://www.equator-principles.com/
index.php/about/governance-and-management>.
[84] Donald H. Schepers, 'The Equator Principles' (2011) 11(1) *Corp. Gov.*, 90,
101.

contain mere recommendations. The EPs are mainly written in 'should' not in 'shall' language, which implies no legal obligations. As a consequence, borrowers and lenders are able to circumvent the contractual obligations of the EPs to avoid being classified as high risk.[85] Banks can redefine their project finance activities as representing something else, such as corporate or export finance and project financiers take the backdoor option and classify their projects as category B or C to avoid a stricter A-classification.[86] Lastly, EPFIs can provide loans in different tranches to avoid the respective financial thresholds.

So far, EP-compliance relies mainly on 'passive' monitoring.[87] NGOs and CSOs function as watchdogs.[88] In case of apparent non-compliance, they might start 'naming and shaming' campaigns that might catch media attention and cause public outcry and negative reputational effects on the involved EPFIs and their clients. However, pro-active and independent monitoring and control, and mandatory and transparent third-party assessment of compliance – e.g., in the form of an independent EP-ombudsperson – are still missing. What is also lacking in EPIII are absolute performance standards and clear, verifiable metrics which are transparently monitored – both of which are a necessity for an impartial and independent verification of conformity. Finally, mandatory grievance- and remedy-mechanisms, which could help to address ineffective implementation and non-compliance, are absent. In short, the EPs are a set of voluntary, legally non-binding guidelines without appropriate accountability, monitoring and auditing systems.

Furthermore, the self-regulatory EP-regime is rather ineffective since a credible deterrent (e.g., in the form of de-listing and exclusion of non-compliant EPFIs) and formal sanctions are lacking. Enforcement, monitoring and sanctions belong together; they form an indissoluble triangle. In all three regards, the EPs lack effective governance mechanisms. The question which comes up with respect to sanctions is whether the EPs have enough legal bite to penalize institutions that fall behind their voluntary socio-environmental commitments. Currently, EPFIs face only minor

---

[85]    Marissa Marco, 'Accountability in International Project Finance' (2011) 34 *Fordham ILJ*, 452, 470.

[86]    Patrick Haack et al., 'Exploring the Constitutive Conditions' (2010) 115 Working Paper Zurich University, 1, 21; Christopher Wright, 'Global Banks, the Environment, and Human Rights' (2012) 12 *GEP*, 56, 68.

[87]    Doug Sarro, 'Do Lenders Make Effective Regulators?' (2012) 13 *GLJ*, 1522, 1542ff.

[88]    Niamh O'Sullivan and Brendan O'Dwyer, 'Stakeholder perspectives on a financial sector legitimation process' (2009) 22 *AAAJ*, 553.

sanctions, should they not comply with the EPs. Until today, only 'naming and shaming' campaigns might put EPFIs and their clients under pressure. NGO/CSO-watchdogs have powerful positions when it comes to reputational pressure. They help to ensure that non-state actors such as MNCs abide by their voluntary commitments and promises. Nevertheless, this passive and *ex-post* way of monitoring (and sanctioning) is not sufficient to prevent 'dodgy deals'.

## 5.  REFORM STEPS

To overcome the institutional shortcomings of the EPs and to move towards a positive impact- and leverage-based CSR-concept, reform steps are to be adopted at the *micro-* (level of the individual corporation including project sponsors and developers), *meso-* (EPA-level) and *macro-levels* ((trans-) national level). The following paragraphs give an overview of the respective reform measures which should be adopted by EPFIs and/or their clients.

### 5.1  Micro-level: EPFIs and Clients

#### 5.1.1  Change in corporate culture
The 'Spirit of the EPs'[89] should not be restricted to project finance alone since it is only a small segment of multinational banks (it commonly accounts for up to 5 per cent of the overall turnover of major banks; as such, the EPs apply only to a small fraction of multinational bank's total activities). The EP-spirit should ideally be applied to all banking activities – including investment banking; that is, EPFIs should aim at '*going beyond project finance*'.

The EP-spirit should also be embedded throughout the whole organization. All levels and sectors of the organization should internalize it. For instance, socio-environmental and human rights risk management and other CSR-activities should be integrated into the company's core businesses; a company's existing risk-management framework, decision-making and governance processes should be extended to also include ESG-issues.

Furthermore, considerable resources are needed for organizational awareness-raising, sensitizing and capacity-building. *Awareness-raising and sensitizing* must have the aim to ensure awareness of ESG-issues and

---

[89]  Conley and Williams (n 8), 547.

responsibilities within the bank at all management levels and across all disciplines. *Capacity-building* deals with building in-house human rights-related knowledge and expertise such as knowledge about international laws and standards, knowledge about client, country, industry, company and asset as well as country- and sector-specific ESG-risks. It achieves this aim via staff and front-line officer training, workshops (e.g., on evaluating human rights conflicts and ethical dilemmas), internal communication, experience and best-practice sharing, feedback-generation, outside consultation, recruitment and budget allocation.

Of particular importance are the *top-level commitment* and senior-level approval: The CEO and other senior managers function as role models. Thus, leadership from the top is essential to embed respect for human rights throughout a company.

A change in the organizational culture should also affect the *incentive structures* and in particular, the bonus payment systems or compensation structures and packages which should be long-term rather than short-term oriented. So far, investment managers are judged according to their quarterly or annual performance and not according to their multiple-years performance.[90]

### 5.1.2   Human rights due diligence (HRDD)

Having a properly functioning HRDD (à la UNGP) which assesses the actual and potential human rights impacts of a company plays a major role. The aim of HRDD is to become aware of, identify, prevent, address and mitigate adverse human rights risks and impacts. HRDD requires the following elements:

- Human rights policy (statement);
- Human rights risk-mapping, Human Rights Impact Assessment (HRIA) and Human Rights Action Plans (HRAP);[91]
- Integration of the human rights perspective into corporate governance structures and corporate decision-making and operational processes;
- Performance tracking including auditing and monitoring; and
- Periodic reporting.[92]

---

[90]   Chan (n 56), 1345.
[91]   EPIII does not require HRIA and HRAP; HRDD is carried out on a voluntary, not mandatory basis.
[92]   UN, 'UNGP' (2011) <http://www.ohchr.org/Documents/Publications/GuidingPrinciplesBusinessHR_EN.pdf>, principles 17–21; Ruggie, *Just Business* (n 26), ch. 3–4; Fasterling/Demuijnck (n 69); Thun Group (n 37), 8ff.

What is essential from a human rights perspective is that all (!) human rights are relevant to HRDD (due to the fact that human rights are indivisible) and that the human rights perspective is applied across all types of products and services and to all company levels. In terms of (EP)FIs, this includes retail and private banking, corporate and investment banking, and asset management. Additionally, HRDD should be carried out on an *ongoing* basis since human rights risks may change over time as operations and contexts evolve (change in human rights risk profile due to unforeseen events). It should also be adapted to the country- and sector-specific risks. There is simply no one-size-fits-all approach to HRDD since local legislation and human rights environments vary from region to region and sector to sector. HRDD is of particular importance in conflict zones, in sectors with strong human rights sensitivities and when vulnerable or marginalized groups such as indigenous peoples are affected.[93]

Potential human rights risks for banks occur, for example, when they provide products and services to governments and/or companies with a challenging human rights track record or projects in sensitive industries and locations. Here, banks should adopt a broader perspective on their human rights impacts. Besides focusing on their own adverse human rights risks and impacts which are directly caused through their own activities, they also need to take into account the potential adverse human rights effects on third-party stakeholders and those risks and impacts which might be caused by their business partners (e.g., clients and other supply-/value-chain actors).

Many human rights impacts of (EP)FIs arise via the actions of their clients and can be addressed through influence, leverage and dialogue.[94] Here, it is decisive to make business partners aware of the corporation's human rights expectations and requirements. What is needed is a commitment from the client (and contractors and suppliers). The client should at least demonstrate conformity with the UNGP, e.g., via human rights policy, HRDD, operational-level grievance mechanisms, reporting on human rights performance, adherence to (inter-) national standards, and performance-track record.[95] Furthermore, human rights clauses should be integrated into business agreements and contracts. If significant human rights risks have been detected, the bank should agree on actions with the client and closely collaborate with it to address and mitigate these human rights risks and impacts. In (extreme) cases, the bank may opt out; that is, it should consider terminating the business relationship (exit option).

---

[93] Thun Group (n 37), 8ff.
[94] (n 37), 20.
[95] (n 37).

### 5.1.3   Stakeholder engagement

EPFIS and especially their clients should adhere to the principles laid down in the IFC PS: The IFC PS (standard 1), and the EPs (principle 5) ask for an encompassing and constant stakeholder dialogue process. Affected stakeholders must have the rights to information, consultation and participation (in decision-making). The stakeholder engagement must take place in a 'culturally appropriate way'; that is, information has to be made readily and publicly available to the affected groups in their local languages. The information disclosure should start as early as possible in the impact-assessment process and operate on a continuous basis. Furthermore, the stakeholder dialogue process must be free from external coercion, interference, intimidation and manipulation.

The overall aim is to respect and protect the legitimate interests and needs of disadvantaged, marginalized and vulnerable (ethnic) groups. One essential element is thus FPIC; the stakeholder dialogue should ideally be based on the *FPIC-paradigm*: FPIC and not the current Informed Consultation and Participation (ICP) paradigm should become the standard procedure for financing, managing and operating projects. FPIC should become mandatory for all projects financed 'under the EPs', not only for those projects with adverse socio-environmental impacts on indigenous peoples ('moving beyond ICP'). Finally, to avoid 'dirty projects' de facto *veto rights* should be granted to affected communities in cases of serious socio-environmental and human rights impacts. What is also needed is a clear-cut rule for decision-making, e.g., a two-thirds majority approval by affected communities.

### 5.1.4   Project-level grievance, complaint and remedy mechanisms

In 2014, FMO, a Dutch development bank, became the first EP-signatory to introduce an independent operational and project-level grievance and complaints mechanism which allows affected communities to hold FMO accountable to its policies. (Non-) judicial grievance, complaint and remedy mechanisms are able to test the robustness of the EPFIs' commitments and can, thus, help to close the gap between theory and practice.[96] Yet, with the exception of FMO, accountability and compliance mechanisms among the EPFIs are mostly lacking. What is urgently needed is a mechanism which allows affected stakeholders as the rights-holders to file complaints of non-compliance with EPFIs and the EPA. This is of particular importance for the most vulnerable and marginalized groups in society such as indigenous peoples.

---

[96]   FMO, 'Project-Related Complaints' (2014) <http://www.fmo.nl/page/1115>.

### 5.1.5 Impact benefit agreements

In practice, mandatory and legally binding revenue-sharing and Impact Benefit Agreements (IBA) between MNCs and indigenous peoples' negotiation committees are required. IBAs go beyond voluntary and informal negotiation protocols or memorandums of understanding. They record in a written form mitigation measures, financial compensation-schemes and benefit-sharing. Typically they

> include commitments and targets in the areas of employment, training, business opportunities, revenue or equity sharing, and environmental protection; and they establish clear, formal channels for communication and dispute resolution . . . Furthermore, some IBAs are re-negotiated periodically throughout the life of a [project], which forces companies to seek and keep community consent beyond the permitting stage.[97]

IBAs should also contain clearly defined community-development plans, e.g., biodiversity action plans, schooling and healthcare programs, to name a few. Additionally, the setup of community liaison officers, grievance officers and resettlement-negotiations committees should be compulsory for the EPFIs' clients.

### 5.1.6 Positive leverage-based responsibility

(EP)FIs are right at the center of the global political economy linking the 'real economy' with the finance sector. They equal economic pacemakers or powerhouses which keep the economic in 'blood' circulation. Financial decision-makers and project sponsors are thus among the most powerful players in the global political economy. By providing financial support to their clients (provision of corporate loans; managing, underwriting and/or assisting with the issuance of shares and bonds; (EP)FIs as shareholders), (EP)FIs exert a substantial leverage over their business partners. This is particularly true prior to deal approval and over the life of the loan. Therefore, (EP)FIs are those institutions which (co-) determine whether or not financial resources are used in an ethical and sustainable manner. They are key actors in the transition towards an ethical and 'green economy'. By voting with their money, they ideally help catalyze the transitional process towards economic, ecological and social sustainability.[98] Equator banks, in particular, have a strong leverage-influence over their clients' behavior: They not only decide which projects get

---

[97] Irene Sosa, 'License to Operate' (2011) <www.sustainalytics.com/sites/default/files/indigenouspeople_fpic_final.pdf>, 13.

[98] Conley and Williams (n 8), 565.

financed but also which ones do not. They also intensively collaborate with their clients over the life of the loan and (help) working out (and monitor) socio-environmental impact assessment, management systems and action plans. Thus, EPFIs have the ability to influence and shape their client's behavior on the ground.

The argument of this chapter to move towards a positive and leverage-based CSR-concept requires EPFIs to exert sufficient leverage prior *and* after deal approval to promote good business practice (this of course demands a strong corporate will and a change in EPFI's/clients' corporate culture as explained above). That is, the chapter asks for human rights advocacy and activism of EPFIs to protect and realize human rights,[99] one that goes beyond the mere negative corporate duty to respect human rights (and which also goes beyond mere HRDD). To put it differently, due to their political power and authority, EPFIs have direct and positive leverage-based human rights duties to fulfill. They should use their powers for the common good. In particular, this requires (EP) FIs to:

- Avoid being (silently) complicit in human rights violations;
- Speak out against ongoing, systematic and severe human rights violations;
- Promote human rights-compatible institutions in home and host countries; and
- Influence institutional change inside the industry branch and in the countries of operation.

One way to exert leverage and influence over business partners in the supply- and value-chain is via business contracts and/or (EP-) *covenants*: Through their contractual business relationships EPFIs can easily build human rights requirements such as HRDD, HRIA, HRAP and IBAs as well as project-level grievance, complaint and remedy mechanisms into their supply- and value-chain management.[100] Another way is to develop and implement adequate and effective *investment policies* which are able to address the harmful business practices of their clients (including human rights monitoring and supply-/value-chain screening). Furthermore, EPFIs should make use of *divestment strategies* as a means of exerting pressure, that is, they should disengage and divest from

---

[99]   Wettstein (n 18).
[100]   Wesley Cragg, 'Ethics, Enlightened Self-Interest, and the Corporate Responsibility to Respect Human Rights' (2012), 22 *BEQ*, 9.

companies which constantly violate international socio-environmental and human rights standards. To avoid being complicit in human rights violations, (EP)FIs have the responsibility to terminate all direct and indirect business relationships and ties to corporations which are notorious for their harmful and detrimental business practices. Instead, they should invest in and foster socio-environmentally friendly and sustainable ('fair trade') industries.

MNCs and in particular EPFIs should take *proactive* (and preventative) measures to help protect and realize the (human) rights of affected communities. One way to do this is via properly implemented value-/supply-chain screening, effective stakeholder-dialogue processes, and project-level grievance and remedy mechanisms. Furthermore, EPFIs could also make use of their political power and authority and lobby for human rights and human rights-compatible institutions: They could promote and lobby for higher industry and governmental standards (e.g., in the form of industry-wide codes of conduct or (trans-) national regulation), engage in public human rights discourses, put pressure on perpetrators and abusive and authoritarian governments, e.g., by making use of diplomatic channels and/or by threatening the host government to withdraw FDIs.[101] Moreover, they could collaborate with NGOs, CSOs as well as home and host countries. For example, they could assist legislatures, governments and jurisdictions in crafting and enforcing legislation and regulation in support of human rights.[102] Last but not least, they could support the work of local human rights activist groups, NGOs and CSOs and/or collaborate with (supra-) national organizations in developing and enforcing binding socio-environmental and human rights standards.

### 5.2 Meso-level: Equator Principles Association

#### 5.2.1 Human rights principle
So far, the EPs keep (mainly) quiet when it comes to HRDD, HRIA and HRAP. Thus, it seems necessary to add a separate human rights principle which is solely devoted to the protection and realization of human rights. This principle should lay down the business-ethical foundations (and expectations) for all the other subsequent principles. To retain a maximum of ten principles, Principles 7 and 9 (independent review and monitoring) as well as principles 9 and 10 (reporting) could be easily combined, thus, creating space for a separate principle solely devoted to human

---

[101]   Cragg (n 100).
[102]   Wettstein (n 18), 42.

rights issues. This principle should then precede all others and serve as an anchoring or guiding principle.[103]

### 5.2.2   Automatic sanctions

What is required is the establishment of an enforcement pyramid[104] as a credible deterrent. This pyramid should start with less coercive means like persuasion (appeal to a client's socio-environmental responsibilities), warnings (highlighting potential consequences of continued EP-violation) and setting deadlines for bringing projects back into compliance. Only when less coercive means fail, should more coercive tactics been employed. They include formal sanctions like penalties and fines. The final stage of such an enforcement pyramid should include the delisting and exclusion of non-compliant EPFIs.[105]

### 5.2.3   Absolute performance standards

Only clear, verifiable metrics that are transparently and independently monitored allow for assessing the socio-environmental and human rights performance of EPFIs and their clients. These performance standards should be developed in close collaboration with the UN Special Representative on Business and Human Rights and transparently monitored by an independent EP-ombudsperson associated with the EPA and/or the UN Human Rights Council.

### 5.2.4   Minimum entry requirements

As of September 2016, no minimum entry requirements exist which have to be met prior becoming an EPA-member. As a consequence, signatories are attracted that are not truly committed to the EP-spirit. In fact, several Equator banks display an opportunistic behavior for strategic reasons such as green-washing and window-dressing. They just mimic the behavior of good EPFIs; yet, they do not have the intention to actually implement their new commitments. Those free-riders gain the benefits of enhanced reputation and reduced threat of government regulations without bearing the implementation and compliance costs.[106] Thus,

---

[103]    BankTrack, 'The Outside Job' (2011) <http://www.banktrack.org/download/the_outside_job/111021_the_outside_job_final.pdf>, 16; BankTrack, 'Tiny steps forward on the Outside Job' (2012) <http://www.banktrack.org/show/pages/equator_principles#tab_pages_documents>, 11.
[104]    Ian Ayres and John Braithwaite, *Responsive Regulation* (Oxford UP, 1992).
[105]    Sarro (n 87), 1549ff.
[106]    Christopher Wright and Alexis Rwabizambuga, 'Institutional Pressure, Corporate Reputation, and Voluntary Codes of Conduct' (2006) 111 *BSR*, 89, 91;

free-riding and opportunistic behavior leads to competitive disadvantages for EP-signatories, since they have to bear compliance and implementation costs while non-compliant corporations do not. Additionally, free-riding negatively affects the collective by lowering the standards of the code and by decreasing the level of compliance. In the end, the EPs' 'brand value' might diminish.[107] Most importantly, project-affected groups suffer from a lack of effectiveness and practical failure of the EPs (including serious human rights violations).The implementation of entry criteria for EP-membership, together with the adoption of absolute performance standards, could help overcoming the problems of free-riding (and adverse selection) and lack of effectiveness. Mandatory entry requirements prior to becoming a member should include HRDD, IBAs, FPIC, and grievance, complaint and remedy mechanisms.

### 5.2.5 Reform of the Equator Principles Association
The existing Equator Principles Association needs reform in several dimensions.

#### 5.2.5.1 Enhanced funding and staffing
The currently available financial and personal resources are insufficient to guarantee proper assistance and advice with regards to EP-implementation and to effectively monitor EP-compliance (the annual membership fee is only GBP £3,575). Thus, higher dedicated resources and more professional staff are required; the lack of professional expertise and limited resources needs to be overcome.[108]

#### 5.2.5.2 Establish an EP-Forum and an EP-Advisory Group
A structural reform of the EPA in the form of creating an EP-Advisory Group with representatives from stakeholders, NGOs and CSOs as well as an EP-Forum for engagement on finance industry sustainability issues seems promising.[109] The inclusion of stakeholders, NGOs and CSOs in decision-making processes of the EPA could help to raise the public accountability and democratic legitimacy of the EPA and the EPFIs. It could also help to overcome confidentiality issues and to raise the overall

---

Richard Macve and Xiaoli Chen, 'The "equator principles"' (2010) 23 *AAAJ*, 890, 895; Schepers (n 84), 93ff.

[107]   Sarro (n 87), 1532.

[108]   Suellen Lazarus and Alan Feldbaum, 'Equator Principles Strategic Review' (2011) <http://www.equator-principles.com/resources/exec-summary_appendix_strategic_review_report.pdf>.

[109]   (n 108), 10; BankTrack, *Outside Job* (n 103), 10; *Tiny Steps* (n 103).

transparency of this CSR-initiative in the field of project finance. The feedbacks which would be generated via the EP-Forum and the EP-Advisory Group would be of great help to overcome practical challenges (e.g., with regards to FPIC- and project-level grievance-mechanism implementation) and to further strengthen the EP-framework.

### 5.2.5.3   *Knowledge-transfer and information-sharing*
The lack of inconsistent EP-implementation could be overcome by facilitating knowledge-transfer, information-sharing and membership capacity-building, especially via the EPA. The EP-homepage is the ideal place to provide EPFIs with case studies and training materials, guidelines and implementation tools and resources. Moreover, best-practice workshops and regional conferences should be organized to help with EP-implementation.[110]

## 5.3   Macro-level: Regulatory Framework

### 5.3.1   Regulatory measures
Voluntary self-regulation and multi-stakeholder CSR-initiatives have proved to be partially ineffective, pointing towards the limits of soft-law regulation. That is why a steering mix consisting of hard and soft law as well as mandatory and voluntary standards is required. Thus, stronger government oversight including (more) legally-binding (human rights) regulation as well as an extension of national legislation (including extra-territorial jurisdiction) to not only include criminal liability of corporations but also human rights liability is indispensable.[111] Governmental regulation should also be accompanied by increasing shareholder pressure; that is, pressure from socially responsible investors (including divestment strategies from companies which violate socio-environmental and human rights standards and shareholders filing lawsuits against senior management), and market-regulation pressure (e.g., denied market access by the SEC and exclusion of non-compliant companies from sustainability indexes).

---

[110]   Lazarus and Feldbaum (n 108), 8.
[111]   Christopher Albin-Lackey, 'Without Rules' (2013) <http://www.hrw.org/world-report/2013/essays/112459>; Cristina Chiomenti, 'Corporations and the International Criminal Court' in Schutter (ed.), *Transnational Corporations and Human Rights* (Hart, 2006); Cragg, *Business and Human Rights* (n 72), 279.

**5.3.2 Third-party beneficiary rights for project-affected communities**[112]

Third-party beneficiary rights for affected communities can enhance external accountability and liability. These rights would allow non-signatories to a contract (affected communities) to enforce their human rights against the contracting parties (EPFIs and clients). A third-party beneficiary status would provide for a right to a promised performance enforceable by a non-signatory to a contract. This approach proposed by Marco[113] would hold both EPFIs and their clients accountable for failing to adhere to the EPs. It thus contains a right to proper EP-implementation. Borrowers and lenders as promisors owe duties of performance to affected communities as local stakeholders, that if breached are enforceable by the respective communities. EPFIs and clients which violate the EPs could be sued.[114] Affected communities would be able to assert their third-party beneficiary rights through breach of contract actions in courts. The overall aim is to curb negative socio-environmental and human rights impacts on local communities and to ensure that affected communities and especially – indigenous peoples maintain their livelihoods.[115]

## 6. CONCLUDING REMARKS

The chapter has argued for a move towards positive impact- and leverage-based human rights responsibilities of MNCs in general and (EP)FIs in particular. While negative obligations impose passive duties to withdraw from certain actions ((corporate) responsibility to respect human rights), positive obligations usually denote active duties, that is, responsibilities to take proactive measures towards the fulfillment of the according obligations (duties to protect and realize human rights). Positive leverage-based (corporate) responsibilities require actors with superior powers and capabilities – such as MNCs – to exert this leverage to influence business partners (in the value- and supply-chain) as well as other (non-) state actors, e.g., with the aim to promote human rights-compatible institutions in home and host countries.

The chapter has also argued for a move towards hardening the soft law

---

[112] Andrew Wilson, 'Beyond Unocal' in Schutter (ed.), *Transnational Corporations and Human Rights* (Hart, 2006); Ruggie, *PRR* (n 26), 206; *Just Business* (n 26).

[113] Marco (n 85).

[114] Andrew Hardenbrook, 'The Equator Principles' (2007) 40 *Vanderbilt JTL*, 197, 218ff.

[115] Hardenbrook (n 114); Marco (n 85).

in the medium and long run. This indicates that soft law CSR-initiatives should gradually transform into hard law to become (more) effective.[116] The proposed reform measures offered here are supposed to lead towards (more) mandatory and legally binding elements of the EPs which might help to fully exploit the potential of this transnational CSR-initiative. The overall aim must be to go beyond Ruggie's PRR-framework and the UNGP (and its negative corporate duty to respect human rights) to also include positive and leverage-based corporate responsibilities. It remains to be seen whether the EPFIs and the EPA will be successful in hardening the EP-framework, e.g., by adopting some of the proposed reform measures, and whether they are willing and are able to align the EPs with the BHR-perspective outlined in this chapter.

---

[116]    Kobrin (n 6), 360–368.

# 6. Group companies: supply chain management, theory and regulation
## Jodie A. Kirshner

## INTRODUCTION

In 1892, 13 years after Thomas Edison patented an electric light bulb, the Edison General Electric Company and its main competitor, Thomson–Houston Electric Company, merged to create the General Electric Company.[1] Today, General Electric (GE) ranks as one of the largest American multinational conglomerate companies. The company earns more than half of its revenues overseas, and, according to the UN Conference on Trade and Development *World Investment Report*, holds more than $500 billion in assets abroad.[2] More than half of its workforce is located outside of the United States.[3]

This chapter will explore the reasons that companies such as GE seek to expand internationally, how companies do so and the ways in which discrete national legal systems strive to keep pace with the international expansions of the companies that they regulate. In summary, companies generally broaden their international reach either to realize economies of scale in production and distribution or to reduce transaction costs. Companies may also expand to access new markets or supplies or to eliminate competition. While some scholars have advanced theories related to companies' gradual expansion, others have more recently documented factors that enable some companies to be 'born global' and enter multiple international markets at once. Limited liability has made expansion through separately incorporated subsidiaries attractive for companies, and many have developed into vast corporate groups with multiple layers of subsidiaries controlled by holding companies. Because the law traditionally has treated each unit of such a corporate group as an independent company, multinational companies have posed a challenge to regulate, and the companies have manipulated their structures to insulate

---

[1] *See*, generally, W. Bernard Carlson, *Innovation as a Social Process: Elihu Thomson and the Rise of General Electric* (Cambridge UP, 1992).
[2] UNCTAD, *World Investment Report*, 2011.
[3] 'Biggest Transnational Companies' *The Economist* (10 July 2012).

assets from tort victims and creditors. Consequently, some legal systems have embraced new approaches to the regulation of corporate groups, such as adapting the law in some areas to regard corporate groups as single, unified entities.

## INCENTIVES FOR INTERNATIONAL EXPANSION

Companies generally seek to earn profits by selling outputs at a higher price than they pay for the inputs needed to produce the outputs.[4] GE, for example, produces jet engines using the metals tin, tantalum and tungsten.[5] In simplified terms, the difference between the sale price of a jet engine and the cost of the metals and other inputs constitutes its profit. Expanding overseas can assist companies in obtaining inputs at a lower cost and in achieving greater sales volumes of outputs. Expanding overseas therefore can increase corporate profits.

### Inputs

Companies potentially can find a range of inputs available abroad at a lower cost than domestically or that are not available domestically. The inputs could include: (1) physical resources, such as minerals, raw materials, agricultural products or financial capital; (2) labor or (3) specialized services, such as technological capabilities.[6] GE, for example, uses rare earth metals from China to manufacture its wind turbines.[7] Labor costs vary among countries, and GE has relocated production facilities to benefit from cheaper production costs. According to its former CEO, Jack Welch, 'Ideally, you'd have every plant you own on a barge to move with currencies and changes in the economy.'[8] GE recently established

---

[4]   *See*, generally, Karl Case, Ray Fair and Sharon Oster (eds), *Principles of Economics* (Prentice Hall, 2014) 155.

[5]   *See, e.g.*, 'GE Sustainability: Action on Conflict Minerals' <http://www.gesustainability.com/wp-content/uploads/2014/04/GE-CM-Cit-report_FINAL-6-6-2014.pdf>.

[6]   *See, e.g.*, John Dunning, *Multinational Enterprises and the Global Economy* (Edward Elgar, 1993) 68; Tarun Khanna, Krishna G. Palepu and Jayant Sinha, 'Strategies that Fit Emerging Markets' *Harvard Business Review* (June 2005); Saskia Sassen, 'The Global City: Introducing a Concept' (2005) 11 *Brown J. World Affairs* 27, 29.

[7]   Tom Miles and Krista Hughes, 'China loses trade dispute over rare earth exports' Reuters (26 March 2014).

[8]   'Welcome Home' *The Economist* (19 January 2013).

an assembly plant in Nigeria, where it manufactures hospital equipment and power plant turbines.[9] It has also responded to falling labor costs in the United States by moving its production of refrigerators from Mexico to Kentucky.[10] The company has further moved to exploit specialized services overseas by, for example, building a research centre in Bangalore, India, where more than a thousand engineers work to develop medical equipment, jet engines and appliances,[11] as well as utilizing specialized underground mining technologies from Australia. In 2012, it acquired the Australian mining equipment manufacturer Industrea.[12]

While companies potentially can acquire cheap foreign inputs from third parties, they also can integrate the production and ownership of foreign inputs into their own corporate structures. Integrating the supply of the foreign inputs into their structures provides companies with control over access to the inputs, which, in turn, may increase the reliability of the supply of the inputs.[13] GE Aviation, for example, recently acquired its Italian parts supplier Avio, as well as two 3D printing companies. 'We want more under our control', the head of supply chain management for GE Aviation said.[14] When companies require inputs from third-party suppliers, they risk shortfalls, losses of intellectual property and the unwillingness of external suppliers to make company-specific investments, leading to inefficiencies.[15] For this reason, for example, the Canadian energy company Husky Energy has integrated ethanol production within its corporate structure.[16] Husky energy has had to comply with legal requirements to blend ethanol into the gasoline it has produced. Rather than deal with independent ethanol producers and risk an inconsistent or

---

[9]   'GE in Nigeria' <http://www.ge.com/africa/company/Nigeria>.

[10]   'As Overseas Costs Rise, More US Companies Are "Reshoring"' *Marketplace* (27 January 2014).

[11]   *See, e.g.*, 'Bangalore, India' <http://www.geglobalresearch.com/locations/bangalore-india>.

[12]   *See, e.g.*, Ed Crooks and Neil Hume, 'GE to Buy Australia's Industrea for A\$700m' *Financial Times* (16 May 2012).

[13]   *See, e.g.*, Günter K. Stahl and Mark E. Mendenhall (eds), *Mergers and Acquisitions: Managing Culture and Human Resources* (Stanford UP, 2005) 25.

[14]   Kate Linebaugh, 'GE Brings Engine Work Back' *Wall Street Journal* (6 February 2013).

[15]   *See, e.g.*, William W.C. Yang et al. (eds), *Supply Chain Management* (Emerald, 2007) 67–68.

[16]   Simon Weseen, Jill E. Hobb and William A. Kerr, 'Reducing Hold-up Risks in Ethanol Supply Chains: A Transaction Cost Perspective' (2014) 17 *International Food & Agribusiness Management Review* 83, 100.

inappropriate supply of ethanol, it has produced its own ethanol to meet its needs.

Integrating the supply of inputs internally also potentially can reduce costs. Transaction costs fall when one part of a company can use the outputs of another part of the same company for its inputs.[17] Transaction costs – the costs associated with carrying out transactions – arise both in preparation for and after a transaction takes place. By providing their own inputs, companies avoid searching for suppliers and negotiating and drafting agreements with suppliers. The companies, furthermore, avoid having to incur monitoring and enforcement costs after transactions with suppliers take place, in order to ensure that the suppliers honor the terms of their agreements. The US wine producer E & J Gallo Winery, for example, manufactures the glass wine bottles in which it bottles its wine itself, because it would be more expensive for the company to buy glass wine bottles from third-party suppliers.[18]

Supply chain integration, however, can also cause losses.[19] Companies may have difficulty coordinating multiple tasks. Furthermore, the inputs that companies require may not achieve volumes sufficient to realise economies of scale, and outside companies may be able to supply the inputs at lower prices. With sales within the company guaranteed, an absence of competition may result in inputs of lower quality.[20]

**Outputs**

Increased sales of outputs, which expansion into international markets potentially can facilitate, directly increase revenues and also potentially can enable companies to realize economies of scale, by making it possible for companies to spread their costs over a greater number of outputs. One study by the global management consulting firm Boston Consulting Group has indicated that doubling output can reduce production costs by as much as 30 per cent.[21] Companies sell outputs in foreign markets by

---

[17]    (n 16) 87.

[18]    'A Glass Act: Gallo Glass Serves Up 1 Billion Bottles Each Year' *Business Wire* (22 September 2004).

[19]    *See, e.g.,* Joel D. Wisner, Keah-Choon Tan and G. Leong, *Principles of Supply Chain Management: A Balanced Approach* (Cengage, 2014) 5.

[20]    *See, e.g.,* John Stuckey and David White, 'When and When Not to Vertically Integrate: A Strategy as Risky as Vertical Integration Can Only Succeed When it is Chosen for the Right Reasons' *McKinsey Glob. Q.* (August 1993).

[21]    *See, e.g.,* Robert M. Grant, *Contemporary Strategy Analysis and Cases: Text and Cases* (Wiley, 2013) 229.

offering products at a lower price than the same domestic products or by offering products unavailable in the domestic market. GE, for example, has developed a hand-held electrocardiogram device for rural India, which it has sold for less than the cost of previously existing electrocardiogram devices in India.[22] After import duties fell in 2008, sales of French wines in Hong Kong have increased dramatically.[23]

While companies can license third parties to sell their products abroad or partner with overseas distributors and retail outlets, often they can gain better control over the quality and timing of the distribution of their outputs by undertaking their own distribution. GE, for example, has sought to acquire the power and grid business of the French electric and rail company Alstom in order to improve its own access to European electric power markets.[24] The Korean conglomerate Samsung maintains an in-house logistics company, Samsung Logitech, which supports the export of Samsung products, and the Anglo–Dutch consumer products company Unilever employs several thousand Indian women to deliver soap in rural Indian villages that more traditional distribution methods cannot reach.[25]

In addition to increasing their production of existing products to sell in overseas markets, companies can expand overseas into new lines of business that also share fixed and overhead costs. The Brazilian mining company Vale, for example, originally mined only iron ore, but it has diversified into other metals by acquiring a Canadian nickel mining company, Canico Resources, and an Australian coal mining company, AMCI Holdings.[26] Diversifying into related areas can enable companies to create synergies from shared resources and skills. Procter & Gamble produces disposable diapers as well as paper towels, and the two products share the expense of developing new technologies to reduce manufacturing

---

[22]   Jeffrey R. Immelt, Vijay Govindarajan and Chris Trimble, 'How GE Is Disrupting Itself' *Harvard Business Rev.* (October 2009).

[23]   Chris Li and Annie Lai, 'Hong Kong Wine Market 2014' USDA Foreign Agriculture Services Grain Report (18 February 2014) 1.

[24]   *See, e.g.*, Richard Clough, Francois de Beaupuy and Alex Webb, 'GE Wins Alstom Energy Bid with France Buying 20% Stake' Bloomberg (22 June 2014); 'A Good Proposal for Alstom, for GE, and for France' <http://www.ge.com/alstom/en/>.

[25]   'Global Value Chain Analysis on Samsung Electronics', Report of the Canadian Embassy in the Republic of Korea (February 2012) 18; for a discussion of Unilever's Project Shakti, see Samar Srivastava, 'Hindustan Lever Rethinks Rural' *Forbes* (1 October 2010).

[26]   Jeff Fick, 'Vale Buys Iron-Ore Stake in Guinea' *Wall Street Journal* (1 May 2010).

costs and also of procuring paper supplies.[27] Some commentators have observed, however, that GE suffered from excessive diversification during the 1970s, which harmed the overall performance of the company.[28] GE began as an electrical company, then expanded backward into electrical generation and backward again into the manufacture of machinery for producing electricity.[29] The company also moved to produce products that use electricity, and then into financing purchases of those products.[30]

## THEORIES OF EXPANSION

Originally, the 'Product Life Cycle Theory' conceived by Harvard economist Raymond Vernon in 1966 provided the prevailing theory of corporate expansion.[31] Later, in 1975, Swedish business scholars sought to update and improve upon the 'Product Life Cycle Theory' with a new 'Uppsala Internationalization Model'; however both the 'Product Life Cycle Theory' and the 'Uppsala Internationalization Model' attracted criticism for their failure to account for the existence of small companies that have operated internationally from their inception.[32] More recently, the 'Born Global Theory' of corporate internationalization has gained ground by explaining their existence.[33]

---

[27]  *See, e.g.*, Michael Porter, *From Competitive Advantage to Corporate Strategy* (Free Press, 2011).

[28]  *See, e.g.*, Charles Harvey and Geoffrey Jones (eds), *Organisational Capability and Competitive Advantage* (Routledge, 2014) 34.

[29]  *See, e.g.*, Thomas F. O'Boyle, *At Any Cost: Jack Welch, General Electric, and the Pursuit of Profit* (Vintage, 1998).

[30]  Louis Grossman and Marianne M. Jennings, *Building a Business through Good Times and Bad* (Praeger, 2002) 146.

[31]  Raymond Vernon, 'International Investment and International Trade in the Product Cycle' (1966) 80 *Quarterly Journal of Economics* 190–207; Raymond Vernon, *Sovereignty at Bay: The Multinational Spread of US Enterprises* (Basic Books, 1971); Raymond Vernon, 'The Product Life Cycle Hypothesis in a New International Environment'(1979) 41 *Oxford Bulletin of Economics and Statistics* 255–267.

[32]  Jan Johanson and Paul F. Wiedersheim, 'The Internationalization of the Firm: Four Swedish cases' (1975) 12 *Journal of Management Studies* 305–322; Jan Johanson and Jan-Erik Vahlne, 'The Internationalization Process of the Firm – A Model of Knowledge Development and Increasing Foreign Market Commitment' (1977) 8 *Journal of International Business Studies* 23–32; Jan Johanson and Jan-Erik Vahlne, 'The Mechanism of Internationalisation' (1990) 7 *International Marketing Review* 11–24.

[33]  *See, e.g.*, Svante Andersson, Jonas Gabrielsson and Ingemar Wictor, 'International Activities in Small Firms: Examining Factors Influencing the

**Product Life Cycle Theory**

According to Vernon's Product Life Cycle Theory, companies start to operate in their home markets and only gradually enter foreign markets.[34] Internationalization thus follows the life cycle of the outputs of companies. Vernon identified three stages of corporate development: First, products are developed in high-income countries, notably the United States, in order to satisfy the needs of local consumers. During the first stage, proximity to the domestic customer base outweighs the importance of finding cost savings through foreign production. Second, companies begin to produce the same products in other advanced economies to serve those local markets. During the second stage, companies strive to realize economies of scale by increasing their production of the products. Third, as production processes become increasingly standardized, companies begin to open manufacturing facilities in less-developed countries in order to save additional costs.[35]

Indeed, GE gained momentum in its international expansion only since 1981, when Jack Welch became CEO.[36] While GE had earlier launched foreign sales operations, Welch pioneered larger investments in developed economies. After Jeffrey Immelt replaced Welch as CEO in 2001, GE expanded its reach into farther-flung international markets.[37] Today, GE operates in roughly 100 countries.[38]

Nevertheless, as differences among countries have decreased and the international breadth of companies has increased, Vernon began to question his own thesis.[39] Companies have appeared, increasingly, to produce products in several markets at once. Among technology companies, for example, it has become increasingly rare to observe companies limiting their markets to their home countries.

---

Internationalization and Export Growth of Small Firms' (2004) 21 *Canadian Journal of Administrative Sciences* 22–34.

[34]   Vernon, 'International Investment' (n 32); Vernon, *Sovereignty at Bay* (n 32).

[35]   Vernon, 'International Investment' (n 32).

[36]   Christopher Bartlett and Meg Wozny, 'GE's Two-Decade Transformation: Jack Welch's Leadership' Harvard Business School Case Study (4 January 2002) 5–6.

[37]   *See, e.g.*, 'A Hard Act to Follow' *The Economist* (28 June 2014).

[38]   'GE Fact Sheet' <http://www.ge.com>.

[39]   Vernon himself stated that 'some of the starting assumptions of the product cycle hypothesis are clearly in question'. See Raymond Vernon, 'The Product Life Cycle Hypothesis in a New International Environment' (1979) 41 *Oxford Bulletin of Economics and Statistics* 55, 260.

**Uppsala Internationalization Model**

The Uppsala Internationalization Model, developed by Jan Johanson and Jan-Erik Vahlne, therefore recast Vernon's Product Life Cycle Theory as a process of adaptation to unfamiliar markets.[40] According to the Uppsala Internationalization Model, while differences in language, culture and politics initially dissuade companies from expanding abroad, over time they gain experience in similar markets that enables them to begin to enter progressively dissimilar markets.[41] Companies therefore begin to grow by entering only the markets that they perceive as least different from their domestic markets.[42] As they begin to enter these additional markets, they gain experiential knowledge that they later can use to identify opportunities in increasingly foreign markets.[43] In line with this theory, GE has entered into markets such as Canada and Australia more quickly and easily than it has entered into China.[44] 'China is big, but it is hard,' Immelt has said.[45]

More recent studies, however, have criticized the Uppsala International ization Model as too simplistic and have noted the frequency with which companies have skipped over stages of the Model.[46] Neither the Product Life Cycle Theory nor the Uppsala International Model has explained the phenomenon of very small internationalized companies. To remedy this situation, analysts at the global consulting firm McKinsey have developed a new Born Global Approach.[47]

---

[40]   Johanson and Vahlne, 'Enterprise Gradually Increases its International Involvement' (1990) 7 International Marketing Rev 11, 11.

[41]   Johanson and Vahlne, 'The Mechanism of Internationalisation' (n 32).

[42]   Johanson and Wiedersheim (n 32).

[43]   Johanson and Vahlne, 'The Mechanism of Internationalisation' (n 32).

[44]   *See, e.g.*, Isaac Pino, 'What's Driving General Electric's Global Growth?' *Motley Fool* (4 November 2013).

[45]   (n 44).

[46]   Andersson, Gabrielsson and Wictor (n 33); Sylvia Chetty and Colin Campbell-Hunt, 'A Strategic Approach to Internationalization: a Traditional Versus a "Born Global" Approach' (2004) 12 *Journal of International Marketing* 57–81.

[47]   McKinsey and Co. and Australian Manufacturing Council, *Emerging Exporters: Australia's High Value-Added Manufacturing Exporters* (1993); Tage Koed Madsen and Per Servais, 'The Internationalization of Born Globals: An Evolutionary Process?' (1997) 6 *International Business Review* 561–583.

**Born Global Approach**

The Born Global Approach has sought to account for the significant number of companies that now operate internationally from their
inception, enter several new markets at once and source supplies and
export finished products into foreign markets.[48] According to the Born
Global Approach, advances in manufacturing techniques, the liberaliza-
tion of trade, improvements in transportation and communications technologies, as well as increases in the international experience of company
managers, have lately facilitated companies in internationalizing swiftly,
rather than gradually.[49] Even small companies now immediately can
compete abroad by providing specialized products, leveraging production
technologies that make small-scale production more cost effective and
using new communication technologies that make it easier for employees
to coordinate their efforts across borders.[50] The speed and adaptability of
Born Global companies has allowed them to compete effectively against
domestic companies to meet the needs of foreign customers.[51]

The computer peripherals company Logitech offers a representative
example of a Born Global company.[52] Two Italians and one Swiss national
founded Logitech and immediately located its operations and research
and development offices in both California and Switzerland, then quickly
expanded production into Ireland and Taiwan.[53] The Logitech mouse
captured 30 per cent of the global mouse market within eight years.[54]

Follow-on studies confirmed and expanded on the Born Global
Approach. The US business school professors Benjamin Oviatt and
Patricia McDougall, for example, noted the increasing ability of entrepreneurs with international relationships and experience to access foreign
resources, including supplies, human capital and financing, to create or

---

[48]   Michael W. Rennie, 'Born Global' (1993) 4 *McKinsey Quarterly* 43–52.

[49]   Chetty and Campbell-Hunt (n 46).

[50]   S. Tamer Cavusgil, 'From the Editor in Chief' (1994) 2 *Journal of
International Marketing* 4–6.

[51]   Cavusgil (n 50).

[52]   *See*, generally, Jeff Jarvis, *What Would Google Do?* (Harper Business, 2009)
111.

[53]   *See, e.g.*, Mason Carpenter and Sanjyot Dunung, *Challenges and
Opportunities in International Business* (Flat World, 2012) 596 <http://catalog.
flatworldknowledge.com/catalog/editions/carpenteribus-international-business-
opportunities-and-challenges-in-a-flattening-world-1-0>.

[54]   Vijay K. Jolly, Matti Alahuhtam and Jean-Pierre Jeannet, 'Challenging the
Incumbents: How High Technology Start-ups Compete Globally' (1992) 1 *Journal
of Strategic Change* 71.

transport new products for sale in foreign markets.[55] Rather than grad-ually evolving into multinational companies, the companies that Oviatt and McDougall identified adopted a multinational approach from their inception. The Danish scholars Tage Koed Madsen and Per Servais explained the existence of these companies as the result of increasingly specialized markets, reduced barriers to global sourcing and the rapid internationalization of finance.[56] Madsen and his Danish colleague Erik Rasmussen also identified as factors in rapid internationalization the shortening of product life cycles, the prevalence of high-tech products that require sales in multiple markets to cover their research and development costs and increased globalization more generally.[57]

## FORMS OF EXPANSION

Companies can enter into a range of different types of relationships with foreign third parties, or they can expand internationally on their own.[58] When companies expand internationally on their own, rather than by licensing or contracting with third parties, for example, they can choose to establish new branches or to incorporate standalone subsidiaries. Companies that establish foreign branch offices simply operate in the foreign countries: Branches do not constitute legal entities independent of their parent companies. Subsidiaries, by contrast, qualify as separate legal entities, distinct from the parent companies that own them, even though parent companies often own most of the shares in their subsidiaries.

The option to form subsidiaries arose relatively recently. Inter-corporate stock ownership originally was outlawed in the United States and Europe, and only natural persons could own shares.[59] In the US, the first holding

---

[55]   Benjamin M. Oviatt and Patricia Phillips McDougall, 'Toward a Theory of International New Ventures' (1994) 25 *Journal of International Business Studies* 45–64.

[56]   Madsen and Servais (n 47).

[57]   Erik S. Rasmussen and Tage Koed Madsen, 'The Born Global Concept', paper for the 28th EIBA Conference, December 2002.

[58]   If they choose to involve outsiders, they can sell or buy goods to and from other entities for forward sale; contract with third parties for supplies, production, or distribution; or utilize licenses that provide royalty payments in exchange for production.

[59]   *See, e.g., Central RR v. Collins*, 40 Ga. 582 (1869); *Hazelhurst v. Savannah, G & NARR*, 43 Ga. 13 (1871); *First National Bank v. National Exchange Bank*, 92 U.S. 122, 128 (1875) ('Dealing in stocks is not expressly prohibited; but such a prohibition is implied from the failure to grant the power'); *Franklin Co. v.*

company act, which allowed companies to buy and hold stock in other companies, was not adopted until 1888.[60] New Jersey was the first state to amend its code and open the door to group companies.[61] To stop the flight of companies to New Jersey from other US states, and the loss of their tax revenues that the moves represented, other states soon followed New Jersey and amended their law.[62]

Unlike in the United States, the law in the United Kingdom did not change at a specific moment in history to allow for corporate groups. Under English law, companies may reserve powers for themselves in their corporate documents that the corporate law does not otherwise grant to them. Companies seem to have begun to award themselves power to acquire and own shares in other companies, and group companies began to show up in English litigation at the turn of the 20th century. An official review of the company law that took place during the 1920s included discussions of concerns specific to corporate groups.[63]

The civil law systems also began to encourage group relationships among domestic companies. In Canada, Latin America, East Asia and much of Europe, many companies have adopted pyramid structures. In a pyramid structure, one company controls another company that in turn holds a controlling stake in a third company. The first company in this chain controls the last company at the end of the chain but does not directly own shares in it.[64]

---

*Lewiston Inst. For Sav.*, 68 Me. 43, 46 (1877); *Rumänischen Eisenbahn case of 1881*, (RGZ 3, 123); *Petroleum case of 1913* (RGZ 82, 308). *Further*, R. Reich-Graef, 'Changing Paradigms: The Liability of Corporate Groups in Germany', 37 *Conn. Law Review* 785 (2005) (discussing fact corporate stock ownership outlawed in Europe and German law unique in changing this in German Stock Corporation Act of 1965).

[60] The New Jersey General Stock Corporation Law as amended in 1888, 1888 N.J. Laws Ch. 269, sec. 1 at 385; Ch. 295, sec. 1 at 445; *further* M. Dearborn, 'Enterprise Liability: Reviewing and Revitalizing Liability for Corporate Groups', 97 *California Law Review* 195, 203 (2009). ('In 1988, New Jersey was the first state to grant permission for any corporation chartered in the state to own stock in any other.')

[61] (n 60).

[62] Eugene Kandel, Konstantin Kosenko, Randall Morck and Yishay Yafeh, 'Business Groups in the United States: A Revised History of Corporate Ownership, Pyramids and Regulation, 1930–1950' (2013) 10 NBER Working Paper Series, Working Paper No. 1969.

[63] David Millman, 'Groups of Companies' in David Millman (ed.), *Regulating Enterprise* (Hart, 1999) 221–222.

[64] *See, e.g.*, Pankaj Ghemawat and Thomas M. Hout, 'Differences in Business Ownership and Governance around the World' Globalization Note Series (2011)

Over time, inter-corporate ownership has enabled companies to cluster into global networks of subsidiaries.[65] Cross-shareholding, in which one corporate entity gains control over another corporate entity within a corporate group by owning its shares, along with inter-enterprise contracts and linked directorships have become common.[66] While international networks of corporate entities linked into groups have seemed to enable more efficient delivery of products, the law in many areas has continued to treat each unit of a corporate group as a separate company, even as many of the networks have operated in a coordinated way and pursued joint strategies.[67]

## BENEFITS OF SUBSIDIARIZATION

Companies deliberately can form subsidiaries, or they can acquire existing subsidiaries and leave them in place. Variations in national laws create idiosyncratic reasons for companies to maintain group structures, and more general benefits of operating though group structures, rather than branching, also exist. Limited liability, for example, underlies many factors that potentially motivate companies to choose to utilize subsidiaries, rather

---

2   <http://www.aacsb.edu/~/media/AACSB/Publications/CDs%20and%20DVDs/GLOBE/readings/differences-in-business-ownership.ashx>.

[65]   *See, e.g.,* O. de Schutter, 'Extraterritorial Jurisdiction as a Tool for Improving the Human Rights Accountability of Transnational Corporations', background paper to the seminar organized in collaboration with the Office of the UN High Commissioner for Human Rights in Brussels on 3–4 November 2006 at 40 ('the multinational corporation appears as a coordinator of the activities of its subsidiaries, which function as a network of organizations working along functional lines').

[66]   *See, e.g.,* J.E. Antunes, 'The Liability of Polycorporate Enterprises' (1999) 13 *Connecticut Journal of International Law* 197, 205 n 29, citing *Investment Trust Corp. Ltd. v. Singapore Traction Co. Ltd.* (1935, 1 Ch. 615) (one share can outvote 399,999 shares); J. Andrews, 'The Interlocking Corporate Director: A Case Study in Conceptual Confusion' (1982) (unpublished MA thesis, University of Chicago); Melvin Eisenberg, *The Structure of the Corporation: A Legal Analysis* (Little, Brown, 1976).

[67]   *See, e.g.,* Detlev Vagts, 'The Multinational Enterprise: A New Challenge for Transnational Law' (1970) 83 *Harvard Law Review* 739; Vivien Schmidt, 'The New World Order, Incorporated: The Rise of Business and the Decline of the Nation State' (1995) 124 *Daedalus* 75 (nation-state becoming less powerful than business); Beth Stephens, 'The Amorality of Profit: Transnational Corporations and Human Rights' (2002) 20 *Berkeley Journal of International Law* 45, 56; Detlev Vagts, 'The Corporate Alien: Definitional Questions in Federal Restraints on Foreign Enterprise' (1961) 74 *Harvard Law Review* 1489, 1526–30.

than branches. Regulatory requirements and tax treatment also provide reasons for companies to operate through group structures.

National legal systems treat branches and subsidiaries differently, although the treatment varies among countries. In Spain, for example, a subsidiary must maintain a minimum capital, while a branch does not.[68] In the UK, closing a subsidiary requires a formal procedure, which a branch does not have to undergo, but the branch must file detailed financial information about its parent company with English regulators, unlike the subsidiary.[69] In Singapore, subsidiaries must have at least one local director.[70]

The legal systems of most countries bestow on companies a separate legal personality and the limited liability that derives from it. The separate legal personality makes a company a discrete entity, distinct from the owners, managers, and employees that comprise the company.[71] As a result of the separate legal personality, the company can own property, sign contracts, pay taxes and sue or be sued in its own name.[72] It can also exist in perpetuity, even as the composition of its shareholders changes.[73] Shareholders buy shares in the distinct corporate entity.

The principle of limited liability has protected the amassed wealth of investors against the liabilities of the companies in which they invest. Specifically, limited liability holds that investors cannot be liable in amounts greater than they deliberately have placed at risk by investing in a company.[74] Limited liability is intended to encourage economic investment. If potential investors had to risk their entire worth, they would, the law assumes, be less likely to provide the financing. Limiting liability, however,

---

[68] A Spanish subsidiary incorporated as an S.A., a limited liability company by shares, must have a minimum capital of €60,102, whereas a subsidiary incorporated as an S.L., a limited liability company by quota, must have a minimum capital of €3,006. A branch is not considered a separate company.

[69] *See, e.g.*, Daniel Reid, 'Setting up in the UK – Branch or Subsidiary?' DRG Chartered Accountants (31 October 2013).

[70] *See, e.g.*, Benjamin Yap, 'Singapore: Memorandum on Setting up of a Branch Office or Subsidiary Company in Singapore' *Mondaq* (25 August 2004).

[71] *See, e.g.*, Arthur Machen, 'Corporate Personality' (1911) 24 *Harvard Law Review* 253, 256.

[72] *See, e.g.*, Elizabeth Martin and Jonathan Law, *Oxford Dictionary of Law*, 7th edn, 'juristic person'.

[73] *See, e.g.*, The Hon T.F. Bathurst, Chief Justice Of New South Wales, Sydney, 'The Historical Development of Corporations Law', Francis Forbes Society For Australian Legal History, Introduction to Australian Legal History Tutorials (3 September 2013) 5.

[74] Frank H. Easterbrook and Daniel R. Fischel, 'Limited Liability and the Corporation' (1985) 52 *University of Chicago Law Review* 89, 90.

may shift losses onto other stakeholders by, for example, protecting assets from the claims of tort victims and creditors or from taxation.[75]

Limited liability has enabled the conduct of business through group structures to result in reduced risk and also has created the potential for conducting business to result in greater financial returns. Group structures made it possible for companies to diversify into different businesses, each operated by a separate unit of the group. The following paragraphs explain how limited liability has incentivized the use of group structures.

Limited liability has facilitated investment in several ways. First, companies that incorporate part of their business as a separate subsidiary, and allow outside investors to acquire shares in the subsidiary, attract capital where it is needed without allowing outside ownership in other parts of the business.[76] Outside share ownership generally carries voting rights and thus opens the door to the dilution of control over decision-making. Group structures, therefore, can also contribute to the entrenchment of the positions of existing management against potential threats from external shareholders.[77] Second, companies can use separate subsidiaries to attract additional investment by moving specific assets into a subsidiary and using the assets to secure loans offered by new creditors.[78] Third, where new subsidiaries engage in risky activities, limited liability encourages investment in other parts of the companies.[79] Limited liability confines the high liability risk to the individual subsidiaries, leaving the assets of the rest of the companies isolated from the liability of the subsidiaries. The creation of separate companies for particular operations, each with their own capital, can also contribute to the avoidance of liabilities to external creditors.

The use of subsidiaries can also facilitate compliance with regulatory requirements. Domestic law may require business to be conducted through companies incorporated within the jurisdiction.[80] Companies

---

[75]   Easterbrook and Fischel (n 74).

[76]   Ian Ramsay and Geof Stapledon, 'Corporate Groups in Australia', Centre for Corporate Law and Securities Regulation, University of Melbourne (1998) 7.

[77]   *See, e.g.*, Randall Morck, Daniel Wolfenzon and Bernard Yeung, 'Corporate Governance, Economic Entrenchment and Growth' (2004) 40 NBER Working Paper No. 10692 <http://www1.worldbank.org/finance/assets/images/yeung_morck_wolfenzon.pdf>.

[78]   *See, e.g.*, 'Finance Fundamentals: Restricted v. Unrestricted Subsidiaries in Loan Agreements', Practical Law <http://us.practicallaw.com/6-532-2747>.

[79]   *See, e.g.*, Alan Dignam (ed.), *Hicks and Goo's Cases and Materials on Company Law*, 7th edn, (Oxford UP, 2011) 486.

[80]   Damien Murphy, 'Holding Company Liability for Debts of its Subsidiaries' (1998) 10 *Bond L. Rev.* 241, 249.

also incorporate separate subsidiaries designed to comply with other local regulations, such as those related to employment law or license holding, while leaving the rest of their operations outside the purview of those regulations.[81]

Another key driver of group structures is their use as a tool for minimizing tax. Losses of one subsidiary can be offset against the income of another, and profits and losses may be pooled among members of corporate groups.[82] Differences among national tax policies therefore often motivate the distribution of assets and liabilities within corporate groups. Lower corporate tax rates or the beneficial tax treatment of specific activities makes it attractive for companies to establish subsidiaries in particular jurisdictions. Companies maximize their profits in jurisdictions with low levels of tax by passing assets and liabilities within the group. Complex structures, therefore, can also conceal the financial position of individual companies in corporate groups from their shareholders and creditors. GE, for example, is rumored to have earned $5.1 billion from its US operations in 2010, yet it paid no US corporate income tax.[83] Canada unsuccessfully has challenged guarantee fees paid by General Electric Canada to the GE parent company in the United States for serving no purpose beyond tax evasion.[84]

## NATURE OF CORPORATE GROUPS

Corporate group structures that result from subsidiarization range from simple to complex. Complex structures entail numerous subsidiaries, both operating and non-operating, as well as sub-subsidiaries and sub-holding companies. Complex structures may also involve other types of entities, such as special purpose entities (SPEs) and joint ventures.

Corporate groups have generally conformed to a vertical hierarchy, but they may also grow horizontally. Vertical groups arise from succeeding layers of parent and controlled companies, which operate at different points in a

---

[81] *See, e.g.*, Hugh Collins, 'Ascription of Legal Responsibility to Groups in Complex Patterns of Economic Integration' (1990) 53 *Modern Law Review* 731.

[82] Damien Murphy, 'Holding Company Liability for Debts of its Subsidiaries' (1998) 10 *Bond Law Review* 241, 249.

[83] *See, e.g.*, David Kocieniewski, 'G.E.'s Strategies Let It Avoid Taxes Altogether' *New York Times* (24 March 2011).

[84] *General Electric Capital Canada Inc. v. The Queen*, <http://www.canlii.org/en/ca/tcc/doc/2009/2009tcc563/2009tcc563.pdf>.

production or distribution process.[85] Horizontal group companies arise from cross-ownership among sibling companies that operate at the same level in different sectors.[86] Keiretsu in Japan, for example, generally comprise a bank, a trading company and a diverse group of manufacturing firms linked through share ownership.[87] Chaebol in Korea typically involve interlocking ownership of companies and centralized control by a single Korean family.[88]

Subsidiaries within group structures possess varying levels of financial and decision-making autonomy. While some groups allow subsidiaries scope to set their own course, others centralize decision-making.[89] A holding company may allocate capital to subsidiaries, set their policies, select their leadership and engage in constant monitoring. In large groups, the holding company may take on the role of an internal capital market, facilitating loans within the group.[90]

In some countries, kinship ties have played a significant role in corporate groups. Family members in these countries sit on the boards of individual companies within the groups. Companies in emerging economies that have lacked liquid capital markets have depended instead on their founding families to reinvest their profits in the companies in order to expand.[91] Roughly 85 per cent of businesses with revenues of more than $1 billion in Southeast Asia, for example, are family run, and roughly 75 per cent of such businesses in Latin America are family-run.[92]

---

[85]    *See, e.g.*, Companies and Securities Advisory Committee, 'Corporate Groups Final Report' (May 2000) 2, <http://www.camac.gov.au/camac/camac.nsf/byheadline/pdffinal+reports+2000/$file/corporate_groups,_may_2000.pdf>.

[86]    (n 85).

[87]    Paul Sheard, 'Keiretsu, Competition, and Market Access' (1997) *Global Competition Policy* 506–508; Dick Nanto, 'Japan's Keiretsu: Industrial Groups as Trade Barriers' (30 January 1994) Congressional Research Service Report No. 94–82 E. ('Both the six conglomerate keiretsu and the many vertical keiretsu use a variety of methods to tie their enterprises together. These include: presidential councils, crossholdings of shares, intra-group financing by a common bank, dispatching of executives and mutual appointments of officers, use of trading companies for marketing and organizing projects, joint investments in new industries.')

[88]    *See, e.g.*, David Murillo and Yun-dal Sung, 'Understanding Korean Capitalism: *Chaebols* and their Corporate Governance' (September 2013) 2, ESADEgeo Position Paper No. 33.

[89]    *See, e.g.*, United National Commission on International Trade Law, UNCITRAL *Legislative Guide on Insolvency Law, Part 3: Treatment of enterprise groups in insolvency* (2010) 10.

[90]    *See, e.g.*, G. Shailaja, *International Finance* (University Press of India, 2008) 239.

[91]    'Business in the Blood' *The Economist* (1 November 2014).

[92]    (n 91).

The structure of many corporate groups illustrates the complexity of potential arrangements. A line-by-line list of the members of the corporate group of GE stretches to seven full pages.[93] The US multinational banking and financial services company J.P. Morgan Chase and Co. comprises investment banking, asset management, private banking, private wealth management, treasury and securities services, credit card services, retail banking and commercial banking.[94] The corporate members of the investment banking division alone account for 52,250 employees in 60 countries.[95]

While formally separate legal entities comprise a group, groups may be managed and marketed otherwise. Rather than conforming to the legal divisions, management can be arranged according to product lines, and product lines might cross over different subsidiaries.[96] The group may use common advertising and maintain a public image of itself as one single entity.[97]

Additional entities, including SPEs and joint ventures, can also form part of a group. Companies use SPEs primarily to isolate financial risk or minimize tax.[98] Companies generally create SPEs to accomplish short-term goals, such as acquiring a stream of specific assets.[99] Typically, the parent company owns the SPE wholly, but by separating the SPE into its own legal structure, the parent can guarantee that its own insolvency will not affect the obligations of the SPE.[100] The assets or liabilities transferred to the SPE exist on its own balance sheet, and not the balance sheet of the parent company.[101]

While best known for their role in the securitization of loans, companies have other uses for SPEs that relate to business strategy.[102] For example, a

---

[93] General Electric, 'Company Snapshot Jan 20, 2015' <http://www.corporateaffiliations.com/Reports/general_electric_company.39328.pdf>.
[94] *See, e.g.*, J.P. Morgan Chase & Co., 'Resolution Plan Public Filing' (1 October 2013) 2 <http://www.federalreserve.gov/bankinforeg/resolution-plans/jpmorgan-chase-1g-20131001.pdf>.
[95] (n 94) 40, 43.
[96] *See, e.g.*, Frank Clarke and G.W. Dean, *Indecent Disclosure: Gilding the Corporate Lily* (Cambridge UP, 2007) 174.
[97] (n 89) 10.
[98] *See, e.g.*, Timothy J. Wilkinson and Vijay R. Kannan (eds), *Strategic Management in the 21st Century* (Praeger, 2013) 181.
[99] *See, e.g.*, International Monetary Fund, *Public Sector Debt Statistics: Guide for Compilers and Users* (IMF, 2011) 77.
[100] *See, e.g.*, Loren Fox, *Enron: The Rise and Fall* (Wiley, 2003) 63.
[101] (n 98) 181.
[102] Over time, companies increasingly have used SPEs to securitize a range of loans, from mortgages to credit card receivables. The SPE takes rights to the revenues from the loans and issues notes, bonds, or other securities to downstream

company may protect its intellectual property by transferring ownership of new technology to an SPE.[103] Ownership by the separate entity ensures that pre-existing license agreements do not extend to the new technology. In 2002, for example, GE held around $55 billion of its $500 billion in assets in SPEs.[104]

Additionally, two or more parties that seek to pursue a joint business can enter a partnership in the form of a joint venture. The venture could relate only to a specific project, or it could extend to a continuing business relationship. The contract generally specifies how the venture is formed, for how long, what each party must contribute, and how revenues, expenses, and control will be apportioned.[105] Joint ventures are common to cross-border situations because some countries condition entry by foreign companies into their markets on the formation of joint ventures with domestic partners.[106] More generally, however, the joint venture can be used to pre-empt competition from the venture partner or to create a stronger entity on the basis of the constituent partners, as well as to allow both partners to diversify.[107] Costs and risks are spread between the two partners, and the venture may be more attractive to financial investors than the individual companies.[108]

Since early 2000, GE, for example, has increasingly utilized joint ventures in its international operations, likely because of the increasing expense of acquiring foreign businesses outright. Joint ventures have also made it possible for GE to enter foreign markets where it has not built up significant expertise, by leveraging the relationships of its local partners in exchange for relinquishing some power and control. GE Money, the retail-lending arm

---

investors, which it pays to the loan originator in exchange for the revenues. The SPE bears the exposure to the risk of non-repayment of the loans, while the originator receives immediate liquidity.

[103]   *See, e.g.*, William J. Kramer and Chirag B. Patel, 'Securitisation of Intellectual Property Assets in the US Market' (2005) *IPO Law Journal*.

[104]   Aswath Damodaran, 'Special-Purpose Entities Are Often A Clever Way to Raise Debt Levels' (21 February 2002) <http://pages.stern.nyu.edu/~adamodar/New_Home_Page/articles/specpurpentity.htm>.

[105]   *See, e.g.*, American Bar Association, 'Model Joint Venture Agreement Checklist' http://apps.americanbar.org/buslaw/newsletter/0049/materials/book.pdf.

[106]   *See, e.g.*, KPMG, *Joint Ventures: A Tool for Growth During an Economic Downturn* (2009) n 3.

[107]   *See, e.g.*, John Chao, Eileen Kelly Rinaudo and Robert Uhlaner, 'Avoiding blind spots in your next joint venture' *McKinsey Insights* (January 2014); James Bamford, David Ernst and David G. Fubini, 'Launching a World-Class Joint Venture' *Harvard Business Review* (February 2004).

[108]   (n 106) 3.

of GE's financial services business, formed a joint venture with Hyundai to provide auto loans, mortgages and credit cards to customers in South Korea. In Spain, GE has pursued joint ventures with local banks, in order to provide consumer loans and credit cards, and in Central America, GE has established a joint venture with BAC-Credomatic, the largest bank in the region.[109]

## REGULATION OF CORPORATE GROUPS

The corporate law systems governing the individual units of corporate groups originated prior to the proliferation of interconnected groups and continue to apply to them.[110] The theory of limited liability developed to encourage individuals to invest, so that companies could pool capital and put it to efficient use.[111] Limited liability, however, still protects corporate owners within group companies, without distinguishing their incentives from those of human investors.[112] While the concept of a corporate group may elude formal definition, different approaches to the regulation of corporate groups have arisen, in some cases to realign the reality of the form with the mode of regulation.

Under a traditional approach to corporate groups, often referred to as 'the separate entity approach', individual parts of a corporate group maintain their own rights and duties, regardless of their connections to

---

[109]　Charles W. Hill, *International Business: Competing in the Global Marketplace* (McGraw-Hill, 2014) 511–512.

[110]　*See, e.g.*, B. Stephens, 'The Amorality of Profit: Transnational Corporations and Human Rights' (2002) 20 *Berkeley Journal of International Law* 45, 54 ('Multinational corporations have long outgrown the legal structures that govern them, reaching a level of transnationality and economic power that exceeds domestic law's ability to impose basic human rights norms'); A. Lowenfeld, *International Litigation and the Quest for Reasonableness* (Clarendon Press Oxford, 1996) 81 ('the law has not kept up with reality . . . law was developed with a view to a single firm operating out of a single state, owned by shareholders who . . . were not other corporations').

[111]　William Groening, *The Modern Corporate Manager: Responsibility and Regulation* (McGraw-Hill, 1981) 11; Henry Manne, 'Our Two Corporation Systems: Law and Economics' (1967) 53 *Virginia Law Review* 259; Frank Easterbrook and Daniel Fischel, 'Limited Liability and the Corporation' (1985) 52 *University of Chicago Law Review* 89; Reinier Kraakmann, 'The Economic Functions of Corporate Liability' in K. Hopt and G. Teubner (eds), *Corporate Governance and Directors' Liabilities* (Walter de Gruyter, 1985) 178.

[112]　*See, e.g.*, Lowenfeld (n 110) 83–85.

the other entities in the group.[113] Each part of the group retains its own separate legal personality, and limited liability protects its shareholders. The assets of the group may not be pooled to cover the debts of another unit of the group.[114]

As corporate groups have becoming increasingly prevalent, the separate entity approach increasingly has not seemed to reflect the economic reality of modern business. While the doctrines of separate legal personality and limited liability have protected individual shareholders against losses that exceed their initial investments, thus encouraging them to invest, the doctrines have had different consequences when they have applied to companies.[115] Multinationals, for example, have exploited the doctrines to shield their parent companies from liability for human rights abuses committed by their foreign subsidiaries.[116] When companies strategically have insulated dangerous activities within separate subsidiaries,[117] the corporate fiction has ensured that each one remained legally separate despite their economic interdependence, and limited liability has protected the parent companies against responsibility.[118]

In addition, as multinational corporate groups have conducted business on a global scale, not only corporate law has failed to keep pace, but jurisdictional law often has too. A mismatch has seemed to develop between the typically territorial scope of jurisdiction and the global nature of

---

[113]　*See, e.g.*, Jenny Dickfos, Colin Anderson and David Morrison, 'The Insolvency Implications for Corporate Groups in Australia: Recent Events and Initiatives' (2007) 16 *International Insolvency Review* 103.

[114]　*See, e.g.*, Henry Peter, Nicolas Jeandin and Jason Kilborn, *The Challenges of Insolvency Law Reform in the 21st Century* (Schulthess Verlag, 2006) 201.

[115]　Phillip Blumberg, *The Law of Corporate Groups* (Aspen, 1995) 7.

[116]　(n 66) 36.

[117]　Joseph Stiglitz, 'Regulating Multinational Corporations: Towards Principles of Cross-Border Legal Frameworks in a Globalized World Balancing Rights with Responsibilities' (2007) 23 *American University International Law Review* 451, 474; J.E. Antunes, 'Enterprise Forms and Enterprise Liability: The Paradox of Corporation Law' at 30 <http://www.direitogv.com.br/subportais/publicaçõe/RDGV_02_p029_068.pdf>. ('In some cases MNCs take a country's natural resources, paying but a pittance while leaving behind an environmental disaster. When called upon by the government to clean up the mess, the MNC announces that it is bankrupt: All of the revenues have already been paid out to shareholders. In these circumstances, MNCs are taking advantage of limited liability.')

[118]　*See, e.g.*, Lowenfeld (n 110). For a private international law perspective on gaps in governance, *see* H. Muir Watt, 'Private International Law as Global Governance: Beyond the Schize, from Closet to Planet' (2011) <http://works.bepress.com/horatia_muir-watt/1>.

commercial markets and corporate activities.[119] The national legal system where harm has occurred often has been unable to exercise jurisdiction over the parent company of a subsidiary that has committed wrongdoing.[120]

In the English case *Adams v. Cape Industries*, for example, a British parent company used an Illinois-based subsidiary to export asbestos from its mines in South Africa to US customers.[121] Cape later divested itself of its shares in the subsidiary. US employees of the US customers became ill from asbestos exposure. When they filed suit in the United States against the English parent company, the parent company refused to participate in the US proceedings because it had no assets in the United States. The US plaintiffs won a default judgment; however, the English courts would not enforce the judgment within the United Kingdom, finding that the British parent company had no presence in the US even though it had the US subsidiary. The English courts declined to disregard the formal separation between the British parent company and its US subsidiary for the purposes of recognizing jurisdiction in the United States, and they rejected arguments by the US employees that the company had sold its shares in the subsidiary in order to avoid liability over the claims of the employees.

Following similar judicial holdings, GE Hitachi Nuclear Energy, for example, took steps to protect its US parent company from liability in case an accident at a Canadian nuclear plant caused damage in the United States. The company forbid its US-based engineers from engaging in any work related to Canadian reactors. It also banned equipment built or designed by the US parent from being integrated into Canadian reactors.[122]

As a consequence of decisions similar to *Adams v. Cape Industries* and actions similar to those of GE Hitachi Nuclear Energy, in some legal areas and in some countries the single entity approach has given way to a 'single enterprise approach'.[123] In contrast to the single entity approach, the single enterprise approach treats corporate groups in a unified way, recognizing that they often operate to further group interests, may offset profits and

---

[119]   *See, e.g.*, Jodie Kirshner, 'Why is the U.S. Abdicating the Policing of Multinational Corporations to Europe?: Extraterritoriality, Sovereignty, and the Alien Tort Statute' (2012) 30 *Berkeley Journal of International Law* 259, 271.

[120]   (n 119).

[121]   *Adams v. Cape Indus. Plc.* (1990) Ch. 433, 434–437 (Eng.).

[122]   Martin Mittelstaedt, 'U.S. Firm Sheds Liability for Canadian Nuclear Peril' *Globe and Mail* (28 November 2009).

[123]   Jenny Dickfos, 'Directors' Duties under an Enterprise Approach', paper presented at Insolvency Seminar Adelaide, September 2009, 3 <file:///C:/Users/deantemp/Downloads/0f31753094b68518f0000000.pdf>.

losses on a group basis, move assets around the group, and leave some subsidiaries undercapitalized.[124]

Australia, for example, overrides the single entity approach in particular instances. Australian law permits group companies to consolidate their accounts at the group level.[125] The law also prohibits public companies from providing financial benefits to other entities in the same corporate group without shareholder approval.[126] In addition, in cases where a parent company should have known that one of its subsidiaries had become insolvent, the parent company can become liable for debts that the subsidiary incurred after it should have entered insolvency proceedings.[127]

Australian law, however, has appeared to confine group treatment of companies to these specific areas and has not permitted more broad imposition of group responsibility. The Australian case, *James Hardie v. Hall*, for example, concerned claims of asbestos-related illness brought by employees of a New Zealand subsidiary of an Australian parent company in an Australian court.[128] The court of first instance in Australia found that the New Zealand subsidiary and the Australian parent company owed a joint duty of care to the plaintiffs, but the judgment was reversed on appeal, even though the Supreme Court of New South Wales found some evidence of control and influence by the parent over the subsidiary.[129]

Germany[130] has also adopted legislation that treats corporate groups as

---

[124]   Phillip Blumberg, Kurt Strasser et al., *Blumberg on Corporate Groups* (Aspen, 2014) 91–93.

[125]   *See, e.g.*, Damien Murphy, 'Holding Company Liability for Debts of its Subsidiaries: Corporate Governance Implications' (1998) 10 *Bond Law Review* 1, 28.

[126]   *See* Section 208 of the Australian Corporations Act, which states, 'for a public company or an entity controlled by a public company to give a financial benefit to a related party of the public company: (a) the public company or controlled entity must: (i) obtain the approval of the members of the public company as provided in sections 217–227; and (ii) give the benefit within 15 months of obtaining such approval; or (b) the benefit must fall within one of the exceptions set out in sections 210–216.'

[127]   *See* § 588G of the Australian Corporations Law; *further* Ian M Ramsay (ed.), 'Company Directors' Liability For Insolvent Trading', Centre For Corporate Law and Securities Regulation Faculty of Law University of Melbourne (2000).

[128]   *James Hardie and Co. Pty Ltd v. Hall* (1998) 43 NSWLR 20 (Aus NSW CA). *Amaca Pty Ltd v. Frost* [2006] NSWCA 173.

[129]   *See, e.g.*, Andrea Boggio, 'Linking Corporate Power to Corporate Structures: An Empirical Analysis' (2012) 22 *Sociology and Legal Studies* 107, 111–16.

[130]   Portuguese law is similar, *see* José Engrácia Antunes, 'The Law of Corporate Groups in Portugal' (May 2008) Institute for Law and Finance, Johann Wolfgang Goethe-Universität, Working Paper Series No. 84.

single enterprises, but also only in specific instances. German law divides corporate groups into three categories, which the law treats in different ways. The first type of corporate group, the integrated group, results when shareholders vote to give a holding company unlimited power to direct its subsidiaries. In return, the law makes the holding company jointly and severally liable for the debts and obligations of the subsidiaries. The second type of corporate group, the contract group, results when two corporate entities contract to give one entity the right to direct the other. German law requires the control of one entity by the other to advance the interests of the parent company or the whole group of companies, and, in return, the law extends special protections to minority shareholders and creditors with enhanced protection. The final type of corporate group, the de facto group, results when one corporate entity exercises direct or indirect influence over another, even if no formal arrangement between them exists. German law treats the de facto group as one entity for purposes of governance and liability.[131]

New Zealand law also includes single enterprise principles. In New Zealand, directors of subsidiaries may act in the interests of their holding companies rather than in the interests of their subsidiaries.[132] Courts have authority to order one unit of a group to contribute to the assets of another insolvent unit of the group.[133] If an entire group collapses, courts also have authority to pool all of the assets and liabilities of the group.[134]

In the United States, courts increasingly have interpreted laws related to corporate groups in light of enterprise principles. US courts have construed legislation to reverse intra-group transactions,[135] support intra-group

---

[131]   *See, e.g.*, René Reich-Graefe, 'Changing Paradigms: The Liability of Corporate Groups in Germany' (2005) 37 *Connecticut Law Review* 785, 788–94.

[132]   *See* Companies Act 1993 § 131(2); Reserve Bank of New Zealand, Corporate Governance Prudential Supervision Department Document BS14 (July 2014) 7.

[133]   Companies Amendment Act 1980 Companies Act 1993 s 315(a); s 271(1)(a). The court exercises discretion and considers the responsibility of the parent company for the problems at the subsidiary.

[134]   Companies Act 1993 § 271(1)(b). The court weighs, among other elements, the extent to which a unit of the group took part in the management of any of the other units in the group; the conduct of the units of the group towards the creditors of the group; the extent to which the business of the units have been combined; and the extent to which the causes of the liquidation of any of the units of the group are attributable to the actions of any of the other units of the group.

[135]   US Bankruptcy Code §547, voiding transfers by an insolvent company, within one year prior to the filing of a bankruptcy petition, to controlling persons and other insiders or affiliates, including the parent corporation.

guarantees[136] and to consolidate corporate assets in bankruptcy.[137] They have also altered the priority of claims in the bankruptcy of one unit of a corporate group by treating intra-group loans as equity rather than debt or by subordinating intra-group loans to the claims of external creditors.[138]

The US case *Amoco Cadiz* illustrates this approach.[139] After an oil tanker caused an oil spill off the cost of France, French plaintiffs lodged negligence claims in the United States against several entities in the Amoco corporate group, including the corporate parent. The US court found subsidiaries and also the parent company liable for negligence because the corporate group was integrated, with the parent company exercising control over its subsidiaries. Decision-making in the company had been centralized to a degree that the subsidiaries could not implement policies without the involvement of the parent company. The court attributed the oil spill to negligence in the design, maintenance and repair of the steering mechanism of the tanker, and to negligent training which had failed to prepare the crew to avoid the spill.

The ability of courts to apply the single enterprise approach in a clear and predictable way, however, depends upon a clear and predictable definition of a corporate group. Given the variations among groups, the law has struggled to define what constitutes a 'corporate group', and this has made the regulation of corporate groups difficult.[140] While legislation on taxation, accounting, or mergers and acquisitions sometimes addresses groups,[141] such legislation has rarely defined corporate groups in a consistent way or regulated them directly.[142] Most legislation and judicial decisions have found group relationships on the basis of ownership, control and influence.[143] Some have required a specific threshold level

---

[136]   US Bankruptcy Code §548, striking down any guarantee given by an insolvent corporation 'without reasonably equivalent consideration'.

[137]   Phillip Blumberg, 'The Increasing Recognition of Enterprise Principles in Determining Parent and Subsidiary Corporation Liabilities' (1996) 28 *Connecticut Law Review* 29, 326.

[138]   (n 137) 328.

[139]   *In re Oil Spill by the Amoco Cadiz off the Coast of France on March 16, 1978* 954 F.2d 1279 (7th Cir. 1992).

[140]   For example, neither the European Insolvency Regulation nor Chapter 15 of the US Bankruptcy Code have defined corporate groups.

[141]   *See, e.g.*, European Market Infrastructure Regulation Article 2(16).

[142]   *See, e.g.*, paras 1.73–1.75 of the Corporate Groups Discussion Paper (December 1998).

[143]   *See, e.g.*, OECD, Glossary of Foreign Direct Investment Terms and Definitions, 'enterprise group' <http://www.oecd.org/investment/investmentfor development/2487495.pdf>; UK Accounting Standards Board, *Statement of Principles for Financial Reporting* (1999) 8.8.

of shareholdings or voting power,[144] while others have examined more closely the substance of the relationship between corporate entities and have explored, for example, the ability of the parent company to affect the composition of the board of directors of the subsidiary, or the ability of the parent company to affect the outcome of a vote of the board of directors of the subsidiary.[145]

Nevertheless, most legal systems and judicial decision-making does not accept the enterprise approach to corporate groups. As a result, multiple layers of limited liability continue to insulate the individual entities in a corporate group from debts and liabilities, leading some to argue that the result was 'a consequence unforeseen when limited liability was adopted long before the emergence of corporate groups'.[146]

## CONCLUSION

Companies frequently have benefited from expanding across borders by gaining access to cheaper supplies, realizing economies of scale and reducing their transaction costs. Increasingly, rather than entering into overseas markets gradually, born global companies have competed immediately in overseas markets. Because limited liability has afforded companies the ability to ring-fence risk, save costs and attract investors, companies often have chosen to establish subsidiaries in order to expand. The resulting vast, transnational corporate groups have challenged traditional approaches to corporate law, jurisdiction and corporate regulation. While a few countries have amended their law in some areas to align it with the increased prevalence of corporate groups, many transnational groups have remained insulated from liabilities to tort victims and creditors.

---

[144]   *See, e.g.*, Article 2359 of the Italian Civil Code. Pursuant to Article 17(2) of the German Joint Stock Companies Act 1965 one company controls another and thus forms part of a group if the company holds a majority interest in the other.

[145]   *See, e.g.*, European Union Seventh Council Directive 1983 Section 1 Article 1(1); Forum Europaeum Konzernrecht, 'Corporate Group Law for Europe' (2000) 1 *European Business Organization Law Review* 31 US Securities Code (1980) § 202(29).

[146]   Philip Blumberg, *The Multinational Challenge to Corporate Law* (Aspen, 1993) 139.

# 7. Global sourcing through foreign subsidiaries and suppliers: challenges for Corporate Social Responsibility

*Andreas Rühmkorf*

## INTRODUCTION

Most transnational corporations increasingly rely on foreign subsidiaries and suppliers for their production of goods.[1] Companies have usually developed a sophisticated and complex global sourcing strategy in order to reduce costs.[2] Following recurrent reports about human rights violations at supplier factories in the developing world, many companies pursue a sustainable supply chain management policy.[3] They publicise information about how they work towards improving working conditions in their corporate group and supply chain. This engagement is usually part of the companies' Corporate Social Responsibility (CSR) agenda.

However, from a legal perspective, the use of foreign subsidiaries and suppliers constitutes significant challenges for the promotion of CSR.[4] The territorial nature of law, the separate legal personality of companies and weak law-enforcement mechanisms in the developing countries where the production takes place create loopholes which make it difficult to hold Western transnational corporations legally accountable for irresponsible corporate conduct within their global production network.[5] This chapter will first look at the challenges for CSR posed by the use of foreign subsidiaries and suppliers in their global sourcing. It will then critically

---

[1]  See L. Mosley, *Labor Rights and Multinational Production* (CUP, 2011) 17.

[2]  A. Millington, 'Responsibility in the Supply Chain' in A. Crane, A. McWilliams, D. Matten et al. (eds), *The Oxford Handbook of Corporate Social Responsibility* (OUP, 2008) 363.

[3]  R. Monczka et al., *Purchasing and Supply Chain Management* (4th edn, South Western, 2010) 377.

[4]  A. Rühmkorf, *Corporate Social Responsibility, Private Law and Global Supply Chains* (Edward Elgar, 2015) 213–233.

[5]  A. Rühmkorf, Global supply chains: the role of law? A role for law! Open Democracy (2 March 2015) <https://www.opendemocracy.net/beyondslavery/andreas-r%C3%BChmkorf/global-supply-chains-role-of-law-role-for-law> accessed 22 June 2015.

discuss to what extent the home state of transnational corporations could fill those gaps by legal regulation.[6] To that end, the chapter will discuss tort law, criminal law and disclosure requirements. It will also critically review if the multi-stakeholder Accord on Fire and Building Safety in Bangladesh, created after the Rana Plaza building collapse, could be a model for the future promotion of CSR.[7] The chapter will argue that it is time that the home states of transnational corporations accept their responsibility for regulating the socially responsible conduct of those companies. In terms of its jurisdictional scope, the chapter focuses on English law.

## GLOBAL SOURCING STRATEGIES: THE USE OF FOREIGN SUBSIDIARIES AND SUPPLIERS

The outsourcing of the production of goods is an important strategic tool of transnational corporations to remain competitive.[8] This is particularly the case in cost-driven industries such as the garment industry or in the production of electronic devices.[9] Whilst in these instances companies try to reduce the cost of manual labour, other industries such as the confectionery industry need the supply of raw materials from overseas, for example cocoa beans.[10] The global sourcing strategy of many transnational corporations includes foreign subsidiaries and/or suppliers, often based in the developing world.

Whilst companies have always sourced raw materials from overseas, the strategic use of manual labour as a cost-saving tool has particularly

---

[6]   The term 'home state' is used in this chapter to refer to the state in which the transnational corporation is incorporated and where it has its administrative centre. The 'host state' is the state in which the transnational corporation operates, either directly or through its subsidiary. See B. Cragg, 'Home is where the halt is: Mandating corporate social responsibility through home state regulation and social disclosure' (2010) 24 *Emory International Law Review* 735, 751.

[7]   Accord on Fire and Building Safety in Bangladesh <http://bangladeshaccord. org> accessed 20 June 2015.

[8]   S. Chopra and P. Meindl, *Supply Chain Management: Strategy, Planning, and Operation* (5th edn, Pearson, 2013) 155.

[9]   I. Mamic, 'Managing Global Supply Chain: The sports footwear, apparel and retail sectors' (2005) 59 *Journal of Business Ethics* 81.

[10]   D. Goodyear, 'The future of chocolate: why cocoa production is at risk' *The Guardian*, Sustainable Business – Fairtrade partner zone <http://www. theguardian.com/sustainable-business/fairtrade-partner-zone/chocolate-cocoa-production-risk> accessed 20 June 2015.

developed since the early 1990s.[11] Transnational corporations employ different global sourcing strategies: They can use directly owned foreign subsidiaries for production or local firms as contractual partners (suppliers).[12] Where trade takes place between transnational corporations and their subsidiaries abroad, and between foreign subsidiaries in different countries, this is referred to as 'intra-firm sourcing'.[13] Over the last decades, many transnational corporations have developed their global production mechanisms in a way that they increasingly use suppliers instead of wholly owned subsidiaries.[14] Under this sourcing strategy, the production relies on independent foreign suppliers.[15] These suppliers are linked to the transnational corporation through contracts and together they form a network of suppliers.[16]

The organisation of the supply chain, which commonly spans over different continents, is described as supply chain management.[17] The supply chain can be developed in a way that the whole production process is outsourced and transnational corporations purely organise the production process and retain the brand. A good example is Nike that has, for decades, designed and marketed shoes in the United States which are all produced in factories abroad where the production costs are lower.[18] This strategic separation of the company's headquarters in the global North and West and the factories in the developing world has now become a standard business strategy, particularly in cost-driven industries such as textiles.

However, whilst there are clear economic benefits of creating a complex global supply chain, there are recurrent reports about human rights violations such as the use of forced labour at foreign factories.

---

[11]    R. Monczka et al., *Purchasing and Supply Chain Management* (4th edn, South Western, 2010) 191.

[12]    Mosley (n 1).

[13]    M. Kotabe and J. Murray, 'Global sourcing strategy and sustainable competitive advantage' (2004) 33 *Industrial Marketing Management* 7, 9.

[14]    See M. Andersen and T. Skjoett-Larsen, 'Corporate social responsibility in global supply chains' (2009) 14 *Supply Chain Management: An International Journal* 75, 77.

[15]    M. Kotabe and J. Murray, 'Global sourcing strategy and sustainable competitive advantage' (2004) 33 *Industrial Marketing Management* 7, 10.

[16]    S. Cavusgil, G. Knight and J. Riesenberger, *International Business: The new realities* (3rd edn, Pearson, 2014) 474.

[17]    For an introduction, see Chopra and Meindl (n 8).

[18]    See for a description of Nike and the athletic footwear industry: R. Locke, *The Promise and Limits of Private Power: Promoting Labour Standards in a Global Economy* (CUP, 2013) 47–51.

Such incidents have had a negative impact on the reputation of Western transnational corporations that source from suppliers in the developing world.[19] As a consequence of increasing public and political pressure, many transnational corporations have developed sustainable supply chain management as a strategic instrument to demonstrate that they are socially responsible in their global sourcing process.[20] Companies with a global supply chain now commonly have CSR policies in place that address issues such as the prohibition of forced labour. To that end, many Western transnational companies have developed their own CSR code of conduct or have signed an international CSR standard.[21] The company's own foreign subsidiaries often adopt the same or a similar code of conduct. As the suppliers are not owned by the transnational corporation, the Western companies, as the buyers in the supply chain, regularly use their bargaining power to incorporate their CSR code of conduct into their supply chain contracts.[22]

Whilst it is evident that transnational corporations have increasingly addressed CSR issues in their global supply chain, the effectiveness of these regimes is a different question. Despite at least two decades of CSR policies, the reports about CSR violations repeat themselves.[23] The 2013 Rana Plaza building collapse is a strong reminder of the fact that we are far off from having achieved responsible corporate conduct throughout global supply chains.[24]

---

[19]   R. Locke et al., 'Beyond corporate codes of conduct: work organization and labour standards at NIKE's suppliers' (2007) 146 *International Labour Review* 21.

[20]   See Andersen and Skjoett-Larsen (n 14).

[21]   D. Wells, 'Too weak for the job: Corporate codes of conduct, non-governmental organisations and the regulation of international labour standards' (2007) 7 *Global Social Policy* 51, 52.

[22]   E. Pedersen and M. Andersen, 'Safeguarding corporate social responsibility (CSR) in global supply chains: how codes of conduct are managed in buyer-supplier relationships' (2006) 6 *Journal of Public Affairs* 228, 237.

[23]   See for example: 'Sweatshops are still supplying high street brands' *The Guardian* (28 April 2011) <http://www.theguardian.com/global-development/poverty-matters/2011/apr/28/sweatshops-supplying-high-street-brands> (accessed 30 June 2015).

[24]   For *The Guardian's* comprehensive coverage of the Rana Plaza disaster, see <http://www.theguardian.com/world/rana-plaza> accessed 25 June 2015.

## LEGAL CHALLENGES FOR CSR THROUGH FOREIGN SUBSIDIARIES AND SUPPLIERS

This situation raises the question of to what extent global sourcing through foreign subsidiaries and suppliers constitute legal challenges for the promotion of CSR.

### No Binding International Law Framework

So far, the legal discussion about CSR and transnational corporations has been particularly prominent in the public international law literature.[25] It is important to note that there is no binding international human rights framework for transnational corporations. International human rights initiatives for transnational corporations are primarily soft law. For example, the UN Global Compact, which is widely adopted by companies as part of their CSR agenda, was not intended to be a 'regulatory instrument'.[26] The Global Compact contains ten principles on human rights, labour standards, environmental protection and fighting corruption, but it is not a code of conduct.[27] Corporations which have subscribed to it are required to submit examples of how they have complied with the Principles on an annual basis.[28] The only control mechanism of the UN Global Compact is that the Global Compact can exclude members who severely violate the principles.[29]

In recent years, the UN Guiding Principles of Businesses and Human Rights have been the focal point of discussions about the responsibilities of transnational corporations for the working conditions at factories abroad that they source from.[30] The Guiding Principles were the result of the six-year mandate of Professor John Ruggie as UN Special

---

[25]    See, for example, J. Zerk, *Multinationals and Corporate Social Responsibility: Limitations and Opportunities in International Law* (CUP, 2006).

[26]    See UN Global Compact <http://www.unglobalcompact.org/AboutTheGC/index.html> accessed 26 June 2015.

[27]    Zerk (n 25).

[28]    UN Global Compact (n 26).

[29]    (n 26).

[30]    The UN Guiding Principles refer to the company's value chain in Principle 17: 'Human Rights Due Diligence', see United Nations, 'Guiding Principles on Business and Human Rights: Implementing the United Nations "Protect, Respect and Remedy" Framework' (New York and Geneva, 2011) <http://www.ohchr.org/documents/publications/GuidingprinciplesBusinesshr_en.pdf> accessed 20 June 2015.

Representative for Business and Human Rights.[31] They have been called 'a landmark in the CSR debate'.[32] The normative contribution of the Guiding Principles lies not in the creation of new international law obligations, but in elaborating the implications of existing standards and practices for states and businesses.[33] The Guiding Principles distinguish between the duties of states and the responsibilities of companies in order to indicate that respecting rights is not an obligation that current international human rights law generally imposes directly upon companies.[34] The Guiding Principles are intended to be implemented by countries and by companies.[35] This aspect is important, as it recognises that there is a role for the home state of transnational corporations to regulate transnational corporations.

**The Limiting Effects of the Shareholder Value Theory for the Promotion of CSR**

Transnational corporations in the United Kingdom or the United States operate within the shareholder value paradigm that is based on an agency model of the company.[36] This theoretical framing of the corporation mandates that it is the primary task of the management to be exclusively accountable to the shareholders and to maximize their profit.[37] Consequently, the shareholders must be prioritized in the decision-making

---

[31] See the website of the Special Representative of the Secretary-General on human rights and transnational corporations and other business at: <http://business-humanrights.org/> accessed 28 June 2015.

[32] J. Ames, 'Taking responsibility' (2011) *European Lawyer* 15.

[33] United Nations, General Assembly, Human Rights Council, Report of the Special Representative of the Secretary-General on the issue of human rights and transnational corporations and other business enterprises, J. Ruggie: 'Guiding Principles on Business and Human Rights: Implementing the United Nations "Protect, Respect and Remedy" Framework' (21 March 2011), Introduction to the Guiding Principles, para 14 <http://www.ohchr.org/documents/issues/business/A.HRC.17.31.pdf> accessed 20 June 2015.

[34] J. Ruggie, 'The construction of the UN 'protect, respect and remedy' framework for business and human rights: the true confessions of a principled pragmatist' (2011) 2 *European Human Rights Law Review* 127, 129.

[35] Office of the United Nations High Commissioner for Human Rights, 'New Guiding Principles on Business and Human Rights endorsed by the UN Human Rights Council'.

[36] A. Johnston, *EC Regulation of Corporate Governance* (CUP, 2009) 21.

[37] S. Sheikh and W. Rees (eds), *Corporate Governance and Corporate Control* (Cavendish, 1995) 10; *Hutton v. West Cork Railway Co. Ltd* [1883] 23 Ch. D. 654, 673.

process.[38] In English law, this theoretical framing of the company is legally embedded in s172 (1) of the Companies Act (CA) 2006, i.e., the duty to promote the success of the company.[39] Whilst this duty allow directors 'to have regard to' the interests of various stakeholders, including suppliers, it requires directors to ultimately prioritise the interests of shareholders.[40]

This purpose of the company directly influences the way company directors engage with CSR in their global supply chain, be it through its own foreign subsidiaries or a network of overseas suppliers. Under this model of the firm, companies will only promote CSR to the extent that it can be based on the business case in the interest of shareholders, i.e., that it promotes the reputation of the firm.[41] The voluntary engagement of transnational corporations with CSR in their global production is therefore limited. Rather, transnational corporations focus on the strategic use of foreign subsidiaries and suppliers as a cost-saving instrument.[42]

**Territorial Limits of the Law and the Legal Structure of Companies**

The violation of CSR principles at factories run by either subsidiaries or suppliers of transnational corporations in the developing world pose a significant challenge due to the territorial nature of the law and the legal personality of companies.

---

[38]   H. Hansmann and R. Kraakman, 'The end of history for corporate law' (2001) 89 *Georgetown Law Journal* 439, 449.

[39]   S172 (1) CA reads as follows: 'A director of a company must act in the way he considers, in good faith, would be most likely to promote the success of the company for the benefit of its members as a whole, and in doing so have regard (amongst other matters) to – (a) the likely consequences of decisions in the long term, (b) the interests of the company's employees, (c) the need to foster relationships with suppliers, customers and others, (d) the impact of the company's operations on the community and the environment, (e) the desirability of the company maintaining a reputation for high standards of business and (f) the need to act fairly between members of the company.'

[40]   See, for a discussion of the duty, A. Keay, 'The duty to promote the success of the company: is it fit for purpose in a post-financial crisis world?' in J. Loughrey (ed.), *Directors' Duties and Shareholder Litigation in the Wake of the Financial Crisis* (Edward Elgar, 2013) 50.

[41]   See A. Kurucz, B. Colbert and D. Wheeler, 'The business case for Corporate Social Responsibility' in A. Crane, A. McWilliams, D. Matten et al. (eds), *The Oxford Handbook of Corporate Social Responsibility* (OUP, 2008) 83–112.

[42]   See, for example, 'The Bangladesh factory collapse: why CSR is more important than ever' *The Guardian* (7 May 2013) <http://www.theguard ian.com/sustainable-business/blog/bangladesh-factory-collapse-csr-important> accessed 22 June 2015.

First, the law that is primarily applicable to irresponsible corporate conduct at factories in the developing world, such as tort law or criminal law, is the law of those countries where the particular incidents have occurred.[43] For example, the laws applicable to the Rana Plaza Building collapse are, first and foremost, the laws of Bangladesh. This situation can constitute a challenge where the substantive law of the country where the violation of CSR principles took place has, for example, lower standards in criminal law and tort law.[44] More often, however, it is not so much the substantive law that is weak in those countries, but rather the law-enforcement mechanisms.

Second, most transnational corporations do not own the factories that produce for them; rather, the production is done by either foreign subsidiaries which are owned by the transnational corporations or by foreign suppliers. The difference between subsidiaries and suppliers is that subsidiaries are owned by the Western transnational company, whereas suppliers are usually completely independent from the transnational company, i.e., they are owned by other people who are not linked to the transnational corporation. The different ownership structures of the two forms – foreign subsidiaries and suppliers – also has consequences for the liability of the transnational corporation. Supplier companies are legally completely independent companies from the transnational corporation as they are owned by different people. However, there is often a strong economic dependence of the suppliers on the transnational corporation as the buyer of their goods.[45] Their conduct could reflect on the transnational corporation in terms of reputation, but not in terms of legal liability.

Foreign subsidiaries, on the other hand, are linked to the transnational corporation through ownership.[46] The transnational corporation holds the majority of the shares of the subsidiary, often it is even the sole shareholder, making the other company its wholly owned subsidiary.[47] The transnational corporation, as the parent company, can decide, for

---

[43] For an introduction to the idea of 'the law of the place of the tort', see: D. McClean and V. Ruiz, *The Conflict of Laws* (8th edn, Sweet and Maxwell, 2012) para 12–003.

[44] Muchlinski notes that the principal jurisdiction level for the regulation of multinational enterprises remains the nation state, see P. Muchlinski, *Multinational Enterprises and the Law* (2nd edn, OUP, 2007) chapters 3 and 4.

[45] See, for example, 'The desperate struggle at the heart of the brutal Apple supply chain' *The Guardian* (14 November 2014) <http://www.theguardian.com/technology/2014/nov/14/sapphire-gt-advanced--brutal-apple-supply-chain> accessed 27 June 2015.

[46] Mosley (n 1) 19.

[47] S1159 (1) Companies Act 2006.

example, who the directors of the subsidiary are, and it benefits from its profits. However, in English law, even wholly owned subsidiaries are legal entities separate and independent from the parent company.[48] This is a consequence of the *Salomon v. Salomon* principle which has established that companies have a separate legal personality from their shareholders.[49] This principle has been expanded to corporate groups with the effect that the parent companies are not vicariously liable for the conduct of their subsidiaries.[50]

## CRITICAL REVIEW OF EXISTING ATTEMPTS TO REGULATE CSR IN GLOBAL SOURCING

In the absence of binding human rights obligations on transnational corporations in international law, other regulatory mechanisms for the promotion of CSR in the global production have been attempted. Most of these are private governance initiatives that are developed and governed in the private sphere between companies, sometimes involving third parties such as non-governmental organisations.[51] Other regulatory initiatives rely on the home state of transnational corporations such as the US Alien Tort Claims Act (ATCA). This section will critically review these measures in terms of their ability to promote the socially responsible conduct of transnational companies.

## CSR BASED ON PRIVATE GOVERNANCE SCHEMES

Many transnational corporations with well-known brands are vulnerable to reputational risks and have therefore voluntarily adopted codes of conduct that address the way they run their business.[52] Such codes of

---

[48]   See *Adams v. Cape Industries plc* [1990] BCLC 479, 513.

[49]   *Salomon v. Salomon & Co. Ltd* [1897] AC 22, HL.

[50]   B. Hannigan, *Company Law* (3rd edn, OUP, 2012) paras 3–35, and 3–43.

[51]   Wells (n 21).

[52]   A study published in 2010 shows that 77 out of the 100 constituent FTSE 100 firms had adopted such codes and many companies have policies about ethical sourcing which they integrate into the supply chain relations with their suppliers, see L. Preuss, 'Codes of conduct in organisational context: from cascade to lattice-work of codes' (2010) 94 *Journal of Business Ethics* 471, 475. Preuss analysed the range of codes that constituent firms of the FTSE100 index use. His findings show that 77 companies used a general, company-wide code of conduct which often also included stipulations for suppliers, 43 companies had adopted ethical sourcing

conduct usually establish principles of good business conduct that the company pledges to comply with.[53] Transnational corporations increasingly incorporate their code of conduct into their business relations with their suppliers, for example through their supply contracts.[54] Depending on how the principles in the codes of conduct are phrased, they can become contractually enforceable clauses.[55]

At first sight, such private governance regimes appear to be a useful tool to achieve greater socially responsible conduct across the global supply chain of transnational corporations. Through codes of conduct, transnational companies can bind themselves to human rights obligations which are otherwise only contained in international soft-law standards.[56] Moreover, by giving these principles contractual force within their supplier contracts, the transnational companies are able to transcend the territorial limits of law, and they can thus impose human rights standards on suppliers in the developing world.

However, despite their widespread use among most transnational corporations, private CSR governance regimes have not prevented the repeated violations of human rights at supplier factories in the developing world. Recent examples of irresponsible corporate conduct at supplier factories include the fire at the textile factory Tazreen Fashions in Bangladesh (November 2012), the widespread use of forced labour in the Thai fishing industry (June 2014), breaches of working time and safety equipment provision in the production of electronic devices in China (July 2014), and, most notably, the deadly Rana Plaza building collapse in Bangladesh (May 2013).[57] All these violations of CSR principles occurred despite

---

policies which specifically contain what companies expect from their suppliers in terms of CSR standards.

[53]   Wells (n 21) 52.

[54]   A. Millington, 'Responsibility in the supply chain' in A. Crane, A. McWilliams, D. Matten et al. (eds), *The Oxford Handbook of Corporate Social Responsibility* (OUP, 2008) 365.

[55]   Rühmkorf (n 4) 79–125.

[56]   See A. Sobczak, 'Are codes of conduct in global supply chains really voluntary? From soft law regulation of labour relations to consumer law' (2006) 16 *Journal of Business Ethics* 167, 168.

[57]   'Bangladesh textile factory fire leaves more than 100 dead' *The Guardian* (25 November 2012) <http://www.theguardian.com/world/2012/nov/25/bangladesh -textile-factory-fire>; 'Trafficked into slavery on Thai trawlers to catch food for prawns' *The Guardian* (10 June 2014) <http://www.theguardian.com/global-development/2014/jun/10/-sp-migrant-workers-new-life-enslaved-thai-fishing>; 'Samsung finds labour violations at dozens of its Chinese suppliers' *The Guardian* (1 July 2014) <http://www.theguardian.com/technology/2014/jul/01/samsung-work ing-practice-breaches-chinese-suppliers>; see the coverage of the Rana Plaza

public awareness of human rights breaches in global sourcing and the CSR policies of most transnational corporations.

Moreover, where the CSR principles have been violated within these private governance systems, the transnational corporations got away with impunity. There is no sanction system such as in state-based regulation that applies in case the CSR principles are violated. Companies only have to face reputational concerns. Where the CSR codes of conduct are incorporated into the contracts between transnational corporations and their suppliers, the monitoring of compliance and the enforcement depends on the Western transnational company as the obligations fall on their suppliers.[58] The workers of the suppliers as the intended beneficiaries of the contractual CSR clauses do not gain any right of enforcement.[59] And while many transnational corporations have increased their efforts to monitor the compliance of their direct suppliers (also called first-tier suppliers), the majority of violations of CSR principles occur further down the supply chain through subcontracting.[60] These factories are beyond the reach of the supply chain contracts between the transnational corporations and their direct suppliers which contain the CSR codes of conduct. The private-governance-based CSR compliance system therefore allows transnational companies to publicly portray themselves as responsible whereas, in reality, subcontracting means that these systems often fail to address those factories where the human rights violations occur.

## THE ACCORD ON FIRE AND BUILDING SAFETY IN BANGLADESH: A MULTI-STAKEHOLDER INITIATIVE

After the deadly Rana Plaza building collapse, serious concerns were raised about the effectiveness of the existing CSR mechanisms in global supply chains. In fact, the building was audited twice by Primark before

---

disaster by *The Guardian*, 'Rana Plaza', <http://www.theguardian.com/world/rana-plaza> accessed 20 June 2015.

[58] See A. Sobczak, 'Are codes of conduct in global supply chains really voluntary? From soft law regulation of labour relations to consumer law' (2006) 16 *Journal of Business Ethics* 167.

[59] Rühmkorf (n 4) 102–107.

[60] See G. LeBaron, 'Subcontracting is not illegal, but is it unethical? Business ethics, forced labor, and economic success' (2014) 20 *Brown Journal of World Affairs* 237, 245.

it collapsed, but the audit did not include a structural survey.[61] This situation illustrates the failure of the existing private governance system of CSR promotion, based on the 'voluntary' inclusion, monitoring and enforcement of CSR by transnational corporations alone.

Due to their failure to prevent the Rana Plaza disaster, the transnational companies in the fashion industry which source ready-made garments from Bangladesh were under significant public and political pressure.[62] In response, the fashion industry came up with different initiatives aimed at improving the situation in Bangladesh. A particularly interesting approach in this context is the Accord on Fire and Building Safety in Bangladesh as a multi-stakeholder initiative.[63] Its structure and mode of operation will be critically assessed here in order to discuss whether or not it could be a model for future CSR mechanisms in global sourcing.

The Accord, established in May 2013, is intended to improve the safety of garment factories in Bangladesh. More than two years after its development, in June 2015, the agreement had been signed by over 200 apparel brands, retailers and importers from over 20 countries, most of which are from Europe; two global trade unions (IndustriALL and UNI); and eight Bangladesh trade unions and four NGO witnesses such as the Clean Clothes Campaign.[64] The International Labour Organisation (ILO) acts as the independent chair of the Accord. This initiative covers all suppliers of the companies that have signed the Accord.[65] It is a five-year legally binding agreement. It stipulates that independent safety inspections must take place at the factories that the signatory companies source from in Bangladesh. The factories are divided into tier 1, tier 2 and tier 3 factories, depending on their share of the signatory company's annual production in Bangladesh by volume.

Where flaws are identified, the signatory company that sources from this factory is under an obligation to require the supplier factory to implement the corrective actions that were identified by the inspectors.[66] Additionally, in the event of safety flaws being identified, the signatory companies also

---

[61]   'How the world has changed since Rana Plaza' *Vogue* (1 April 2014) <http://www.vogue.co.uk/news/2014/04/01/bangladesh-rana-plaza-anniversary-fashion-revolution-day> accessed 21 November 2014.

[62]   'Bangladesh pressed on factory safety' *The Guardian* (6 June 2013) <http://www.theguardian.com/global-development/2013/jun/06/bangladesh-garment-industry-scrutiny-factory-collapse> accessed 28 June 2015.

[63]   Accord on Fire and Building Safety in Bangladesh <http://bangladeshaccord.org/> accessed 2 July 2015.

[64]   ibid, Signatories.

[65]   ibid, Scope.

[66]   ibid, Credible Inspection, 9.

commit to ensuring that sufficient funds are available for the corrective actions and that those who work at the factories in question continue to be paid.[67] The Accord also provides transparency by the regular publication of the list of all suppliers in Bangladesh used by the signatory companies, written inspection reports for all factories inspected under the Accord and quarterly aggregate reports that summarise both aggregate industry compliance data.[68]

The work of the Accord is funded through an annual membership fee paid by the signatory companies which depend on their yearly volume of sourcing from Bangladesh.[69] The signatory companies commit to maintain their sourcing relationships with Bangladesh. The Accord is governed by a Steering Committee which consists of equal representation chosen by the trade union members and company members of the agreement (maximum three seats each) and a representation from and chosen by the ILO as a neutral chair.[70] Disputes are regulated in the way that, in the first instance, the Steering Committee decides by majority vote within a maximum of 21 days of a petition being filed. By request of either party, the decision of the Steering Committee may be appealed to a final and binding arbitration process. The arbitration award is enforceable in a court of law of the domicile of the signatory against whom enforcement is sought.[71]

Through the involvement of different stakeholder groups in its governance structure and through the provision of remedial action, the Accord goes beyond the previous attempts to promote CSR standards at factories in the developing world. The Accord is a clear improvement as it does not rely on the transnational corporations alone. It can therefore be argued that future credible approaches to better promoting CSR principles in global supply chains should build on these positive features of the Accord.

However, the Accord has several weaknesses. First, it does not have universal reach among transnational companies in the textile industry. Its signatory companies are primarily European textile companies,

---

[67]   Workers who lose their job as a consequence of working for a factory that is unsafe are promised to be supported, for example, by being offered employment with safe suppliers, see Accord, Remediation, 14.

[68]   ibid, Transparency and Reporting, 19. The reports can be found at <http://accord.fairfactories.org/ffcweb/Web/ManageSuppliers/InspectionReportsEnglish.aspx> accessed 30 June 2015.

[69]   ibid, Financial Support, 24.

[70]   ibid, Governance, 4.

[71]   It is also subject to The Convention on the Recognition and Enforcement of Foreign Arbitral Awards (The New York Convention) where applicable.

whereas the majority of US-American companies that source ready-made garment from Bangladesh did not agree to this initiative.[72] Instead, they created the Alliance for Bangladesh Worker Safety which relies on a voluntary, business-driven structure.[73] In effect, the Alliance, by and large, continues to operate in the same way that the companies addressed CSR prior to Rana Plaza. Second, the Accord is a five-year plan with no clarity, yet what is going to happen after its expiry date? It is quite possible that the signatory companies involved might then declare that sufficient improvements have been made so that, in their view, the scheme would not need to be renewed. It is not sure how much interest the public will take in the issue in a few years' time. Third, the Accord is only a single-issue initiative that is restricted to one country. It is a reaction to a much reported disaster as companies felt the pressure to publicly demonstrate commitment to engage with the cause of the factory collapse, i.e., the poor health and safety standards at factories in Bangladesh. It is important to bear in mind that global supply chains with poor health and safety standards exist in many other countries of the developing world, too.[74] Moreover, the violations of CSR principles in the global supply chain are not restricted to health and safety breaches alone; there are many other pressing issues that urgently need to be addressed, too, such as the use of forced labour.[75] Finally, first reports about the effectiveness of the Accord indicate that the initiative does not cover the large-scale subcontracting that it still taking place in the industry.[76] The inspections 'fail to address the greatest risks of this system' which occur further down the supply chain.[77]

---

[72]   'Major US names missing as retailers sign deal to improve Bangladesh safety' *The Guardian* (8 July 2013) <http://www.theguardian.com/business/2013/jul/08/retail-bangladesh-factories-improve-safety-deal> accessed 26 June 2015.

[73]   Alliance for Bangladesh Worker Safety <http://www.bangladeshworker-safety.org/>; 'Battling for a Safer Bangladesh' *New York Times* (21 April 2014) <http://www.nytimes.com/2014/04/22/business/international/battling-for-a-safer-bangladesh.html?_r=0> accessed 23 June 2015.

[74]   See, for example, 'Improving worker conditions in the global supply chain is good business' *The Guardian* (7 August 2013) <http://www.theguardian.com/sustainable-business/improve-worker-conditions-supply-chain-china> accessed 27 June 2015.

[75]   A. Crane, 'Modern slavery as a management practice: exploring the conditions and capabilities for human exploitation' (2013) 38 *Academy of Management Review* 49, 56.

[76]   S. Labowitz and D. Baumann-Pauly, 'Business as usual is not an option' NYU Stern Center for Business and Human Rights (April 2014) <http://www.stern.nyu.edu/sites/default/files/assets/documents/con_047408.pdf> accessed 24 June 2015.

[77]   (n 76).

Two years after Rana Plaza and the development of the Accord, transnational corporations have still not worked together to create similar multi-stakeholder initiatives for other CSR issues and other countries. This situation shows that though the Accord is an improvement of the pre-Rana Plaza world, we are still far from witnessing a new era in the promotion of CSR.

## TORT LAW: THE LIABILITY OF THE PARENT COMPANY

Due to the challenges that many tort victims of foreign subsidiaries and suppliers experience with access to justice in their home countries, there is an ongoing discussion about the tortious liabilities of transnational corporations that source from factories where CSR principles are violated.[78] Companies are liable in tort through vicarious liability.[79] This is not a tort in its own right, but a rule of responsibility which means that the company is liable for the actions of other people such as employees.[80]

The prospect of making claims against the transnational corporation at the head of the global supply chain is attractive for the promotion of CSR, as these companies usually have better financial means and are based in Western countries which often provide easier access to justice. Moreover, transnational corporations with well-known brands are concerned about the reputational damage that results, for example, from losing a case linked to human rights violations. It is exactly for these reasons that transnational corporations are commonly strongly opposed to be subjected to claims by victims of torts committed at the factories of their subsidiaries and suppliers.[81] However, the structure of global supply chains makes it difficult to hold transnational companies liable. Although companies can be sued for torts committed by other people, the challenge for legal

---

[78]   See, for example, M. Anderson, 'Transnational corporations and environmental damage: is tort law the answer?' (2002) 41 *Washburn Law Journal* 399.

[79]   P. Giliker and S. Beckwith, *Tort* (4th edn, Sweet and Maxwell, 2011) para 7–022.

[80]   D. French, S. Mayson and C. Ryan, *French and Ryan on Company Law* (28th edn, OUP, 2011–12) para 19.7.2.

[81]   An example of the opposition by businesses is the lobbying in the United States against the Alien Tort Claims Act (ATCA). See D. McBarnet and P. Schmidt, 'Corporate accountability through creative enforcement: human rights, the Alien Torts Claims Act and the limits of legal impunity' in D. McBarnet, A. Voiculescu and T. Campbell (eds), *The New Corporate Accountability: Corporate Social Responsibility and the Law* (CUP, 2007) 175.

liability for the relevant torts here is that they occur at factories operated by subsidiaries and suppliers abroad. In the case of suppliers, this situation means that the tort is committed by a company which is legally completely separate from the transnational corporation as there is no link between the two through ownership.

Even where the torts are committed by the foreign subsidiaries of transnational corporations, the tort victims do not have a cause of action against the transnational corporation in English law either.[82] All companies in a group of companies are separate legal entities, even in cases of wholly owned subsidiaries with only little paid-up share capital and a board of directors which predominately or solely consists of directors who are also directors of the parent company.[83] Corporate group structures enable parent companies to reduce their liability risk in tort.[84] The consequence of this approach is that tort victims of a subsidiary company might not be able to recover their loss, if the subsidiary is undercapitalised.[85] In *Adams v. Cape Industries plc*, the Court of Appeal applied a strict approach to the question of piercing the corporate veil in corporate groups and dismissed the idea of a single economic unit between the parent company and its subsidiaries.[86] The court held that the corporate veil could in only be pierced where special circumstances exist which indicate that the corporate veil is a mere façade concealing the true facts, i.e., where the corporate structure is used to evade rights of relief that third parties may in the future acquire.

Slade LJ noted:

> There is no general principle that all companies in a group of companies are to be regarded as one. On the contrary, the fundamental principle is that "each company in a group of companies (a relatively modern concept) is a separate legal entity possessed of separate legal rights and liabilities: see *The Albazero* [1975] 3 All ER 21, 28."[87]

Slade LJ also stated that the use of the corporate group by a parent company as a means to ensure that legal liability in respect of future activities of the group will fall on another member of that group was 'inherent in our corporate law'. The consequence is that the risk is allo-

---

[82]   See *Adams v. Cape Industries plc* [1990] BCLC 479, 513.

[83]   Hannigan (n 50) para 3–35.

[84]   (n 50) para 3–44.

[85]   S. Lo, 'Liability of directors as joint tortfeasors' (2009) 2 *Journal of Business Law* 109, 120.

[86]   (n 82).

[87]   (n 82) 508.

cated to the poorer risk taker, the tort victim.[88] This approach does not only disregard the fact that it puts tort victims as involuntary creditors at a severe disadvantage; it also overlooks that limited liability was developed in the 19th century to promote business activities by investors, whereas nowadays parent companies strategically use corporate group structures with a range of (foreign) subsidiaries as an instrument to reduce their liability risks.[89] Moreover, the rejection of the idea of group liability ignores the economic realities of corporate groups. Parent companies usually maintain close ties with their subsidiaries and they effectively control the running of these companies. The parent companies therefore benefit from the gains made by the subsidiaries whilst they avoid liability for their obligations. English law is also not coherent in its strict application of the *Salomon v. Salomon* principle as parent companies must prepare group accounts pursuant to s399 (2) CA 2006.[90]

This approach of English courts to group liability constitutes a significant challenge for the promotion of CSR, as tort victims are unable to make a claim against the transnational corporation as the parent company for the torts committed by its foreign subsidiaries. This approach needs to be changed in order to promote greater social responsibility of transnational corporations. The strategic use of subsidiaries to limit their liability risks contributes to the irresponsible conduct that continues to occur at factories in the developing world.

A potentially different avenue to address the same issue is to hold transnational corporations primarily liable in tort for the working conditions at the factories of their subsidiaries. In the case *Chandler v. Cape plc*, it was held that a parent company can owe a primary duty of care in negligence to the employees of its subsidiary.[91] In this case, the defendant *Cape plc*, as the parent company, was directly and jointly liable with its subsidiary (which had been dissolved in the meantime) in negligence for asbestos-related injuries inflicted on the subsidiary's previous employee (the claimant). Prior to this decision, there had been a longstanding debate about the question of whether or not such a primary duty exists in English law, but this issue was never formally decided by a court as the

---

[88]   P. Muchlinski, 'Limited liability and multinational enterprise: a case for reform?' (2010) 34 *Cambridge Journal of Economics* 915, 918, 923.

[89]   S. Baughen, 'Multinationals and the Export of Hazard' (1995) 58 *Modern Law Review* 54, 70.

[90]   S404 CA2006.

[91]   [2012] EWCA Civ 525 which affirms [2011] EWHC 951 (QB).

cases were either settled or struck out for other reasons.[92] The difference between this case and the previous discussion about group liability is that, in *Chandler v. Cape plc*, the parent company was held to have breached a duty of care which it directly owed to the employees of its subsidiary company. This duty of care was imposed on the parent company on the basis of an assumption of responsibility as the parent company had superior knowledge of the asbestos-related risks that the employees of its subsidiary were exposed to. Moreover, it dictated the overall health and safety policy of its subsidiaries and it also exercised control over their business behaviour to an extent that it had the ability to intervene.

The imposition of a direct duty of care on the parent company is distinct from any question of piercing the corporate veil as this approach respects the separate legal personality of the two companies. Rather, parent companies are liable for their own failure to protect the employees of its subsidiaries which resulted in their harm. *Chandler v. Cape plc* sets an important precedent for the legal responsibility of parent companies as it restricts the ability of parent companies to completely outsource their liability where they clearly have superior knowledge and are the dominant force within the group. However, it is unclear to what extent this precedent, which concerned a particularly dangerous industry related to asbestos, might be applied to other business areas and to cases between UK-based transnational corporations and their foreign subsidiaries as the facts underlying this decision occurred in the UK.

## TORT LAW: THE US ALIEN TORT CLAIMS ACT

Whilst this chapter focuses on English law in its jurisdictional scope, it is important to briefly consider the US Alien Tort Claims Act (ATCA) in this context as this statute has, for some time now, captured the interest of those interested in the home state liability of transnational corporations for torts committed abroad.[93] This Act is, so far, the most successful

---

[92]   However, it was already argued in the academic literature that a parent company could owe a primary duty of care to tort victims of its affiliates. See, for example: Zerk (n 25) 216.

[93]   See, for example, D. McBarnet and P. Schmidt, 'Corporate accountability through creative enforcement: human rights, the Alien Torts Claims Act and the limits of legal impunity' in McBarnet, Voiculescu and Campbell (n 81) 148.

example of holding parent companies liable in tort law.[94] The ATCA was enacted in 1789, but only rediscovered and creatively used by NGOs during the late 20th century. The ATCA confers jurisdiction on the US District Court in respect of 'any civil action by an alien for a tort only, committed in violation of the law of nations or a treaty of the United States'. Parent companies based in the United States can be held accountable for human rights violations by their subsidiaries abroad under the ATCA.

In *Filartiga v. Pena-Irala* the court decided that non-American citizens could be punished for tortious acts committed outside the United States which were in violation of public international law or any treaties to which the United States is a party.[95] This decision is important as it extends the jurisdiction of US courts to tortious acts committed around the world. A further significant step for the use of the ATCA was the decision in *Sosa v. Alvarez*.[96] Here, the US Supreme Court allowed courts to hear claims by private individuals for breaches of international law committed in other countries. These decisions were followed by a significant increase of claims against US parent companies. However, the courts have been reluctant to assume jurisdiction in cases where the claimants were not resident in the United States.

At present, the future use of the ATCA for tort liabilities of parent companies for tortious acts committed outside the United States is uncertain. In *Kiobel v. Royal Dutch Petroleum Co.* the Supreme Court decided in April 2013 that the Act would only apply to conduct within the United States or on the high seas.[97] It would not create jurisdiction for a claim regarding conduct that occurred in the territory of a foreign sovereign. This decision effectively means that a presumption against extraterritoriality applies to claims under the Act. After this decision it is unclear if the ATCA will play a significant role for liability related to torts committed at factories of foreign subsidiaries of US transnational corporations. This development is unfortunate as the Act was able to fill an accountability vacuum.

Notwithstanding the decision in *Kiobel*, there is, at the time of writing, ongoing litigation under the ATCA concerning the use of forced labour at cocoa firms which supply the confectionery industry. In September 2014, a US appeal court held in *Doe v. Nestlé USA Inc. et al.* that the claimants

---

[94]   A discussion of the Act can be found at A. de Jonge, *Transnational Corporations and International Law: Accountability in the Global Business Environment* (Edward Elgar, 2011) 99–106.
[95]   630 F 2d 876 (2d Cir. 1980).
[96]   542 US 692 (2004).
[97]   133 S.Ct. 1659 (2013).

were allowed to amend their claim against Nestlé, ADM and Cargill so that the defendant companies could be held to account for aiding and abetting child slavery in Ivory Coast.[98] The court reinstated a lawsuit filed by three citizens of Mali in 2005 who claim that they were forced to work as child slaves on cocoa plantations in the Ivory Coast. This judgment overrules a previous decision by a district court which had dismissed the case on grounds that US courts had no jurisdiction for abuses committed by companies outside the territory of the United States. The court held in this case that at least parts of the act occurred in the United States. It remains to be seen, however, how the case is finally decided in light of *Kiobel*.

In summary, tort law is, at least in theory, an attractive avenue for the promotion of greater social responsibilities of transnational corporations as it provides remedies for tort victims. However, changes are necessary for English tort law to better promote CSR in global sourcing, for example group liability would be a strong incentive for transnational companies to use their power to improve working conditions at their foreign subsidiaries.

## EXTRATERRITORIAL CRIMINAL LIABILITY: THE BRIBERY ACT

Criminal law is another area of the law that has much potential to improve the working conditions in the global production chain of transnational companies. English law applies criminal law to corporations.[99] Where corporations are criminally liable, the requirements of the criminal act (*actus reus*) and the criminal mind (*mens rea*) are found in a person acting on behalf of the corporation such as the relevant officer.[100] As companies cannot be imprisoned, they are, if convicted, sanctioned with a monetary fine. Like tort law, criminal law is, first and foremost, bound to the territory of the jurisdiction where the crime occurs.[101] Generally speaking, where crimes are committed at factories in the developing world, the crime is prosecuted under the laws of that jurisdiction. The advantage of criminal law vis-à-vis tort law is that the prosecution is initiated by the state. It does not depend on the action being brought by a private individual and therefore, by definition, has a broader reach than tort law.

---

[98]  10–56739 (9th Cir. Sept. 4, 2014).
[99]  Hannigan (n 50) para 3–89.
[100]  Hannigan (n 50).
[101]  See the discussion of jurisdiction in Muchlinski (n 44) chapters 3 and 4.

Moreover, the threat of criminal conviction acts as a strong deterrence, not just because of the financial consequences of convictions, but also because of the reputational concerns.

Extraterritorial criminal liability of transnational corporations in their home state is therefore an attractive idea to better promote CSR in global sourcing. In English law, this approach has been introduced in the UK Bribery Act 2010. Common to all cases of bribery in the Bribery Act is the offer or taking of a 'financial or other advantage'.[102] The Act has a near-universal jurisdiction. This approach makes it possible to prosecute an individual or a company with links to the United Kingdom, regardless of where the crime occurred. In particular, the Act makes it an offence for commercial organisations which have business in the UK to fail to prevent bribery by a person associated with it.[103] The associated person can be an employee, agent, subsidiary or supplier.[104] However, the Act also provides a defence for a commercial organisation if it can prove that it had adequate procedures in place designed to prevent persons associated with it from undertaking such conduct.[105] The government has published guidance about what 'adequate procedures' could be.[106] The guidance, *inter alia*, recommend companies to use due diligence mechanisms such as anti-bribery terms and conditions in their supply contracts.[107]

The interesting feature of this approach in terms of promoting CSR is that companies can protect themselves against liability through taking active steps to prevent bribery in their supply chain. The risk of liability combined with the defence of 'appropriate procedures' effectively forces companies to take measures aimed at preventing bribery in their supply chain. As the Bribery Act directly addresses the transnational corporations, it overcomes the limits caused by the territoriality principle and the

---

[102]   G. Sullivan, 'Legislative comment: The Bribery Act 2010: Part 1: an overview' (2011) *Criminal Law Review* 87, 89.

[103]   s7 (1) UK Bribery Act 2010.

[104]   s8 Bribery Act 2010. S8 (3) stipulates that an 'associated person' may (for example) be an employee, an agent or subsidiary. The list is non-exhaustive, as indicated by 'for example'. Suppliers can therefore be an 'associated person' for the purpose of ss7, 8 of the Act.

[105]   s7 (2).

[106]   s9 (1).

[107]   See Ministry of Justice, The Bribery Act 2010: Guidance about procedures which relevant commercial organisations can put into place to prevent persons associated with them from bribing (section 9 of the Bribery Act 2010) (March 2011) para 39 <https://www.justice.gov.uk/downloads/legislation/bribery-act-2010-guidance.pdf> accessed 24 June 2015.

separate legal personality. Transnational corporations cannot outsource their legal responsibility for bribery in their supply chain.

However, as this liability only concerns bribery, it will not force companies to address other CSR issues in their supply chain with the same caution. The range of CSR violations in their supply chain goes beyond the committing of bribery. It is a missed opportunity that the legislator did not follow the model of the Bribery Act for the UK Modern Slavery Act 2015. There was a discussion about how forced labour in the supply chain of UK-based transnational corporations should be addressed in the Act.[108] One of the options discussed was to create criminal liability modelled on the Bribery Act. However, this idea was eventually rejected and, instead, a supply chain transparency clause was included in the Act.[109]

# DISCLOSURE: CSR REGULATION THROUGH TRANSPARENCY

Corporate reporting on CSR, both mandatory and voluntary, has grown exponentially over the last years. Based on public pressure and reputational concerns, companies increasingly voluntarily report their engagement with CSR, including their global supply chains. However, NGOs often criticise these voluntary reports for being public relations instruments that are written in rather vague language and that are not verified. At the same time, mandatory reporting requirements have been an increasingly popular instrument for governments to require companies to report on their engagement with their social responsibilities.

In English law, the strategic report,[110] which was previously the business review,[111] has the purpose of informing members of the company how the directors have performed their duty under section 172 CA (duty to promote the success of the company). As this duty refers to a range of stakeholders, the strategic report could be an instrument to better promote CSR. In case of a quoted company, the strategic report must, to the extent necessary for an understanding of the development, performance or position of the company's business (a) include the main trends and factors likely to affect the future development, performance and position of the company's

---

[108] Joint Committee on the Draft Modern Slavery Bill, Draft Modern Slavery Bill: Report (Session 2013–14, HL Paper 166, HC 1019, April 2014) 85–90.

[109] s54 of the Modern Slavery Act 2015. The clause will be discussed in the next section.

[110] s414A CA.

[111] s417 CA.

business and (b) (i) include information about environmental matters (including the impact of the company's business on the environment), (ii) the company's employees and (iii) social, community and human rights issues, including information about any policies of the company in relation to those matters and the effectiveness of those policies.[112] However, if the review does not contain information regarding these issues, it must only state which of these categories it does not contain.

This last sentence of the section shows that quoted companies do not have to report on the range of CSR issues such as human rights in the strategic report as long as they declare that their report does not contain this information. This is a severe limitation for the promotion of CSR. In effect, the reporting about CSR is degraded to a voluntary exercise for directors. Moreover, the law remains very vague about what needs to be included in it. The danger is that directors can comply with their reporting duty even if they make rather neutral statements.[113] Research about the predecessor of the strategic report, the business review, confirms this sceptical view. A study by Villiers and Aiyegbayo, based on semi-structured interviews with key corporate governance actors such as investor relations managers and corporate governance directors from institutional investment firms, showed that the business review made little difference to the quality of reports.[114] The authors of this study conclude that companies are struggling to report effectively about their non-financial key performance indicators.[115]

The continuing debate about the need to require transnational companies by law to be more socially responsible has been taken up by the European Union. A new Directive on non-financial information disclosure, adopted in 2014, requires public-interest companies with more than 500 employees to disclose relevant and material environmental and social information in their annual reports from 2017 onwards.[116] The Directive stipulates that the annual report of these companies must include a non-financial statement containing information relating to at least environmental, social and employee matters, respect for human rights, anti-corruption and bribery matters.[117] This statement must include a description of the

---

[112]    s414C (7) CA.

[113]    C. Villiers, 'Narrative reporting and enlightened shareholder value under the Companies Act 2006' in J. Loughrey (ed.), *Directors' Duties and Shareholder Litigation in the Wake of the Financial Crisis* (Edward Elgar, 2013) 108.

[114]    C. Villiers and O. Aiyegbayo, 'The enhanced business review: has it made corporate governance more effective?' (2011) *Journal of Business Law* 699, 712.

[115]    (n 114).

[116]    Article 1 (1) (a) of the Directive.

[117]    (n 116).

policy pursued by the company in relation to these matters, the results of these policies and the risks related to these matters and how the company manages those risks. Companies that do not pursue policies in relation to one or more of these matters shall provide an explanation for not doing so.[118]

The Directive goes beyond the strategic report as it is more prescriptive and as it applies the 'comply or explain' approach to CSR reporting which means that companies have to give an explanation in case they do not pursue policies. Although the Directive fails to require external verification of the company's CSR reporting, it will expand the quantity of disclosure on those issues by transnational corporations. The Directive can create a level playing field among companies across the European Union as it expects companies to have a policy on CSR issues. Still, it remains to be seen to what extent companies are going to use this reporting duty as a genuine opportunity to openly and critically reflect on their CSR policies.

The increasing focus on global supply chains has led to the inclusion of a transparency-in-supply-chains clause in the Modern Slavery Act 2015.[119] This clause requires companies of a size that, at the time of writing, is yet to be determined to prepare a slavery and human trafficking statement for each financial year of the organisation.[120] In order to comply with this reporting duty, companies must either describe the steps that they have taken during the financial year to ensure that slavery and human trafficking is not taking place in any of their supply chains, and in any part of its own business, or make a statement that they have taken no such steps.

The strength of the transparency in supply chains clause is that it recognises the important role of transnational corporations for the eradication of forced labour in global supply chains. However, the clause is rather vague and leaves much discretion to the companies. It fails to establish a requirement that companies must have external third-party verification of their forced labour statement. It is likely that, in most cases, companies will be able to continue to report in the same way about how they combat forced labour in their supply chain as they already do in their voluntary CSR report. In actual fact, the transparency in supply chains clause resembles many features of the California Transparency in Supply Chains Act 2010 which, too, requires disclosure on the efforts of a company on combatting forced labour in its supply chain. However, it is also rather

---

[118]   (n 116).

[119]   s54 of the Act.

[120]   Home Office, 'Modern slavery and supply chains consultation' (12 February 2015) <https://www.gov.uk/government/consultations/modern-slavery-and-supply-chains> accessed 2 July 2015.

soft, with no enforcement power and no requirement to have the report externally verified.[121]

The various reporting requirements pertaining to CSR issues that have been introduced in the past years demonstrate that, at the moment, the legal regulation of CSR in global sourcing is primarily transparency laws. Whilst these initiatives are positive steps towards recognising that transnational corporations have social responsibilities for the working conditions at the factories of their foreign subsidiaries and suppliers, they all lack stringency.

## CONCLUSION

Recurrent reports about irresponsible corporate conduct by foreign subsidiaries and suppliers of Western transnational corporations demonstrate that the mainly voluntary, business-driven, private govern-ance regime of CSR in global production chains has failed. Transnational corporations are able to hide behind their foreign subsidiaries and sup-pliers. The division between the corporate headquarters in the global North and West and the production in the developing world presents challenges for the law to adequately address violations of CSR principles. Transnational corporations outsource both the production and the legal responsibility. Whilst foreign subsidiaries already pose a significant chal-lenge for holding transnational corporations as the parent companies legally accountable, this situation is even more difficult in case of suppliers which are owned by third parties.

Despite its weaknesses, the Accord on Fire and Building Safety in Bangladesh as multi-stakeholder initiative displays some features that future CSR regimes should build on such as its inclusion of different stakeholder groups and its access to remedies. However, two years since its development, no similar scheme for other countries and other CSR issues has been developed. The danger is that the Accord remains a single-issue initiative that resulted from significant public and political pressure in the wake of the Rana Plaza disaster.

In the absence of a binding international human rights framework for transnational corporations, there is a growing consensus that the home state of transnational corporations has got a more important role to play in the promotion of CSR. The home state could fill some of the legal

---

[121]    The Act is available at: <http://leginfo.ca.gov/pub/09–10/bill/sen/sb_0651–0700/sb_657_bill_20100930_chaptered.html> accessed 15 February 2015.

loopholes of global sourcing. However, at present, the regulation of CSR issues is focused on disclosure laws which are not stringent enough to ensure that transnational corporations go beyond their present efforts. The chapter has shown that tort law and corporate criminal law could be an important part of the legal promotion of CSR, as they have the potential to hold transnational corporations legally accountable for irresponsible conduct at factories run by subsidiaries and/or suppliers. However, in order to use their full potential, both areas need amendments in English law.

# PART II

# TNC BEHAVIOR AND STRATEGY IN THE 21ST CENTURY: INDUSTRY CASE STUDIES

# 8. How the transnational pharmaceutical industry pursues its interests through international trade and investment agreements: a case study of the Trans Pacific Partnership

*Deborah Gleeson, Pat Neuwelt,*
*Erik Monasterio and Ruth Lopert*

## INTRODUCTION

This chapter explores the strategies used by transnational pharmaceutical companies and their industry associations to advance their economic interests through international trade and investment agreements. We begin by characterizing the research-based pharmaceutical industry as a transnational industry with a concerted global agenda to expand and extend monopolies over its products, thereby increasing returns for its shareholders. We describe the broad set of strategies employed to meet these objectives. We then give an historical overview of attempts by the industry to use international trade agreements to expand intellectual property rights and constrain the operation of pharmaceutical coverage programs. Focusing specifically on the Trans Pacific Partnership Agreement (TPP), we explore the ways in which pharmaceutical industry bodies in the United States and other TPP countries have sought to influence the negotiations to further their agenda and protect and promote the industry's interests.

## THE PHARMACEUTICAL INDUSTRY AS A TRANSNATIONAL INDUSTRY

In this part of the chapter, we describe the large and growing market for medicines, and the nature and global distribution of the highly profitable industry engaged in research and development, manufacturing, sales and distribution of patented medicines. We focus particularly on the research-based pharmaceutical industry (hereafter, 'the pharmaceutical industry' or 'the industry') rather than generic medicines manufacturers.[1] The two parts of the industry have different objectives in relation to international trade agreements, and our purpose in this chapter is to explore the influence of intellectual property owners in the context of trade negotiations – in particular, the Trans Pacific Partnership Agreement.

## The Global Pharmaceutical Market

The global pharmaceutical market is large and reported to be expanding rapidly, with spending on pharmaceuticals estimated at US$965 billion in 2012 and likely to reach almost $1.2 trillion by 2017, according to projections by the IMS Institute for Healthcare Informatics.[2] While high-income countries account for most of the current spending on pharmaceuticals, expenditure growth in these countries has slowed in recent years due to a combination of factors including patent expiries, increasing use of generics, cost containment measures and the long term impact of the global economic crisis. Global pharmaceutical expenditure is expected to begin increasing after 2014, primarily due to fewer patent expiries.[3] It is expected to grow most rapidly in middle-income countries, particularly China, Brazil, Russia and India, as their economies and healthcare systems develop.[4] In 2012, originator products made up almost two-thirds of global spending on pharmaceuticals; however, future increased spending on generic medicines in emerging economies is expected to lead to generics making up a growing share of the market.[5]

Health expenditure generally accounts for a large proportion of each country's spending, and pharmaceutical expenditure in turn accounts for a large proportion of health spending. In 2012, the average expenditure on health for Organisation for Economic Co-operation and Development

---

[1]    We use the term 'research-based pharmaceutical industry' to refer to that part of the pharmaceutical industry which is engaged in research, manufacturing, promotion and sale of patented medicines. In many cases there is an overlap between the two parts of the industry, particularly given the increasing tendency towards mergers and acquisitions. Some generic manufacturers also hold secondary patents.

[2]    IMS Institute for Healthcare Informatics, 'The Global Use of Medicines: Outlook through 2017' (2013) <http://www.imshealth.com/deployedfiles/imshealth/Global/Content/Corporate/IMS%20Health%20Institute/Reports/Global_Use_of_Meds_Outlook_2017/IIHI_Global_Use_of_Meds_Report_2013.pdf> accessed 22 July 2015.

[3]    (n 2).

[4]    (n 2).

[5]    (n 2).

(OECD) countries was 9.3 per cent of GDP, with the United States (US) having the highest health expenditure at 16.9 per cent.[6] In the same year, OECD countries spent on average 15.9 per cent of their health expenditure (or $498 PPP per capita) on pharmaceuticals.[7]

**Nature and Global Distribution of the Pharmaceutical Industry**

While the pharmaceutical industry is transnational in nature, manufacturing and research and development (R&D) activity is concentrated in certain countries, notably the United States, Japan and France.[8] According to the International Federation of Pharmaceutical Manufacturers and Associations (IFPMA), Europe is the biggest exporter of pharmaceuticals.[9]

Publicly available statistics describing the state of the global research-based pharmaceutical industry are difficult to obtain – particularly aggregate data estimating profits and spending on marketing and promotion. To understand the shape and structure of transnational pharmaceutical companies, we must examine the configuration and activities of particular companies.

In stark contrast to the difficulty of obtaining data on sales, revenue and profits, figures for R&D spending abound. Industry reports suggest that almost $137 billion was invested in R&D by the 'research-based pharmaceutical industry' in 2012.[10] According to the IFPMA, R&D spending in the United States has steadily increased over a decade and a half, amounting to more than twice the spending of the National Institutes of Health by 2014.[11]

It is, however, very difficult to ascertain the actual costs of drug

---

[6] OECD, 'OECD Health Statistics 2014 How Does the United States Compare?' <http://www.oecd.org/unitedstates/Briefing-Note-UNITED-STATES-2014.pdf> accessed 13 August 2015).

[7] (n 6).

[8] IFPMA, 'The Pharmaceutical Industry and Global Health: Facts and Figures 2014' (International Federation of Pharmaceutical Manufacturers & Associations) 41 <http://www.ifpma.org/fileadmin/content/Publication/2014/IFPMA_-_Facts_And_Figures_2014.pdf> accessed 22 July 2015).

[9] (n 8) 46.

[10] Evaluate Pharma (2013), cited in International Federation of Pharmaceutical Manufacturers & Associations, 'The Pharmaceutical Industry and Global Health: Facts and Figures 2014' (IFPMA, 2014) <http://www.ifpma.org/fileadmin/content/Publication/2014/IFPMA_-_Facts_And_Figures_2014.pdf> accessed 22 July 2015).

[11] IFPMA (n 10) 13.

development. The few published estimates are highly contested. The most recent figure of $2.6 billion (representing an increase of 145 per cent over a decade) as the cost of bringing a new drug to market was estimated by the Tufts Center for the Study of Drug Development in November 2014.[12] This figure included around $1.4 billion in direct drug development costs and $1.2 billion in 'time costs' (i.e. the opportunity costs associated with foregone returns to investors during the development process).[13] The Tufts Center estimate has been heavily criticized, as the industry data on which it is based (provided by ten pharmaceutical companies) have not been made publicly available.[14, 15] In fact, the report itself has not yet been released; to date only a press release, slide show and background paper about the study's methodology have been made available.[16]

**Company Structures and Relationships**

As shown in the Pfizer example in Box 8.1, large transnational pharmaceutical companies tend to operate by establishing a large number of subsidiary organizations incorporated in different countries. The relationship between the subsidiaries and the parent company are often quite opaque. So, too, are the transfer pricing arrangements by which transnational pharmaceutical companies set the prices of the products they provide to their subsidiaries in other jurisdictions. Manipulation of transfer pricing (by setting arbitrary prices for intra-company transactions) has long been a strategy transnational corporations have used to minimise the profits of subsidiaries in higher tax countries while moving taxable income to countries with lower tax rates.[17]

---

[12]   Tufts Center for the Study of Drug Development, 'Briefing: Cost of Developing a New Drug', (2014) <http://csdd.tufts.edu/files/uploads/Tufts_CSDD_briefing_on_RD_cost_study_-_Nov_18,_2014.pdf> accessed 22 July 2015).

[13]   Tufts (n 12).

[14]   Knowledge Ecology International, 'KEI comment on the new Tufts Study on Drug Development Costs' <http://keionline.org/node/2127> accessed 13 August 2015).

[15]   Médecins sans Frontiéres, 'R&D Cost Estimates: MSF Response to Tufts CSDD Study on Cost to Develop a New Drug' <http://www.doctorswithout-borders.org/article/rd-cost-estimates-msf-response-tufts-csdd-study-cost-develop-new-drug> accessed 13 August 2015).

[16]   Tufts Center for the Study of Drug Development, 'Briefing: Cost of Developing a New Drug' (webcast) <http://csdd.tufts.edu/news/complete_story/cost_study_press_event_webcast> accessed 24 August 2015).

[17]   Harry Grubert and John Mutti, 'Taxes, Tariffs and Transfer Pricing in Multinational Corporate Decision Making' (1991) 73 *Review of Economics and Statistics* 285–293.

---

BOX 8.1    PFIZER: A CASE STUDY OF A TRANSNATIONAL
PHARMACEUTICAL COMPANY

As one of the world's largest pharmaceutical companies, Pfizer provides a useful case study demonstrating the transnational nature of the industry. Pfizer's head office is based in New York, but the majority of its manufacturing takes place in Ireland, representing an investment of over US$7 billion in that country.[18] Its Global Financial Services Centre and Global Treasury are also located there. The bulk of Pfizer's R&D activity, however, takes place in the United States and the United Kingdom. With almost 600 subsidiaries in many different countries,[19] Pfizer has grown to its current size partly through a large number of mergers and acquisitions – the most recent being Hospira, a large generic company acquired in 2015. For the first six months of 2014 Pfizer Inc. (the US parent company) reported revenues of more than $24 million and net income of over $5.2 million.[20] This represents a tiny fraction of the income of the global conglomerate. The combined reported revenues of Pfizer Inc. and its subsidiary companies were $49.6 billion in 2014, and its net income was $9.1 billion (18.4 per cent of revenues).[21] In November 2015, Pfizer announced its intention to merge with Allergan, a company based in Ireland, to create the world's biggest pharmaceutical company.[22] This merger, which would have enabled the establishment of the merged company's base in Ireland (which has a much lower company tax rate), was expected to reduce its US tax liability by tens of billions of dollars.[23] Plans for the merger were later abandoned following a change to US tax rules for corporations.[24]

---

[18]    Pfizer, 'About Pfizer in Ireland' <http://www.pfizer.ie/about_pfizer_in_ireland.cfm> accessed 24 August 2015.

[19]    US Securities and Exchange Commission, 'Company Search' <http://www.sec.gov/edgar/searchedgar/companysearch.html> accessed 22 July 2015.

[20]    (n 19).

[21]    Pfizer, '2014 Financial Review: Pfizer Inc. and Subsidiary Companies', 16.

[22]    Ransdell Pierson and Ankur Banerjee, 'Pfizer to buy Allergan in $US160 billion deal that will create world's largest drugmaker' *Sydney Morning Herald* (24 November 2015) <http://www.smh.com.au/business/world-business/pfizer-to-buy-allergan-in-us160-billion-deal-that-will-create-worlds-largest-drugmaker-20151123-gl63g8> accessed 28 February 2016.

[23]    Lynnley Browning, 'Pfizer seen avoiding $48 billion in tax through Allergan merger', *Sydney Morning Herald* 26 February 2016 <http://www.smh.com.au/business/world-business/pfizer-seen-avoiding-48-billion-in-tax-through-allergan-merger-20160225-gn46s3.html> (accessed 28 February 2016).

[24]    Charles Riley and Chris Isidore, 'Pfizer-Allergan merger scrapped after Obama cracks down on tax breaks', CNN Money, 6 April 2016 <http://money.cnn.com/2016/04/06/investing/allergan-pfizer-merger/index.html> (accessed 22 September 2016).

These practices recently came under scrutiny in Australia during a Senate inquiry into corporate tax avoidance. A Parliamentary Library report provided to the Senate Committee, according to a June 2015 article in the *Sydney Morning Herald*,[25] reported that 'The five biggest suppliers of publicly subsidised medicines in Australia recorded sales of nearly $5 billion last year but paid an average of just $10 million each in company tax.'

Pfizer was one of the companies brought before the Inquiry. Fairfax Media reported in 2014[26] that 'Pfizer's cost of sales as a percentage of revenues is four times higher in Australia than in the United States.' In a public hearing before the Senate Inquiry, representatives of Pfizer described the company's affiliations as follows:

> Pfizer Australia Holdings is owned by a combination of two Netherlands companies and a Luxembourg company. They hold particular portions of shares. The ultimate holding company of those companies is Pfizer Inc. That is a US company.[27]

Asked to describe the origins of the company's drugs, the Chairman and Managing Director of Pfizer Australia Pty Ltd responded: 'of 90 per cent of our medicines, 67 per cent come from Ireland; I think 14 per cent or 15 per cent from Singapore; and eight per cent from Spain; the other 10 per cent come from various sources.'[28]

Citizens for Tax Justice reported in 2014[29] that:

> Over the past five years for example, [Pfizer] has reported that it lost about $14.5 billion in the United States, while at the same time it earned about $75.5 billion abroad. Is the United States just a really bad market for Pfizer? It's unlikely given that Pfizer also reports that around 40 per cent of its revenues are

---

[25]   Heath Ashton, 'Pharmaceutical Companies Called on to Explain Tiny Tax Contribution' *Sydney Morning Herald* (3 June 2015) <http://www.smh.com.au/federal-politics/political-news/pharmaceutical-companies-called-on-to-explain-tiny-tax-contribution-20150602-ghf59s.html> accessed 14 August 2015.

[26]   Michael West, 'Pfizer is a Tax Fizzer' *Sydney Morning Herald* (20 May 2015) <http://www.smh.com.au/business/comment-and-analysis/pfizer-is-a-tax-fizzer-20150519-gh4t7t.html> accessed 14 August 2015.

[27]   Tony George, Head of Finance Operations, Australia and New Zealand, Pfizer Australia Pty Ltd, evidence to the Senate Economic References Committee Inquiry on Corporate Tax Avoidance. *Hansard* (1 July 2015) 4.

[28]   David Gallagher, Chairman and Managing Director, Pfizer Australia Pty Ltd, evidence to the Senate Economic References Committee Inquiry on Corporate Tax Avoidance. *Hansard* (1 July 2015) 6.

[29]   Richard Phillips, 'Why Does Pfizer Want to Renounce Its Citizenship?' *Citizens for Tax Justice* (30 April 2014) <http://www.ctj.org/taxjusticedigest/archive/2014/04/pfizer_is_a_bad_corporate_citi.php> accessed 14 August 2015.

generated in the United States. The more realistic explanation is that Pfizer is aggressively using transfer pricing and other tax schemes to shift its profits into offshore tax havens.

Pharmaceutical companies, such as Pfizer, also function as members of industry associations in the countries in which they are based. Operating as a collective of business interests, it is primarily through these associations that they exert influence on international trade agreements.

**Industry Associations**

The research-based pharmaceutical industry is represented by industry associations in many countries, such as the Pharmaceutical Research and Manufacturers of America (PhRMA) and the European Federation of Pharmaceutical Industries and Associations (EFPIA). The International Federation of Pharmaceutical Manufacturers and Associations (IFPMA) represents the industry's interests at the global level.

At the time of writing, PhRMA's membership included 31 biopharmaceutical (pharmaceutical and biotechnology) companies and 16 'research associate members'.[30] The membership of industry associations in countries like Australia and New Zealand is primarily comprised of subsidiaries of transnational pharmaceutical companies. For example, in 2014, at least 12 of Medicines New Zealand's 19 full member organisations were affiliated with corporations that were also members of PhRMA.[31]

## PHARMACEUTICAL INDUSTRY STRATEGIES TO MAXIMISE PROFITS

The business model of the pharmaceutical industry, which seeks to maximise profits and returns to shareholders, is often in direct conflict with the public health model, which focuses on the health, safety and well-being of entire populations. The two models do not sit comfortably together, and tension between them threatens the ability of governments to provide equitable and affordable healthcare for their citizens. Healthcare systems throughout the world rely heavily on medications and vaccines for preventing and treating infectious diseases and chronic health conditions.

---

[30]  PhRMA, '2015 Profile: Biopharmaceutical Research Industry' 61–62.
[31]  Pat Neuwelt, Deborah Gleeson and Briar Mannering, 'Patently Obvious: A Public Health Analysis of Pharmaceutical Industry Statements on the Trans Pacific Partnership International Trade Agreement' *Critical Public Health* (2015).

Expenditure on pharmaceutical products in the United States has increased exponentially in the past 15–20 years and accounts for a substantial part of healthcare expenditure.[32] Spending is largely driven by branded and patented drugs, which are generally priced much higher than generics, accounting for 20 per cent of prescriptions, but 80 per cent of costs.[33] In 2011, the National Health Service in the UK spent £13.6 billion (US$21 billion) on medicines, of which about £10 billion was spent on branded or proprietary products.[34] This problem of rising prescription drug costs has become a critical health policy issue. For example expenditure on just two new products used to treat hepatitis C, Sovaldi and Harvoni, amounted to $12.4 billion in the United States in 2014. Existing patents on the two products, held by the manufacturer, Gilead Sciences, will not expire until 2028.[35]

The extent to which the pharmaceutical industry strategy puts self-interest and profit ahead of public health has become the subject of specialized scientific enquiry attracting highly regarded researchers. In his recent book *Deadly Medicines and Organised Crime: How Big Pharma has Corrupted Healthcare*, Peter Gøtzsche (a physician and head of the Nordic Cochrane Centre) convincingly argues that the pharmaceutical industry has corrupted the scientific process to exaggerate the benefits and downplay the harms of its products.[36] Many other books and peer-reviewed articles, for example by Dr Ben Goldacre and the former editors of the *New England Journal of Medicine*, have reached similar conclusions and, in addition, provide comprehensive analysis of industry strategy to maximise profits.[37, 38, 39]

This section of the chapter describes the more common strategies

---

[32]   Aaron S. Kesselheim, 'Rising Health Care Costs and Life-Cycle Management in the Pharmaceutical Market' (2013) 10 *PLoS Medicine* <http://dx.doi.org/10.1371/journal.pmed.1001461> accessed 22 November 2016.

[33]   Kesselheim (n 32).

[34]   Association of the British Pharmaceutical Industry, 'UK NHS medicines bill projection 2012–15' (2015) <http://www.abpi.org.uk/our-work/library/industry/Pages/medicines-bill-projection.aspx> accessed 1 September 2015.

[35]   Jeffrey Sachs, 'The Drug That Is Bankrupting America' *Huffington Post* (16 February 2015) <http://www.huffingtonpost.com/jeffrey-sachs/the-drug-that-is-bankrupt_b_6692340.html> accessed 14 September 2015.

[36]   Peter C. Gøtzsche, Richard Smith and Rennie Drummond, *Deadly Medicines and Organised Crime: How Big Pharma Has Corrupted Healthcare* (Radcliffe London, 2013).

[37]   Ben Goldacre, Bad Pharma: How Drug Companies Mislead Doctors and Harm Patients (Macmillan, 2014).

[38]   Jerome P. Kassirer, On the Take: How Medicine's Complicity with Big Business Can Endanger Your Health (Oxford UP, 2004).

[39]   Marcia Angell, 'Drug Companies & Doctors: A Story of Corruption' (2009) 56 *New York Review of Books* 8.

employed by the pharmaceutical industry to maximise profits. The industry's substantial financial resources also enable it to further its own interests through extensive (and expensive) political lobbying. We do not attempt a comprehensive account here but provide some examples of the types of strategies used by the industry, in order to contextualise the industry's efforts in relation to trade agreements, specifically the Trans Pacific Partnership Agreement.

Landmark legal cases brought by the US Department of Justice have highlighted the extent to which the largest drug companies have repeatedly and systematically engaged in strategies of questionable legality to promote drug sales. These include ostensibly illegal promotion of medications for off-label uses, misrepresentation of research results, withholding data on harms, and Medicaid and Medicare Fraud.[40] These activities are widespread and recurrent. It is argued that some of these behaviours may be resistant to external regulatory approaches.[41, 42] In 2012 GlaxoSmithKline (GSK) agreed to plead guilty and pay a record $3 billion in penalties for unlawful promotion of prescription drugs, failure to report safety data, and false price reporting. It also signed a 123-page corporate integrity agreement with the US Department of Justice that regulates its activity for the next five years.[43] Of the top 10 drug companies, in July 2012 only Roche was not bound by such an agreement.[44]

Commenting on a recent legal case against AstraZeneca, US Attorney General Eric Holder said that illegal acts by drug companies 'can put the public health at risk, corrupt medical decisions by healthcare providers, and take billions of dollars directly out of taxpayers' pockets.'[45]

---

[40]   Peter C. Gøtzsche, 'Corporate Crime in the Pharmaceutical Industry Is Common, Serious and Repetitive' (2012) 345 *British Medical Journal* e8462.

[41]   Goldacre (n 30).

[42]   Aaron S. Kesselheim, Michelle M. Mello and David M. Studdert, 'Strategies and Practices in Off-Label Marketing of Pharmaceuticals: A Retrospective Analysis of Whistleblower Complaints' (2011) 8 *PLoS Medicine* 553.

[43]   US Department of Justice, 'GlaxoSmithKline to Plead Guilty and Pay $3 Billion to Resolve Fraud Allegations and Failure to Report Safety Data' (2 July 2012) <http://www.justice.gov/opa/pr/glaxosmithkline-plead-guilty-and-pay-3-billion-resolve-fraud-allegations-and-failure-report> accessed 15 September 2015.

[44]   Peter C. Gøtzsche, 'Big Pharma Often Commits Corporate Crime, and This Must Be Stopped' (2012) 345 *British Medical Journal*.

[45]   Janice Hopkins Tanne, 'AstraZeneca Pays $520 M Fine for off Label Marketing' (2010) 340 *BMJ*.

## Promoting Off-label Use of Medications

Off-label prescribing refers to the use of a medication outside the indications approved by the regulatory authority; it is costly, potentially harmful and of questionable benefit.[46] It is now clear that pharmaceutical companies strongly encouraged off-label prescribing at a time when this type of promotion was not permitted.[47] Pharmaceutical companies have extended sales into unapproved indications and drug doses; a series of recent publications based on the analysis of whistle-blower complaints, as well as civil and criminal charges, have exposed the use of systematic, sophisticated and far-reaching promotional methods.[48]

The significant worldwide expansion in the use of atypical antipsychotic medications for off-label indications illustrates the success of industry marketing strategies over evidence-based practice. Antipsychotic medications have a considerable side-effect burden and are intended for the treatment of psychoses and psychotic spectrum disorders, which are rare conditions affecting around 2 per cent of the general population. They are licensed for few additional indications and not for the bulk of the conditions for which they are prescribed.[49] Monasterio et al noted that:

> Antipsychotics global sales were US$25.4 billion and the seventh biggest therapeutic group in 2010; Seroquel™ (quetiapine), Zyprexa™ (olanzapine) and Abilify™ (aripiprazole) were the 5th, 10th and 13th biggest selling pharmaceuticals, with sales of US$6.8; US$5.7 and US$5.4 billion respectively. Even recent record-breaking fines imposed on the industry are unlikely to act as a significant deterrent in the face of such profitable sales.[50]

Pharmaceutical industry marketing appears to have influenced the rapid expansion in off-label prescribing of psychotropic drugs to paediatric and adolescent populations, often by overstating benefits and obscuring known harms.[51] This trend is occurring at a time when the US Food and Drug

---

[46]   Andrew McKean and Erik Monasterio, 'Off-Label Use of Atypical Antipsychotics' (2012) 26 *CNS Drugs* 383.

[47]   Kesselheim, Mello and Studdert (n 42).

[48]   (n 42).

[49]   McKean and Monasterio (n 46).

[50]   E. Monasterio and D. Gleeson, 'Pharmaceutical Industry Behaviour and the Trans Pacific Partnership Agreement' (2014) 127 (1389) *New Zealand Medical Journal* 6–12, 10.

[51]   Erik Monasterio and Andrew McKean, 'Use of Quetiapine in Child and Adolescent Populations–Response to Letter from Dr Lambe' (2013) 47 *Australian and New Zealand Journal of Psychiatry* 1084.

Administration (FDA), by virtue of a recent court decision[52] is planning to relax restrictions on off-label advertising,[53] despite being criticized for its poor monitoring of drug companies' promotion of on-label uses of medicines.[54]

### Medical Ghostwriting and Withholding Data on Harms

Medical 'ghostwriting', a mechanism by which pharmaceutical companies covertly author journal articles published under the bylines of academic researchers, has contributed to public health harms by manipulating research data.[55] For example, the influential Study 329, which stimulated the prescribing of Specific Serotonin Reuptake Inhibitors (SSRIs) to adolescents, was ghostwritten, over-stated benefits and withheld information on harms.[56]

### Outcome Reporting and Publication Bias in Industry-sponsored Trials

The pharmaceutical industry designs, funds and controls a significant proportion of medical research. It exerts considerable influence over the publication and dissemination of results, prescribing patterns, and the direction of subsequent clinical research. Although in the United States there are ethical and legal requirements to disclose research findings promptly, a recent report found that only 17 per cent of research funded by industry was published within the legally required one-year period.[57] Selective reporting bias increases the likelihood that interventions will appear to be effective and safe when they are not. A number of examples illustrate this point, including the following: misleading reports of the effectiveness

---

[52]   John Osborn. 'The FDA Settles With Amarin: Precursor To An Actual Policy On Off-Label Information?' http://www.forbes.com/sites/johnosborn/2016/03/10/the-fda-settles-with-amarin-precursor-to-an-actual-policy-on-off-label-information/#30b5a8bf2731 accessed 29 September 2016.

[53]   Ed Silverman. 'FDA to hold long-awaited meeting to review off-label marketing' https://www.statnews.com/pharmalot/2016/08/31/fda-off-label-marketing/ accessed 29 September 2016.

[54]   Tracy Hampton, 'Experts Weigh in on Promotion, Prescription of Off-Label Drugs' (2007) 297 *JAMA* 683.

[55]   Jeffrey R. Lacasse and Jonathan Leo, 'Ghostwriting at Elite Academic Medical Centers in the United States' (2010) 7 *PLoS Med* e1000230.

[56]   Joanna Le Noury, John M. Nardo, David Healy, Jon Jureidini, Melissa Raven, Catalin Tufanaru and Elia Abi-Jaoude, 'Restoring Study 329: Efficacy and Harms of Paroxetine and Imipramine in Treatment of Major Depression in Adolescence' (2015) *British Medical Journal* h4320.

[57]   Monique L. Anderson et al., 'Compliance with Results Reporting at ClinicalTrials.gov' (2015) 372 *New England Journal of Medicine* 1031.

of gabapentin (Neurontin) for a range of off-label indications; under-statement of the increased cardiovascular risk associated with the use of medicines like rosiglitazone (Avandia) (for type II diabetes) and rofecoxib (Vioxx) (as an anti-inflammatory); and withholding of clinical trial data regarding the limited efficacy of oseltamivir (Tamiflu) for the prevention and treatment of influenza. Each of these examples of the industry selec-tively reporting or misreporting its research findings has led to public harm and a considerable cost burden.[58]

**Life-cycle Management, 'Evergreening'**

Life-cycle management occurs when a manufacturer extends market exclusivity (and thus delays market entry of cheaper generic products) by applying a range of strategies that include slight changes to formula-tions or different salts of the same base, but without any requirement to show therapeutic superiority over the existing product. These new formulations can, nonetheless, be protected by additional patents. For example, eight commonly prescribed drugs subject to these evergreening strategies in the public hospital system of the canton of Geneva were estimated to cost an additional €30 million (over the generic selling price equivalent) between 2000 and 2008, without demonstrating any additional clinical benefits for the additional expenditure.[59] Lifecycle management of two medications (protease inhibitors) widely used worldwide for patients with HIV may extend their market exclusivity to 2028 – 12 years beyond the expiration of the patents on their base compounds.[60]

**Legal Action against Licensing Authorities**

In 2012 AstraZeneca filed a lawsuit against the FDA in a bid to delay the entry into the market of generic versions of the antipsychotic medication Seroquel. AstraZeneca argued that the generic versions should be required to carry the same warnings about the risks of high blood sugar levels

---

[58]   Peter Doshi, Tom Jefferson and Chris Del Mar, 'The Imperative to Share Clinical Study Reports: Recommendations from the Tamiflu Experience' (2012) 9 *PLoS Med* e1001201.

[59]   Nathalie Vernaz et al., 'Patented Drug Extension Strategies on Healthcare Spending: A Cost-Evaluation Analysis' (2012) 10 *PLoS Medicine* e1001460.

[60]   Tahir Amin and Aaron S. Kesselheim, 'Secondary Patenting of Branded Pharmaceuticals: A Case Study of How Patents on Two HIV Drugs Could Be Extended for Decades' (2012) 31 *Health Affairs* 2286–2294.

and suicidal ideation as the branded drug, and because these warnings were the result of the company's own clinical trials, they were protected by a marketing exclusivity period. Although the lawsuit was eventually unsuccessful, this approach highlights the pharmaceutical industry's strategies to maintain monopoly for their products.[61]

## Negotiating Settlements with Generic Companies

Despite the uncertain legal future of pay-for-delay settlements, manufacturers of originator medicines and generic-drug manufacturers continue to enter into arrangements whereby financial settlements leave the patents intact and the generic version off the market. These outcomes result in substantial costs to patients and payers.[62]

## Promotion

Recent estimates indicate that pharmaceutical companies spend as much as 25 per cent of their sales revenue on promotion and marketing – almost twice as much as they spend on R&D.[63] The range of promotional activities include intense marketing to medical students and residents, contributions to continuing medical education and the development of clinical practice guidelines, and, in the United States and New Zealand, direct-to-consumer advertising.[64] Pharmaceutical companies also commonly use drug coupons as a marketing tool to stimulate demand for brand-name medications and reduce patient cost sharing.[65]

'Disease mongering', a process that extends the boundaries of what is considered illness in order to expand markets for new products and medical interventions, is another tactic taken by the industry. It can include

---

[61]   Kurt R. Karst, 'DC Circuit Rules for FDA in SEROQUEL Exclusivity Case; AstraZeneca Not Entitled to 3-Year Exclusivity' *FDA Law Blog* <http://www.fdalawblog.net/fda_law_blog_hyman_phelps/2013/04/dc-circuit-rules-for-fda-in-seroquel-exclusivity-case-astrazeneca-not-entitled-to-3-year-exclusivity.html> accessed 22 September 2015.

[62]   Marc-André Gagnon and Joel Lexchin, 'The Cost of Pushing Pills: A New Estimate of Pharmaceutical Promotion Expenditures in the United States' (2008) 5 *PLoS Med* e1.

[63]   (n 62).

[64]   Emmanuel Stamatakis, Richard Weiler and John Ioannidis, 'Undue Industry Influences That Distort Healthcare Research, Strategy, Expenditure and Practice: A Review' (2013) 43 *European Journal of Clinical Investigation* 469.

[65]   David Grande, 'The Cost of Drug Coupons' (2012) 307 *JAMA* 2375.

turning ordinary ailments into medical problems, by promoting mild symptoms as serious and risks as diseases.[66]

## Lobbying for Expanded Intellectual Property Rights

Another strategy used by pharmaceutical companies to maximise profits and returns for shareholders – and a particularly important one in the context of the transnational corporation – is to lobby for expanded intellectual property rights, including patent extensions and longer periods of protection of clinical test data. This strategy has been pursued both within nation states (particularly countries with large pharmaceutical sectors) and at the global level through international trade agreements.

The justification for granting intellectual property rights is to provide incentives for investment in R&D.[67] 'The cost of developing a new drug is high and must be compensated in order to stimulate innovation, which is in the public interest', the argument goes. It is clearly in the interests of the research-based pharmaceutical industry to lobby for strong intellectual property protections in order to prolong their monopolies and exclude competitors from the market. However, there is a trade-off between providing monopoly rights and enabling access to affordable medicines.[68] Intellectual property rights are an imperfect instrument for promoting investment in R&D; while they may provide incentives for investment in therapies for chronic conditions in wealthy markets where there is a good return on investment, they do not stimulate development of vaccines and treatments primarily of benefit to people in developing countries.[69]

Jurisdictions where large transnational pharmaceutical companies are headquartered – particularly the United States, the European Union and Japan – tend to have stronger intellectual property protections for pharmaceuticals than countries that are primarily importers of medicines. But the global nature of the pharmaceutical industry and the availability of international trade agreements as a vehicle for altering domestic intellec-

---

[66]  Ray Moynihan, Evan Doran and David Henry, 'Disease Mongering is Now Part of the Global Health Debate' (2008) 5 *PLoS Med* e106.

[67]  Hans Löfgren and Philip Soos, 'Financing Pharmaceutical Research and Development: Alternatives to the Patent System', *The Politics of the Pharmaceutical Industry and Access to Medicines: World Pharmacy and India* (Social Science Press, 2013) 302–327.

[68]  Susan K. Sell, 'TRIPS-Plus Free Trade Agreements and Access to Medicines' (2007) 28 *Liverpool Law Review* 41.

[69]  Kenneth C. Shadlen et al., Globalization, Intellectual Property Rights, and Pharmaceuticals: Meeting the Challenges to Addressing Health Gaps in the New International Environment (Edward Elgar, 2011).

tual property settings is leading to the rapid spread of strong IPRs around the globe.

Taken together, these findings must caution against allowing greater influence to be exerted by the pharmaceutical industry, through weakening of government drug pricing and reimbursement policies and changes to intellectual property laws, pursued through trade and investment agreements. The industry's history of aggressively pursuing opportunities to expand markets and maintain high prices suggests that any opportunities presented by trade negotiations will be fully exploited.

## THE US PHARMACEUTICAL INDUSTRY'S ATTEMPTS TO INCREASE INTELLECTUAL PROPERTY PROTECTIONS AND INFLUENCE PHARMACEUTICAL COVERAGE PROGRAMS THROUGH TRADE AGREEMENTS: FROM TRIPS TO THE TPP

The World Trade Organization's TRIPS Agreement on Trade Related Aspects of Intellectual Property Rights (TRIPS), which came into force in 1995, represented a concerted and sustained effort by the pharmaceutical industry to achieve global harmonisation of intellectual property protections, which until then had been largely confined to developed countries.[70] Drahos describes how US pharmaceutical companies, including Pfizer, played a key role in campaigning for the inclusion of intellectual property rights within trade agreements – a campaign that was pursued largely through national and international industry bodies and conservative think tanks.[71] TRIPS represented a significant shift in global IP norms as it mandated 20-year patent terms for both product and process patents, in all fields of technology.[72] The global expansion of IP rights via TRIPS was hotly contested by non-government organisations and some developing countries, however, and this resulted in the inclusion of key flexibilities allowing nation states significant leeway to determine the implementation

---

[70]   (n 69).

[71]   Peter Drahos with John Braithwaite, 'Who Owns the Knowledge Economy? Political Organising Behind TRIPS' (2004) 32 *Corner House Briefing*.

[72]   Ellen F.M. 't Hoen, The Global Politics of Pharmaceutical Monopoly Power: Drug Patents, Access, Innovation and the Application of the WTO Doha Declaration on Trips and Public Health (AMB Publishers 2009) <http://apps.who.int/medicinedocs/documents/s20963en/s20963en.pdf>.

of the obligations in their respective domestic laws.[73] The rights of member countries to utilise these flexibilities were re-affirmed in the 2001 Doha Declaration on the TRIPS Agreement and Public Health.[74]

Despite TRIPS establishing significant standards of protection globally, it fell well short of both US and pharmaceutical industry aspirations, particularly as it provided phase-in provisions for less-developed states, some of which were major producers of generic medicines. The two decades since TRIPS have seen successive efforts to 'ratchet up' IP standards, effectively circumventing TRIPS through bilateral and plurilateral trade agreements, particularly those involving the US and the European Union.[75, 76] 'TRIPS-plus' IP provisions have been key elements of a US post-TRIPS agenda that effectively began with the Jordan-US free trade agreement (FTA) in 2000.[77] It has since advanced virtually unchecked, to the extent that the provisions of TRIPS seem modest in comparison with the US push in the TPP.

### The 'May 10' Agreement: A Brief Interruption to the IP Trajectory

A notable exception to this trend occurred in 2007 with the bipartisan New Trade Policy agreed between Congress and the White House. The so-called May 10 agreement moderated some of the more egregious IP demands pursued in US trade agreements, but was only available to some developing countries.[78] The former expansionist trajectory was quickly restored, with the Korea–US Free Trade Agreement (KORUS) (concluded

---

[73]  't Hoen (n 72). Even though the TRIPS Agreement imposed new standards of protection and enforcement of intellectual property, signatories nonetheless retained a number of important flexibilities in interpretation and implementation, including options to: determine the grounds for issuing compulsory licenses; allow parallel importation; apply general exceptions to infringement, such as 'early working' for regulatory approval of generic products (also known as the Bolar provision) or experimental use; and for developing countries, a longer transition periods for implementation of the treaty obligations.

[74]  Sell (n 68).

[75]  Peter Drahos, 'Four Lessons for Developing Countries from the Trade Negotiations over Access to Medicines' (2007) 28 *Liverpool Law Review* 11.

[76]  Ruth Lopert and Deborah Gleeson, 'The High Price of "Free" Trade: US Trade Agreements and Access to Medicines' (2013) 41 *The Journal of Law, Medicine & Ethics* 199.

[77]  Oxfam International, 'All Costs, No Benefits: How TRIPS-plus Intellectual Property Rules in the US-Jordan FTA Affect Access to Medicines' Oxfam (2007) <https://www.oxfam.org/sites/www.oxfam.org/files/all%20costs,%20no%20benefits.pdf> accessed 2 October 2015.

[78]  Lopert and Gleeson (n 76).

in 2007 and ratified in 2012) containing some extensive TRIPS-Plus provisions, despite South Korea's per capita GDP being roughly half that of the United States.[79]

### The Australia-US Free Trade Agreement: A New and Alarming Element

The negotiation of the Australia–US Free Trade Agreement (AUSFTA) in 2003–2004 represented a shift in an alarming new direction. The AUSFTA negotiations represented the first US bid to introduce provisions intended to directly influence the operation of a pharmaceutical coverage program of another country.[80] Through the AUSFTA, Washington attempted to undermine reimbursement formulary listing and pricing mechanisms and gain greater influence over pharmaceutical decision-making in Australia's national drug coverage program, the Pharmaceutical Benefits Scheme (PBS). The PBS is an effective monopsony and operates a closed formulary with strict cost effectiveness criteria as a prerequisite for listing medicines. The industry legitimised the pursuit of such provisions in a free trade agreement by claiming that the PBS represented a technical barrier to trade in the Australian market. Australia fended off this attempt, however, and successfully protected the drug selection and pricing mechanisms of the PBS, acceding only to changes in process and transparency, many of which were either already in process or planned. Nevertheless, the inclusion of provisions targeting a pharmaceutical coverage program set a highly unfortunate precedent, and the United States was able to introduce more intrusive provisions in the 2007 KORUS Agreement.[81]

### A Brave New World: The Trans Pacific Partnership

The commencement of the Trans Pacific Partnership negotiations in 2010 – an ambitious multilateral trade and investment agreement involving the United States and 11 other countries around the Pacific rim, in aggregate representing 40 per cent of the global economy – provided a new forum for the further expansion of IP protections. Not surprisingly, initial US proposals included a wide range of substantially TRIPS-plus (as well as AUSFTA and KORUS plus) provisions. Text leaked in February 2011 showed the US seeking to require parties to make patents available for new forms of existing products, without requiring any demonstration

---

[79]   (n 76).
[80]   (n 76).
[81]   (n 76).

of improved efficacy or performance, and the elimination of exclusions from patent–ability (preserved in both the AUSFTA and KORUS) for diagnostic, therapeutic and surgical methods of treatment. The leaked text also showed the US seeking extensions to patent terms to compensate both for delays in the granting of patents and in the marketing approval processes, with extensions required not just for molecule patents but also for method and use patents.[82] Other draft provisions included the elimination of pre-grant patent opposition; minimum periods of data exclusivity of five years for new products and three years for new uses of existing products;[83] and a patent linkage provision that included a requirement for drug regulatory authorities to scan for existing patents, provide notification to patent holders and delay marketing approval until the conclusion of dispute settlement proceedings.[84] The text also contained a placeholder for a separate data exclusivity provision for biologics to be added at a later stage. Washington, as anticipated, was seeking a period of 12 years, consistent with the period of exclusivity conferred on these products in the United States.[85]

In addition to expanding IP protections, successive leaked texts revealed US ambitions in relation to the pharmaceutical coverage programs of its TPP partners.[86] An initial US proposal for an annex to the 'Transparency' chapter ('the Transparency Annex'), applying to pharmaceutical products and medical devices, articulated a number of provisions intended to constrain TPP countries in setting drug coverage policies and their approaches to selecting and pricing the medicines to be covered.[87] While several TPP countries do not yet have coverage or reimbursement programs in place, the draft provisions appeared to target New Zealand's Pharmaceutical

---

[82]    (n 76).

[83]    Sean Flynn et al. 'Public Interest Analysis of the US TPP Proposal for an IP Chapter. Draft Version 1.3. 2011.'

[84]    Burcu Kiliç and Peter Maybarduk, 'Comparative Analysis of the United States' TPPA Intellectual Property Proposal and Australian Law' *Public Citizen* (29 August 2011).

[85]    Biologics are therapeutic products derived from living organisms and include drugs, blood products, tissues and vaccines. Biological medicines are typically much more expensive than small molecule chemically synthesized medicines and represent the fastest growing segment of the pharmaceutical market. In the United States biologics currently receive four years of data exclusivity and a total 12 years of market exclusivity.

[86]    'Transparency Chapter – Annex on Transparency and Procedural Fairness for Healthcare Technologies. [Leaked Draft Text]' (*Trans-Pacific Partnership*, 22 June 2011) <http://www.citizenstrade.org/ctc/wp-content/uploads/2011/10/Trans PacificTransparency.pdf> accessed 17 September 2015.

[87]    Lopert and Gleeson (n 76).

Management Agency (PHARMAC) and Australia's PBS. If agreed to, the provisions would have seriously circumscribed both these programs, and any program other TPP partners might have chosen to develop in future.

The US ambitions did not go unchecked, however. The final text of the Transparency Annex[88] reveals that many of the more problematic demands had been withdrawn or mitigated in the course of negotiations. The final Annex is largely similar to AUSFTA Annex 2-C, albeit capturing medical devices (although these are exempted for some parties including Australia and New Zealand) as well as medicines. While it will not require changes to Australia's PBS, it will require PHARMAC to introduce administrative changes including a review process and a specified timeframe for considering applications.

There has also been substantial evolution in the pharmaceutical provisions of the IP chapter, with leaks of later iterations of the text showing a significant degree of resistance among the other TPP parties. This resistance led to the tabling of a (largely TRIPS-consistent) counterproposal in 2013 and the withdrawal or moderation of some of the provisions in 2014.[89]

Nevertheless, text leaked by Wikileaks and published by Knowledge Ecology International in mid-2015 revealed that crucial elements of the US proposal had remained to the final stages of the negotiations.[90] By mid-2015, a key obstacle to the conclusion of the agreement lay with US demands for data exclusivity for biologics, despite suggestions of a US 'compromise' of eight years.[91] However, with the exception of Japan and Canada, this still represented a substantial increase in the monopoly periods for these very expensive products, with some TPP countries having only five

---

[88]   Trans Pacific Partnership, 'Annex 26-A: Transparency and Procedural Fairness for Pharmaceutical Products and Medical Devices', New Zealand Ministry of Foreign Affairs and Trade (26 January 2016) <https://www.mfat.govt. nz/assets/_securedfiles/trans-pacific-partnership/text/26.-transparency-and-anti-corruption-chapter.pdf> accessed 28 February 2016.

[89]   Krista Cox, 'TPP Negotiating Parties' Counterproposal to the US on Medicines Represents a More Flexible Approach' *Knowledge Ecology International* (14 November 2013) <http://www.keionline.org/node/1826> accessed 24 August 2015.

[90]   'May 11, 2015 Consolidated Text of Intellectual Property Chapter for TPP' *Knowledge Ecology International* <http://keionline.org/tpp/11may2015-ip-text> accessed 24 August 2015.

[91]   Burcu Kiliç and Courtney Pine, 'Decision Time On Biologics Exclusivity: Eight Years Is No Compromise' *Intellectual Property Watch* (27 July 2015) <http://www.ip-watch.org/2015/07/27/decision-time-on-biologics-exclusivity-eight-years-is-no-compromise> accessed 22 September 2015.

years of exclusivity in place, and others, none at all. Despite the US Trade Representative's ongoing push for prolonged exclusivity for biologics, successive White House budgets have sought a reduction of the term within the US from 12 to seven years. The 2016 White House budget proposal estimates that reducing data protection to seven years, together with prohibiting additional periods of exclusivity for biologics due to minor re-formulations, would save $16 billion in federal spending alone over the next decade.[92]

The final text of the TPP's intellectual property chapter[93] reveals that the initial US proposals were significantly pared back in the final stages of the negotiations. However, the pharmaceutical industry was successful in securing many provisions which extend and entrench monopoly periods, such as mandatory secondary patents (Article 18.37.2), patent term extensions (Arts. 18.46 and 18.48) and data exclusivity (Arts. 18.50 and 18.51). The final biologics provisions (Art. 18.51) are problematic and ambiguous, with a 'two-track' outcome that appears to commit parties to eight years of market exclusivity for biologics whichever option they choose. While several developing countries have secured transition periods to implement some of the chapter's more onerous provisions, these are both short and inflexible.

The TPP will also provide an opportunity for the pharmaceutical industry to contest future national pharmaceutical policy-making, which recent experience suggests will be quickly exploited. The TPP's investment chapter[94] includes an investor–state dispute settlement clause allowing foreign corporations to sue governments for monetary compensation if they perceive that a policy change has affected the value of their investments. Investments are defined very broadly and include intellectual property rights. Eli Lilly and Company, a US-based pharmaceutical company, has used a similar mechanism in the North American Free Trade Agreement (NAFTA) to seek CAD $500 million in compensation after Canadian courts invalidated patents for two of its drugs.[95]

---

[92]   United States Government, 'Fiscal Year 2016 Budget'<https://www.white-house.gov/sites/default/files/omb/budget/fy2016/assets/budget.pdf> accessed 24 August 2015.

[93]   Trans Pacific Partnership, 'Chapter 18: Intellectual Property' New Zealand Ministry of Foreign Affairs and Trade, 26 January 2016 <https://www.mfat.govt.nz/assets/_securedfiles/trans-pacific-partnership/text/18.-intellectual-property-chapter.pdf> accessed 28 February 2016.

[94]   Trans Pacific Partnership, 'Chapter 9: Investment' New Zealand Ministry of Foreign Affairs and Trade, 26 January 2016 <https://www.mfat.govt.nz/assets/_securedfiles/trans-pacific-partnership/text/9.-investment-chapter.pdf> accessed 28 February 2016.

[95]   *Eli Lilly and Co. v. The Government of Canada*, UNCITRAL, ICSID Case No. UNCT/14/2 <http://www.italaw.com/cases/1625> accessed 24 September 2015.

# THE PHARMACEUTICAL INDUSTRY: AGENDA SETTING IN THE TPP

### The Influence of Big Pharma over the TPP Negotiations

The pharmaceutical industry[96] has played a key role in shaping the US negotiating position in the TPP. This can be seen in the similarity between the initial US proposals for the intellectual property chapter of the TPP and the industry's submissions to the USTR advocating for strong IP protections.[97] Many commentators have suggested that the US proposals simply reflect an industry 'wish list'.[98, 99]

### How US-based industry sought to influence the TPP negotiations

The pharmaceutical industry actively tried to shape the US position through direct input to the negotiations via several of the 28 US trade advisory committees. PhRMA is represented on the Industry Trade Advisory Committee on Intellectual Property Rights (ITAC15)[100] which, at the time of writing, also had representatives from several pharmaceutical and biotechnology corporations including Gilead Sciences, Johnson and Johnson, as well as from the Biotechnology Industry Organization (BIO), but no representation from non-government organisations or academics. The Industry Trade Advisory Committee on Chemicals, Pharmaceuticals, Health/Science Products and Services (ITAC3)[101] and

---

[96] The biotechnology sector has also been very important in this context, and to a large extent their interests and activities overlap with those of the pharmaceutical industry. For the purpose of this chapter however, we focus specifically on the pharmaceutical industry.

[97] See, for example, 'PhRMA Written Comments Concerning the Proposed Trans-Pacific Partnership Free Trade Agreement with Singapore, Chile, New Zealand, Brunei Darussalam, Australia, Peru and Vietnam', *Docket Id: USTR-2009–0002* (2009) <http://infojustice.org/wp-content/uploads/2011/02/PhRMA-Comments-032009.doc>.

[98] Phillip Dorling, 'Trade Deal Could Be Bitter Medicine' *Sydney Morning Herald* (14 November 2013).

[99] Jeff John Roberts, 'Obama Trade Bill Would Boost Biotech Patents, Leak Suggests' *Fortune* (1 July 2015).

[100] US Department of Commerce and the Office of the United States Trade Representative, 'Industry Trade Advisory Committee on Intellectual Property Rights ITAC15' <http://www.ita.doc.gov/itac/committees/itac15.asp> accessed 16 July 2015.

[101] US Department of Commerce and the Office of the United States Trade Representative, 'Industry Trade Advisory Committee on Chemicals,

the Advisory Committee for Trade Policy and Negotiations[102] also include pharmaceutical company representation.

These committees are comprised of cleared advisors who have access to the negotiating texts on which they are providing advice.[103] An analysis of the membership of the trade advisory committees published in the *Washington Post* in February 2014[104] indicated that 85 per cent of the trade advisors on these committees were industry representatives. In response to criticism about the imbalance, in February 2014 the USTR belatedly announced that it would establish a 'Public Interest Trade Advisory Committee ('the Committee') to provide policy advice on issues involving trade and from the perspective of those concerned with public interest issues',[105] however this development has been greeted with some scepticism by non-government organisations regarding the extent to which this could truly rebalance the input to USTR decision-making.[106]

Other, less overt avenues of influence have also been demonstrated between the industry and the USTR. Confidential emails obtained by Intellectual Property Watch via a Freedom of Information Act request[107] have shown frequent informal interactions between industry executives (including pharmaceutical and biotechnology company executives) and

---

Pharmaceuticals, Health/Science Products and Services ITAC3' <http://www.ita.doc.gov/itac/committees/itac03.asp> accessed 16 July 2015.

[102]    Office of the United States Trade Representative, 'Advisory Committee for Trade Policy and Negotiations' <https://ustr.gov/about-us/advisory-committees/advisory-committee-trade-policy-and-negotiations-actpn> accessed 16 July 2015.

[103]    In July 2015, Politico reported that cleared advisors on the trade advisory committees had been provided with access to complete draft texts for the TPP. See Victoria Guida, 'USTR Clears Advisers to Read TPP Draft' *Politico* (9 July 2015) <http://www.politico.com/morningtrade/0715/morningtrade19070.html> accessed 16 July 2015.

[104]    Christopher Ingraham, 'Interactive: How Companies Wield Off-the-record Influence on Obama's Trade Policy' *Washington Post* (28 February 2014) <http://www.washingtonpost.com/blogs/wonkblog/wp/2014/02/28/how-companies-wield-off-the-record-influence-on-obamas-trade-policy/> accessed 16 July 2015.

[105]    Office of the United States Trade Representative, 'Requests for Nominations: Public Interest Trade Advisory Committee' Regulations.gov (25 February 2014) <http://www.regulations.gov/#!documentDetail;D=USTR-2014–0005–0001> accessed 16 July 2015.

[106]    Knowledge Ecology International, 'KEI Comments Regarding USTR Public Interest Trade Advisory Committee' *Knowledge Ecology International* (25 March 2014) <http://keionline.org/node/1983> accessed 16 July 2015.

[107]    William New, 'Confidential USTR Emails Show Close Industry Involvement In TPP Negotiations' *Intellectual Property Watch* (6 May 2015) <http://www.ip-watch.org/2015/06/05/confidential-ustr-emails-show-close-industry-involvement-in-tpp-negotiations/> accessed 16 July 2015.

USTR officials. One email from a senior USTR official specifically asked an industry executive to lobby New Zealand's trade minister for strong IP protections at an upcoming event; in another email exchange, an industry executive sent a draft of a lobbying letter to USTR seeking comment.[108] Most tellingly, large sections of many emails were redacted, suggesting the email exchanges included a significant amount of confidential information concerning the issues under negotiation – a level of information to which non-government stakeholders do not have access.

Commentators and researchers have also pointed out a longstanding 'revolving door' between USTR and the industry, with USTR staff frequently moving directly into industry from their USTR roles, and many USTR staff coming directly from industry positions.[109] The *Washington Post* reported in November 2013 that 'Since the turn of the century, at least a dozen USTR officials have taken jobs with pharmaceutical companies, filmmakers, record labels, and technology companies that favor stronger patent and copyright protection'.[110] The article documents several instances where longstanding, senior USTR officials had been engaged as pharmaceutical industry executives and vice versa.

The combination of close relationships between USTR and industry personnel, along with asymmetries in information access and opportunities for input between industry and non-industry stakeholders can be seen to lead to a situation of 'regulatory capture'.[111] An elite set of domestic industry stakeholders with vested interests and direct input to the trade negotiating process is able to effectively manipulate government processes for its own ends:

> This subset of IP stakeholders, with access to current information and the ability to discuss negotiating proposals with U.S. negotiators, is able to nudge the law in free trade agreements toward the kind of IP law they would prefer existed domestically. Accordingly, the making of international IP law has been captured through the U.S. trade negotiating regime.[112]

This regulatory capture is exacerbated by certain institutional and governance features of USTR:

---

[108]   New (n 107).

[109]   Margot E. Kaminski, 'The Capture of International Intellectual Property Law through the US Trade Regime' (2014) 87 *Southern California Law Review* 977.

[110]   Timothy Lee, 'Here's Why Obama Trade Negotiators Push the Interests of Hollywood and Drug Companies' *Washington* Post (26 November 2013).

[111]   Kaminski (n 109) 980.

[112]   Kaminski (n 109).

By statutory design and by some chance, the USTR is not subject to the same transparency, input or oversight requirements as other agencies. Consequently, the USTR is structurally subject to information capture by its limited industry advisors, with little or no countervailing textual input by opposing industries, the public, or public interest groups.[113]

The absence of transparency, in particular, undermines both account- ability and legitimacy with the public. At the international level, Kaminski argues that it 'co-opts the authority of the United States on the interna- tional stage for private interests'.[114] Jasso-Aguilar and Waitzkin observe that 'In many instances the U.S. government has acted more as a sales representative, aggressively promoting U.S. corporations' interests abroad, rather than as a political negotiator.'[115]

In addition to direct avenues of influence through the USTR, the indus- try also uses more traditional lobbying avenues. The Sunlight Foundation undertook an analysis of lobbying reports in 2014 and found that the pharmaceutical industry (including its industry associations) had been by far the most active industry in lobbying for the TPP:

> From 2009 until mid-2013 (the time during which the language of the agreement was still reasonably fluid), drug companies and associations men- tioned the trade agreement in 251 separate lobbying reports – two and a half times more than the next most active industry (at least measured by lobbying reports).[116]

As would be expected, PhRMA was the most vocal, topping the list of organisations (across all industries) with the most lobbying reports mentioning the TPP.[117]

The pharmaceutical industry spends large amounts of money on lobbying: data compiled by the Center for Responsive Politics indicates that the 'pharmaceuticals and health products' industry spent a total of almost $231 million on lobbying in 2014 alone, with PhRMA the

---

[113]   (n 109) 993.
[114]   (n 109) 1035.
[115]   Rebeca Jasso-Aguilar and Howard Waitzkin, 'Multinational Corporations, the State, and Contemporary Medicine' (2011) 20 *Health Sociology Review* 245, 249.
[116]   Lee Drutman, 'How Big Pharma (and others) Began Lobbying on the Trans-Pacific Partnership Before You Ever Heard of It', Sunlight Foundation (13 March 2014) <https://sunlightfoundation.com/blog/2014/03/13/tpp-lobby/> accessed 17 July 2015.
[117]   Drutman (n 116).

largest spender at $16.6 million.[118] Pfizer Inc. made over $1.5 million in campaign contributions (to both Democrats and Republicans) in the 2013–2014 financial year.[119] It is hardly surprising in this context that a key component of pharmaceutical industry strategy in the context of the TPP negotiations was to persuade members of Congress to write letters advocating for strong intellectual property protections, such as the 2011 letter from 40 Members of Congress to President Obama[120] and another in 2015 to Ambassador Froman, the United States Trade Representative.[121] Public interest organisation Knowledge Ecology International obtained, via a Freedom of Information Act request to the USTR, a total of 13 letters from members of Congress advocating for stronger monopolies on biologics sent during the period 27 July 2011 to 8 August 2013.[122]

### Pharmaceutical industry influence in countries other than the US

The degree of influence of the pharmaceutical industry over the negotiating positions of the other TPP countries appears to have been far more limited, with the possible exception of Japan, which has its own large, research-based pharmaceutical industry. Japan's domestic intellectual property laws already include a range of TRIPS+ intellectual property protections, and its negotiating position in the 2014 leaked TPP intellectual property chapter was more closely aligned with the US position than that of any of the other countries (and *vice versa*).[123]

In Australia and New Zealand, the local industry associations (Medicines Australia and Medicines New Zealand) have both echoed some of PhRMA's demands in the TPP. For example, for some years, Medicines Australia has been lobbying for extensions to data protection, particularly

---

[118] Center for Responsive Politics, 'Pharmaceuticals/Health Products Industry Profile 2014' <http://www.opensecrets.org/lobby/indusclient.php?id=h04&year=2014#> accessed 17 July 2015.

[119] (n 118).

[120] Letter from 40 Members of Congress to President Obama, 27 July 2011 <http://phrma.org/sites/default/files/pdf/ttpbioletterfinal072711.pdf> accessed 24 September 2015.

[121] Letter from 11 US Senators to Ambassador Froman, United States Trade Representative, 15 May 2015 <http://www.phrma.org/sites/default/files/pdf/051315-tpp-biologics-letter-to-ustr.pdf> accessed 24 September 2015.

[122] Knowledge Ecology International, 'Money Speaks: USTR Releases Letters from Congress Backing PhRMA on Exclusive Rights Biologic Test Aata in TPP' KEI (4 August 2014) <http://www.keionline.org/node/2069> accessed 17 July 2015.

[123] 'US and Japan Lead Attack on Affordable Cancer Treatments' Wikileaks (16 October 2014) <https://wikileaks.org/tpp-ip2/attack-on-affordable-cancer-treatments.html> accessed 17 July 2015.

following the failure to gain any ground in the Australia–US Free Trade Agreement.[124] Medicines New Zealand has been primarily seeking changes to PHARMAC's processes, arguing for greater transparency and industry input to decision-making.[125]

## PHARMA LOBBYING AND THE USE OF DISCOURSE

The patent-holding pharmaceutical industry uses a particular common rhetoric in its efforts to influence trade negotiations. The language used entirely masks its business interests. Instead, it promotes the industry as working in the interests of national, even international, economic development and in favour of population health.

### Framing the Issues as Problems: TPP as the Solution

In a study of industry discourse with regard to the TPP, Neuwelt, Gleeson and Mannering asked the question 'How has the industry used language and ideas to attempt to influence the TPP negotiations?'[126] We undertook a critical discourse analysis[127] of publicly available texts about the TPP produced by peak bodies representing the Industry in the United States and New Zealand (NZ): the Pharmaceutical Research and Manufacturers of America (PhRMA) and Medicines New Zealand (Medicines NZ, formerly the Researched Medicines Industry or RMI). Documents analysed included submissions to trade negotiating authorities, media releases and annual reports. Documents dated between November 2008 and March 2013 were identified through website searches.

We found that PhRMA and Medicines NZ portrayed the TPP provisions as needing to address a number of 'problems'. First, the TPP would tackle the supposed 'unfair' treatment of the industry by governments (outside of the

---

[124] 'An Open Letter to the Australian Parliament: Australia's Economic Prosperity Relies on Innovation and Innovation Needs Strong Intellectual Property Protections' AusBiotech, Research Australia and Medicines Australia (20 March 2015) <http://www.researchaustralia.org/documents/item/714> accessed 17 July 2015.

[125] Media release: 'Access to Medicine and the Trans-Pacific Partnership' Medicines New Zealand (2 October 2012) <http://www.medicinesnz.co.nz/mediareleases/> accessed 17 July 2015.

[126] Pat Neuwelt, Deborah Gleeson and Briar Mannering, 'Patently Obvious: A Public Health Analysis of Pharmaceutical Industry Statements on the Trans-Pacific Partnership International Trade Agreement' (2015) *Critical Public Health* <10.1080/09581596.2015.1022510> accessed 24 September 2015.

[127] Carol Bacchi, *Women, Policy and Politics* (Sage Publications, 1999).

United States), and the resulting restricted access to 'innovative medicines'. Second, the TPP would address the US economic crisis, in part by expanding the US-based patent-holding pharmaceutical industry. These 'problems', for which the TPP was regarded as the solution, were framed in particular ways. The industry was personified as the victim of unfair treatment, as the protector of the public good and as economic saviour for the US (and later, for other nations as well). These were the major discourses identified.

### 'The Unfair Treatment of the Industry'

The industry personified itself as comprised of 'researchers and innovators', who have received inequitable treatment by governments in comparison to the generic pharmaceutical industry. In so doing, its business agenda remained hidden, in the interests of persuading negotiators and government ministers that the United States is a victim of other nations' overly restrictive regulatory environments. As each nation applied to the Office of the USTR to enter into the TPP negotiations, PhRMA made a submission critiquing that nation's 'climate for innovative medicines', identifying the ways its regulatory environment unfairly limited the US industry's ability to market 'new' medicines. Further, PhRMA expressed clear expectations that the TPP provisions would ensure that no TPP nation could offer preferential regulatory treatment to its own local pharmaceutical manufacturers, over US-based transnational pharmaceutical companies.

PhRMA's call for stronger intellectual property protections was said to be a response to the 'need to be doing more to champion researchers and innovators who rely on strong [intellectual property] protections'.[128] These 'people' were represented to be victims whose rights have not, to date, been adequately protected by governments beyond the United States. In a 2009 submission to the USTR, PhRMA stated:

> PhRMA believes that the TPP FTA negotiations [. . .] could help ensure that US-based biopharmaceutical products have as fair and equitable access to foreign markets as foreign products have to ours.[129]

---

[128] Media release: 'PhRMA Urges Trans-Pacific Partnership Negotiators to Adopt a Strong Intellectual Property Framework' PhRMA (5 March 2013) <http://www.phrma.org/press-release/phrma-urges-trans-pacific-partner ship-negotiators-to-adopt-a-strong-intellectual-property-framework> accessed 20 August 2015.

[129] 'PhRMA Written Comments Concerning the Proposed Trans-Pacific Partnership Free Trade Agreement with Singapore, Chile, New Zealand, Brunei Darussalam, Australia, Peru and Vietnam' PhRMA (3 November 2009) <http://

This language of fairness and equity extended to the framing of PHARMAC activities in New Zealand. In a 2008 submission about the TPP to the Ministry of Foreign Affairs and Trade, the Researched Medicines Industry Association (Medicines NZ's predecessor) complained about perceived inequities in PHARMAC's processes. It cast the industry in the role of victim and suggested a punitive (and therefore unfair) motive for PHARMAC's activities.

### 'The Industry as Global Protector of Patient Rights, Public Good and Economic Development'

In both PhRMA and Medicines NZ documents discussing the TPP, the industry presented PHARMAC's processes as a breach not only of industry rights, but also of patient rights – by delaying patient access to newer, so-called innovative medicines. It failed to mention the inequitable impact of high-cost medicines, in general, and on people's access to medicines. Further, the industry represented itself as contributing to the global public good, and to US economic security, through the development of new medicines. In positioning itself as protector of the public good, PhRMA used language to set up a 'crisis' that PhRMA, through the TPP, would solve. For example, PhRMA referred to itself as 'offering new hope to those suffering from life-threatening disease or disability'.[130] The sense of urgency created in language, such as 'timely access to medicines for patients', framed stronger IP protection as being imperative in order to save lives now.

What remains unsaid is that every day of delay in getting a medicine to market costs the industry millions of dollars in revenue. Further, claims about the TPP leading to economic growth, jobs and prosperity in the TPP countries were often made in the same sentences as claims about health outcomes. The TPP was presented as a 'win–win' for population health and economic development:

> Such policies will help ensure timely patient access to advanced life-saving medical discoveries, support improvements in quality of life and productivity, and serve as an engine for future economic growth.[131]

---

infojustice.org/wp-content/uploads/2011/02/PhRMA-Comments-032009.doc> accessed 24 August 2015.

[130]   Jay Taylor (13 January 2012) 'PhRMA letter to the Office of the US Trade Representative' in response to USTR Request for Request for Comments on Mexico's Expression of Interest in the Proposed Trans-Pacific Partnership Trade Agreement Fed. Reg. 76479 (7 December 2011).

[131]   PhRMA (n 129).

In a US Business Association letter to the US president, PhRMA made unsubstantiated claims that all trading nations would benefit equally from the TPP, as in the following quote:

> the adoption of strong IP protections by all countries in the TPP more widely promotes strong benefits for all[132]

Medicines NZ also claimed that stronger IP protections in the TPP would explicitly benefit the New Zealand economy. However, since the pharmaceutical industry in NZ largely comprises branch offices of transnational corporations, the talk of harnessing innovative ideas for NZ's economic benefit obscures the real transnational beneficiaries of such arrangements.

### Re-defining 'Access to Medicines' in Its Own Interests

The study found that PhRMA and Medicines NZ had redefined the term 'access to medicines' to mean 'access to new (on-patent) medicines'. The term usually refers to people having equitable access to affordable medicines. Access to medicines is generally defined by organisations such as the World Health Organization in terms of 'equitable availability and affordability of essential drugs'.[133] The industry's reconstruction of the term was designed to gain support from clinicians, policy-makers and politicians; perhaps also from patient groups concerned about access to new medicines, for example for rare diseases. The conflation of terms, or intentional re-construction of their meaning, is evident in a recent Medicines NZ study. The term 'waiting list', usually reserved for patients waiting to receive healthcare, is used to refer to the 'unfair' time that medicines wait for public funding by PHARMAC in New Zealand.[134]

Neuwelt, Gleeson and Mannering noted that the industry's personification of itself as both victim (of regulation) and protector (of patients, of a healthy economy) appeared to be directed at a number of audiences. While discourses were aimed at convincing the Office of the USTR to prosecute

---

[132]  Media release: 'PhRMA Urges President Obama to Secure an Ambitious Trans-Pacific Partnership Agreement' (PhRMA, 8 May 2012) <http://www.phrma.org/media/releases/phrma-urges-president-obama-secure-ambitious-trans-pacific-partnership-agreement> accessed 20 August 2015.

[133]  World Health Organization, 'How to Develop and Implement a National Drug Policy' (2003) <http://www.who.int/management/background_4b.pdf> accessed 20 August 2015.

[134]  Jacqueline Barber and Kevin Sheehy, 'Uptake of New Medicines in New Zealand: Evidence of a Waiting List' (2015) 128 (1412) *New Zealand Medical Journal* 10.

its case in the negotiations, some were also aimed at the medical profession, patient groups lobbying for increased access to high cost new medicines, and members of the US Congress. The industry's use of language to appeal to a sense of 'fair play' in international trade actually obscured that the policies promoted by industry would likely have the effect of decreasing access to medicines and health equity for already-disadvantaged population groups.[135, 136] The industry's agenda for the TPP would reduce access to medicines globally, by ensuring that the IP rights of the industry are paramount to the rights of patients to be able to access affordable medicines.

The discourses identified by Neuwelt, Gleeson and Mannering continue to be evident in industry statements on the TPP since 2013. In fact, the industry language is also evident in politicians' letters to President Obama about pharmaceutical patent protection in the TPP, USTR reports and even in leaked TPP chapters. Industry influence in the negotiations, direct and indirect, is expressed in the similarity of the language and ideas presented in each. Some examples will now be provided.

The PhRMA website[137] contains articles which make strong assertions about biologics. A US proposal to extend the period of data exclusivity on biologic medicines was still 'on the table' in the TPP negotiations at the final stages. However, even more pertinent to this discussion are the letters to the US President or to the USTR about the TPP published on the website. Eighteen letters dated between 2011 and 2015, and signed by governors, senators and other members of Congress, strongly urged the US President or the USTR to ensure 12 years of exclusivity for biologic drugs as part of the intellectual property settings in the TPP. By 2015, for the first time, the letters contained national figures on biopharmaceutical industry employment and economic output, suggesting increasing PhRMA desperation to influence this aspect of the negotiations. Discourses in the letters parallel those of the industry, as is evident in the following excerpt from a May 2015 letter signed by 11 US senators:

---

[135]    Deborah Gleeson, Ruth Lopert and Papaarangi Reid, 'How the Trans Pacific Partnership Agreement could undermine PHARMAC and Threaten Access to Affordable Medicines and Health Equity in New Zealand' (2013) 112 *Health Policy* 227.

[136]    Erik Monasterio and Deborah Gleeson, 'The Trans Pacific Partnership Agreement: Exacerbation of inequality for patients with serious mental illness' (2014) 48 *Australian and New Zealand Journal of Psychiatry* 1077.

[137]    Pharmaceutical Research and Manufacturers of America <http://www.phrma.org/> accessed 5 August 2015.

The US innovative biologics industry supports 3.4 million US jobs and exports of $50 billion worth of medicines each year. These treatments offer new hope to patients suffering from cancer, arthritis, and rare diseases . . . Biologics are the future of medicine . . . Not offering adequate protections that will continue to spur innovation and investment will ultimately lead to companies taking fewer risks, and patients globally not receiving treatments that may have been developed under an appropriate standard. We strongly believe that standard should be 12 years.[138]

The industry discourse was also mirrored by the Office of the USTR in its 2015 annual Special 301 Report dealing with intellectual property issues. PHARMAC was explicitly identified as a target:

With respect to New Zealand, U.S. industry has expressed serious concerns about the policies and operation of New Zealand's Pharmaceutical Management Agency (PhARMAC), including, among other things, the lack of transparency, fairness, and predictability of the PhARMAC pricing and reimbursement regime, as well as the negative aspects of the overall climate for innovative medicines in New Zealand.[139]

The industry language of 'negative climates for innovative medicines' had been adopted, along with the discourse of equity with regard to pharmaceutical regulations.

## CONCLUSION

The contemporary large pharmaceutical company is typically a transnational conglomerate with a head office in one state, R&D and manufacturing activities in several and a large number of subsidiaries scattered across the globe. These corporations and their industry associations employ a variety of strategies to maximise their profits and the returns for their shareholders.

An increasingly important strategy for the industry is the pursuit of expanded intellectual property rights at the global level through international trade agreements. Trade negotiations provide fertile ground for pharmaceutical industry lobbying, particularly in the United States

---

[138] Senator Rob Portman et al., 'Letter from US Senators to USTR about the TPP and Biologics' (13 May 2015) <http://www.phrma.org/sites/default/files/pdf/051315-tpp-biologics-letter-to-ustr.pdf> accessed 20 August 2015.

[139] Michael Froman, '2015 Special 301 Report' Office of the United States Trade Representative (25 April 2015) <https://ustr.gov/sites/default/files/2015-Special-301-Report-FINAL.pdf> accessed 20 August 2015.

where regulatory capture is enabled by close relationships between the trade negotiating authority and industry, opaque negotiating processes, and advisory structures that allow privileged access to industry. The consequences of this capture can be seen in the 'ratcheting up' of IPRs in successive US free trade agreements, culminating in the US proposals for the Trans Pacific Partnership.

The industry also employs a range of rhetorical devices and discursive flourishes – terms such as 'access to medicines' and 'win–win outcomes' – to persuade policy-makers to adopt its proposals, while attempting to obscure its strategic objectives in the TPP negotiations. Much of this rhetoric has been reflected in recent letters from members of Congress to President Obama, as well as in the negotiating positions taken by USTR, indicating that it has been influential at least in the US. This rhetoric, however, has been contested in many of the non-US TPP countries, which generally put up strong resistance to the US proposals, at least until the late stages of the negotiations. Despite this resistance and the resulting mitigation of some provisions, many key objectives of the pharmaceutical industry were still achieved in the final text of the TPP.

# 9.    A case in supply chain and business sustainability: Samsung's management of human rights in consumer electronics manufacturing

*Anna Chou*


## INTRODUCTION

The United Nations's Universal Declaration of Human Rights[1] proclaimed the world's obligation to combat human rights abuses in 1948. Actors on the global stage are now accountable for human rights abuses in a number of different ways. In today's globalized economy, though national sovereigns remain primarily responsible for the protection of human rights, transnational corporations (TNCs) also have a responsibility to respect human rights in their business operations. John Ruggie's 'Protect, Respect and Remedy' framework outlines principles for collaboration among States and corporations.[2] In particular, TNCs should evaluate and manage potential implications of their activities on human rights. Ruggie promotes that companies 'must take proactive steps' by performing 'human rights impact assessments' and integrating human rights policies.[3] Specifically, they should define initiatives in their corporate social responsibility (CSR) programs.

The basic idea of corporate social responsibility is that business decisions can be more than completely self-serving. Companies use CSR strategies to address social and environmental concerns while simultaneously pursuing business objectives.[4] CSR challenges the traditional definition of marketing because the impact and intention extends beyond the

---

[1]  'Universal Declaration of Human Rights' UNGA Res 217 A(III) (10 December 1948).

[2]  John Ruggie, 'Protect, Respect and Remedy: a Framework for Business and Human Rights' 7 April 2008. *Human Rights Council*, Eighth session, agenda item 3. <http://shiftproject.org/publication/protect-respect-and-remedy-framework-business-and-human-rights> accessed 16 October 2014.

[3]  Ruggie (n 2) 18.

[4]  Keith Davis, 'Can Business Afford to Ignore Social Responsibilities?' (1960) 2/3 *California Management Review* 70.

relationship of the consumer and corporation to the world at large. The typical understanding of marketing is an exclusive relationship between a company and its target consumer. Marketing campaigns are for economic gains, an extrinsic motivation for enterprises. CSR, however, is about accomplishing a good in addition to profit.

The global consumer electronics supply chain requires consideration of human rights impacts because of concerns for conflict minerals and worker conditions. The need for minerals ties many actors and interest groups into a complex problem in the consumer electronics industry. Mineral sourcing raises issues of the political economy, consumerism and profit-driven decision-making. Among the many stakeholders, manufacturing companies emerge as very important players. Their operations depend on minerals as production inputs. This case study evaluates Samsung Electronics's efforts to prevent human rights abuses in its supply chain. The profits earned from selling minerals to Samsung can be connected to violence in the Democratic Republic of Congo (DRC) and surrounding countries. Human rights considerations concern the relationship between mineral trade and civil conflict as well as worker rights more broadly. First, an overview of conflict minerals provides the foundation for this discussion. This evaluates the local and political structure in the DRC. The problem arises from conditions in the local area but is further fueled by consumers and corporations from afar. Understanding the nature of this issue frames it as a corporate social responsibility concern. After establishing the need to address conflict minerals, codes of conduct and publications from the United Nations, the International Conference of the Great Lakes Region, and national governments provide a framework for approaching the problem. These guidelines establish a reference point to judge and analyze Samsung's actions. Samsung's own 2014 sustainability report was the primary source used to understand its CSR activities. This study answers the question of how a company can set up its strategy and operations to protect against human rights risks in its supply chain.

Case studies serve to spark a conversation and provoke further critical thinking. Reading theoretical literature on conflict mineral management and evaluating its practical application through Samsung's business strategy introduces readers to the tradeoffs in CSR strategies. It demonstrates that key values can conflict with each other, inviting readers to contemplate different facets of the decision-making and judgment process. Specifically, modern-day supply chain analyses demand a comparison of the cost of human rights violations against business profits. Furthermore, how can a firm's culpability for human rights abuses be calculated in a multi-linked and global supply chain? Finally, what intrinsic responsibilities do corporations hold while courting consumer demand? In hard circumstances, deciding on the best practice is a difficult task. First, without an overarching governing body, planning and executing a solution is challenging. Second, it is not easy to confirm if a particular plan of action was the best choice. Nevertheless, regardless of actually achieving the optimal result, it is important for firms to at least aspire to it.

## EXPLAINING THE CORE ISSUE OF CONFLICT MINERALS

Before evaluating potential solutions and ensuing actions, we must first understand the nature of a problem. This phenomenon affects all players in the consumer electronics market. In this chapter, the term 'conflict minerals' describes minerals that are connected to human rights abuses in the Democratic Republic of Congo and surrounding countries. The production of modern-day technological devices demands four key minerals: gold, tantalum, tungsten and tin.[5] The DRC is abundant in these resources. However, these inputs are linked to armed groups and their ensuing violence in Congo. These rebel groups, not affiliated with the political sovereign, campaign for self-serving economic and political objectives. The story starts in 1996 with a political and ethnic war between the Rwandan faction and the Congolese regime. The dispute evolved into a competition for control of the DRC's natural resources. Three major groups vied for control in Congo: the Rwandan Hutu Democratic Forces for the Liberation of Rwanda (FDLR), the Rwanda and Uganda-backed M23, and various local 'Mai Mai' groups.[6] Since, efforts from the Congolese government and the United Nations ended the activities of M23 in 2013. Rebel groups need financial resources to perpetuate their campaigns and activities. The minerals in Congo are a major source of revenue for these groups. Competing against other armed groups, they use violence and intimidation tactics to maintain control of mines, resulting in disturbing human rights violations. These include murder, rape, child labor and recruitment of youth soldiers. Sales of minerals further sustain these atrocities. Rebel groups control and tax the mines as well as the illegal smuggle points.[7] Because these minerals are in such high demand, trade is very lucrative. This income equips them

---

[5]   Enough Project, 'Conflict Minerals 101' 18 November 2009. <https://www.youtube.com/watch?v=aFsJgcoY20> accessed 24 July 2014.

[6]   Enough Project, 'Armed Groups' *Raise Hope for Congo*, 2014 <http://www.raisehopeforcongo.org/content/armed-groups> accessed 10 August 2014.

[7]   (n 5).

with more weapons and influence, further strengthening their ability to terrorize civilians. Estimates predict that armed rebel forces collectively funnel about US$183 million each year,[8] an ample budget for continuing their activities. Conflict minerals taint the electronics supply chain with human rights abuses at the beginning acquisition stage.

The consumer electronics supply chain has several links. Conflict minerals are raw resources at the very beginnings of the supply chain. After their extraction in the DRC and the surrounding areas, minerals are sent to smelting companies in Thailand, Malaysia, China and India.[9] Smelters combine large stocks of minerals during processing. There is no discrimination among minerals imported from around the world. As a result, supply-chain tracking is challenging. The smelting process combines original inputs from many different mines. Once the minerals are smuggled out of Congo and accepted by smelters in Asia, there is no way to distinguish between the conflict-free and conflict minerals. Therefore, the refined forms of tin, tantalum, gold and tungsten have unknown levels of conflict-sourced inputs. Mineral tracing would have to follow resources from their origins at the mines to smelters and suppliers before reaching consumer electronics manufacturers. This multi-step processing chain complicates attempts to remain conflict free.

Because the global supply chain network is distant and widespread, it creates an illusion of moral disconnect, forming a screen that absolves actors of their responsibility. The problem is geographically far removed, which creates a misleading psychological effect. Because corporations and consumers do not see or experience the violence in Africa, the issue seems less pressing. However, location is a morally arbitrary factor. Geographic distance does not dilute the intensity of human rights atrocities happening in the Democratic Republic of Congo. Consumers who demand these products are physically far removed from the effects in the DRC. Yet, their connection to conflict minerals is very direct. Furthermore, the complexity of having many actors obscures the responsibility of each. Actors in the supply chain might try to assign fault to others also involved. Therefore, they are less likely to initiate resolution. The lack of ownership in the supply chain thus perpetuates the conflict mineral crisis.

---

[8]    Mike Ramsdell, 'Reality is a Simple Story Realized – Congo and Conflict Minerals' 29 January 2012 YouTube <https://www.youtube.com/watch?v=kkMN P2tUWoo>.
[9]    (n 5).

# CURRENT CODES OF CONDUCT, REGULATIONS AND CERTIFICATION SYSTEMS

The human rights abuses that arise from this situation are grave. Efforts to address the conflict mineral crisis in Congo come from several different channels: the United Nations, international non-governmental organizations (NGOs) and national governments. Pressure to address conflict minerals comes from consumers and grassroots activist groups. However, they are not key players in designing and coordinating resolution for these problems. They initiate awareness but lack resources, organization and authority to hold the supply chain accountable. This section examines the actors involved in conflict mineral resolution. The position and efforts of the United Nations mark a starting point. Following, the focus zooms in to understand local efforts from the International Conference on the Great Lakes Region (ICGLR) in Africa. These organizations offer mere recommendations of conduct, lacking legal backing. On the other hand, governments have also taken action against conflict minerals. Particularly, these are policies from the United States, European Union and China. Additionally, understanding the requirements of different certification schemes highlights the high-risk links in the mineral supply chain. This achieves a grasp of the current status quo.

# INTERNATIONAL CODES OF CONDUCT

International and non-governmental organizations provide guidance for managing conflict minerals. Their recommendations establish a paradigm of what should be done. However, without legitimate sovereignty, they lack a viable system to enforce or monitor compliance. There is no legal obligation for firms to act in accordance with these guidelines. Therefore, for firms to abide, they must be motivated, either by the desire for a competitive advantage or a sense of obligation.

These standards are important to the discussion of responsible supply chain strategy because they provide guidance for its content. For corporations starting their discussion of how to manage conflict minerals, standards provide guidance and suggestions of best practices. These standards are written in the context of today's business environment, taking into account particular opportunities and threats corporations face. They highlight issues that corporations must anticipate to remain viable in the future. However, these recommendations require nothing of companies. Without a threat of punishment for non-compliance, they lack legal weight. Nevertheless, these standards cannot be disregarded. Written in the context of current events and developments, they remain relevant because they illuminate salient issues for corporations to address.

### Resolutions and Undertakings from the United Nations

The United Nations has established a discourse on corporate social responsibility and transnational corporations. In 2000, the UN Global Compact outlined guidelines of proper and ethical business practices for 21st-century enterprises. This is the largest initiative for corporate social responsibility. Its official statement of purpose is to call 'companies everywhere to voluntarily align their operations and strategies with ten universally accepted principles in the areas of human rights, labor, environment, and anti-corruption.'[10] The Global Compact's ten principles outline the ideals. The first two principles regarding human rights set the foundation for later publications on conflict mineral management. Explicitly, the Global Compact explains that 'businesses should support and respect the protection of internationally proclaimed human rights; and make sure that they are not complicit in human rights abuses.'[11] Coming from an organization of international collaborators, this publication prioritized the need address human rights infringements in business operations.

The UN followed up with literature specific to the exploitation of natural resources. In 2001, the UN Security Council produced the 'Report of the Panel of Experts on the Illegal Exploitation of Natural Resources and Other Forms of Wealth of the Democratic Republic of the Congo.' It explains the pre-existing and current structures that enable the exploitation of minerals, agriculture, forests and ivory products in the DRC. Furthermore, it clarifies the classification of illegality as any violation of existing laws and regulations or the disregard of sovereignty. It explains that any extraction, production, commercialization or export of Congo's natural resources is illegal if it occurs without the consent of the legitimate government.[12] Evaluating the link between the exploitation and continuing conflict, there are six general categories of recommendations for resolution:

---

[10]   Carrie Hall, 'Global Corporate Sustainability Report 2013' United Nations Global Compact Office (September 2013) 2.

[11]   (n 10).

[12]   'Report of the Panel of Experts on the Illegal Exploitation of Natural Resources and Other Forms of Wealth of the Democratic Republic of the Congo' (12 April 2001) UN Doc S/2001/357.

(1)  Sanctions against countries and individuals involved in the illegal activities;
(2)  preventative measures to avoid a recurrence of the current situation;
(3)  reparations to the victims of the illegal exploitation of natural resources;
(4)  design of a framework for reconstruction;
(5)  improvement of international mechanisms and regulations governing some natural resources; and
(6)  security issues.[13]

Sanctions are a method of reducing the demand for conflict minerals and exploited natural resources. There are several types of sanctions. The first is a restriction on imports and exports of Congo's natural resources. Other countries that violate this embargo would face consequences as well. Next, sanctions also include freezing the financial assets of rebel groups, corporations or individuals complicit in illegal activities. Finally, an embargo on imports of weapons to the DRC aims to reduce rebel groups' power to terrorize civilians. Though the UN initiated these recommendations to address the problem in Congo, it depends on national governments to enforce them. This demonstrates the UN's lack of authority to implement its policies. To address this dearth, MONUC (UN Organization Mission in the Democratic Republic of the Congo) was formed in November 1999 to enforce the Lusaka Ceasefire Agreement of the Second Congo War.[14] MONUC also served to oversee the implementation and acceptance of several UN Security Council resolutions. In July 2010, the Security Council aptly renamed MONUC to MONUSCO (UN Organization Stabilization Mission in the Democratic Republic of the Congo) to reflect the advancements achieved in Congo. The mission of MONUSCO remained generally the same, working to protect civilians and supporting the DRC government against insurgents.[15] This body provides force behind the UN's efforts to maintain peace.

The UN's initial report spoke broadly of natural resources in the DRC. About a decade later, in November 2010, Resolution 1952 substantiated the policies against conflict minerals in particular. It first reaffirmed many of the prior recommendations regarding sanctions. It highlighted

---

[13]  (n 12) 3.
[14]  'MONUSCO Background' United Nations Organization Stabilization Mission in the Democratic Republic of the Congo (2014) <http://www.un.org/en/peacekeeping/missions/monusco/background.shtml> accessed 24 August 2014.
[15]  (n 14).

that the DRC government is primarily responsible for 'ensuring security in its territory and protecting its civilians with respect to the rule of law, human rights and international humanitarian law',[16] but with support and collaboration from the international community. More significantly, however, it additionally addressed importers, processors and consumers, some of the many stakeholders involved in the supply chain. Each contributes to the human rights abuses that occur in the conflict minerals supply chain. As a result, resolving this issue requires a comprehensive effort.

Efforts from the United Nations are slowly making progress in ending the conflict and bringing peace and stability to the Democratic Republic of Congo. The United Nations, working with the Congolese government, successfully disarmed the M23 group on 5 November 2013.[17] This is a small, but significant, milestone that demonstrates success in upholding the International Declaration of Basic Human Rights.

### Collaboration Through the International Conference on the Great Lakes Region (ICGLR)

UN Resolution 1952 mentions the International Conference of the Great Lakes Region for its initiatives to promote peace and stability. ICGLR does this through a collaborative effort among the DRC and eleven surrounding countries (Angola, Burundi, Central African Republic, Republic of Congo, Kenya, Uganda, Rwanda, Republic of South Sudan, Sudan, Tanzania and Zambia).[18] This intergovernmental organization, formed in 2000, works towards a vision of peace, security, democracy and development. It is important because it establishes cooperation and solidarity among multiple sovereigns in the African Great Lakes Region. By broadening support behind the mission to achieve peace in Congo, rebel groups have fewer channels and options to continue their violent campaigns. Combining the efforts of many countries, the ICGLR set up programs to address peace and security, democracy and good governance, economic development and regional integration, humanitarian and social

---

16    UNSC Res 1952 (2010) 2.

17    Michael J. Kavanagh, 'Congo's M23 Says Rebellion Over After Government Victories' Bloomberg News (5 November 2013) <http://www.bloomberg.com/news/2013-11-05/congo-s-m23-declares-end-to-rebellion-after-government-victories.html> accessed 25 August 2015.

18    'Background: Who We Are' International Conference on the Great Lakes Region <http://www.icglr.org/index.php/en/background> accessed 25 August 2014.

issues, genocide prevention, and natural resources.[19] As opposed to global, high-level efforts from the United Nations, the ICGLR contributes solutions as a local actor, representing the views of the people most impacted by worker rights and mining issues.

## GOVERNMENT LEGISLATION TO REGULATE MINERALS IN THE SUPPLY CHAIN

The United Nations and the ICGLR offer valuable discourse and valiant recommendations on the conflict mineral crisis. However, their initiatives lack enforcement capabilities. In contrast, sovereigns have legitimate power, as well as a duty to counter human rights abuses. This section evaluates their legislative efforts to restrict and combat the conflict mineral crisis in the electronics supply chain. The world superpowers got involved in this issue because of the concern for international human rights. Typically, CSR activities are voluntary, proactive measures initiated by corporations as a means to achieve a competitive advantage. It is a form of market differentiation, creating a reputation that differs from comparable firms. Government regulation concerning conflict minerals aims to raise awareness through disclosure and labeling. However, it is not a definitive ban against conflict minerals. Instead, this method might reduce demand by increasing consumer knowledge. Regulations and sanctions from government bodies can slowly starve rebel groups of the means to continue their activities. This theme underpins regulations by the United States, European Union, and China.

### Requirements of the US SEC Dodd–Frank Act: Section 1502

The 2012 decision by the US Securities and Exchange Commission (SEC) reflects consumer transparency. The Dodd–Frank Wall Street Reform and Consumer Protection Act addresses conflict minerals in section 1502. This legislation, proposed and passed in 2010, requires 'persons to disclose annually whether any conflict minerals that are necessary to the functionality or production of a product . . . originated in the Democratic Republic of the Congo or an adjoining country.'[20] Furthermore, if conflict minerals

---

[19] International Conference on the Great Lakes Region, 'Programs' <http://www.icglr.org/index.php/en/peace-and-security> accessed 20 October 2014.

[20] 'Specialized Corporate Disclosure' US Securities and Exchange Commission 30 May 2013 <http://www.sec.gov/spotlight/dodd-frank/speccorpdisclosure.shtml> accessed 26 August 2014.

are present in the supply chain, corporations are required to follow up with a report about their efforts to eliminate such products from the supply chain. The SEC explains that an independent private sector auditor must also confirm reports of being 'DRC Conflict Free'. This Congressional action provides a rare government mandate for corporate social responsibility. To date, such involvement is uncommon but serves as a precedent for future CSR regulations.

### The European Union's Voluntary 'Responsible Importer' Label

The European Union also established a program to address the conflict mineral problem. However, its impact appears weaker. Rather than establishing a legal liability for corporations to comply, it is a voluntary, self-reporting system. Instead of a comprehensive evaluation of the supply chain and corresponding report that the Dodd–Frank Act requires, the EU guideline sets up a 'responsible importer' label. As long as metals and minerals enter the EU through a 'responsible importer', they are regarded as conflict-free. This simplifies verification. Instead of checkpoints at each link of the mineral supply chain, the EU guideline reduces tracking to only one point – importation.[21] In practice, this approach essentially absolves corporations in the European Union of their responsibility to trace mineral sourcing, leaving the onus and cost of tracking on importers.

The EU's model is much weaker compared to the Dodd–Frank Act. Not all companies comply with voluntary guidelines because of the costs. Conflict-free certified minerals have a higher price. This premium for ethical sourcing arises from both the greater demand for them and the limited supply of them. Smaller companies are at a disadvantage in implementing ethical supply chain guidelines. They might not be able to afford these higher costs or have the administrative resources to implement new requirements.[22] Instead of enacting definitive requirements, the EU only recommends a voluntary labeling scheme. Considering the abundance of pre-existing certification systems, this effort is redundant and ineffective, only adding to the lack of solidarity in managing conflict minerals.

---

[21]    Ian Weekes, 'Conflict Minerals: New EU Rules Simpler Alternative to US Regulation' *The Guardian* (26 March 2014) <http://www.theguardian.com/sustainable-business/blog/eu-regulations-conflict-minerals-trade> accessed 26 August 2014.

[22]    Hall (n 10) 17.

## Ethical Sourcing Guidelines from China's Chamber of Commerce

Concerns about conflict minerals in China come from the Chamber of Commerce of Minerals, Metals and Chemical Importers and Exporters (CCCMC).[23] This governmental department offers voluntary guidelines for CSR strategies regarding processing operations and overseas mines. There is no sanction for non-compliance. Instead, CCCMC hopes to encourage guideline adoption by rewarding the best-performing Chinese companies. CCCMC's recommendations are based on the ten principles of the UN Global Compact and the International Organization for Standardization's (ISO) publication on social responsibility.[24] CCCMC calls on 'ethical and transparent behavior to effectively manage the social and environmental impact from mineral exploration, extraction, processing, investment cooperation and related activities.'[25] Specifically, the guiding principles are:

(1)   Ensure compliance with all applicable laws and regulations.
(2)   Adhere to ethical business practices.
(3)   Respect human rights and protect the rights and interests of employees.
(4)   Respect nature and protect the environment.
(5)   Respect stakeholders.
(6)   Strengthening responsibility throughout the value chain.[26]

This report also has specific approaches and actions that are means to fulfilling these high-level ends. For example, such actions include setting 'targets for responsible procurement and formulat[ing] relevant company policies' and ensuring 'non complicity in human rights violations.'[27] The principles are the categorical ends to achieve. The CCCMC elaborates on these principles by explaining actions and methods to reach these ends.

China's announcement is not a leader in the discussion of conflict

---

[23]   Geraint Roberts, 'China Draws Up Minerals Sourcing Guidelines' Chemical Watch Global Risk and Regulation News (15 May 2014) <http://chemical watch.com/19669/china-draws-up-minerals-sourcing-guidelines> accessed 25 August 2014.

[24]   International Organization for Standardization, 2010. ISO26000.

[25]   'Guideline for Social Responsibility in Chinese Outbound Mining Investments' China Chamber of Commerce of Metals, Minerals, and Chemical Importers and Exporters (6 March 2014) 1 <http://www.syntao.com/Uploads/file/Public-Consultation_Draft_Guideline.pdf> accessed 25 August 2014.

[26]   (n 25) 3–4.

[27]   (n 25) 9, 10.

minerals. Instead, it reflects decisions from the United States and the European Union. In fact, China's initiatives are for its own economic interests, not concern for the people of the DRC. China owns a significant portion of mineral smelters and has connections to other international mines.[28] China is a link in the overall supply chain for consumer electronics. Because the United States and European Union have set up stricter guidelines regarding conflict mineral transparency, Chinese operations must also follow suit in order to maintain their business. China's own economic interests are tied to the conflict in the DRC, which explains the motive behind Beijing's efforts.

A response from China shows the growing commitment to ending conflict minerals. It is also demonstrates the business consequences of ignoring this problem. There are far-reaching implications of the violence occurring in Congo. Corporate responsibility is important for a stakeholder's own financial interests. Policies against conflict minerals protect China's own economic security while helping to resolve the ensuing conflict. This demonstrates the dual bottom-line that is found in CSR activity of the globalized economy.

## EICC AND ICGLR CERTIFICATION SYSTEMS

The European Union manages imports of conflict minerals through a voluntary certification scheme. This policy merely echoes the attempts of many other organizations. This section explains the certification systems recommended by the Electronic Industry Citizenship Coalition (EICC) and ICGLR, as well as their scopes of application.

The Electronics Industry Citizenship Coalition and the Global e-Sustainability Initiative (GeSI) founded the Conflict-Free Sourcing Initiative (CFSI) in 2008. This program is the most utilized resource for managing conflict minerals in corporate supply chains. Over 150 companies across seven industries have pledged to follow EICC's Conflict-Free Sourcing Program.[29] Overall, CFSI is comprised of several different programs: the Conflict-Free Smelter Program (CFSP), the Conflict Minerals Reporting Template (CMRT), due diligence guidance, and stakeholder engagement. The Conflict-Free Smelter Program is its most significant initiative. It uses third-party audits to identify smelters and refiners

---

[28]   Roberts (n 23).
[29]   'About the Conflict-Free Sourcing Initiative' Conflict Free Sourcing (2014) <http://www.conflictfreesourcing.org/about/> accessed 25 August 2014.

determined conflict-free.[30] Audit parameters include government-issued certifications of origin, government authorization of extraction activities, shipping documentation and receipts of sales volume and inventories. These checkpoints audit the legality of mineral sourcing. The details of the audit procedures and protocols for each mineral are easily accessible on CFSI's website.[31] Smelters and refiners are cleared based on these thorough expectations. This published list of compliant organizations is instrumental for companies looking for a simple way to check the links of their supply chain.

Another aid to transparency is the Conflict Minerals Reporting Template, a tool for corporate self-reporting. Users can download the template from CFSI's website as an Excel spreadsheet. Its questions guide a declaration process to determine the presence of conflict minerals within the supply chain. Finally, the emphasis on stakeholder engagement enhances collaboration on this issue. Workshops and discussions spread information about industry best practices and upcoming issues in the supply chain. In summary, the Conflict-Free Sourcing Initiative facilitates the efforts of corporations trying to operate in the modern business environment.

The International Conference on the Great Lakes Region (ICGLR) was previously discussed in the context of intergovernmental organizations. It also developed a certification mechanism. ICGLR intends for its regional certificates to be 'the sole acceptable document for intra-regional mineral shipments.'[32] This would simplify and consolidate all other efforts to label minerals. ICGLR explains that the abundance of initiatives to address conflict minerals is overwhelming and thus collectively confusing. Other labeling schemes vary in scope, covered minerals and approach. Instead of disregarding previous frameworks, ICGLR guidelines are fully compatible with them. Specifically, these are the German Federal Institute for Geosciences and Natural Resources (BGR) certification system for artisanal mine sites, the Certified Trading Chains from the Office of Geology and Mines of Rwanda and BGR, the Tin Supply Chain Initiative from the International Tin Research Institute, and the OECD's (Organisation

---

[30] 'Conflict-Free Smelter Program' Conflict Free Sourcing (2014) <http://www.conflictfreesourcing.org/conflict-free-smelter-program/> accessed 25 August 2014.

[31] 'Audit Protocols and Procedures' *Conflict Free Sourcing* (2014) <http://www.conflictfreesourcing.org/audit-protocols-procedures/?> accessed 25 August 2014.

[32] Shawn Blore and Ian Smillie, 'Taming the Resource Curse: Implementing the ICGLR Certification Mechanism for Conflict-prone Minerals' *Partnership Africa Canada* (March 2011) 37.

for Economic Co-operation and Development) Due Diligence Guidance for Responsible Supply Chains of Minerals from Conflict-Affected and High-Risk Areas. From these evaluations, ICGLR proposed its Regional Certification guidelines to guarantee that minerals 'were mined under acceptable conditions, in areas free of conflict, and have exited their countries of origin in a legal fashion with all dues and taxes paid.'[33] This end is supported by five guiding principles:

(1)   Transparency
(2)   Burden of proof falls primarily on exporters, secondly on governments
(3)   Mandatory third-party audits
(4)   Adapt current systems
(5)   Design for adaptability[34]

ICGLR identifies these as key characteristics of a viable system to track conflict minerals. The ICGLR system aims to be comprehensive and complete, covering all the concerns related to conflict minerals and challenges in certification.

## SAMSUNG ELECTRONICS: COMPANY OVERVIEW

The preceding discussion explained the conflict mineral crisis and general attempts for management. An overview of Samsung's operations, market position and strategy provides context for understanding how it manages conflict minerals in its supply chain. Samsung Electronics, based in South Korea, is a leader in the global consumer electronics industry. As of 2014, its market value is US$186.47 billion.[35] About 227,000 employees make up its operations in 75 countries,[36] manufacturing and selling a diverse basket of goods. Its product line includes consumer electronics, mobile communications and information technology, and device solutions (i.e., LED screens and memory cards).[37] Furthermore, Samsung performs

---

[33]   (n 32) 37.
[34]   (n 32) 34–35.
[35]   'Samsung Electronics' *Forbes* (May 2014) <http://www.forbes.com/companies/samsung-electronics/> accessed 19 August 2014.
[36]   'Samsung Value and Code of Conduct' Samsung Electronics <http://www.samsung.com/us/aboutsamsung/sustainability/sustainablemanagement/samsung-valsamsungvaluecod/> accessed 19 August 2014.
[37]   Global Public Affairs Group, 'Sustainability Report 2014' Samsung Electronics (30 June 2014).

well as a global leader in its industry. In 2013, revenues increased by 13.7 per cent and operating profits by 27 per cent.[38] This type of growth for a well-established market player is a commendable feat. Booz & Co. ranked Samsung as the third most innovative company in the world for 2013, behind Apple and Google.[39] This marks significant progress since its ninth-place standing in 2010. These metrics and rankings confirm the success of Samsung's overall business strategy.

A corporate business strategy guides long-term market decisions and initiatives. It establishes what a corporation ultimately wants to be known for. Samsung defined its 'Vision 2020' in 2009, branding its goals to 'inspire the world, create the future.'[40] Its corporate literature further explains its mission 'to inspire the world with [its] innovative technologies, products, and design that enrich people's lives and contribute to social prosperity by creating a new future.'[41] This is the guiding doctrine of Samsung's business decisions.

**The Key to CSR Strategy Definition**

This section discusses the general approach modern firms can take in forming a CSR strategy as a component of its business strategy. The first step is to establish an honest and authentic intention to achieve positive social or environmental good. Today's CSR strategy maintains the spirit of the dual bottom line, creating a positive impact in conjunction with business success. CSR strategy is approached as a business strategy that contributes to the 'core business objectives and core competencies of the firm.'[42] The overarching goal of producing social and environmental good can be intimidating. Firms must be wary of avoiding 'a random collection of unfocused, unlinked, and unrelated strategies'[43] in pursuit of an overly broad end goal of social and environmental change. This explains the importance of how CSR strategy should integrate with the

---

[38]   (n 37); Global Public Affairs Group, 'Sustainability Report 2014' Samsung Electronics (30 June 2014).

[39]   Booz and Company, 'Highlights from the 2013 Global Innovation 1000 Study: Navigating the Digital Future' (2013) <http://www.strategyand.pwc.com/media/file/Strategyand_2013-Global-Innovation-1000-Study-Navigating-the-Digital-Future_Media-Report.pdf> accessed 12 September 2014.

[40]   (n 38) 18.

[41]   (n 38) 19.

[42]   Kellie McElhaney, 'A Strategic Approach to Corporate Social Responsibility' (2009) 52 *Leader to Leader* 31.

[43]   (n 42) 32.

business objectives of the firm. CSR strategies offer a clear and compelling contribution to improved business performance.

### Samsung's CSR Strategy for Global Harmony

Samsung's CSR strategy is the guiding principle driving its initiatives and activities relating to the public good. Samsung has produced sustainability publications since 2000. The scope and success of Samsung's CSR strategy has since been substantiated as business literature and discourse on CSR has increased. Samsung's announced CSR vision is 'global harmony with people, society, and environment,'[44] hoping to reorganize society where these components coexist in concord. Samsung regards people as employees, shareholders, investors, and labor and human rights organizations. In society, key stakeholders are business partners, governments and local communities. Next, Samsung considers customers, NGO, and international organizations in its environment category. Initiatives to fulfill its CSR vision are social contributions, partner collaboration, integrity management, competitive products and services and green management. As a large transnational corporation, Samsung has a variety of programs to fulfill its overarching CSR vision. In 2013, its investments across its CSR programs totaled around US$500 million (536.3 billion KRW).[45] Samsung's CSR reports encompass a wide scope of issues: human resources, health and safety, eco-products, water management, shared growth, suppliers' compliance, conflict minerals, product accessibility and global social contribution. This study of human rights considerations in the supply chain specifically focuses on Samsung's efforts for safe worker conditions and ethical mineral supplier standards.

### A Vision in Response to Various Drivers

There are several factors driving Samsung's CSR activities. First, there is internal motivation from Samsung itself. Internal reasons are the actor's own choice, not in response to an outside influence or mandate. One important motive for developing a CSR strategy is for the business advantage. Higher profits are correlated with successful corporate social

---

[44] 'CSR Vision and Organization' *Samsung: Sustainability Management* 2014, <http://www.samsung.com/us/aboutsamsung/sustainability/sustainablemanagement/csrvisionorgacsrvisio/index.html> accessed 17 August 2014.
[45] (n 37) 109.

responsibility programs.[46] Therefore, economic gains are an extrinsic reason. On the other hand, the intrinsic reason for corporate social responsibility stems from moral obligations. This is the viewpoint that corporations are inherently bound by moral expectations.[47] It associates corporations with a higher degree of altruism than typically acknowledged. Interpreting CSR from this perspective treats the corporate entity as a global citizen with ethical expectations and limitations. It is difficult to quantify the contribution of intrinsic versus extrinsic factors driving Samsung's CSR behavior. Nevertheless, these possible explanations show that CSR can be a self-motivated initiative.

In addition to internal motivations, expectations for CSR also come from external market and government pressures. In a connected, globalized world, international trade makes the market more competitive, providing consumers with more buying power. Pressure from consumer groups about human rights atrocities in Africa drives corporations to react because of the threat of losing market share. Consumers create pressure for corporate responsibility. They can choose not to buy from a company, which eventually leads to lower profits and poorer stock performance. In comparison, government regulations can force compliance with more immediate consequences. Governments are interfering in the consumer electronics market because of a responsibility to international human rights. Direct intervention by means of sending forces to the DRC is a costly alternative to address this problem. Instead, they are trying to reduce the demand for conflict minerals through disclosure requirements on the market side. Weighting the strength of each of these forces is a separate research endeavor. However, all of these influences are drivers for Samsung's corporate responsibility initiatives.

## Samsung's CSR Activities

Samsung's sustainability report summarizes its annual accomplishments regarding corporate social responsibility. There are at least two possible forms of human rights abuses in a consumer electronics supply chain – worker conditions and conflict minerals. Samsung's efforts in relation to worker conditions are aimed at improving the safety of mines, processing locations, and factories. These are typical concerns that any type of

---

[46] Chin-Huang Lin, Ho-Li Yang and Dian-Yan Liou, 'The Impact of Corporate Social Responsibility on Financial Performance: Evidence from Business in Taiwan' (2009) 31 *Technology in Society* 56–63.
[47] (n 4) 70.

corporation needs to act proactively against. Regarding the electronics industry specifically, companies must additionally consider the local political situation in the DRC. As previously discussed, profits from conflict minerals fuel the extended warfare in the DRC. In this section, describing Samsung's corporate social responsibility strategy and operations allows for later evaluation of its approach and success. Information about Samsung's activities is summarized from publications and statements easily accessible on its official website.[48]

### Samsung's Advances in Worker Conditions

In the CEO message of its 2014 Sustainability Report, Samsung declared that its top priority is 'to ensure the health and safety of [its] employees and the communities where [it] operates.'[49] Regarding the consumer electronics supply chain, Samsung is concerned about the safety conditions of the mines, any use of child labor and employee wages. It emphasizes these principles in its supplier code of conduct. That is, it 'requires all suppliers to provide safe and healthy working conditions for all employees.'[50] This includes a zero-tolerance policy for child labor and mandatory age identification checks on new hires. Samsung expects its suppliers to abide by local laws and regulations to define the limitations of minors' employment. This code of conduct also mandates that suppliers compensate workers at least minimum wage plus overtime hours, social insurance and rest days.

In 2013, third-party audits found inadequate safety precautions regarding minors working at supplier sites. They also found that 39 suppliers had failed to provide overtime pay. In response, Samsung directed violators to correct their policies and set up preventative policies against future infringements.[51] These considerations in workplace safety, environment and labor rights are typical to most supply chains of transnational corporations. In the electronics supply chain specifically, there are violent atrocities associated with gold, tantalum, tungsten and tin mining. This is the other concern in human rights management.

---

[48] 'Corporate Social Responsibility' Samsung Electronics <http://www.samsung.com/us/aboutsamsung/investor_relations/corporate_governance/corporatesocialresponsibility/> accessed 28 August 2014.
[49] (n 37) 5.
[50] (n 49) 67.
[51] (n 49) 69.

**Samsung on Conflict-free Mineral Sourcing**

Samsung reacted quickly to the growing outcry against conflict minerals. Compared to the most recent 2014 report, the firm's 2013 Sustainability Report had sparse literature on conflict minerals. The 2013 version briefly mentioned eliminating conflict minerals in its high-level list of major issues from customers. The only additional information on conflict minerals was a short paragraph explaining its participation in the EICC's programs to develop investigation methods and certification programs of smelting factories. In the 2014 Sustainability Report, Samsung's discussion and explanation of its actions against conflict minerals strengthened significantly.

In 2014, Samsung wrote more substantially about its involvement with the Conflict-Free Sourcing Initiative. In light of Dodd–Frank Section 1502, Samsung set a basic policy of 'providing consumers with products that go through a legitimate and ethical distribution process.'[52] It pursues this principle through five key actions. The first is raising supplier awareness. To guarantee that final products are conflict free, Samsung needs to evaluate smelters and mines that its suppliers buy from. Some 3,000 of its global suppliers pledged to abide by its conflict-free policy. Second, Samsung conducts audits on the use of conflict minerals in its supply chain. Unfortunately, in 2014, 601 smelters were found to be sourcing from conflict mines. In response, Samsung reiterated its commitment for materials suppliers to source from certified conflict-free smelters. As of April 2014, only 3 per cent of suppliers used tantalum in their products sold to Samsung.[53] As a member company of the EICC, Samsung's actions against conflict minerals also involve collaboration with other governments, industry actors and non-profit organizations. In conclusion, Samsung's efforts against conflict minerals are multi-channeled, requiring audits *and* transparency while partnering with other stakeholders.

# CRITICAL ANALYSIS OF SAMSUNG'S CSR VISION AND MANAGEMENT OF CONFLICT MINERALS

At this point, the phenomenon and actors involved in conflict minerals and the consumer electronics supply chain should be clear. This chapter started with an explanation of the war and violence in the Democratic Republic of Congo among a wealth of natural resources. Illegal exploitation in

---

[52]  (n 37) 73.
[53]  (n 37).

this region has far-reaching effects on various stakeholders committed to human rights. They have each made efforts to address this problem. These efforts include voluntary certification schemes and mandatory government statutes. The previous section explained Samsung's reported business strategy, overall corporate social responsibility vision and specific activities to protect human rights in its supply chain. The following section seeks to critically evaluate Samsung's supply chain management in relation to its corporate obligation to protect human rights and compare its efforts to three other transnational consumer electronics corporations.

**Merits and Areas for Growth**

Samsung's awareness and activities in conflict mineral management match industry expectations. Its publications explain the violent crisis in the DRC and surrounding countries and then further connect it to the impact on its supply chain. The language is reminiscent of the themes established by principles from the EICC, ICGLR and Chinese Chamber of Commerce. These touch on third-party audits, adherence to local laws, human rights interests of workers, environmental protection and reporting. As a member of the EICC, Samsung's stance on supplier sourcing aligns with the Conflict-Free Sourcing Initiative program. This means buying only from certified smelters. Samsung Electronics is not covered in the scope of the Dodd–Frank Act directly,[54] but the legislation applies to Samsung's corporate partners. Therefore, Samsung also abides by Section 1502's disclosure requirements. In each aspect of CSR strategy and practices, Samsung merely meets expectations. They are a leader in consumer electronics but fail to transform the conversation on CSR.

Regarding reporting, Samsung is transparent about its findings. It established its ideal state but remains realistic in the gradual change towards it. Third-party audits for compliance found that the reality of Samsung's CSR efforts falls short of its goals. This is reasonably expected due to implementation lag times. Nevertheless, Samsung includes these findings in its annual sustainability report along with reactions to account for them. By being honest about shortcomings, Samsung signals its authenticity and genuine intentions. Therefore it continues to build consumer trust.

---

[54]  'Mineral Sourcing' Samsung Electronics <http://www.samsung.com/us/about samsung/sustainability/suppliers/conflictminerals/> accessed 28 August 2014.

**Comparative Industry Analysis**

The quality of Samsung's management of human rights can be judged by comparing it to LG Electronics, Apple and Intel. Comparing a corporation with its competitors gauges if a company is fulfilling its potential and keeping up with industry standards. This is a general practice to track business performance metrics such as revenue growth and market share. Specifically, comparative analyses are useful in evaluating corporate social responsibility initiatives because CSR is predominantly self-motivated. That is, within an industry, corporations pursue CSR because of internal motivations rather than in response to legal regulations. Intel and Apple have better defined human rights management practices than Samsung. In relation to LG Electronics, Samsung falls about on par as a mid-tier performer.

These competitors have policies in their CSR literature to uphold labor and human rights. Apple, for example, emphasizes education to empower workers, bans 60-hour workweeks at supplier sites and runs the Apple Supplier EHS (environment, health, and safety) Academy to improve workplace safety and health standards in its supply chain.[55] LG Electronics writes about its stance prohibiting child labor and surveys of supplier violations. It also performs supplier audits 'to identify unsafe conditions and practices and to support suppliers' improvement efforts.'[56] Finally, Intel's efforts regarding human rights are based on the UN's 'Guiding Principles on Business and Human Rights.' By manufacturing products in its own factories, it can enforce its Code of Conduct and human rights expectations. Regarding external suppliers, it collaborates with actors to implement 'system-level improvements on issues such as working hours.'[57] In general, firms in the electronics industry are aware of concerns about worker conditions, safety and supplier codes of conduct.

Specific to conflict mineral management, at a minimum, all four firms are associated with the Conflict-Free Smelter Program. Adherence to these guidelines is the industry expectation. Beyond this, firms have

---

[55] 'Supplier Responsibility: 2014 Progress Report' Apple Inc. (January 2014) <https://www.apple.com/supplier-responsibility/pdf/Apple_SR_2014_Progress_Report.pdf> accessed 18 October 2014.

[56] 'LG Electronics' Statement on Conflict Minerals' LG.com (5 August 2013) <http://www.lg.com/global/sustainability/business-partner/conflict-minerals> accessed 16 October 2014.

[57] '2013 Corporate Responsibility Report' Intel Corporation (2013) 104 <http://csrreportbuilder.intel.com/PDFFiles/CSR_2013_Full-Report.pdf> accessed 22 October 2014.

differentiated themselves through the intensity of their mineral tracing programs, reporting, collaboration with governments and NGOs, and public relations interface. LG's statements and policies on conflict minerals include joining the EICC coalition, a supplier code of conduct, analyzing the materials supply chain and conducting due diligence of smelters associated with conflict minerals.[58] LG's approach is based on a model of supplier consulting. It works with suppliers on their corporate social responsibility practices by conducting assessments and providing recommendations for improvement. The weakest component of LG's policy is the mandate for responsible sourcing only 'when there is an adequate number of CFS smelters/refiners.'[59] This language creates a huge loophole that permits the use of conflict minerals under certain circumstances.

Though it is younger and smaller than Samsung, Intel emerges as an industry leader in human rights management. It was 'one of the first companies to address the issue of conflict minerals in its supply chain,' initiating supply chain surveys in 2009.[60] Since then, it has focused on smelters and refiners as the key link to ensuring conflict-free products. In January 2014, Intel reached the industry milestone of manufacturing the first conflict-free microprocessor.[61] Uniquely, LG's and Intel's CSR literature includes the additional consideration of unintended consequences of conflict-free labeling. They realize that the increased concern for due diligence 'may unintentionally drive down demand for all minerals' from the Great Lakes Region, which can 'inadvertently hurt the economic opportunities for artisanal and other legitimate miners operating in that region.'[62] LG Electronics encourages responsible sourcing of minerals from the DRC to 'prevent an embargo and associated worsening of economic conditions and human suffering.'[63] The concern of a 'de facto embargo' reflects local views on mining reform.[64] Furthermore, Intel has impressive accessibility for consumer transparency, offering

---

[58]    (n 56).

[59]    (n 58).

[60]    'Intel's Efforts to Achieve a "Conflict Free" Supply Chain' Intel White Paper (August 2014) <http://www.intel.com/content/dam/doc/policy/policy-conflict-_miner als.pdf> accessed 18 October 2014.

[61]    (n 60).

[62]    (n 60).

[63]    (n 56).

[64]    makeITfair, 'Voices from the Inside: Local Views on Mining Reform in Eastern DR Congo' *Finnwatch & Swedwatch* (October 2010) 36 <http://somo.nl/publications-en/Publication_3586/at_download/fullfile> accessed 18 October 2014.

convenient links[65] for curious consumers to make inquiries or download documentation.

Apple also has similar policies enforcing a supplier code of conduct for responsible mineral sourcing. Speaking to worker health and safety, it hopes to 'eradicate unethical hiring and exploitation of workers – even when local laws permit such practices.'[66] This outperforms Samsung's policy. Regarding wage and benefit expectations, Samsung's guidelines are for suppliers to abide by 'local laws and regulations.'[67] At face value, this seems commendable because of the expectation for legal compliance. However it is not innovative. It does not exceed the minimum require-ments by law. In fact, this referral to local law is operationally inefficient and inadequate. First, varying standards create an administrative burden for audits. Since guidelines are relative to the geographic location of the supplier, audit processes cannot be universal. There is also ambiguity when suppliers operate in several countries. Furthermore, by referring to local laws, Samsung risks falling short of ideal corporate behavior. Given the variance in legislation across countries, Samsung's global suppliers are held to different standards. A better approach is to set the same expectations for all suppliers, regardless of geographic location. By merely referring to local regulations, Samsung's supplier code of conduct is vulnerable to short-comings. Given their reach and influence, TNCs could function as global political actors, setting standards that apply like law. Such is the new reign in the global market.

There are several factors to consider when explaining performance dif-ferences. All four firms compete in the global consumer electronics indus-try. However, they vary in revenue, years since founding and company headquarters. Samsung, the oldest of these firms, has a market value of US\$186.47 billion.[68] Intel (market value of US\$129.22 billion)[69] and Apple (US\$483.15 billion)[70] are both US companies headquartered in California. LG Electronics, headquartered in South Korea, has the smallest market value of US\$10.03 billion.[71] These differences are not direct indicators of a company's corporate social responsibility efforts. According to the

---

[65]   See http://www.intel.com/content/www/us/en/corporate-responsibility/csr-report-builder.html; http://www.intel.com/content/www/us/en/forms/corporate-responsibility-contact-us.html.

[66]   (n 55) 10.

[67]   (n 37) 69.

[68]   (n 35).

[69]   (n 68).

[70]   (n 68).

[71]   (n 68).

UN Global Compact, company size has the most significant influence on sustainability performance because of greater financial and knowledge resources.[72] However, it does not guarantee performance. In other words, a company's monetary value can signal its potential for CSR success but does not explain why one competitor may perform better than another. LG's subpar CSR performance might be because its market value is vastly smaller than the other three players. However, this correlation is inconclusive. Beyond these influences, a better factor to determine a corporation's CSR success is how genuine its commitment to valuable improvements is. Yet, this is a factor that cannot be measured directly.

Comparing Samsung's activities to pre-existing standards of conduct and other industry players' actions, Samsung meets but does not exceed expectations. It voluntarily satisfies the recommendations discussed beforehand but does not lead the field in conflict mineral management. It urges its suppliers to switch to certified conflict-free smelters, as well as encourages all smelters to be certified. These activities are merely sufficient. The world looks to Samsung as an industry leader in electronics sales. Its reputation can challenge competitors to match its initiatives. Furthermore, Samsung has the financial and human capital resources to make a more substantial effort. Due to its size and financial success, Samsung is positioned to make a significant change in conflict mineral usage and human rights. First-tier CSR strategies are rated as such because they have elements that exceed the industry norm, looking a few extra steps ahead of their competitors. Though Samsung keeps up with industry norms, it does not yet contribute innovation in the corporate social responsibility sphere.

### The Impact of CSR Activity for Samsung

So far, this analysis has evaluated how Samsung approaches human rights concerns in the supply chain through CSR programs and conflict mineral management. It is also valuable to study what these initiatives mean for the corporations' performance. The key theme of 21st-century corporate social responsibility is to produce a social benefit in conjunction with improved business performance. In communicating about material issues, Samsung emphasizes that it wants 'to create value through corporate sustainability management . . . while also strengthening its position as a market innovator for the future.'[73] This embodies the dual bottom line of CSR. Corporate social responsibility adds value to the firm through public

---

[72]    (n 10) 16.
[73]    (n 37) 33.

image and risk management. These are internal benefits achieved while pursuing a greater good.

Externally, CSR contributes to developing a corporation's public image and reputation. It becomes a part of corporate branding. CSR can achieve 'competitive differentiation,' generating a unique identity associated with the company.[74] This contributes to market performance. Efforts in CSR can steal market share from competitors or create an opportunity to enter a new market. As the Millennial generation overtakes the consumer population, these strategies are a way to respond to demands of the new consumer.[75] Consumers today expect a connection that is more than a mere goods and payment exchange.

Managing conflict minerals in the supply chain is necessary for sustainable business. For the electronics industry, conflict minerals are important because they pose a business risk. Resolving human rights violations is a necessary component of Samsung's business strategy. Ultimately, this CSR translates to business sustainability in two ways. First, Samsung protects its market share by responding to consumer pressures. Due to increased awareness about conflict minerals from non-profit organizations and the Dodd–Frank Act, consumers are more conscious of mineral sourcing. Second, managing conflict minerals is dually important because it relates directly to supply chain sustainability. The circumstances in the DRC make the supply of crucial raw resources volatile and undependable. Conflict mineral management ensures that its operations have the necessary materials to manufacture products without huge variations in price. Political conflict, violence and instability in the DRC make conflict minerals management necessary for both corporate image and supply chain security. Samsung's commitment to human rights is a way to ensure economic sustainment and future progress.

### Samsung, a Potential Leader

Evaluating Samsung's performance in the consumer electronics marketplace, it is clear that, in business terms, it is an industry leader. As a leader in the technology market, Samsung can also shape industry expectations for corporate behavior. As a large company, competitors and customers look to Samsung for its initiatives in social responsibility. Market leaders play a key role in defining industry paradigms.

---

[74]   (n 42) 31.
[75]   (n 42) 31.

The 'institutional isomorphism model as the normative factor'[76] could redefine industry approaches to conflict minerals. This is when competition causes mirroring and adoption of practices throughout the whole industry. Powerfully, Samsung's CSR achievements could stimulate comparable actions by other consumer electronics companies. Therefore, competition may create a form of collective governance. In trying to outperform each other, corporations continually raise general expectations for CSR activity. Specifically, because of the continual challenge to match initiatives against conflict minerals, the industry can slowly starve rebel groups out of their revenue.

## CONCLUSION

Evaluating human rights considerations in a transnational supply chain requires multiple perspectives. Stakeholders involved are civilians, workers, rebel groups, governments in the DRC and surrounding area, transnational corporations, intergovernmental organizations, global superpowers, non-profit organizations, and individual consumers. As a global issue, there are many uncoordinated streams for resolution. Non-profit and intergovernmental organizations offer numerous different certifications. Regulations from different national sovereigns vary in scope and severity. Each of these actors has their own agenda of priorities. Thus, this is not a simple issue. It is a tough balance for companies to understand their level of complicity, set and enforce guidelines without destroying the local economy in the DRC.

This was a focused case study of how an industry leader addresses human rights in its supply chain. It started by explaining the specific human rights abuses that arise from sourcing. Then, it looked at efforts to resolve this issue. These established expectations to evaluate Samsung's efforts. Doing so explained how corporations can manage human rights in their business operations. They can set a CSR strategy according to regulations and industry practices, as well as innovating new programs and approaches. This case study did not intend to assign or measure levels of moral culpability of those involved. Instead, agreeing that actions against conflict minerals are necessary, this is research into what these actions can be.

---

[76]    Michael Ewing and Lydia Windisch, 'Corporate Social Responsibility in China' (2007) paper presented at Anznac Conference, University of Otago, New Zealand.

The idea of corporate citizenship frames transnational corporations as entities responsible to the world. Conflict minerals are a domestic issue with global reach. Without the global demand for consumer electronics, rebel groups would not target mines as a lucrative revenue stream. The ultimate end is not to prohibit the use of conflict minerals. Rather, managing conflict minerals is a means to the ultimate goal of ending human rights atrocities in the DRC. People, not profits, are the end. In a globalized economy, transnational corporations are prominent actors. Tied to other stakeholders through economic dependence and human rights obligations, they are increasingly influential and well-positioned to make a global impact.

# PART III

# TNC BEHAVIOUR AND STRATEGY IN THE 21ST CENTURY: COUNTRY CASE STUDIES

# 10. China's investment traditions and the modern transnational corporation
*Megan Bowman, George Gilligan and Justin O'Brien*[1]

## INTRODUCTION

China has emerged as a prominent investment actor in the contemporary global economy. It is a significant recipient of foreign direct investment (FDI) and one of the largest outward investors in foreign jurisdictions, both of which have stimulated China's importance as a global investment actor across markets and continents today. However, while China's economic prowess in terms of attracting inward FDI and expanding trade surplus is reasonably well understood, academic attention has been given to China's role as an outward investor and its outward foreign direct investment (ODI) ambitions only in more recent years.[2] This chapter contributes to the growing body of literature on the duality of Chinese FDI–ODI by adding an historical perspective to the state capital story and examining China's trade and investment patterns through a longitudinal lens. Specifically, it analyzes FDI and ODI data in the context of China's Five-Year Plans, which have to date been an underutilized prism through which to view the patterns and ambitions of trade and investment from a Chinese national perspective. This chapter discusses how China has become a modern global investment force by documenting its historical record and where China's ODI ambitions are likely to focus in the future.

[1] The authors acknowledge the financial support of the Centre for International Finance and Regulation (for project 'Enter the Dragon: Foreign Direct Investment and Capital Markets, E002'), which is funded by the Commonwealth of Australia and NSW State Government and other consortium members (see http://www.cifr.edu.au/). They also thank Ms. Lisa Soo for additional research assistance.
[2] See, for example: Yin-Wong Cheung and Xingwang Qian, 'Empirics of China's Outward Direct Investment' (2009) 14 *Pacific Economic Review* 318–319; Raphael Kaplinsky and Mike Morris, 'Chinese FDI in Sub Saharan Africa: Engaging with Large Dragons' (2009) 24 *European Journal of Development Research* 554–555; Leonard K. Cheng and Zihui Ma, 'China's Outward Foreign Direct Investment' in Robert C. Feenstra and Shang-Jin Wei (eds), *China's Growing Role in World Trade* (University of Chicago Press, 2010) 547–549.

Importantly, we also explore the role and implications of TNCs as modern vehicles for politically motivated ODI strategies.

We start by documenting the emergence of China as a global investment force. We trace China's investment and trade traditions back to the 12th century and through succeeding centuries into the post-war 'globalized' boom of the 1930s, then to the relative isolation under Mao Zedong in the 1950s, the 'open door' FDI policy of the 1980s, and the 'going global' ODI strategy of the current era. We then explore the strategy behind China's global investment behaviour. Utilizing extant empirical data we analyze the global sectors and jurisdictions in which China has invested and show that significant Chinese investments have occurred in both developed and developing nations but more so in the former; and in mining/natural resources but with emerging diversification toward energy, agriculture and commercial real estate. Specifically, the data demonstrate that state-owned enterprises (SOEs) have been the primary modality of Chinese ODI, which have been highly scrutinized TNCs for their potential as politically motivated corporations even while pursuing commercial opportunities. We conclude by discussing how China's increasing middle-class consumer demand, together with declining domestic supply, will be relevant factors that shape China's strategic investment priorities in the future.

## CHINA'S EMERGENCE AS A GLOBAL INVESTMENT FORCE

### China's Traditions of Outward Trade

China has a longstanding tradition of external trade. For example, in the 12th to 14th centuries it enjoyed economic advancement and dynamism far exceeding its Western counterparts.[3] During this period China reputedly established a professional navy and vigorous international trade into India, Asia, Arabia and East Africa.[4] By the early 15th century, however, trade missions had become costly for the Chinese Government and with the death of Emperor Zhu Zhanji 朱瞻基 in 1435 the fleets were recalled.[5] Griswold asserts that by 1477 China had begun a path towards self-

---

[3]   China's per capita GDP has been estimated as higher than that of Europe before 1280: Cheung and Qian (n 2) 312.

[4]   As attested by Marco Polo: Daniel Griswold, 'Trade and the Transformation of China', paper presented at the James and Margaret Tsend Loe Chinese Studies Center Conference, St Vincent College, PA (6 November 2002) 1–2.

[5]   (n 4).

sufficiency that comprised 'cultural and economic inwardness, a closed and centralized political system, and an anti-commercial culture' that lasted for more than 400 years.[6] Yu clarifies the purpose of nationalism to this process as 'key to repelling foreign invasions and maintaining China's full sovereignty.'[7] Nonetheless, Cheung and Qian note that China still ran a substantial trade balance surplus during the 16th and 17th centuries,[8] and Maddison estimates that China accounted for nearly one-third of world GDP output from 1700 to 1820.[9]

In the early 1840s, foreign powers such as Great Britain pressured China to open its economy to receive international trade through a series of treaties that pried open ports to allow transactions with foreigners. For example, the 1842 Treaty of Nanking permitted foreign trade with China through five ports and stipulated a 5 per cent tariff on almost all goods leaving and entering the country.[10] Nonetheless, the scale of Chinese trade and production was relatively small until China's 1895 defeat in the Sino–Japanese War, which precipitated the Treaty of Shimonoseki that permitted Japanese businesses to invest directly in China and to produce goods and services that could be sold within China and abroad. Soon after, this privilege was extended to other foreign nations via most-favored nation agreements, with the result that foreign capital financed China's industrialization by injecting funds into its telecommunications, railroad and shipping industries. By the early 20th century, 48 Chinese cities had been opened to foreign trade.[11]

As ports opened up and foreigners were allowed to invest and trade, China transitioned from a closed to an open economy. Cheng estimates that from 1900 to 1913 the total value of Chinese trade grew twice as much as it had during the previous 40 years and that China's trade growth was faster than the world average in the first three decades of the 20th century.[12]

---

[6]  (n 4) 3.

[7]  Miin-ling Yu, 'From Two Camps to Three Worlds: The Party Worldview in PRC Textbooks (1949–1966)' (2013) 215 *China Quarterly* 682.

[8]  (n 3).

[9]  Angus Maddison, *Chinese Economic Performance in the Long Run* (OECD Development Centre, 1998).

[10]  See <http://china.usc.edu/ShowArticle.aspx?articleID=405&AspxAutoDetect CookieSupport=1>.

[11]  Kris James Mitchener and Se Yan, 'Globalization, Trade and Wages: What Does History Tell Us About China?' (2012) National Bureau of Economic Research, Working Paper No. 15679, 5, Figure 1.

[12]  China's share of world trade increased from 1.5% around 1898 to 3.44% by 1928. See Yu-Kwei Cheng, *Foreign Trade and Industrial Development of China* (University Press of Washington, DC, 1956).

Indeed, Mitchener and Yan claim that the period 1901–1930 was comparable with the present period of globalization in trading terms.[13] Specifically, the exogenous shock of World War I dramatically raised the price of Chinese exports and increased the demand for its goods abroad. For example, China's exports to the United States grew at an annual rate of 6 per cent before World War I, but boomed after the war started, growing by approximately 27 per cent per year; similarly, exports to Japan grew at 5.8 per cent per year pre-war and then jumped to 17.4 per cent per year after 1913. Trade costs declined when the war ended in 1918, which, in turn, led to a rise in China's terms of trade and further growth in its export sector, particularly in exports of unskilled, intensive manufactures, mining and agricultural products. Indeed, while the war disrupted trade in many other parts of the world, it created 'new markets for Chinese goods that had previously been served by producers in belligerent countries'.[14] China's total trade as a share of GDP almost tripled during the period 1903–1928.[15] China would not experience this pace again for nearly 60 years.

**The Long March into Isolation**

On 1 October 1949 Mao Zedong 毛泽东, having led the Communists to victory against the Nationalists, proclaimed the founding of the People's Republic of China. At this time, the worldview of the Chinese Communist Party (CCP) was anti-imperialism, anti-colonialism, and focused on Sino–Soviet relations to the exclusion of the United States.[16]

During the late 1940s and early 1950s, China followed the Soviet model of centralized economic development, emphasizing heavy industry at the expense of consumer goods.[17] However, Mao disapproved of Khrushchev's 1956 de-Stalinization policy and the principle of peaceful coexistence and competition with the United States.[18] By the late 1950s Mao had developed different ideas for how China could directly advance to Socialism through

---

[13]   Mitchener and Yan (n 11) 2–3, 6. Their data show that an exogenous shock to the price of traded goods can boost unskilled industries more so than skilled industries; and that the observed decline in the skill premium in China in the 1920s is consistent with China's changing terms of trade.

[14]   (n 11) 3.

[15]   (n 11) 38, 41, 43, 48, Appendix (Figure 1).

[16]   Yu (n 7) 687.

[17]   Chi-Kwan Mark, 'Ideological Radicalization and the Sino-Soviet Split, 1958–64' in *China and the World Since 1945: An International History* (Routledge, 2012) 45–57, 45.

[18]   Yu (n 7) 691.

the mobilization of China's workers; ideas that precipitated China's Great Leap Forward in 1958 and the contemporaneous Sino–Soviet split.[19]

In terms of trade and economic measures, the Great Leap Forward introduced human labour intensive industrialization and collectivized farming and was initially intended as a five-year economic plan (see Table 10A.1); however, it was abandoned after only two years due to economic breakdown following poor harvests and mass starvation.[20] Six years later, in 1966, Mao instigated the Cultural Revolution, which continued until his death in 1976. During this time diplomatic and trade relations warmed between Beijing and Washington, culminating in a declared desire by both countries to normalize relations when President Richard Nixon visited Beijing in 1972.[21]

Under the leadership of Deng Xiaoping 邓小平, far-reaching economic reforms were instigated from 1977, which included the 'open door' policy designed to encourage foreign trade and FDI via market-oriented measures[22] (see Table 10A.1). By the late 1970s Chinese policy-makers were cooperating with foreign oil companies regarding access to offshore oil and gas fields within China's sovereign seas. Howson notes that this commercial initiative precipitated intense internal political debate regarding China's potential loss of control over strategic natural resource assets in a context of hidden foreign political agendas; ironically, these concerns would be echoed by US constituents *vis-à-vis* Chinese acquisition of US assets nearly 40 years later.[23]

Nonetheless, China continued to enter into production sharing contracts

---

[19]   Lorenz M. Luthi, 'Mao's Challenges, 1958' in *The Sino-Soviet Split: Cold War in the Communist World* (Princeton UP, 2008) 80–113, 80. Relations between China and the Soviet Union remained strained until then-Soviet leader Mikhail Gorbachev visited Beijing in 1989.

[20]   Nicholas R. Lardy and John K. Fairbank, 'The Chinese Economy Under Stress, 1958–1965' in Roderick MacFarquhar (ed.), *The People's Republic, Part 1: The Emergence of Revolutionary China 1949–1965* (Cambridge University Press, 1987). See also Jisheng Yang, 'The Fatal Politics of the PRC's Great Leap Famine: The Preface to Tombstone' (2010) 16 *Journal of Contemporary China* 755–776.

[21]   Nixon titled the visit 'the week that changed the world' and the US Public Broadcasting Service reported that 'For eight days and nights, American television audiences tuned in to a spectacular parade of images from China, the first they had seen in more than twenty years': http://www.pbs.org/wgbh/amex/china/sfeature/nixon.html.

[22]   Linda Yueh, 'China's "Going Out, Bringing In" Policy: the Geo-economics of China's Rise', paper presented at the IISS Seminar, International Institute for Strategic Studies, Manama (23–25 March 2012) 2.

[23]   Nicholas C. Howson, 'China's Acquisitions Abroad – Global Ambitions, Domestic Effects' (2006) 48 *Law Quadrangle Notes* 73, 75.

with US oil companies such as Mobil, Chevron and Exxon in order to explore and access Chinese offshore oil and gas resources. The prime commercial entity established by the Chinese government for these purposes was the China National Offshore Oil Corporation (CNOOC) Ltd,[24] which is an SOE that plays a prominent role today as a Chinese ODI actor abroad.

### China's Economy Opens Up and Trade Imbalances Spur Outward Investment

Apart from domestic economic and law reform, a key element of China's 1979 'Reform and Opening to the Outside World' policy emphasized increased trade with foreign nations and inward FDI into China. Unlike the earlier opening of the 19th century, this strategy was unilaterally initiated by China.

Policy reform of inward FDI began with China's creation of Special Economic Zones (SEZs) in 1979–1980. SEZs were introduced in the coastal provinces of Fujian and Guangdong; they permitted preferential treatment (with regard to corporate income tax and duty free imports) to foreign invested companies.[25] Subsequently, Economic and Trade Development Zones (ETDZs) were created in 1985 in port cities along China's eastern coastline, which granted preferential investment as well as import treatment.[26] The creation of SEZs and ETDZs greatly facilitated FDI to China, particularly in consumer electronics and computer-related goods.[27]

Some commentators argue that China viewed inward FDI very strategically at this time. Howson asserts that it was seen 'as a way to attract hard currency financing for China's bankrupt state-owned or controlled assets, and gain additional benefits like foreign technology, management know-how, distribution and marketing skills, and foreign sales channels for hard currency earning exports.'[28] Moreover, Yueh notes that China exerted significant control over the form and destination of inward FDI; for example, the Chinese partner often held 51 per cent of shares in joint

---

[24]   Indeed, disaggregation of the Ministry of Petroleum resulted in the creation of three new major SOEs: CNOOC Ltd. (1982), China Petrochemical Corporation (1983) and China National Petroleum Corporation ('CNPC') (1988). Kjeld Erik Brødsgaard, 'Politics and Business Group Formation in China: The Party in Control?' (2012) 211 *China Quarterly* 624, 627.

[25]   Yueh (n 22) 2–3.

[26]   For a comprehensive list, see <http://www.china.org.cn/e-china/openingup/sez.htm>.

[27]   Yueh (n 22) 4.

[28]   Howson (n 23) 76.

ventures, which were only approved if two criteria were satisfied: first, the foreign partner had superior technology of interest to China; second, the manufactured products were export-quality and had demand in global markets.[29] In this way, China was able to mitigate foreign takeovers while developing domestic technological capacity.

In the 1990s, China began to look beyond inward FDI to international capital markets in order to raise finance for state assets as it was 'no longer content to be the workshop of the world'.[30] Accordingly, in 1997–1998 Chinese authorities initiated a 'national team' (*guojia dui* 国家队) of large internationally competitive Chinese enterprises that could compete with the large multinational companies dominating global production chains. These companies were selected from strategically important sectors such as oil and gas, iron and steel, electricity generation and telecommunications.[31] Interestingly, however, hallmarks of ODI are not notably evidenced in China's Five-Year Plans until the 9th Five-Year Plan, which commenced in 1996.

The situation changed radically in the early 2000s when China initiated its 'going out' or 'going global' strategy.[32] This strategy was launched in China's 10th Five-Year plan in 2001, the same year that China acceded to the World Trade Organization. At this time, three major initiatives were instigated which indelibly changed the role and nature of China as a global investment actor.

First, China started issuing shares in its major SOEs on foreign exchanges. For example, PetroChina (a subsidiary of CNPC) was listed on the New York and Hong Kong exchanges in 2000; in the following year, Sinopec (a subsidiary of Sinopec Corporation) and CNOOC were listed on the New York, Hong Kong and also London exchanges. Brødsgaard notes that these listings created huge capital gains for the subsidiaries and their parent companies such that these SOEs 'became powerful in terms of their ability to generate capital and to augment their value in terms of market capitalization.'[33]

---

[29] Yueh (n 22) 3.

[30] Brødsgaard (n 24) 628.

[31] (n 24) 634.

[32] The Chinese word is *zouchuqu*, which literally means 'go out' (as adopted by some authors such as Howson [n 23]), but it can also be interpreted as 'go global', as other authors have done, such as KPMG and the University of Sydney, *Demystifying Chinese Investment: Update August 2012* (University of Sydney China Studies Centre and KPMG, 2012). On this point, see also Cheng and Ma (n 2) 550.

[33] Brødsgaard (n 24) 630.

Second, the Ministry of Commerce was established as responsible for domestic and international trade and international economic cooperation, and the Chinese State-owned Assets Supervision and Administration Commission (SASAC) was created to exercise ownership over China's largest SOEs and to ensure their pursuit of overall national interests.[34]

Third, President Jiang Zemin 江泽民 announced that the 'going out' policy included increased ODI, undertaking construction and engineering projects abroad, and exporting labor services.[35] While it is difficult to catalogue exact policy measures due to a lack of publicly available information, initial measures certainly included relaxation of investment restrictions abroad and increasing financial support for the national team of corporate champions.[36]

The effect of China's going out policy was almost immediate: China's ODI stock reached approximately US$36 billion and ranked sixth among 118 emerging economies by late 2002.[37] In 2004 a gradual liberalization of the ODI regulatory regime began with the 'reform of the investment system'.[38] This process comprised multiple prongs, including decentralization of investment verification and approval at the provincial level, relaxation of foreign exchange controls and stimulus packages to ease the transition of Chinese companies onto the world stage.[39]

Importantly, the going global strategy motivated Chinese SOEs to actively seek to *acquire* foreign assets and equity interests, as opposed to merely *trading* in global commodities and raw materials.[40] This global acquisition strategy continues today, with high-profile examples including CNOOC's successful acquisition of Nexen in Canada (2012) and the

---

[34]   (n 24) 630–631.

[35]   Cheng and Ma (n 2) 550.

[36]   (n 2).

[37]   Eunsuk Hong and Laixiang Sun, 'Go Overseas via Direct Investment: Internationalization Strategy of Chinese Corporations in a Comparative Prism' (2004) 6, University of London, Department of Financial and Management Studies, School of Oriental and African Studies, Discussion Paper No. 40.

[38]   People's Republic of China State Council, 'Decision of the State Council on Reform of the Investment System' (2004) National Development and Reform Commission, Guofa Paper No. 20.

[39]   Cristelle Maurin and Pichamon Yeophantong, 'Going Global Responsibly? China's Strategies towards "Sustainable" Overseas Investment' (2013) 86 *Pacific Affairs* 281, 286–287.

[40]   Howson (n 23) 73; Hong and Sun (n 37).

multi-jurisdictional penetration of Huawei Technology services into 45 of the world's 50 largest telecoms operators.[41]

Importantly, China has never been in arrears on foreign debt. Its foreign borrowing is relatively modest and predominantly medium-to-long term.[42] Moreover, China's foreign reserves are significant. In 2007 China had accumulated huge foreign exchange reserves of $1.2 trillion,[43] which nearly tripled to $3.1 trillion in 2012 or 45 per cent of its annual GDP.[44] As a result, China has been able to become a significant foreign investor and also world banker. For example, as of 30 June 2013, China held nearly $1.5 trillion of US long-term debt, representing the largest single foreign country holding of same.[45]

## CHINA'S GLOBAL INVESTMENT STRATEGY AND SECURING SUPPLY

### The Scale and Spread of Chinese Overseas Investment

Despite the fact that China is a relatively new outward investor, it now 'has a market presence in virtually every country in the world; this presence has grown in almost every market in recent years.'[46] Accordingly, this global external trading presence has stimulated a significant rise in

---

[41]  Ashlee Vance and Bruce Einhorn, 'At Huawei, Matt Bross Tries to Ease US Security Fears' *Business Week* (15 September 2011) <http://www.businessweek.com/magazine/at-huawei-matt-bross-tries-to-ease-us-security-fears-09152011.html> accessed 25 November 2015.

[42]  From 1979 to 2005 China's foreign borrowing totaled only US$147 billion: Angus Maddison, *Chinese Economic Performance in the Long Run: 960–2030 AD* (OECD Publishing, 2007) <http://www.oecd.org/dev/chineseeconomicperformanceinthelongrunreformistpoliciessince1978producedthreedecadesofdynamicgrowth.htm>.

[43]  See <http://www.oecd.org/dev/chineseeconomicperformanceinthelongrunreformistpoliciessince1978producedthreedecadesofdynamicgrowth.htm>.

[44]  Kenneth Rapoza, 'China's Cash Hoard Nearly Half its GDP' *Forbes* (25 May 2012) <http://www.forbes.com/sites/kenrapoza/2012/05/25/chinas-cash-hoard-nearly-half-its-gdp/>.

[45]  US Department of the Treasury, 'Foreign Portfolio Holdings of US Securities as of June 30, 2013 Total Holdings of Long-Term and Short-Term Securities, by Country of Holder, Table 1 (preliminary data, February 28, 2014) <http://www.treasury.gov/ticdata/Publish/shlptab1.html>.

[46]  Steven Husted and Shuichiro Nishioka, 'China's Fare Share? The Growth of Chinese Exports in World Trade' (2013) 149 *Review of World Economics* 565–585, 567.

China's importance as an investment actor across markets and continents. Interestingly, the recent rapid growth in Chinese ODI flows has come from a small base. UNCTAD data show that China's ODI stock in 2008 was $183 billion – 1.11 per cent of world stock and placing China 19th in global rankings;. However it has increased year-on-year to reach $509 billion in 2012,[47] which equated to 2.16 per cent of total world stock, placing China 13th in global rankings.[48] Thus, while China's ODI stock has been quite small relative to other nations, it is clearly growing.

Moreover, Chinese investment activity has clearly changed over time. Prior to 2005, China's ODI share of the manufacturing sector fell from 60 per cent in 1993–1995 to less than 15 per cent in 2005.[49] During the same period, resources exploration grew from approximately 5 per cent of Chinese ODI stock in 1993–1995 to 15 per cent in 2005.[50] From 2005 to 2012, energy, power and metals together accounted for over 70 per cent of Chinese ODI, and real estate, construction and agriculture have become areas of growing interest.[51]

In terms of target jurisdictions, there are several recipients of large amounts of Chinese investment. Data from both the Chinese Ministry of Commerce (MOFCOM) and the US Heritage Foundation show that Australia and the United States have been leading recipients of Chinese investment, and engineering and construction contracts (2005–2012), with other major recipients being Canada, Brazil and Indonesia (see Table 10.1).[52]

---

[47]    UNCTADSTAT, 'Inward and Outward Foreign Direct Investment Stock, annual, 1980–2012 (2012)' <http://unctadstat.unctad.org/TableViewer/tableView. aspx>. UNCTAD data for China is displayed separately from the China Special Administrative Regions (SARs), being Hong Kong and Macao, and Taiwan.

[48]    Note that Hong Kong's global ODI stock was ranked fifth in 2012: UNCTADSTAT (n 47).

[49]    Cheung and Qian (n 2) 317–318.

[50]    Cheung and Qian (n 2).

[51]    Derek Scissors, 'Chinese Investment in the US: Facts and Motives', Heritage Foundation (9 May 2013) <http://www.heritage.org/research/testimony/2013/05/chinese-investment-in-the-us-facts-and-motives>. See also OECD Development Centre, 'Chinese Economic Performance in the Long Run: reformist policies since 1978 produced three decades of dynamic growth' (n.d.) <http:// www.oecd.org/dev/chineseeconomicperformanceinthelongrunreformistpolicies since1978producedthreedecadesofdynamicgrowth.htm> accessed 25 November 2015.

[52]    Scissors (n 51). The Heritage Foundation tracks investments of US$100 million or more from the beginning of 2005. The dataset does not include bond purchases, trade, loans, or aid. The Heritage Foundation notes that its investment figures are similar to those published by MOFCOM since 2005.

*Table 10.1*    *Top Ten Country Recipients of Chinese Investment,*
                     *Engineering and Construction Contracts in 2012*

| Ranking | Country | US$ billions |
| --- | --- | --- |
| 1. | United States | 54.2 |
| 2. | Australia | 53.5 |
| 3. | Canada | 36.7 |
| 4. | Brazil | 27.5 |
| 5. | Indonesia | 25.0 |
| 6. | Iran | 16.8 |
| 7. | Nigeria | 15.6 |
| 8. | Britain | 14.7 |
| 9. | Kazakhstan | 14.0 |
| 10. | Venezuela | 13.9 |

*Source:*    Heritage Foundation, 'China Global Investment Tracker dataset' (January 2013)
<http://www.heritage.org/~/media/Images/Reports/2013/01/b2757/map-1_750px.ashx>.

Moreover, the geographic distribution of Chinese ODI has changed over time. Cheung and Qian demonstrate that Asia's share increased to nearly half of total Chinese ODI in 2005, up from 16 per cent in 1991.[53] During the same period, Australia, the United States and Canada accounted for a decreasing aggregate share of Chinese ODI stock, which fell to less than 10 per cent in 2005 from over 40 per cent in 1991.[54] Derek Scissors of the Heritage Foundation notes that 'Chinese enterprises have shown a clear tendency to move in packs' regarding geographic distribution of ODI.[55]

### Strategic Investment Priorities for China

The preceding data demonstrate that Chinese ODI has been substantially directed into energy, power and metals in the past decade and that certain jurisdictions are favoured investment destinations. These empirics reflect Chinese policy.

In the 11th Five-Year plan (2006–2010), China's energy policy approach focused on developing domestic supply as the primary means of meeting its energy demands, supplemented by foreign energy sources. Pursuant to

---

[53]   Cheung and Qian (n 2) 316–317.
[54]   (n 2) 317.
[55]   Scissors (n 51).

China's Policy on Mineral Resources (2003)[56] and Policies for Development of Iron and Steel Industry (2005),[57] government support has been given to Chinese investments in foreign mining assets[58] in the form of preferential loans granted to SOEs through the China Development Bank and China Exim Bank.[59] The result has been twofold. First, there was a surge in global resources investments by China during this policy timeframe with China's ODI stock in the mining sector (oil, gas and minerals) rising starkly from $5.94 billion in 2004 to $44.66 billion in 2010.[60] Second, the prominent

---

[56] See <http://www.gov.cn/english/official/2005–07/28/content_17963.htm>.

[57] National Development and Reform Commission, 'Policies for development of iron and steel industry: order of the National Development and Reform Commission No. 35' (8 July 2005) <http://www.asianlii.org/cn/legis/cen/laws/pfdoiasi501/> accessed 28 November 2015.

[58] China's 'Policy on Mineral Resources' focuses on domestic utilization of minerals within China as well as the opening up of Chinese minerals resources to foreigners. Nonetheless, Item IV of that Policy provides that: 'The Chinese government encourages domestic enterprises to take part in international cooperation in the sphere of mineral resources, and in exploration, exploitation and utilization of foreign mineral resources. It will promote and protect investments in mineral resources prospecting and exploitation outside China'. Art. 30 of the 'Policies for Development of Iron and Steel Industry' states that: 'We should, according to the principles of making their advantages complement each other and achieving the win–win situation, intensify the international cooperation regarding overseas mineral resources. We should support those large backbone enterprise groups to establish overseas production and supplying bases of iron mines, chrome ore mines, manganese mines, nickel ore mines, waste steel and coking coal, etc. by way of setting up solely-funded enterprises, joint-equity enterprises, contractual enterprises and purchase of mineral resources ... Where two or more domestic enterprises are engaged in vicious competition for overseas resources, the state may adopt administrative coordination to hold alliance or select one of them to make investment so as to avoid vicious competition. The relevant enterprises shall be subject to the administrative coordination of the state'.

[59] National Development and Reform Commission and China Import and Export Bank, *Circular on Credit Support Policy to Key Offshore Investment Projects Encouraged by the State* (National Development and Reform Commission and China Development Bank, 2005); *Circular on the Issues on Offering More Financing Support to Key Overseas Investment Projects* (NDRC and CDB, 2005).

[60] Ministry of Commerce of People's Republic of China, '2010 statistical bulletin of China's outward foreign direct investment' (16 September 2011) <http://english.mofcom.gov.cn/article/statistic/foreigninvestment/201109/20110907742320.shtml> accessed 28 November 2015. Note, also, that China has relied on construction and engineering contracts as well as ODI to secure foreign supply of oil, gas and minerals. Cheng and Ma state that China even 'swapped' its construction projects for oil when it agreed in 2004 to invest US$1 billion in Brazilian port facilities in return for Brazil's oil, iron ore, bauxite and other raw materials. See Cheng and Ma (n 2) 560.

modality of Chinese foreign investment has been SOEs, which accounted for approximately 70 per cent of China's ODI stock in 2009.[61]

Indeed, the central role of SOEs in the rise of China's ODI continued to flourish under the 12th Five-Year plan (2011–2015) which built on the 'going out' strategy by stipulating that China gradually increase the level of international operations of its multi-jurisdictional corporations and financial institutions, particularly in the agricultural and construction sectors. The data detailed above for Chinese ODI in the global agriculture, real estate and construction sectors reflect this policy emphasis. The 13th Five-Year plan (2016–2020) reflects China's economic rise to become the world's second largest economy with per capita GDP increasing to $7,800. The core goal of the latest plan is to enhance national governance through modernization; this will likely include a shift to increased ODI by privately owned enterprises.[62]

These trends are likely to continue according to international predictions. For example, the OECD–FAO *Agricultural Outlook 2013–2022* report focused on China in the context of projected production, consumption, stocks, trade and prices for agricultural products for the period 2013 to 2022.[63] The OECD–FAO Report sets out key data and analysis in Chapter 2 titled 'Feeding China: Prospects and challenges in the next decade'.[64] A clear message is the increasing symbiosis between global markets and China's appetite and output. The OECD predicts that although China should remain self-sufficient in the main food crops (such as rice and sugar), overall agricultural output growth from China will slow in the next decade even as Chinese demand rises due to a rapidly growing and urbanizing population.[65]

---

[61]   David M. Marchick and Daniel R. Bowles, 'The State of Chinese Investment in the United States' (2011) 11, paper presented at the conference on China's Economic and Trade Relations, Columbia University, New York, 10 November 2011). Interviews with businessmen in Beijing by Cheng and Ma also confirmed the advantages enjoyed by Chinese SOEs with regard to energy-related ODI: Cheng and Ma (n 2) 561.

[62]   Permanent Mission of the People's Republic of China to the UN, 'Highlights of Proposals for China's 13th Five-Year Plan' <http://www.china-un.org/eng/zt/China123456/> accessed 28 November 2015. On increasing levels of privately owned ODI see, for example, (n 32).

[63]   OECD and Food and Agriculture Organization of the United Nations, *OECD–FAO Agricultural Outlook 2013–2022* (OECD Publishing, 2013). The report was a collaborative effort of the OECD and the United Nations Food and Agriculture Organization (FAO) with assistance from the Chinese Ministry of Agriculture and the Chinese Academy of Agricultural Sciences.

[64]   (n 63).

[65]   (n 63).

Part of the issue is that China now lacks the rural workforce needed for more complex large-scale farming operations; its rural sectors have been drained of modern, skilled agricultural workers due to land tenure policies and higher urban wages.[66] Moreover, there are serious constraints to any further expansion of agricultural production. Increased urbanisation will likely limit the usage of arable land, and the quality of extant cultivated land is deteriorating.[67] The OECD Report concludes that the net result will be limited productivity within the decade, which will necessarily curb supply from China.[68]

Concomitantly, however, the rapid increase in China's urban population will continue to affect global food demand patterns. The OECD projects a total population explosion to 1.392 billion by 2022, comprising a potential significant urban population increase.[69] And urbanization has significant ramifications for food demand and global markets. Urban zones are associated with higher incomes and larger food consumption rates, including meat, dairy and fish. Indeed, while China is expected to remain the largest fish exporter and maintain its aquaculture leadership at 63 per cent of global production, it is also predicted to become the world's leading consumer of pig meat per capita, surpassing the European Union by 2022.[70]

The result of reduced domestic supply and increased domestic demand is just simple economics: China's policy choices will need to address domestic resource constraints, which necessarily entails higher foreign imports. China may well import more meat in order to contain environmental problems associated with livestock production and to limit the growth in feed requirements while lowering competition for land associated with high intensity crop production by importing more coarse grain to meet rising demand.[71] Such a policy choice would expedite China's transition from an export-driven economy to a consumer-based one in the next 10–30 years, an aspiration confirmed by China's Prime Minister Li Keqiang 李克强 during the 2013 Fortune Global Forum.[72]

---

[66]   Regarding the *hukou* (household registration) system in relation to population mobility and its social and economic ramifications, see Tiejun Cheng and Mark Selden, 'The Origins and Social Consequences of China's *hukou* System' (1994) 139 *China Quarterly* 644.

[67]   Specifically, cereals productivity will likely decline, such as maize and coarse grains for livestock feed: (n 63) 65, 70.

[68]   (n 63).

[69]   (n 63).

[70]   (n 63).

[71]   (n 63) 84.

[72]   See <http://www.fortuneconferences.com/global-forum-2013/>.

The opening of 'soft resources' commodities markets in China represent timely new opportunities for Western meat, dairy and grain producers. A prime example was the 2013 merger agreement between Smithfield Foods, Inc. (Smithfield) and Shuanghui International Holdings Limited (Shuanghui). US-based Smithfield is the world's largest pork processor and hog producer, and one of the biggest and oldest pork producers in the United States. Hong Kong-based Shuanghui is the majority shareholder of China's largest meat processor, Henan Shuanghui Investment and Development, which is publicly listed on the Shenzhen Stock Exchange. The total proposed deal was valued at $7.1 billion, pursuant to which Shuanghui agreed to pay $34 per share and assume Smithfield's debt. The US Committee on Foreign Investment (CFIUS) reviewed the proposal for potential national security concerns about, among other things, whether the takeover places Shuanghui in a position to disrupt food supply in the United States before approving the takeover on 6 September 2013.[73] It represented the largest Chinese takeover of an American company in US history.

It is yet to be seen to what extent the US decision will influence foreign policy in other recipient jurisdictions. The OECD–FAO Report is certainly optimistic, predicting that soft commodities markets will become increasingly open and integrated within the decade.[74]

**Supply Priorities in China's Global Investment Strategy**

Arguably, the focus on sectoral investment in resources (particularly in metals and mining) with diversification into energy (particularly gas) and food production indicates China's national interest in supporting a rapidly urbanizing population that exceeds per capita indigenous resources. In this regard, some commentators argue that China has a coordinated state strategy beyond simply seeking higher financial return, given that China is a

---

[73] There is an initial 30-day review following notification of a potential acquisition after which CFIUS has the option to extend the process for up to 45 days longer in accordance with the 1988 Exon-Florio Amendment to the US *Omnibus Trade and Competitiveness Act 1988*. For analysis of implications of the proposed takeover and eventual CFIUS decision, see Megan Bowman, 'One more time: the ongoing investment review of Smithfield-Shuanghui', Centre for Law, Markets & Regulation Portal, UNSW Australia, (16 August 2013) <http://www.clmr.unsw.edu.au/article/risk/one-more-time-ongoing-investment-review-smithfield-shuanghui> accessed 15 November 2015.

[74] (n 63) 87.

*Table 10.2    Chinese Completed Investment in Australia: 1 January 2006 –*
*31 December 2012 (AU$ millions)*

| 2006 | 2007 | 2008 | 2009 | 2010 | 2011 | 2012 | Total |
|------|------|------|------|------|------|------|-------|
| 550 | not published | 3,643 | 9,058 | 12,944 | 14,404 | 16,741 | **57,340** |

*Source:*   Australian Bureau of Statistics, '5352.0 – International Investment Position,
Australia: Supplementary Statistics 2012, Table 2' (2 May 2013) <http://www.abs.gov.au/
AUSSTATS/abs@.nsf/DetailsPage/5352.02012?OpenDocument>.

latecomer playing global catch-up in procuring natural resources[75] and that
it seeks ownership of commodities sources to ensure continuous supply of
necessary imports.[76]

Sino–Australian investment provides a useful case-study for examining
China's investment strategy. Natural resources and mining sector investments have traditionally dominated the Australia–China FDI landscape.
Regarding Chinese strategic investment in Australia, 78 per cent of completed Chinese investments from January 2005 to December 2012 were
for the purpose of securing supply to an underlying commodity; and the
largest recipient (73 per cent of all Chinese investment) was the mining
sector.[77] Overall, Chinese FDI in Australia increased significantly year-
on-year from 2006 to 2012 (Table 10.2) partly due to resurging energy and
metals investments.[78]

In 2012 alone, however, total Chinese investment into Australia con-
sisted of 48 per cent into mining and 42 per cent into gas, which reflected
an increased global demand for LNG in conjunction with China's plan
to diversify its energy consumption structure beyond coal.[79] Importantly,
Sinopec, an SOE predominantly owned by central government, operates
solely in the energy (gas and oil) sector and was Australia's third-largest

---

[75]   See, for example, Jiangyong Lu, Xiaohui Liu and Hongling Wang,
'Motives for Outward FDI of Chinese Private Firms: Firm Resources, Industry
Dynamics, and Government Policies' (2010) 7 *Management and Organization
Review* 223, 330.

[76]   See, for example, Scissors (n 51).

[77]   Jonathan Li, 'Digging Deep: Chinese Investment in Australian Energy
and Resources' Clayton Utz (2013) 5 <http://www.claytonutz.com.au/publica-
tions/edition/14_march_2013/20130314/digging_deep_chinese_investment_in_
australian_energy_and_resources.page> accessed 12 November 2015.

[78]   KPMG and the University of Sydney (n 32) 3–4, 7. Note, however, that for
the first time in 2014 commercial real estate transactions comprised nearly half of
Chinese investment in Australia.

[79]   (n 32) 9.

Chinese investor based on accumulated investment figures from February 2005 to December 2012.[80]

## The SOE Conundrum

Despite the national benefits that can accrue to investee nations from increased FDI, the intrinsic nature of an SOE has tended to cause media and policy concerns in recipient nations.[81] This is because an assumed investment priority of SOEs is political purchase rather than commercial strategy. This was seen clearly at the time of Chinese acquisitions (attempted and actual) during 2004–2005, including CNOOC's failed bid for Unocal (2005), which raised 'fierce political opposition' in the United States[82] and resulted in US–China political tensions.[83] Concerns also manifested in Australian media and policy debates. For example, headlines in Australia in 2012–2013 included 'China's state-owned enterprises obtain FIRB approval by stealth';[84] and the former Australian Prime Minister Tony Abbott commented that there should be no 'colour bar' on investors, which was an implicit reference to local concerns over Chinese FDI into Australia.[85]

Why is there such concern? Some understanding of SOEs is relevant at this point. Oi describes the evolution of the Chinese 'corporate state' from the initial local town and village enterprises (TVE) to show that Chinese SOEs were traditionally an organizational form, not a legal one.[86]

---

[80] Heritage Foundation, 'Chinese outward investment: China Global Investment Tracker, Dataset 1 Investments' (2013) <http://www.heritage.org/research/projects/china-global-investment-tracker-interactive-map> accessed 12 November 2015.

[81] See George Gilligan and Megan Bowman, 'State Capital: Global and Australian Perspectives' (2014) 37 *Seattle University Law Review* 597.

[82] David Barboza, 'China Backs Away from Unocal Bid' *New York Times* (3 August 2005) <http://www.nytimes.com/2005/08/02/business/worldbusiness/02iht-unocal.html?_r=0> accessed 13 November 2015.

[83] For example, Michael Rowland, 'China-US Tension Mounts over Unocal Takeover Bid', ABC News (6 July 2005) <http://www.abc.net.au/worldtoday/content/2005/s1408416.htm> accessed 14 November 2015. See also Howson (n 23) who gives excellent coverage of these deals and associated political concerns.

[84] Bryan Frith, 'China's State-owned Enterprises Obtain FIRB Approval by Stealth' *The Australian* (13 March 2013) <http://www.theaustralian.com.au/business/opinion/chinas-state-owned-enterprises-obtain-firb-approval-by-stealth/story-e6frg9kx-1226595937750> accessed 13 November 2015.

[85] Mr. Abbott made this comment as then-opposition leader of the Coalition Party during the final leadership debate prior to the September 2013 Australian federal election, which was won by the Coalition Party.

[86] Jean C. Oi, 'The Role of the Local State in China's Transitional Economy' (1995) 144 *China Quarterly* 1132, 1138–1139. See also Howson (n 23).

Specifically, Oi describes the county as similar to 'a large multi-level corporation . . . at the top of a corporate hierarchy as the corporate headquarters, the township as the regional headquarters, and the villages as companies within the larger corporation'.[87] Importantly, TVEs were forms of government not private ownership. Traditionally, therefore, an SOE did not have separate legal personality nor issue stock or equity ('ownership') in itself; instead it was administratively controlled by the state, which had the right to appoint management and appropriate revenues or profits.

Since the commencement of the Chinese corporatization program, as expressed in the 1994 Company Law and 2006 PRC Company Law, Chinese companies can take the form of a company limited by shares, limited by liability or wholly owned by a state agency. However, corporatization is still not synonymous with privatization,[88] and an SOE is now administratively *and* financially controlled by an entity of the state (central or local). Indeed, in 2012 top executives at 53 of the most important central SOEs held ministerial-level status and equal rank to provincial governors.[89] By implication, a controlling shareholder of a Chinese SOE has political as well as economic dominance, which has important implications for the nature of a state-controlled corporation and who it seeks to serve.

For these reasons, uneasiness around SOEs has not been confined to foreign investee nations; the Chinese middle class is also concerned about domestic favouritism toward SOEs to the detriment of private entrepreneurship.[90] For example, some Chinese scholars argue that Deng Xiaoping's plan for the country's development has been reversed by SOE dominance if the main beneficiaries of SOE growth are corrupt officials and not the Chinese public.[91] Cheng Li further notes that bank loans and preferential policies have been almost exclusively available to SOEs.[92]

Thus, a challenge for commentators of state capital is to discern and appreciate the impacts of three factors when ascribing political and/or nefarious motives to SOEs that facilitate ODI in foreign jurisdictions.

---

[87] Oi (n 86) 1138.

[88] Nicholas C. Howson, '"Quack Corporate Governance" as Traditional Chinese Medicine: The Securities Regulation Cannibalization of China's Corporate Law and a State Regulator's Battle Against State Political Economic Power' (2014) 37 *Seattle University Law Review* 667.

[89] Brødsgaard (n 24) 634.

[90] Cheng Li, 'The End of the CCP's Resilient Authoritarianism? A Tripartite Assessment of Shifting Power in China' (2012) 211 *China Quarterly* 595, 608.

[91] See, for example, the blog by Xu Xiaonian (an economics and finance professor at the China Europe International Business School in Shanghai) <http://xuxiaonian.blog.sohu.com/158818651.html>.

[92] Li (n 90) 608.

First, China's increasing need to secure supply for its domestic demand is no secret: it requires resources, technology and national champions to go out and expand overseas. Scissors writes that: 'The foundations for Chinese outward investment are neither subtle nor, except for advanced dual-use technology, dangerous.'[93]

Second, tensions may exist between the goals of central and provincial government entities. The above depiction of local (not central) government actors as germane to the commercial success of traditional TVEs/SOEs are telling.[94] Indeed, Oi terms China's state-led growth as *local state corporatism* whereby local governments in China are *economic* and not merely administrative actors with the result that 'the entrepreneurial interests of local governments have compromised their role as agents of the central state'.[95] Accordingly, the fragmentation of SOE ownership and thus potentially competing priorities between levels of government add complexity to SOE investment behaviour.

Third, SOEs may be exercising independence from the government entities that formally own or control them. In March 2012, SASAC issued regulations requiring central state-controlled SOEs to: register with SASAC before undertaking 'key investment projects' in their core businesses; obtain SASAC approval prior to investing overseas in non-core areas of business; and lodge details with SASAC of sources of investment and financing for proposed non-core area investments.[96]

---

[93]   Scissors (n 51).

[94]   On this point see also: Teemu Ruskola, *Legal Orientalism: China, the US and Modern Law* (Harvard UP, 2013).

[95]   Oi (n 86) 1139.

[96]   State-owned Assets Supervision and Interim Measures on the Supervision and Administration of Overseas State-Owned Equity Interests of Central SOEs Administration Commission, '*Interim Measures On The Supervision and Administration of Outbound Investments by Central SOEs*', Circular No. 28 (2012) Circular No. 28 was issued on 18 March 2012 and came into force on 1 May 2012. It builds on extant SASAC regulations: State-owned Assets Supervision and Administration Commission, Interim Measures on the Supervision And Administration of Overseas State-Owned Assets of Central SOEs, Circular No. 26 (14 June 14 2011) and 'State-owned Assets Supervision and Administration Commission', Circular No. 27 (14 June 2011). These measures regulate: foreign investments by central SOEs from their initial decision-making through project management and operation, as well as the way in which equity interests in foreign investment projects are managed and monitored by central SOEs and SASAC. For details, see Wei Chen and Jiahao Xie, 'New SASAC Rules Enacted to Consummate Outbound Investment Supervisory System for Central SOEs', (4 July 2012) <http://xbma.org/forum/chinese-update-new-sasac-rules-enacted-to-consummate-outbound-investment-supervisory-system-for-central-soes/> accessed 14 November 2015.

Yet despite the SASAC framework, there is some evidence to suggest that the Going Out strategy is being led by Chinese firms rather than central government. Brødsgaard suggests that Chinese companies listed abroad operate under international (not domestic) market conditions and that powerful SOEs have blocked state initiatives that may be contrary to their own economic interests, preferring instead to garner 'legitimacy by symbolizing China's economic rise'.[97] Howson makes a similar claim, citing the action of CNOOC in bidding for Unocal in 2005 despite central government opposition.[98] Similarly, KPMG argues that 'Chinese SOEs abroad have shown strong commercial motivations, similar to those of multinational corporations from developed countries'.[99] Commercial motivations are evinced by SOE capital investments to secure stable and high-quality supplies of natural resources, mergers and acquisitions to acquire new brands and technology, accessing new markets and exporting Chinese brands.[100]

Moreover, in practice, multiple external parties are involved in Chinese SOE investment decision-making abroad, including domestic consultants, corporate partners and financiers, such that decisions cannot be made solely by a government entity. Importantly, management may remain local. For example, Australian statistics show that Chinese investors have relied heavily on local talent to manage Australian companies in which the investor gains a controlling interest. Specifically, during the period 1 January 2005 to 31 December 2012, Chinese nationals were appointed as chief executive officer only in 32 per cent of corporate acquisitions in the Australian energy and resources sectors, and chief operating officer in only 10 per cent of the same.[101]

Thus, based on the empirical evidence, Chinese SOEs appear to be pursuing commercial opportunities in source-rich foreign jurisdictions with

---

[97]   Brødsgaard (n 24) 633.

[98]   Howson (n 23) 73, makes this point in relation to the CNOOC bid for Unocal, which was opposed by Chinese central government actors.

[99]   KPMG and University of Sydney (n 32) 13. See also Theodore Moran, Barbara R. Kotschwar and Julia Muir, 'Chinese Investment in Latin American Resources: The Good, the Bad, and the Ugly', (2012) Peterson Institute for International Economics, Working Paper No. 12–3.

[100]   Nonetheless, the regulatory framework is designed to set the parameters for the economic activities of large enterprises, and the CCP still controls the appointment of CEOs and presidents of the most important companies. See Brødsgaard (n 24) 633.

[101]   Li (n 77). However, it is important that, as a sign of potential investment practice change, Chinese private sector investment in Australia exceeded SOE investment in 2014, both in terms of volume (85% of total) and value (66% or AU$6.23 bn), see KPMG and University of Sydney (n 32) 3.

governmental blessing in much the same way as Western multinational corporations have done and continue to do.

## CONCLUSION

China's emergence as a prominent global investment actor – in terms of both FDI and ODI – is a phenomenon that can be better understood using a longitudinal lens. This chapter has sought to contribute to the growing body of literature on the duality of Chinese FDI–ODI by adding an historical perspective to the state capital story in order to look forward. By analyzing FDI and ODI data in the context of China's Five-Year Plans, which have to date been an underutilized contextual tool, we have viewed trade and investment patterns and ambitions from a Chinese perspective to shed light on China's role as an outward investor and its strategic ODI ambitions.

Data detailed and discussed throughout this chapter show that: Chinese investments have occurred predominantly in mining/natural resources with emerging diversification toward energy, agriculture, and commercial real estate; and SOEs have been the primary modality of Chinese ODI abroad. Indeed, the advent of the 2001 'going global' policy animated Chinese SOEs to move beyond mere trading relationships to active foreign asset and equity acquisition. In so doing, China has become a pervasive investment actor in nearly all markets and continents. Although SOE investment behaviour has triggered political concerns in some recipient nations, empirical data indicate that these SOEs appear to be pursuing commercial opportunities abroad as Western multinational corporations have done and continue to do. Indeed, it may be argued that concerns about the prevalence and potentially political nature of China's SOEs reflect (and perhaps mask) deeper concerns about the increasing significance of China on the world stage.

Nonetheless, international predictions regarding global food security and China's changing domestic demand–supply make clear that China's significance as a global foreign investor, as well as a recipient of global soft commodities, will only continue to rise.

Arguably, these developments are consistent with China's long-standing traditions of trade and ODI, albeit with different emphases over different decades as evidenced in the Five-Year Plans and documented throughout this chapter. From the economic advancement of the 12th century to the post-war boom of the 1930s, from the relative isolation under Mao Zedong to the 'open door' FDI policy under Deng Xiaoping, to the 'going global' ODI strategy initiated under Jiang Zeming, it is clear that China's significance as a key global investment actor is remarkable and ever-evolving.

# APPENDIX

*Table 10A.1   Viewing China's Five-Year Plans through an Investment Lens*

| Five-Year Plan | Leader | Inward FDI | Outward ODI |
|---|---|---|---|
| **13th** (2016–2020)[1] | President Xi Jinping (2013–)  Premier Li Keqiang (2013–) | • Competition to be further improved in certain national monopoly sectors including electricity, telecommunications and transport. <br> • Financial reforms to be accelerated. <br> • Green finance to be promoted. | • Renmimbi's inclusion in the IMF's special drawing rights to be promoted to achieve convertible capital account. <br> • International coordination of macroeconomic policy to be strengthened. |
| **12th** (2011–2015)[2] A 'very green' plan; Focused on drawing value from local consumers rather than investment.[3] | Presidents Xi Jinping (2013–)  Hu Jintao (2003–2013)  Premiers Li Keqiang (2013–)  Wen Jiabao (2003–2013) | • Continue dual strategies 'bringing in' and 'going out'. Equal attention to both FDI in China and Chinese ODI. <br> • Guide foreign investment towards modern agriculture, high-end technology, advanced manufacturing, energy conservation, new energy, modern service industry, especially in middle and western parts of China. <br> • Encourage different means to acquire domestic enterprises. E.g. Buying shares, joint ventures. <br> • Bring in senior talent and advanced technology from overseas and encourage foreign enterprises to set up research and development (R&D) centres in China in order to learn advanced international management concepts and systems. | • Continue dual strategies 'bringing in' and 'going out'. Equal attention to both FDI in China and Chinese ODI. <br> • Speed up the implementation of the 'going out' strategy <br> • Speed up formulation of laws and regulations concerning overseas investments. <br> • Deepen development of international energy resources and mutually beneficial processing cooperation. <br> • Support technology research and development (R&D) investments abroad. <br> • Encourage leading manufacturing industry enterprises to conduct foreign investment to create internationalised marketing and sales channels and brands. <br> • Enlarge international cooperation in the agricultural sector and develop overseas engineering contracts. <br> • Engage in labour cooperation and cooperation projects that can improve living standards in local areas. |

*306*

| Plan | Leadership | Foreign capital / domestic | 'Going out' / outward |
|---|---|---|---|
| **11th** (2006–2010)[4] | President Hu Jintao (2003–2013) Premier Wen Jiabao (2003–2013) | • Improving the quality of foreign capital by guiding foreign investment direction and diversifying the modes of foreign capital utilisation. <br> • Focus on the import of foreign advanced technologies, managerial know-how and high quality talents. <br> • Integrating foreign capital utilization through the upgrading of domestic industrial structure and technology. | • Gradually develop own cross-country corporations and cross-country financial institutions to increase level of international operations. <br> • Conduct research in relation to overseas investments, including enhancement of scientific evaluation methods. <br> • Actively discuss and sign mutual agreements on investment protection and agreements to avoid double taxation. <br> • Increase facilitation for enterprises to invest overseas while protecting China's reputation abroad and minimising investment risks. <br> • 'Going out' enterprises should comply with good standards of corporate social responsibility. <br> • Promote international economic cooperation by implementing the 'going out' strategy and promoting regional economic cooperation. <br> • Improve mechanisms and policies to promote the cross-border flow and optimized allocation of production factors (labour, land, etc.) <br> • Actively develop economic and technological cooperation with neighbouring countries and economies for mutual benefit. |
| **10th** (2001–2005)[5] Implemented strategies for outward FDI | Presidents Hu Jintao (2003–2013) Jiang Zemin (1993–2003) Premiers Wen Jiabao (2003–2013) | • Reform of the Investment System (2004). <br> • Gradually open up the service sector to foreign-investment. <br> • Encourage foreign investment in high-tech industries and infrastructures, and encourage setting up of R&D centres in China to participate in restructuring and renovation of SOEs. | • Implement 'going out' strategy (2001), encouraging enterprises with comparative advantages to make investments abroad, to establish processing operations, to exploit foreign resources with local partners, to contract for international engineering projects, and to increase the export of labour. <br> • Support the listing of eligible enterprises on overseas stock markets. |

*Table 10A.1* (continued)

| Five-Year Plan | Leader | Inward FDI | Outward ODI |
|---|---|---|---|
| | Zhu Rongji (1998–2003) | • The 'Western development strategy': encourage more investment in central and western regions, which otherwise are least likely to attract aid on their own. [6] | • Provide supportive policy framework to create favourable conditions for enterprises to establish overseas operations.<br>• Strengthen supervision and prevent loss of state assets. |
| **9th** (1996–2000)[7] Transition to greater levels of private ownership and corporatisation in increasingly market economy. | President Jiang Zemin (1993–2003) Premiers Zhu Rongji (1998–2003) Li Peng (1988–1998) | • Special policy regarding SEZs and the Shanghai Pudong New Area will remain unchanged.<br>• Gradually open the domestic market including finance, commercial outlets and tourism.<br>• Recruit overseas intelligence.<br>• Gradually give foreign-funded enterprises the same treatment as Chinese counterparts; standardize taxation system and levy taxes fair and reasonable to both Chinese and foreign enterprises. | • Establish a unified and standardized system of foreign economic affairs in line with generally accepted international practices.<br>• Develop economic and trade relationships with other countries (noting that some western countries are determined to exclude China from WTO). |

**8th**
(1991–1995)

President
Jiang Zemin
(1993–2003)
Yang Shangkun
(1988–1993)
Premier
Li Peng
(1988–1998)

- Attract advanced technology and managerial expertise from abroad to help improve production technology and management.
- Rapid growth in international tourism.[8]

**7th**
(1986–1990)

Presidents
Yang Shangkun
(1988–1993)
Li Xiannian
(1983–1988)
Premiers
Li Peng
(1988–1998)
Zhao Ziyang
(1980–1988)

- Open up further to the outside world, combining domestic economic growth with expanding external economic and technologic exchanges.[9]
- Continued emphasis on innovation and economic expansion.
- Foreign loans declined as result of Tiananmen incident.

309

*Table 10A.1* (continued)

| Five-Year Plan | Leader | Inward FDI | Outward ODI |
|---|---|---|---|
| **6th**<br>(1981–1985)[10]<br>Central government opened China's economy to FDI for the first time.[11] | President<br>Li Xiannian<br>(1983–1988)<br>Acting President<br>Ye Jianying<br>(1981–1983)<br>Premier<br>Zhao Ziyang<br>(1980–1998) | ● Continue to expand trade, economic and technological exchanges with the outside world in accordance with the principles of equality and mutual benefit, of unified plan and policy and of concerted action toward foreign counterparts.<br>● Use foreign loans efficiently, encourage FDI via joint ventures in order to increase the use of foreign funds to a suitable extent.<br>● Overarching goal to raise capacity for self-reliance, not impair development of national economy.<br>● The Government 'placed large numbers of key projects in the coastal areas, causing 47 per cent of total investment to gravitate to those areas'.[12]<br>● From 1980, SEZs created in Southern coastal areas. | |
| **5th**<br>(1976–1980)<br>Introduced opening up of the communist economic system | Acting President<br>Ye Jianying<br>(1976–1981)<br>Premier<br>Hua Guofeng<br>(1976–1980) | ● Opening up of the communist economic system.<br>● Moving away from Soviet-style command economy and gradual introduction of market reforms. | |

| Plan | Leaders | Focus |
|---|---|---|
| **4th** (1971–1975) | Acting President Dong Biwu (1968–1975)<br>Premier Zhou Enlai (1949–1976) | • Focus on internal economic strengthening in industry and agriculture, rather than FDI. |
| **3rd** (1966–1970) | Acting President Song Qingling (1968–1972)<br>Premier Zhou Enlai (1949–1976) | • Focus on internal economic strengthening, rather than FDI. |
| **2nd** (1958–1962) Abandoned almost immediately after inauguration[13] | Presidents Liu Shaoqi (1995–1968) Mao Zedong (1954–1959)<br>Premier Zhou Enlai (1949–1976) | • Focus on internal economic strengthening, rather than FDI.<br>• Continued industrial construction with focus on heavy industry as foundation for socialist industrialization.[14] |
| **1st** (1953–1957) Perfecting Soviet Style Marxist Communism | President Mao Zedong (1954–1959)<br>Acting President Mao Zedong (1949–1954)<br>Premier Zhou Enlai (1949–1976) | • Aimed to develop state-directed growth of heavy industry, particularly coal, steel and petrochemicals.<br>• Many plants and equipment purchased from Soviet Union.<br>• Increase of government control over industry. E.g. nationalization of banking system; no privately owned companies in China by 1956. |

*Table 10A.1* (continued)

*Notes:*

1 Permanent Mission of the People's Republic of China to the UN, *Highlights of Proposals for China's 13ʰ Five-Year Plan* <http://www.china-un.org/eng/zt/China123456/> accessed 28 November 2015.

2 KPMG, *China's 12th Five-Year Plan: Overview (2011–2015)* (KPMG, March 2011) <http://www.kpmg.com/cn/en/issuesandinsights/articlespublications/publicationseries/5-years-plan/pages/default.aspx> accessed 20 November 2015.

3 Stephen S. Roach, 'A Giant Step Towards Solutions' *China Daily* (22 March 2011) <http://usa.chinadaily.com.cn/opinion/2011–03/22/content_12207694.htm> accessed 15 May 2014.

4 National Development and Reform Commission of the People's Republic of China, *The Outline of the Eleventh Five-Year Plan: For National Economic and Social Development of the People's Republic of China* (NDRC, n.d.) <http://en.ndrc.gov.cn/hot/t20060529_71334.htm> accessed 20 November 2015.

5 Zhu Rongji, *Report on the Outline of the Tenth Five-Year Plan for National Economic and Social Development (2001)* 5 March 2001 <http://english.gov.cn/official/2005–07/29/content_18334.htm> accessed 19 November 2015.

6 Markus Taube and Mehmet Ogutcu, *Main Issues on Foreign Investment in China's Regional Development: Prospects and Policy Challenges* (OECD Publishing, 2002) 2.

7 Li Peng, 'Report on the Outline of the Ninth Five-Year Plan (1996–2000) for National Economic and Social Development and the Long-range Objectives to the Year 2010 (excerpts)' *China.org* (5 March 1996) <http://www.china.org.cn/95e/95-english1/2.htm> accessed 18 November 2015.

8 (n 7).

9 'The 7th Five-Year Plan (1986–1990)' *gov.cn* (5 April 2006) <http://www.gov.cn/english/2006–04/05/content_245695.htm> accessed 18 November 2015.

10 Zhao Ziyang, 'Report on the Sixth Five-Year Plan for National Economic and Social Development' (1985) 18(4) *Chinese Economy* 3–61.

11 Australian Bureau of Resources and Energy Economics, Tourism Research Australia, *Resources, Energy and Tourism China Review: June 2012* (Commonwealth of Australia, 2012) 12.

12 Xiaojuan Jiang, *FDI in China: Contributions to Growth, Restructuring, and Competitiveness* (Nova Science Publishers, 2004) 90.

13 W.K., 'China's Third Five-Year Plan' *China Quarterly* 25 (1966) 171–175.

14 <http://www.china.org.cn/english/MATERIAL/157606.htm>.

# 11. Capital market disclosure regimes: advancing accountability for Chinese TNCs

*Virginia Harper Ho\**

## INTRODUCTION

One of the most significant economic transformations of the modern period is that global economic power is no longer wielded exclusively by sovereign states, but also by transnational corporations (TNCs), global corporate networks whose operations span jurisdictional and geographic boundaries. In response to the limits of jurisdictionally bounded legal systems, regulatory networks grounded on comity, international law and mutual assistance commitments have emerged as local regulators, and enforcement authorities work with their counterparts in other jurisdictions to reach the TNC on its own terms. Firm self-regulation and voluntary regimes, such as the Global Compact, complement these responses by harnessing TNCs' reputational interests and market incentives to drive corporate accountability. Within these evolving regulatory networks, the transnational nature of capital and information flows makes global capital market regulation an important source of accountability for TNCs, and one that directly shapes TNC's market incentives.

Capital market regulation, a field that extends broadly to include rules governing investment products, trading mechanisms and the oversight of investment professionals and financial institutions, is grounded on disclosure obligations that lie at the heart of domestic securities laws and stock exchange listing rules. Beyond the level of accountability produced by core financial disclosure, public reporting requirements in many markets have expanded to include non-financial information on the firm's environmental, social and governance (ESG) practices that may reflect its long-term financial health, risk management practices and impact on stakeholders.[1]

\*   Professor, University of Kansas School of Law. This chapter benefited from helpful comments by Zheng Lin, Zhu Kejun, and representatives of SynTao and of the GRI-China office. Able research assistance was provided by Lin Lei.
[1]   The term 'ESG' is widely used to refer to a broad range of non-financial

This chapter examines how both traditional and emerging disclosure obligations for listed firms serve as an important source of TNC accountability to investors and other stakeholders. It then presents a case study of the adoption of mandatory and voluntary reporting requirements by stock exchanges and securities regulators in mainland China. The potential role of capital market disclosure regimes in driving accountability for Chinese TNCs is particularly interesting because of the growing influence of Chinese TNCs in the global economy. China is also a leader among global capital markets, and its influence is likely to deepen with new reforms that are expanding access for foreign investors. China's experience highlights the advantages of disclosure-based regimes as a source of accountability for TNCs even in institutional contexts that limit the effectiveness of external monitoring and traditional regulatory tools.

## CAPITAL MARKET DISCLOSURE REGIMES AND TNCs

As global firms, TNCs rely on public capital markets not only to fund their operations, but also to elevate their brand recognition in local markets and demonstrate their status as industry leaders. By going public, a TNC parent or subsidiary subjects itself to the listing requirements of the securities exchange and to regulatory authorities in each jurisdiction where its securities are traded. As a result, the TNC as a global organization becomes subject to greater scrutiny by investors and other stakeholders around the world.

Disclosure is central to the triple mission of modern securities law: 'protecting investors; ensuring that markets are fair, efficient and transparent; and reducing systemic risk.'[2] Strong securities markets require that minority investors have adequate information about the company's business and that they enjoy protections from insider self-dealing and opportunism.[3] The prevalence of disclosure requirements in modern capital markets also rests on the view most famously articulated by Louis Brandeis that

---

indicators beyond environmental, social or governance factors, including human rights and sustainability.

[2]   International Organization of Securities Commissions (IOSCO), *Objectives and Principles of Securities Regulation* (June 2010) 3 <http://www.iosco.org/library/pubdocs/pdf/IOSCOPD323.pdf>.

[3]   Bernard Black, 'The Legal and Institutional Preconditions for Strong Securities Markets' (2001) 48 *UCLA Law Review* 781, 783.

'sunlight is . . . the best of disinfectants' and a deterrent to fraud.[4] In addition, accurate and timely information on the risk and potential return of investments enables capital to be efficiently allocated in the market and reduces market volatility.[5]

Accordingly, TNC affiliates that issue securities to the public must assume initial and ongoing reporting obligations.[6] In addition, stock exchange listing rules impose corporate governance requirements, such as shareholder voting rights, that protect outside investors in listed firms. Firms that fail to comply with the listing standards of the exchange can be denied entry or, once admitted, can be sanctioned or de-listed.

### Transparency as a Regulatory Tool

By encouraging firms to alter practices that investors might view negatively, transparency mandates designed to advance the primary goals of securities regulation can also directly incentivize changes in corporate behavior.[7] For example, mandating or encouraging disclosure of greenhouse gas (GHG) emissions may cause companies to voluntarily reduce pollution. Disclosure rules also help firms identify issues they might otherwise have failed to monitor. Disclosure can therefore motivate self-regulation and align companies with broader public policy goals. These reporting obligations are also backed by the enforcement power of securities regulators and, in many jurisdictions, by shareholder litigation.

As a driver of accountability to investors, and indirectly to other stakeholders, disclosure-based regimes offer a number of advantages over traditional regulation of TNCs by home or host governments:

### Global reach

The global integration of capital flows, investor networks and information has placed TNCs within market systems whose power and reach exceed the bounds of traditional regulation. Public company reporting rules have

---

[4]   Louis D. Brandeis, *Other People's Money and How the Bankers Use It* (F.A. Stokes, 1914) 92.

[5]   *See* Gerard Hertig, Reinier Kraakman and Edward Rock, 'Issuers and Investor Protection' in Reinier Kraakman et al. (eds), *The Anatomy of Corporate Law: A Comparative and Functional Approach* (2nd edn, Oxford UP, 2009) 279–280 (surveying empirical evidence).

[6]   In the United States, the Securities Act of 1933, 15 U.S.C. § 77 *et seq.*, and the Securities Exchange Act of 1934, 15 U.S.C. § 78 *et seq.*, establish the basis for these requirements.

[7]   Cynthia Williams, 'The Securities and Exchange Commission and Corporate Social Transparency' (1999) 112 *Harvard L. Rev.* 1197, 1209–1246.

enterprise-wide reach across the TNC and extend beyond any disclosure requirements that might apply to the TNC parent and its directors and officers under local corporate and securities law. Under consolidated reporting rules, ongoing reporting by a publicly traded TNC parent or subsidiary provides information about both the listed entity and any affiliates that it owns or controls.[8] Some public reporting requirements extend further to contracting parties of the TNC, such as suppliers.[9]

### Good governance

Transparency and other dimensions of good corporate governance are mutually reinforcing, promoting greater efficiency that benefits all corporate constituencies. Disclosure regimes obligate firms to adopt internal monitoring and reporting systems that facilitate better monitoring across the TNC, and the strength of these internal systems and procedures determines, in part, the power of disclosure as a self-regulatory tool. Disclosure also facilitates corporate governance by enabling minority shareholders to exercise their voting rights on an informed basis.

### Market signals

In efficient markets, market prices provide signals to investors about the future value of the firm and give firm management an indication of investors' reaction to new information about the firm or changes in market conditions. If executive compensation is tied to clear performance measures that include both financial and non-financial indicators, market signals may better align management incentives with both short- and long-term firm value.

### Peer benchmarking

Because mandatory disclosures must conform to specific format, content and timing requirements, they allow corporate performance to be readily measured against industry peers and other benchmarks. Benchmarking creates direct incentives for firm management, particularly when tied to executive compensation. Requiring specific disclosures regarding corporate governance matters, such as executive compensation, board structure and related party transactions, can also motivate firms to adopt best practices.

---

[8]   In general, majority-owned subsidiaries are included in consolidated reporting. Regulation S-X, Rule 3A-02(a), 17 C.F.R. § 210.3A-02 (2011) (U.S.); International Financial Reporting Standard 10, May 2011.

[9]   European Parliament, 'Directive on Disclosure of Non-financial and Diversity Information by Large Companies and Groups' (15 April 2014).

## Flexibility

In contrast to costly and potentially ineffective one-size-fits-all mandates, reporting requirements can be applied by firms of different scale and impact. Listed firms are industry leaders, so introducing new requirements for listed firms first also allows them to be tested by firms with the greatest capacity to comply. 'Comply or explain' disclosure rules widely used in the United Kingdom, Europe and Asia, which require companies to either comply with a reporting obligation or explain why they do not, allow for even greater flexibility in application. Reporting requirements are also more flexible than direct regulation, in that they reach beyond a single regulatory space, such as environmental protection.

## Public oversight

Disclosure complements direct public regulation by simultaneously facilitating investor and regulator oversight, as well as direct monitoring by the public, NGOs and other interested stakeholders. Harnessing market pressure and the threat of reputational harm in this way can directly impact TNC practice, often on a global basis.

## The Scope of Disclosure and Accountability for Stakeholder Impacts

The extent to which disclosure can motivate greater TNC accountability depends in part on its power to focus TNCs on costs, risks and impacts that might not otherwise have been adequately monitored or mitigated. However, the goal of the public reporting rules is not complete disclosure, but rather disclosure of all *material* information necessary to comply with reporting requirements and to render those disclosures not misleading, including material non-financial information . The US Supreme Court has defined information as material if it is substantially likely to be 'viewed by the reasonable investor as having significantly altered the "total mix" of information made available' to them.[10] Although definitions vary somewhat across jurisdictions, international and US materiality standards are substantively the same.[11] False or misleading disclosures and material omissions can subject the firm or its principals to administrative, civil or criminal penalties, or to civil damages claims by the firm's shareholders.

Mandatory reporting for listed firms has historically been limited

---

[10]    *T.S.C. Industries, Inc. v. Northway, Inc.*, 426 U.S. 438, 449 (1976).

[11]    Michael P. Krzus, 'Reporting and Standards: tools for stewardship', in James P. Hawley et al. (eds), *Cambridge Handbook of Institutional Investment and Fiduciary Duty* (Cambridge UP, 2014) 415, 426.

to financial measures and other material information that might affect investors' risk–return calculation and the future value of the listed company, although some of this information may require firms to account for their impact on corporate stakeholders. For example, in 2010, the US Securities and Exchange Commission (SEC) issued policy guidance emphasizing the potential materiality of climate change impacts for listed firms and linking climate change impacts to existing financial reporting requirements.[12] Pending legal or administrative claims and known and quantifiable risks may arise from poor ESG practices, and prospective or 'forward-looking' information based on management's best estimates of market changes may also relate to sustainability or other ESG factors.[13] However, the rules governing financial reporting in most markets have not directly taken into account the stakeholder-oriented concerns that motivate standard debates on the accountability of global firms, and stakeholder impacts in many jurisdictions are communicated to the market largely through voluntary sustainability or ESG reporting.

A key limitation of current disclosure-based regimes in advancing accountability for TNCs is the poor quality of information available to the capital markets about firms' management of non-financial, stakeholder-related risks and other ESG factors.[14] To be meaningful to the markets, information must be material, timely, reliable, comparable and presented in a consistent way over time. Financial reporting generally satisfies these conditions because it is produced in accordance with accounting standards, such as International Financial Reporting Standards (IFRS) or US Generally Accepted Accounting Principles, and it is backed by mandatory audits using standardized procedures. A number of standard-setting organizations, including the Sustainability Accounting Standards Board (SASB) in the United States and global organizations, such as the International Standards Organization (ISO), the International Integrated Reporting Council (IIRC) and the Global Reporting Initiative (GRI), have developed tools designed to standardize reporting of material non-financial indicators, but the quality and comparability of non-financial

---

[12]    Commission Guidance Regarding Disclosure Related to Climate Change, Securities Act Release No. 3 3–9106, 75 Fed. Reg. 6292 (Feb. 2, 2010) (codified at 17 C.F.R. pts. 211, 231, 241).

[13]    Securities regulations in the US require the management discussion and analysis (MD&A) to disclose 'known trends or uncertainties' that might have a material impact on future financial performance. Reg. S-K, Item 303, 17 C.F.R. § 229.303 (1982).

[14]    Robert G. Eccles, et al., 'The Need for Sector-Specific Materiality and Sustainability Reporting Standards' (2012) 24 *J. Applied Corporate Finance* 65–71.

reporting within and across markets lags behind standard financial measures.

However, regulators, investors and other market participants increasingly acknowledge the potentially material effect of companies' attention to employees, creditors, communities and other stakeholders on long-term corporate financial performance, investment risk and return, and even systemic risk to entire economies.[15] Stakeholder impacts and related regulatory compliance are also widely recognized as within the scope of the risk management function and the duty of corporate boards to monitor management and the firm's legal and compliance risk.[16] These conclusions are supported by a growing academic literature demonstrating that firms that operate more responsibly, manage risk effectively and adopt sound corporate governance practices can obtain financing from lenders and investors at lower cost.[17] Such firms may also do better at preserving value for investors than other firms of comparable size and financial strength.[18] Empirical studies also support a link between good corporate governance, widely recognized as essential to long-term financial success, and responsible or sustainable business practice.[19]

Over 50 governments, including emerging markets like India, South Africa and indeed, China, have already endorsed these findings by introducing mandatory ESG reporting requirements.[20] Others, such as the US SEC, have enacted disclosure rules directed at specific stakeholder concerns, such as human rights impacts, as part of standard financial

---

[15] Gunnar Friede et al., 'ESG and Financial Performance: Aggregated Evidence from More Than 2000 Empirical Studies' (2015) 5 *J. Sustainable Finance* 210.

[16] COSO, Enterprise Risk Management– Integrated Framework, Executive Summary (Sept. 2004) <http://www.coso.org/documents/coso_erm_executivesummary.pdf>.

[17] Sadok El Ghoul et al., 'Does Corporate Social Responsibility Affect the Cost of Capital?' (2012) 35 *J. of Banking & Finance* 2388; Allen Goss and Gordon S. Roberts, 'The Impact of Corporate Social Responsibility on the Cost of Bank Loans' (2011) 30 *J. of Banking & Finance* 1794.

[18] Paul C. Godfrey et al., 'The Relationship Between Corporate Social Responsibility and Shareholder Value: An Empirical Test of the Risk Management Hypothesis' (2009) 30 *Strategic Management J.* 425.

[19] Allen Ferrell et al., 'Socially Responsible Firms' (2014) ECGI working paper.

[20] William Bartels et al., 'Carrots and Sticks: Global Trends in Sustainability Reporting Regulation and Policy' (2016) 14 <https://assets.kpmg.com/content/dam/kpmg/pdf/2016/05/carrots-and-sticks-may-2016.pdf>; Sustainable Stock Exchanges (SSEI), 'Sustainability Reporting Policies' (2015) <http://www.sseinitiative.org/sustainabilityreporting/>.

reporting but do not mandate more comprehensive ESG disclosures.[21] Stock exchanges in most developed markets and a growing number of emerging markets, including Brazil, India, South Africa, Mexico and Thailand, have committed to improving ESG disclosure and performance among listed companies.[22] These measures have added to growing pressure from investors, consumers and interest groups, leading to significant increases in the level of non-financial reporting over the past decade, deepening corporate accountability for material stakeholder impacts and related indicators that may ultimately affect financial performance.[23]

## CAPITAL MARKET DISCLOSURE REGIMES IN CHINA: A STAKEHOLDER PERSPECTIVE

Any discussion of TNC accountability must take into account the role of Chinese TNCs and Chinese capital markets. Chinese TNCs are not only global leaders in foreign direct investment in developed markets such as Australia, Europe and the United States, but their influence is also deeply felt in Africa and other parts of the developing world. Most Chinese TNCs are publicly traded domestically, as well as in Hong Kong and on other leading exchanges. In addition, China now ranks second globally after the United States based on the combined market capitalization of listed companies on China's two primary exchanges in Shenzhen and Shanghai.[24] In 2010, China surpassed the United States as the largest market for initial public offerings (IPOs) globally, reflecting a broader shift in public listings from developed to emerging markets.[25]

China's regulatory regime for listed firms has relied heavily on disclosure since its inception, and most Chinese TNCs also produce sustainability reports that reflect to some extent the firm's attention to stakeholder

---

[21]   David M. Lynn, 'The Dodd-Frank Act's Specialized Corporate Disclosure: Using the Securities Laws to Address Public Policy Issues' (2011) 6 *J. of Business and Technology Law* 327; Erika R. George, 'Influencing the Impact of Business on Human Rights' in Lara Blecher et al. (eds), *Corporate Responsibility for Human Rights Impacts: New Expectations and Paradigms* (ABA Publishing, 2014).

[22]   Bartels et al., *Carrots and Sticks* (n 20); SSEI, *Sustainability Reporting* (n 20).

[23]   KPMG, *The KPMG Survey of Corporate Responsibility Reporting 2015* (KPMG International December 2015) 5, 28–37; Ioannis Ioannou and George Serafeim, 'The Consequences of Mandatory Sustainability Reporting: Evidence from Four Countries' (2014) HBS Working Paper No. 1.

[24]   CSRC Annual Report [中国证券监督管理委员会年报] (2014) 12, tbl. 2–1.

[25]   '"Equity sans frontiers": Trends in Cross-border IPOs and an Outlook for the Future', Price Waterhouse Cooper (November 2012) 8, 16.

interests.[26] While the weaknesses of standard financial reporting are mirrored in the poor quality of ESG reporting by Chinese firms, deeper integration of local and global capital markets and concerns about market volatility are increasing pressure on firms and on China's securities regulator, the China Securities Regulatory Commission (CSRC), to strengthen reporting practices and market oversight. Although these pressures alone cannot transform TNC practice, China's experience suggests that capital market disclosure regimes can be an important driver of accountability for emerging market TNCs.

## Disclosure Regimes for Listed Firms

Capital market regulation is arguably more important than company law in the governance and oversight of Chinese TNCs. Since Chinese firms first began to list their shares in Hong Kong and then on the mainland in the early 1990s, capital market regulation and, in particular, securities law, has been the dominant force in the formation of Chinese corporate governance principles for listed firms.[27] Although the 1993 version of China's Company Law imposed only general disclosure obligations on a corporation's supervisors, directors or officers,[28] Chinese authorities recognized early on that information disclosure was essential to the creation of viable public capital markets. In the late 1990s, the Shanghai Stock Exchange took the lead by introducing disclosure concepts that directly influenced the CSRC's 2001 Code of Corporate Governance for Listed Companies, China's first national corporate governance standard.[29]

### Financial reporting

China's Securities Law and related regulations establish a system of ongoing reporting for all listed firms on an annual, semi-annual and

---

[26] SynTao, 'A Journey to Discover Values 2015: A Study of CSR Reporting in China' [价值发现之路 2015: 中国企业社会责任报告研究] (2015).

[27] Nicholas C. Howson, '"Quack Corporate Governance" as Traditional Chinese Medicine – the Securities Regulation Cannibalization of China's Corporate Law and a State Regulator's Battle Against Party State Political Economic Power' (2013) 37 *Seattle L. Rev.* 675–689.

[28] Company Law of the People's Republic of China [中华人民共和国公司法], St. Committee, Nat'l People's Cong., prom. 29 Dec.1993, arts. 140, 156, as amended 28 Dec. 2013, arts. 134, 145.

[29] Jane Fu, *Corporate Disclosure and Corporate Governance in China* (Kluwer Law, 2010) 5, 12; CSRC, State Economic & Trade Commission, Code of Corporate Governance for Listed Companies [上市公司治理准则], No. 1 [2002], prom. & eff. 7 Jan. 2002.

interim basis. These rules require disclosure of various aspects of corporate governance, including executive compensation, director independence, the composition of the board, the identity of controlling shareholders and other blockholders, and related party transactions.[30] As in other markets, periodic reporting also requires some reference to matters that relate to the firm's impact on stakeholders, including management's discussion and analysis addressing major events and risks affecting the firm, as well as material disputes, investigations, losses or similar events.[31]

Financial reporting is based on Chinese accounting and audit standards, which now converge substantially with IFRS and international audit standards.[32] All disclosures must be authentic, accurate and complete without any false or misleading statement or material omission, as attested by the company's directors and senior managers, and a listed firms' directors, supervisors and senior managers bear joint and several liability for any misleading statements or material omissions.[33]

The CSRC approves new issues, exercises enforcement authority over listed firms and oversees the stock exchanges, financial intermediaries and auditors.[34] Chinese TNCs that are publicly traded within China are also subject to the listing requirements of its major exchanges: the Shanghai Stock Exchange (SHSE), the Shenzhen Stock Exchange (SZSE), and China's over-the-counter market, the National Equities Exchange and Quotations (NEEQ). Although particular requirements apply to separate indices and boards, the listing rules' disclosure provisions are largely uniform across the exchanges.

### ESG reporting and accountability for stakeholder impacts

Capital markets regulation is also a key component of China's sustainability policies and state-driven approach to corporate social responsibility (CSR), and its role is likely to deepen as the Chinese government

---

[30]   Primary sources include: PRC Securities Law [中华人民共和国证券法], prom. Nat'l. People's Cong., 27 Oct. 2005, effective 1 Jan. 2006, as amended 31 Aug. 2014, arts. 63–72, Sect. III; CSRC, Administrative Measures for Information Disclosure of Listed Companies [上市公司信息披露管理办法], eff. 30 Jan. 2007; Code of Corporate Governance (n 29), arts. 87–90.

[31]   PRC Securities Law, art. 67; CSRC, *Administrative Measures*, ibid., arts. 21(7)-(8), 22 (4)-(5), 30.

[32]   OECD, 'Governance of Listed Companies in China: Self-Assessment by the CSRC' (OECD Publishing, 2010) 51–75.

[33]   PRC Securities Law (n 30), arts. 63, 68–69.

[34]   (n 30) ch. X.

implements its 2016 framework for establishing a green financial system.[35] Although not directly enforceable, this emphasis is already reflected in the Company Law and in the CSRC's Code of Corporate Governance for Listed Companies, which encourage listed companies to consider stakeholder interests, in addition to legal compliance and adherence to business ethics.[36] Since 2006, China has also adopted a number of sustainability initiatives and ESG reporting requirements for state-owned enterprises (SOEs) and other large firms. These measures reflect central policies promoting sustainable development and the global competitiveness of Chinese TNCs, and they complement voluntary sustainability reporting regimes created by international and domestic organizations and by local trade associations and governments across China.[37] Although ESG reporting guidelines in China are generally voluntary, ESG reporting is explicitly mandatory for most Chinese TNCs, either because of their status as listed firms or as SOEs, or because of their industry sector or scale.

Beginning in the early 2000s, the State Environmental Protection Agency (SEPA), now known as the Ministry of Environmental Protection (MEP), joined with several other administrative agencies to promote better environmental compliance by large Chinese firms under a series of green finance policies. Among these was a green securities policy formalized by the CSRC and the MEP between 2007 and 2009, which required environmental disclosures and performance assessment for listed firms. It also included a Green IPO component, which required companies in highly polluting industries that wished to launch an IPO or make a later offering of securities to pass an environmental assessment.[38] Although the Green

---

[35]   People's Bank of China, China Ministry of Finance, National Development and Reform Commission, China Ministry of Environmental Protection, China Banking Regulatory Commission, China Securities Regulatory Commission, China Insurance Regulatory Commission (2016), Guidelines for Establishing the Green Financial System [关于构建金融体系的指导意见], prom. 31 Aug. 2016; People's Bank of China, United Nations Environment Programme, Establishing China's Green Financial System: Final Report of the Green Finance Task Force (2015) 13.

[36]   CSRC, Code of Corporate Governance (n 29), arts. 81–86, 88; PRC Company Law (n 28) art. 5.

[37]   Virginia Harper Ho, 'Beyond Regulation: A Comparative Look at State-Centric Corporate Social Responsibility and the Law in China' (2013) 46 *Vanderbilt Transnational Law Journal* 375.

[38]   Numerous guidance documents issued by the MEP and the CSRC beginning in 2001 implement the Green IPO policy. *See* Wang Qiguo [王起国] 'Green Securities Law Research' [绿色证券法研究] (2013) 15 *Journal of Southwest*

IPO policy was discontinued in late 2014, while it was in force the CSRC aggressively enforced it to block listings of polluting firms.[39] Other MEP environmental disclosure guidelines remain in effect for listed firms and are slated to be expanded and more closely linked to financing opportunities for Chinese firms under the 2016 recent green finance policy guidelines and new rules designed to help "green" companies access public capital markets.[40]

In 2008, the SHSE also adopted environmental disclosure guidelines that are mandatory for firms in certain extractive sectors, companies that are included in the SHSE Corporate Governance Index, companies that are cross-listed in China and on a foreign market, and financial companies.[41] These guidelines cover firm environmental performance and encourage disclosure of information regarding pollution levels and mitigation efforts; reporting is, however, required for all firms on the MEP's list of serious polluters. In addition, all listed companies must report within two days on any environmental liability or investigation, serious environmental risk events, or other circumstances that may have a significant impact on the stock price.[42] These interim disclosures alert investors of potential risk exposure and give authorities additional notice of serious environmental incidents.

In addition, the 2016 green finance framework reinforces broader obligations toward stakeholders that are explicitly referenced in guidelines adopted initially by the stock exchanges and later by the Ministry of Finance, the CSRC and the National Audit Office regarding internal financial controls and enterprise risk management systems, which are

---

*University of Political Science and Law* [西南政法大学学报] 79–81 (compiling these sources).

[39]   Notice of the MEP Regarding Reform and Adjustment of the Green Listing Inspection System [环境保护部关于改革调整上市环保核查工作制度的通知], No. 149, 19 Oct. 2014. Hua Wang and David Bernell, 'Environmental Disclosure in China: An Examination of the Green Securities Policy' (2013) 22 *J. Environment & Development* 339, 343. Other sources report, however, that in some years, all applicants passed the environmental screening. *See* Wang (n 38) 80, tbl. 2.

[40]   (n 35). MEP guidance for listed firm environmental disclosure is available at <http://wfs.mep.gov.cn/gywrfz/hbhc/zcfg/s>.

[41]   Shanghai Stock Exchange (SHSE) (2008), Notice on Strengthening Listed Companies' Assumption of Social Responsibility and on Issuing the Guidelines on Listed Companies' Environmental Information Disclosure [关于加强公司社会责任承担工作暨发布'上海证券交易所上市公司环境信息披露指引'], prom. 14 May 2008.

[42]   Ibid. arts. 2–3.

mandatory for all listed firms in China, and for certain other large firms.[43] In contrast to most Western jurisdictions, the relevant guidelines explicitly require monitoring of financial and non-financial risks that relate to corporate stakeholder impacts.

Beyond the SHSE's environmental disclosure guidelines, both stock exchanges have also adopted CSR reporting guidelines for listed firms that urge them to protect the interests of creditors, employees and other stakeholders and to issue regular ESG disclosures.[44] Although sustainability reporting is voluntary for most firms under these CSR guidelines, it is in fact mandatory for Chinese TNCs that are in the Shenzhen 100 Index or, in Shanghai, for firms on the SHSE Corporate Governance Index, other listed firms that are cross-listed abroad, and financial companies.[45] In 2009, both exchanges added incentives for voluntary reporting by introducing separate sustainability indices, which encourage firms to adopt governance and disclosure best practices and signal their credibility to the market.[46] New green indices, rating systems, environmental reporting requirements and green investment vehicles building on ESG measures are contemplated by the 2016 green finance framework.[47]

Additional sustainability reporting requirements already apply to SOEs under the administrative oversight of China's State-owned Assets

---

[43]   Guidelines of SHSE for the Internal Control of Listed Companies [上海证券交易所上市公司内部控制指引], prom. 5 June 2006, eff. 1 July 2006, at Ch. II; Guidelines of Shenzhen Stock Exchange (SZSE) for the Internal Control of Listed Companies [深圳证券交易所上市公司内部控制指引], No. 118, eff. 1 July 2007, superseded by Guidelines of the SZSE for Standardized Operation of Companies Listed on the Main Board [深圳证券交易所主板上市公司规范运作指引] and the SME Board [深圳证券交易所中小企业上市公司规范运作指引] prom. 28 July 2010, eff. 1 Sep. 2010; Ministry of Finance, China Securities Regulatory Commission, National Audit Office, China Banking Regulatory Commission, China Insurance Regulatory Commission, Basic Internal Control Norms for Enterprises [企业内部控制基本规范], No. 7, prom. 22 May 2008, eff. 1 July 2009.

[44]   SZSE, Social Responsibility Instructions for Listed Companies [深圳证券交易所上市公司社会责任指引] No. 115, 25 Sept. 2006, superseded by SZSE Main Board Guidelines, ibid. ch. 9, and SZSE SME Board Guidelines, ibid. ch. 9; SHSE, *Listed Companies' Environmental Disclosure* (n 41).

[45]   Shanghai Stock Exchange (SHSE) (2013), Notice on Doing Good Job in Listed Companies' Annual Reports of 2013, 31 Dec. 2013, par. II (VI)(4).

[46]   In Shanghai, firms within the SHSE Corporate Governance Index that produce voluntary sustainability reports and rank among the top 100 firms on its unique social value indicator are eligible for inclusion in the SHSE social responsibility index. SHSE Social Responsibility Index Methodology: <http://www.csindex.com.cn/sseportal_en/csiportal/xzzx/file/000048hbook.pdf>.

[47]   People's Bank of China (n 35) 13.

Supervision and Administration Commission (SASAC).[48] The 2008 SASAC CSR Guidelines for Centrally Managed SOEs encourage the integration of CSR practices into corporate governance and strategy, as well as voluntary ESG reporting. In 2012, SASAC began to mandate ESG reporting for SOEs directly controlled by the central government.[49]

The level of sustainability reporting has risen rapidly in China in recent years, driven by these regulatory mandates and demand from international consumers, global industry leaders and state policy.[50] Nearly 80 per cent of China's top 100 firms now produce sustainability reports, on par with leading Western firms.[51] As of the end of 2016, over 500 Chinese companies were signatories of the United Nations' Global Compact, discussed separately in this volume, which requires participating firms to report annually on progress toward mitigating stakeholder-related risks.[52]

### Institutional Context and the Limits of Disclosure

Beyond its core function in promoting the efficiency, stability and equity of public capital markets, disclosure's potential as a regulatory tool depends on its power to motivate corporate behavioral change. However, as a self-regulatory tool, disclosure is subject to firm discretion regarding what and how to report. Unreliable information weakens market signals and incentives for firms to alter their underlying conduct, undermining the market's ability to allocate capital efficiently in a manner that accurately reflects investment risk.

These concerns are particularly salient in China. Although China's disclosure regime follows global models and the informational efficiency of its capital markets has improved,[53] inadequate, misleading, and even

---

[48]   SASAC, Notice of the Guiding Opinion Regarding the CSR Implementation of Centrally Managed Enterprises [关于印发《关于中央企业履行社会责任的指导意见》的通知] [SASAC CSR Notice], prom. 29 Dec. 2007, eff. 4 Jan. 2008, arts. 1–8, 18–19.

[49]   Harper Ho (n 37) 409, n. 79.

[50]   SynTao, *CSR Reporting* (n 26) 3–4. A similar percentage applies to private firm reporting, ibid.

[51]   KPMG (n 23).

[52]   *See* <http://www.unglobalcompact.org/what-is-gc/participants/>. This number nearly equals the number of US corporate signatories.

[53]   Jennifer N. Carpenter et al. 'The Real Value of China's Stock Market' (2015) NBER working paper No. 20957.

fraudulent disclosure practices remain endemic.[54] Accounting scandals and disclosure violations continue to dog Chinese firms cross-listed in the United States and other global markets. Similarly, numerous studies of ESG reporting in China find that while the quantity of ESG reporting by Chinese firms has risen dramatically since 2008, its overall quality remains weak, with wide industry variation[55] Relatively few firms report quantitative indicators or negative events such as regulatory investigations or penalties.[56] Less than five per cent of the sustainability reports produced by firms in China are independently audited by a third party.[57] Although voluntary and mandatory reports are publicly available either on company websites or directly through the stock exchanges, and global ESG investment analytics are beginning to incorporate data from Chinese-listed firms, integration of ESG information directly into investment analysis is in its infancy and is made more challenging because of the dearth of quantifiable, comparable metrics.

Part of the explanation for the low quality of mandatory reporting in China is that the institutional context of China's capital markets limits effective external monitoring and enforcement that might motivate higher quality reporting and deter fraud. Like other markets where concentrated ownership is the norm, Chinese firms exhibit an insider governance model, with control wielded by management and controlling shareholders who do not stand to benefit from greater transparency.[58] The dominant role of the state in the governance of Chinese TNCs and other listed firms may also affect disclosure quality,[59] since by some estimates, over 80 per cent of Chinese-listed firms, which include most Chinese TNCs, are indirectly, if not directly, state-owned or controlled.[60] The opacity of related party

---

[54]   Benjamin L. Liebman and Curtis J. Milhaupt, 'Reputational Sanctions in China's Securities Market' (2008) 108 *Columbia L. Rev.* 929; Joseph D. Piotroski, (2014), 'Financial Reporting Practices of China's Listed Firms' (2014) 26 (3) *J. Applied Corporate Fin.* 53–60.

[55]   Lin Zheng, N. Balsara and H. Huang, 'Pressure, Blockholders, and Corporate Social Responsibility (CSR) Disclosures in China' (2014) 10 (2) *Social Responsibility Journal* 226–245; SynTao, *CSR Reporting* (n 26).

[56]   Lopin Kuo et al., 'Disclosure of Corporate Social Responsibility and Environmental Management: Evidence from China' (2012) 19 *Corporate Social Responsibility and Environmental Management* 27 3–87; SynTao, *CSR Reporting* (n 26) 16.

[57]   SynTao (n 26) 1, 4.

[58]   Alice de Jonge, *Corporate Governance and China's H-Share Market* (Edward Elgar, 2008) 82–83.

[59]   Zheng et al., *CSR Disclosures* (n 55).

[60]   Xi Chao, *Corporate Governance and Legal Reform in China* (Wildy, Simmonds and Hill, 2009) 24–25, 49–51.

transactions, in particular, can expose minority investors and other corporate stakeholders to a greater risk of tunneling, managerial rent-seeking and other forms of expropriation by controlling shareholders.[61] This reality is in tension with the informational demands of public capital markets and the interests of minority investors, who enjoy formal legal protections under China's Company Law.[62]

In markets that rely on disclosure regimes, the power of ongoing reporting requirements lies in the anti-fraud requirements of the securities laws, which are backed by the enforcement authority of securities regulators and the stock exchanges, by the threat of civil and criminal liability for individual directors and officers and for listed firms, and by the gatekeeping role of accountants, lawyers and auditors. Disclosure regimes are also informally enforced through reputational sanctions, since listed firms seek to maintain investor confidence, and markets react negatively to public investigations.

In China, however, none of these mechanisms are robust. Traditional gatekeepers have proven unable or unwilling to promote transparency, the market for corporate control does not effectively constrain controlling shareholder opportunism, and the threat of private legal remedies remains weak.[63] Although China's Securities Law gives investors harmed by false or misleading disclosures the right to claim damages from the company and its directors, supervisors, officers or other employees, such claims are rarely brought against widely held listed firms.[64] Alternative dispute resolution mechanisms have been established to resolve securities-related disputes,[65] but procedural limits, the relative weakness of the Chinese courts, and the challenge of litigating against powerful local and state interests dissuade

---

[61]    Xi, *Corporate Governance*, ibid., 53–61; Flora X. Huang and Horace Yeung, 'Regulatory Cooperation Between Securities Commissions: A Reflection from Hong Kong' (2013) 1 (1) *Chinese Journal of Comparative Law* 112, 134.

[62]    PRC Company Law (n 28) art. 20 (prohibiting controlling shareholders from prejudicing the interests of minority shareholders and providing remedies for shareholder abuse of the corporate form that disadvantages creditors).

[63]    Donald C., Clarke, 'Law Without Order in Chinese Corporate Governance Institutions,' (2010) 30 *Northwestern J. Intl. L. and Bus.* 131; Zhong Zhang, 'Legal Deterrence: the Foundation of Corporate Governance' (2007) 15 *Corporate Governance* 41.

[64]    Donald C. Clarke and Nicholas C. Howson 'Pathway to Minority Shareholder Protection: Derivative Actions in the People's Republic of China' in D. Puchniak et al. (eds), *The Derivative Action in Asia: A Comparative and Functional Approach* (Cambridge UP, 2012).

[65]    CSRC, *Annual Report 2014* (n 24), 49 (reporting on dispute resolution levels).

private enforcement by investors. In addition, individual retail investors, who tend to adopt short-term, speculative investment strategies, hold 80 per cent of the tradable shares of listed firms, by market capitalization.[66] In other emerging markets, institutional investors, who are more likely to have an influence on listed firms, hold on average around 40 per cent of the shares.[67]

As a result, the burden of policing disclosure quality and protecting minority investors falls to the stock exchanges, the CSRC and its local subdivisions. The CSRC has the authority to issue warnings and correction orders, disqualify financial intermediaries, levy fines on listed firms and individual supervisors, directors and officers, as well as suspend or de-list a firm.[68] The CSRC also has the authority to sanction accountants, auditors and lawyers in connection with disclosure or other violations of the securities laws, in addition to litigation by investors. In contrast to securities regulators in other markets who do not engage in merit review of mandatory disclosures, the CSRC also conducts regular onsite visits to listed firms, and selected review of financial disclosures in annual reports for approximately 20 per cent of all listed firms each year.[69] Serious disclosure violations may give rise to criminal liability, and in recent years the CSRC has referred nearly half of the case leads it received to the police for criminal investigation.[70]

Since the late 1990s, a significant number of investigations by the CSRC have involved disclosure violations.[71] One study by Liebman and Milhaupt of CSRC enforcement strategies also found that reputational sanctions against individuals are an effective deterrent.[72] Despite heightened regulatory enforcement in recent years, however, serious penalties against firms, responsible individuals or their advisors are relatively rare, and available administrative sanctions are too weak to discourage violators.[73]

---

[66]   IOSCO, Development and Regulation of Institutional Investors in Emerging Markets FR04/12 (June 2012) 5. Institutional investors account for over half of the trading volume on the Hong Kong Stock Exchange (HKEx), where subsidiaries of Chinese TNCs commonly list. HKEx *Fact Book* (2015) 787 <https://www.hkex.com.hk/eng/stat/statrpt/factbook/factbook2015/fb2015.htm>.

[67]   IOSCO (n 66) 4–6.

[68]   PRC Securities Law (n 30), arts. 180, 193; CSRC, Administrative Measures on Information Disclosure by Listed Companies [上市公司信息披露管理办法], No. 40 (30 Jan. 2007) Ch. VI.

[69]   CSRC (n 24) 27. These figures are consistent with prior years.

[70]   (n 24) 33.

[71]   Fu (n 29) 101–102.

[72]   Liebman and Milhaupt (n 54).

[73]   Clarke (n 63). On recent sanctions trends, see CSRC (n 24) 31, tbl. 3–2.

Another explanation for the deficiencies in current reporting practices is that protecting minority investors matters less to Chinese-listed firms and to the state since, as in Europe, equity markets are less important sources of funding for large Chinese firms than banks or intra-group financing outside the public markets.[74] The CSRC is also hampered by personnel and resource constraints, as well as the need to coordinate with other agencies, such as the MEP, the Ministry of Public Security and other financial regulators to enforce disclosure rules.[75] Studies of mandatory environmental disclosures under the green securities program suggest that compliance with the basic reporting obligation might be more consistent if the CSRC had not left enforcement largely to the relatively weak MEP.[76] For all of these reasons, reporting practices in China lag behind international standards.

**Toward Accountability for Stakeholder Impacts**

The observed weaknesses in core financial reporting and the limits of external monitoring by the CSRC and outside investors would seem to challenge the argument that capital markets' disclosure rules can meaningfully constrain TNC managers and promote greater accountability to corporate stakeholders. However, measuring the implementation of capital markets regulation in China against more mature markets may not be the best comparison. A better question is how effective capital markets regulation is relative to other sources of oversight for Chinese TNCs, and from this standpoint, capital markets regulation in fact enjoys a comparative advantage. Its strength lies in the potential for disclosure-based rules to shape listed firm incentives, as outlined earlier, and also in the positive pressure the CSRC and other state agencies face to improve investor confidence, attract global capital and raise the reputation the Chinese capital markets themselves.

**Institutional power**

Transparency mandates are an important driver of greater accountability for Chinese TNCs because the institutional position of the CSRC gives it greater influence over TNCs than most other state agencies. The state's strong interest in bolstering confidence and stability in Chinese capital markets has allowed the CSRC to deepen reforms favoring minority

---

[74]   Clarke (n 63). On Europe, see Hertig (n 5) 302.
[75]   de Jonge (n 58) 59.
[76]   Wang and Bernell (n 39).

investors against other entrenched state interests, and the CSRC's technical expertise and its mandate to improve confidence in China's public capital market also enable the CSRC to introduce rules that constrain state-controlled firms in a way that other agencies and the courts cannot.[77] Because the securities exchanges and direct administrative enforcement of the securities laws are both under the CSRC's authority, it has greater power than its counterparts elsewhere to move listed firms toward transparency and better governance.

**Direct state oversight of leading TNCs**
In addition, the state has direct external and internal control over many of China's leading TNCs that goes beyond the regulatory oversight of the CSRC. In China, SASAC and its local branches exercise the governance rights of shareholders, as well as administrative and personnel oversight over SOEs. The alignment of state regulatory policy in areas like environmental protection is therefore an important driver behind recent trends in ESG reporting by Chinese TNCs. Although empirical evidence of the effect of state ownership on disclosure quality in China is mixed, some studies suggest that state control improves disclosure of environmental performance and other ESG factors that are aligned with state sustainable development policies.[78]

Because many Chinese TNCs are large, state-sector firms that are expected to adopt global standards, top-down mandates have proven particularly powerful in expanding the scale of sustainability reporting. Over half of sustainability reports are produced by state-owned firms,[79] and empirical studies have shown that the 2008 SASAC CSR Guidelines had an observable effect on the level of sustainability reporting by listed SOEs even before they became officially mandatory in 2012.[80] This evidence points to the strong state influence over SOE disclosure practices. At the same time, even centrally controlled SOEs are more likely to issue sustainability reports when the firm is subject to stock exchange

---

[77] Howson (n 27) 709–713.
[78] Lei Gao and Gerhard Kling, 'The Impact of Corporate Governance and External Audit on Compliance to Mandatory Disclosure Requirements in China' (2012) 21 *Journal of International Accounting, Auditing & Taxation* (2012) 17, 27 (finding lower disclosure by SOEs but higher disclosure by other firms with concentrated ownership); Zheng et al., *CSR Disclosures* (n 55); Kuo et al. (n 56) 281 (reporting SOEs outperform private firms on some CSR disclosures but not others); SynTao (n 26) 16 (finding that SOEs controlled by the central government produce the highest quality ESG reports).
[79] SynTao (n 26) 4–54.
[80] Ioannou et al. (n 23).

mandates.[81] The emphasis by SASAC and by the stock exchanges on sustainability reporting therefore appears to be mutually reinforcing.

In addition, national policy priorities on sustainability and a desire to take greater leadership on the international stage have led the Chinese government to engage actively with international standard-setting bodies focused on the development of integrated reporting frameworks and other sustainable finance tools. China's 2016 green finance guidelines are a prime example. They build on prior green finance policies and outline far-reaching goals designed to encourage the CSRC, the stock exchanges, and financial institutions to direct capital toward investments that promote environmental sustainability and a transition toward a green economy. The 2016 guidelines also signal new demand for ESG analytics and sustainability information from regulators and market participants.

**Capital market competition and institutional investor influence**
An important shift in Chinese capital markets that might motivate better implementation of existing disclosure rules is the growing presence of institutional investors. One recent survey by the International Organization of Securities Commissions (IOSCO) found that its members in emerging markets, including China, view foreign institutional investors as having a positive impact on market liquidity, corporate governance and financial innovation.[82]

Several reforms over the past decade have strengthened listed firms' potential responsiveness to market oversight by increasing the public float of listed firms and expanding the space for foreign ownership of Chinese TNC shares. Historically, shares of Chinese-listed firms were strictly divided into separate markets, with trading in A shares denominated in RMB limited to domestic investors and trading in dollar-denominated B shares limited to foreign investors. In addition, until the late 2000s, non-tradable shares, largely held by various governmental entities ('state shares') or by industrial firms or other institutions ('legal person shares') accounted for over two-thirds of listed company shares, leaving public investors particularly vulnerable to exploitation.[83] Far fewer shares are now restricted from trading, and the aggregate public float of listed firms on the Shenzhen and Shanghai stock exchanges represents over 80 per cent of the total outstanding shares.[84]

---

[81]   Zheng et al. (n 55).
[82]   IOSCO (n 66) 50.
[83]   Xi (n 60) 114.
[84]   CSRC (n 24) 83, tbl. 1.

Although still relatively small, the size of institutional investment in the Chinese market has increased steadily since the early 2000s, as has the willingness of some institutional investors to engage listed companies directly on corporate governance matters.[85] China's 2016 green finance framework also contemplates new measures mandating that state-owned institutional investors incorporate environmental indicators into investment analysis and encouraging others to do so.[86]

In addition, since 2002, qualified foreign institutional investors (QFIIs), and since 2011, QFIIs with RMB accounts (RQFIIs), have been permitted to trade in restricted shares of domestic firms denominated in RMB ('A shares') through a quota system.[87] Although less than 2 per cent of A shares are currently held by QFIIs,[88] QFIIs' presence in the market creates reputational incentives for the CSRC, SASAC and other regulators to improve the quality of public listings and strengthen minority investor protections.

In 2014, China raised the bar higher by introducing the Shanghai–Hong Kong Stock Connect program, which opened a broader segment of China's domestic capital markets to foreign capital, mediated through Hong Kong-based brokers and the Hong Kong Stock Exchange (HKEx).[89] The program, which is being expanded to Shenzhen at the time of this writing, also allows wealthy Chinese investors to invest in firms listed in Hong Kong, creating greater competition between the HKEx and mainland exchanges. Allowing domestic markets to compete more directly with Hong Kong and exposing them to higher transparency demands may increase pressure on mainland firms to improve reporting quality and also pave the way for proposed plans to allow foreign firms to list locally, a change which could make public capital more expensive for firms with weak transparency. These developments raise the prospect that China

---

[85]   Xi (n 60) 108–149; Huang and Yeung (n 61) 134–135.

[86]   PBOC (n 35); PBOC and UNEP (n 35) 5–6.

[87]   The QFII program was originally authorized by the CSRC Interim Measures on the Administration of Domestic Securities Investment by Qualified Foreign Institutional Investors (expired) [合格境外机构投资者境内证券投资管理的办法], Nov. 5, 2002, and the RQFII program, by the CSRC, People's Bank of China, State Administration of Foreign Exchange, Pilot Program Measures for Domestic Securities Investment by Fund Management Companies & Securities Companies that are RMB Qualified Foreign Institutional Investors (expired) [基金管理公司，证券公司人民币合格境外机构投资者境内证券投资试点办法], No. 76, 16 Dec. 2011.

[88]   CSRC (n 24) 21.

[89]   Shanghai-Hong Kong Stock Connect <http://english.sse.com.cn/investors/shhkconnect/introduction/definition>.

will follow the experience of continental Europe, where the expansion of outside minority investors led to improvements in mandatory and voluntary disclosure by listed firms.[90]

**Peer benchmarking and public oversight**

Public reporting also facilitates stakeholder monitoring, and in China, direct public oversight of firm's compliance with local environmental, labor or consumer protection regulation through traditional and online media, petitioning government agencies, and even public protest, is increasingly common. There is also some evidence in China that peer benchmarking and spillover effects from industry leaders to other firms are driving observed improvements in the level of non-financial reporting by Chinese TNCs, and to a smaller extent, in its quality.

Voluntary firm adoption of international reporting standards by some Chinese firms also signals a deeper level of commitment to accountability for stakeholder impacts. Nearly 70 per cent of sustainability reports produced by Chinese TNCs and other reporting firms are based on an independent third-party standard.[91] Although a growing number of Chinese TNCs issue sustainability reports through the Global Compact or other regimes, the primary non-financial reporting standards used in China are the GRI standards and reporting standards developed by the CSR Research Center of the Chinese Academy of Social Sciences.[92] The GRI standards are explicitly designed to make sustainability reporting standard practice globally for all organizations.[93] In other emerging markets, such as South Africa, South Korea and Brazil, 90 per cent of leading firms use the GRI, and many governments recommend or require GRI-based reporting.[94] The number of Chinese TNCs based in mainland China that use the GRI itself has risen from only 13 in 2008 to nearly 2000 in 2016.[95]

Top-down pressure does not explain these trends. Although the 2008 SASAC CSR Guidelines and existing environmental reporting rules encourage adoption of international standards, they do not require any particular

---

[90]   Hertig (n 5) 303.

[91]   SynTao (n 26) 4; GRI Disclosure Database <http://www.globalreporting.org> (n 91).

[92]   GRI and CASS CSR Research Center, 'Linking CASS-CSR 3.0 and GRI's G4 Sustainability Reporting Guidelines' (2014) <http://www.globalreporting.org>.

[93]   'Who We Are – About GRI' <http://www.globalreporting.org>.

[94]   KPMG (n 23) 12.

[95]   GRI Disclosure Database <http://www.globalreporting.org> (n 91). By way of comparison, the number of GRI-based reports produced by US firms increased three-fold over the same period, from 130 to over 500.

standard, nor mandate independent third-party auditing of sustainability reports. Instead, benchmarking with local and global peers may be driving firms to move gradually toward international ESG reporting standards.[96]

New analytical tools are now being developed by state agencies, local organizations within China, and international organizations, such as the GRI, to evaluate the quality of ESG reporting in China in order to facilitate the use of ESG metrics by firms, external stakeholders and, eventually, investment analysts.[97] The GRI and CASS have coordinated their two leading standards,[98] and the most recent green finance framework outlines plans to institute a state-funded system for standardizing environmental cost accounting metrics and to establish a publicly accessible database of reported data that can be accessed by institutional investors, regulators, rating agencies and companies themselves.[99] As these metrics improve, firms will face increasing pressure from industry peers and administrative authorities to improve the quality of voluntary and mandatory ESG reporting.

### Cross-listing and bonding
Foreign capital markets and their regulators are another important source of accountability and oversight for Chinese TNCs. Cross-listing gives TNCs and their affiliates access to cheaper and more diverse sources of capital, and companies may also choose to list on a foreign exchange with a reputation for tougher governance and transparency requirements in order to achieve a bonding effect.[100] According to conventional bonding theory, firms can obtain capital more cheaply by assuring investors that they are subject to tougher oversight that is perceived to be lacking in their home market. Although limited cross-border enforcement capacity weakens bonding effects in practice,[101] cooperation among regulators and

---

[96]   Although this hypothesis has yet to be tested empirically, it is supported by other studies of voluntary disclosure by Chinese firms, finding that industry peer influence and reputational factors affect firms' decision to produce ESG disclosures. S.X. Zeng et al., 'Factors that Drive Chinese Listed Companies in Voluntary Disclosure of Environmental Information' (2012) 109 *Journal of Business Ethics* 309–321.

[97]   SynTao (n 26).

[98]   GRI and CASS (n 92).

[99]   PBOC and UNEP 'Detailed Recommendations 10' (n 35).

[100]   *See* John C. Coffee, 'The Future as History: The Prospects for Global Convergence in Corporate Governance and its Implications' (1999) 93 *Northwestern U. L. Rev.* 641 673–677; Licht, Amir, 'Cross-Listing and Corporate Governance: Bonding or Avoiding' (2003) 4 *Chicago Journal of International Law* 141.

[101]   Jordan Siegel, 'Can Foreign Firms Bond Themselves Effectively by Renting U.S. Securities Laws?' (2005) 75 *Journal of Financial Economics* 319.

exchanges, as well as market discipline from foreign investors, investment intermediaries, and external auditors and other gatekeepers create new sources of external monitoring for cross-listed TNCs. Firms cross-listed in more developed markets or those that are highly covered by investment analysts also exhibit better social performance, perhaps because of their improved transparency.[102]

The potential effect of external oversight is significant since Chinese TNCs list their shares on foreign exchanges in record numbers. Because of its proximity, cultural affinity and established institutions, Hong Kong has historically been the leading international market for mainland Chinese firms since the early 1990s when the first SOEs were authorized to go public. Nearly 400 mainland Chinese firms or their subsidiaries are listed in Hong Kong, accounting for over 40 per cent of the market capitalization on the HKEx main board and around 10 per cent of its Growth Enterprise Market (GEM).[103] Approximately 200 of these Chinese TNCs also list in New York, London or other global markets.[104]

Like other major markets, Hong Kong has a disclosure-based system that depends upon self-regulation by the HKEx and on the gatekeeping function of market intermediaries, acting under regulatory oversight.[105] Mainland Chinese firms that wish to list overseas directly must obtain approval from the CSRC and comply with additional governance and accounting rules under both Chinese domestic law and the listing rules of the foreign securities exchange.[106] In Hong Kong, listing rules for mainland firms impose heightened corporate governance standards, such as mandating the presence of an internal compliance advisor, extending fiduciary duties to the supervisory board and providing for preemptive rights and arbitration.[107] To facilitate cross-border enforcement, Hong Kong's securities regulator, the Securities and Futures Commission, has entered

---

[102]   Ioannou et al. (n 23) 854–856.
[103]   HKEx, 'Market Capitalisation of China-related Stocks (Main Board and GEM) (2016) <https://www.hkex.com.hk/eng/stat/smstat/chidimen/cd_mc.htm>; HKEx, 'China Dimension' (2016) <https://www.hkex.com.hk/eng/stat/smstat/chidimen/chidimen.htm>.
[104]   CSRC (n 24) 26.
[105]   Huang and Yeung (n 61) 126, 154.
[106]   (n 61) 119–120. The CSRC is transitioning away from the current pre-approval system to a registration system for Chinese firms that wish to list domestically or to cross-list abroad. CSRC (n 24) 83, tbl. 1. TNCs can also avoid the current approval requirements by using offshore affiliates.
[107]   HKEx, Listing Rules and Guidance: Equity Securities – Issuers Incorporated in the People's Republic of China, Ch. 19A <http://www.hkex.com.hk/eng/rules-reg/listrules/rulesandguidelines.htm>.

into cooperative consultation agreements with the CSRC, as have US regulators.[108]

Like Shenzhen, Shanghai and other Asian stock exchanges, the HKEx has also introduced measures to promote listed firm attention to sustainability or ESG issues in recent years, including a Corporate Sustainability Benchmark Index, guidance encouraging institutional investor monitoring of investee companies' ESG performance, and mandatory ESG reporting for listed firms.[109] Consistent with its 2014 revised Companies Ordinance, Hong Kong's ESG reporting requirements were introduced as voluntary guidelines but now apply to all issuers on a 'comply or explain' basis.[110]

Although the evidence on whether Hong Kong offers better investor protection is mixed,[111] cross-listing has subjected Chinese TNCs to higher scrutiny, particularly with regard to the quality of their public reporting. Studies of non-financial reporting also find that reporting quality is highest for firms listed on the HKEx, followed by firms listed on the Shanghai Exchange.[112] Although information gaps may weaken bonding effects, Chinese TNC subsidiaries cross-listed in the United States have also come under increasing scrutiny from US regulators in the wake of accounting and disclosure scandals involving Chinese firms, and regulators in both the US and in Hong Kong have suspended or de-listed a number of Chinese companies.[113] In contrast to other areas of foreign host–state regulation, securities disclosure regimes can bring market forces and host state enforcement capacity more directly to bear on listed TNCs.

## CONCLUSION

Stock exchanges, securities regulators, leading institutional investors and other international organizations recognize the power of disclosure regimes to promote greater accountability for TNCs. Investors in global companies are also facing growing demand from regulators and the public

---

[108] Huang and Yeung (n 61). *See, e.g.* 'PCAOB Enters into Enforcement Cooperation Agreement with Chinese Regulators' (24 May 2013) <https://pcaobus.org>.
[109] HKEx Rules and Guidance (n 107).
[110] HKEx. 'Environmental, Social and Governance Reporting Guide' (2016), app. 27.
[111] Huang and Yeung (n 61).
[112] SynTao (n 26) 13.
[113] *See, e.g.* Luo Weifeng, 'HKEx Gets Tough with Listing Regime' *ChinaDaily Asia* (1 June 2016); SEC, Investor Bulletin: Reverse Mergers, June 2011, <http://www.sec.gov/investor/alerts/reversemergers.pdf>.

for transparency and accountability regarding how they deploy capital and how they monitor the firms in which they invest.[114] Most critically, authorities in emerging markets around the world are adopting disclosure-based tools to refocus TNCs and institutional investors toward the long-term and to improve monitoring of ESG risks and stakeholder impacts.[115] Leaders in this space include regulators in South Africa and Brazil, as well as China's Asian neighbors – Japan, Singapore, Malaysia, Thailand and South Korea, among others.[116] Like China, these regulators are increasingly transitioning from voluntary ESG reporting to mandatory standards that more readily lend themselves to peer benchmarking and verification.

At the same time, the persistence of accounting scandals and securities fraud in Western markets shows that disclosure-based regimes are not a substitute for tough enforcement of basic home and host state regulation. The quality of core financial reporting also depends on strong market-based incentives and external institutions, which are not uniform across global capital markets. These challenges are heightened for ESG reporting, and, as China's latest green finance framework recognizes, regulatory mandates may be needed to improve the use of materiality standards and comparable quantitative indicators.

However, China's experience shows that disclosure obligations, a key condition for access to public capital markets, can be an important source of TNC accountability even where internal governance and external oversight are weak. It also shows that the need to ground strong capital markets and compete internationally can in fact motivate governments to adopt minimum transparency and governance standards within home state law. Implementation challenges certainly persist, but as the gap between the long-term interests of investors and stakeholders narrows, global capital market networks will play an increasingly important role in shaping TNC incentives, operations and impacts.

---

[114] Examples include stewardship codes adopted by the United Kingdom and a number of other governments. Fin. Reporting Council (FRC), The UK Stewardship Code (2012), <https://www.frc.org.uk/Our-Work/Publications/Corporate-Governance/UK-Stewardship-Code-September-2012.pdf>.

[115] Bartels et al., *Carrots and Sticks* (n 20) 11.

[116] Ibid.; KPMG (n 23).

# 12. Transnational corporations and mining tax reform: the story of the Australian mineral resources rent tax revolt

## Roman Tomasic

In a global economy where multinational enterprises (MNEs) play a prominent role, governments need to ensure that the taxable profits of MNEs are not artificially shifted out of their jurisdiction and that the tax base reported by MNEs in their country reflects the economic activity undertaken therein.

– OECD[1]

The Great Crash [of 2008] raises fundamental questions about the capacity of contemporary Governments of democratic capitalist countries to implement policies in the public interest that are contested by powerful private interests . . . We [are] back in the old world, in which policy was the resultant of pressure from vested and other sectional interests.

– Professor Ross Garnaut[2]

[BHP Billiton's CEO Marius] Kloppers assumed the leadership role in the anti-tax campaign . . . [BHP Billiton] . . . felt that the RSPT [Resources Super Profits Tax] had global ramifications: if this was not done in Australia, other nations would follow . . . Kloppers' aim was to dismantle the RSPT by a punitive assault, an extraordinary step for his company. It revealed the complete breakdown between the world's biggest mining company and the Rudd Government.

– Paul Kelly[3]

---

[1]  Organisation for Economic Co-operation and Development, *Transfer Pricing Guidelines for Multinational Enterprises and Tax Administrations* (OECD, 2010) <http://www.oecd.org/ctp/transfer-pricing/transfer-pricing-guidelines.htm> accessed 21 February 2015. Also see J. Mathew, 'OECD unveils measures to tackle tax avoidance by multinational companies' *International Business Times* (17 September 2014) <http://www.ibtimes.co.uk/oecd-unveils-measures-tackle-tax-avoidance-by-multinational-companies-1465802> accessed 21 February 2015.

[2]  R. Garnaut, 'The new Australian resources rent tax' *The Australian* (21 May 2010).

[3]  P. Kelly, *Triumph and Demise – The Broken Promise of a Labor Generation* (Melbourne University Press, 2014) 308.

## INTRODUCTION

Globalisation has encouraged transnational corporations (TNCs) to seek to minimize their overall tax liabilities, and they do so in a number of ways. One of these is to seek to locate their operations in a low tax jurisdiction such as Ireland or Singapore. Many countries actively try to offer tax incentives to encourage TNCs to set up their operations in their jurisdictions. Another strategy is to manipulate the costs of inputs in different jurisdictions and seek to ensure that profits are made in a low-taxing jurisdiction through the use of transfer pricing strategies.[4] TNCs are very sensitive about the amount of tax that they have to pay; this is especially where risks, exploration costs and mining costs are high, and where ore prices can be volatile. As a result TNCs will often threaten moving to other countries if these costs are too high. Alternatively, they may go to great lengths to undermine government efforts to introduce new taxes.[5] This was a choice that confronted multinational mining companies in Australia when the Australian Labor Government sought to introduce a minerals resources rent tax in 2010. Due to fiscal crises, national governments are increasingly in need of revenues; yet, they are often easily intimidated by threats or campaigns from mining industry multinationals or TNCs.

Due to declining government revenues as a result of tax base erosion and profit shifting (BEPS), the payment of taxes by transnational corporations has been a matter of increasing concern to governments around the world; however, governments have been reluctant to act unilaterally in imposing additional taxes upon powerful TNCs.[6] Where national governments do seek to act unilaterally against TNCs from powerful countries, such as US internet companies, the companies may seek protection from their own national governments.[7]

As a result, collective governmental action to deal with this problem through multilateral bodies, such as the Organisation for Economic Co-operation and Development (OECD), has been preferred, but these

---

[4]   See further, N. Acocella, *Economic Policy in the Age of Globalisation* (Cambridge UP, 2009) 456.

[5]   See, for example, D. Pinto, 'Governance in a globalised world: Is it the end of the National State' in R. Biswas (ed.), *International Tax Competition – Globalisation and Fiscal Sovereignty* (Commonwealth Secretariat, 2002) 66, 85.

[6]   Dominque Strauss-Kahn, 'Preface' in P. Daniel, M. Keen and C. McPherson (eds), *Taxation of Petroleum and Minerals: Principles, Problems and Practice* (Routledge, 2010) xiv.

[7]   See generally, S. Schechner, 'Europe targets US Web firms' *Wall Street Journal* (27 November 2014) <http://www.wsj.com/articles/french-german-officials-call-for-fresh-look-at-internet-giants-1417110508>.

actions have been slow to bear fruit. Globalization has meant that TNCs operate in many jurisdictions and, as rational economic actors, seek to minimize their tax obligations by any legal mechanisms available to them. It has been estimated that at least 60 per cent of international trade takes place within rather than between transnational corporations.[8]

In seeking to minimize their tax liabilities, TNCs often seek to curtail efforts by national governments to subject them to higher or even more efficient taxes. The use of mechanisms such as transfer pricing has helped to minimize the tax liabilities of companies within corporate groups by adjusting prices charged for transactions within the group so that the income is recorded in the accounts of the subsidiary located in a low-tax jurisdiction or in a tax haven.[9] Whilst transfer pricing is not necessarily illegal, mispricing transfers may well be illegal. Shifting profits from a high-tax to a low-tax jurisdiction has also been seen as an attractive means for corporate groups to minimize their overall tax obligations.

This remained a problem for Australian governments after the multi-nationals successfully defeated the federal government's resources rent tax as illustrated by State government complaints that companies such as BHP Billiton would sell minerals from Australia at a low price to a subsidiary company (a marketing hub) located in Singapore, and then that company would sell these minerals to its customers in the international market at a much higher price. The TNC, however, paid mining royalties based on the lower price, rather than the eventual sale price.[10]

The taxing of multinational mining companies has also been a matter

---

[8]   See 'Transfer Pricing' Tax Justice Network <http://www.taxjustice.net/topics/corporate-tax/transfer-pricing/> accessed on 21 February 2015. Also see, OECD/G20, *Base Erosion and Profit Shifting Project, Guidance on Transfer Pricing Documentation and Country-by-Country Reporting* (OECD, 2014).

[9]   See, for a discussion of transfer pricing problems, S. Picciotto, *International Business Taxation* (Weidenfeld and Nicholson Ltd, 1992) 171–229; also see: J. Wittendorff, *Transfer Pricing and the Arm's Length Principle in International Tax Law* (Kluwer Law International, 2010); OECD, *Transfer Pricing Guidelines for Multinational Enterprises and Tax Administrations* (OECD, 2010); OECD, *Guidance on Transfer Pricing Documentation and Country-by-Country Reporting* (OECD, 2014); J. Henshall, *Global Transfer Pricing: Principles and Practice* (2nd edn, Bloomsbury Professional, 2013); A. Miller and L. Oats, *Principles of International Taxation* (4th edn, Bloomsbury Professional, 2014).

[10]   In one such case, BHP Billiton was sued by the Queensland State government for a $288 million shortfall in coal royalty payments to the State due to the use of a pricing structure such as this. At the same time, the Australian Taxation Office (ATO) in 2015 was also seeking to reclaim some $522 million in back taxes from BHP Billiton as a result of its use of its Singapore marketing hub; see further, B. Fitzgerald, 'BHP in $288m royalty row with Queensland' *The Australian* (13

of heated debate in Australia for over half a century. These debates have come to a head as governments have found themselves struggling to deal with declining national tax revenues. Dominque Strauss-Kahn, the former managing director of the International Monetary Fund, has argued that:

> The International Monetary Fund has for many years paid close attention to the special challenges faced by resource-rich countries. Those relating to macroeconomic and budgetary management have long figured in our surveillance work and lending arrangements, and we continue to champion initiatives towards greater transparency in the extractive industries. And in our technical dialogues with resource-rich countries, the design of fiscal regimes has also been a central topic – an especially lively and active one in the last few years of high, and, more especially, volatile, commodity prices.[11]

The OECD and the G20 have combined to seek solutions, such as creating the 'Base Erosion and Profit Shifting Project'.[12] However, tax minimization schemes do not only affect G20 countries; developing countries lose over $100 billion as a result of such measures each year.[13]

Tax base erosion and profit shifting (BEPS) schemes used by TNCs have been of increasing concern globally.[14] In 2014, the meeting of the G20 held in Brisbane discussed measures to combat such BEPS schemes.[15] Later that year, the Australian Treasurer at that time, Joe Hockey, suggested that Australia should follow the UK in imposing the so-called Google tax

---

November 2015) 20; also see N. Chenoweth and L. Tingle, 'BHP reveals $522m Singapore tax bill' *The Australian Financial Review* (28 April 2015) 10.

[11]   'Preface' in P. Daniel and M. Keen (eds), *Taxation of Petroleum and Minerals, Principles, Problems and Practice* (IMF, 2011).

[12]   OECD, 'Action Plan on base erosion and profit shifting' (OECD Publishing, 2013) <http://dx.doi.org/10.1787/9789264202719-en> accessed, 21 February 2015. *OECD/G20 Base Erosion* (n 8), see further at: <http://www.oecd-ilibrary.org/taxation/oecd-g20-base-erosion-and-profit-shifting-project_23132612> accessed 21 February 2015.

[13]   See further, R. Press, 'Developing nations lose $100bn in tax revenue each year – will G20 reforms help?' *The Guardian* (4 November 2014) <http://www.the-guardian.com/sustainable-business/2014/nov/03/developing-nations-lose-100bn-tax-revenue-g20-reforms-avoidance> accessed 21 February 2015.

[14]   See generally, A Creighton, 'The future of tax reform in a shifting world' *Weekend Australian* (14–15 March 2015) 18; A. Creighton, 'The complex battle to make global companies pay more tax' *Weekend Australian* (12–13 April 2015) 16; and J. Shapiro, 'The macroeconomics of multinational sins' *Australian Financial Review* (21 April 2015) 44–45.

[15]   A. White, 'Big firms urged to pay fair tax share' *The Australian* (23 September 2014) 21.

on multinationals which shifted their profits to low-taxing jurisdictions.[16] Subsequently, the UK introduced its 'diverted profits tax' measures, and the Australian government introduced the Tax Laws Amendment (Combating Multinational Tax Avoidance) Bill which includes a targeted anti-avoidance law in Part IVA of the Income Tax Assessment Act 1936 (Cth) aimed at multinationals that artificially avoid having a taxable presence in Australia.

Treasurer Hockey was reported to have said that he was 'absolutely determined to ensure that companies that earn their profits in Australia pay tax to the Australian government.[17] Australian government leaders, such as the former federal Treasurer Joe Hockey, have continued to search for a more modern system for taxing multinationals companies in a globalised world.[18]

Australia's opposition Labor party was also concerned that $2 billion in taxes had been evaded by multinational companies operating in Australia.[19] However, industry groups, such as the Minerals Council of Australia, the Australian Chamber of Commerce and Industry and the Business Council of Australia, were critical of Labor's efforts to crack down on tax avoidance by multinationals operating in Australia.[20] Chris Jordan AO, the Commissioner of the Australian Taxation Office (ATO) also took an interest in this issue.[21]

Mining company BHP Billiton was one of the companies under scrutiny by the ATO; this TNC had earlier led the revolt in Australia against the imposition of the Minerals Resources Rent Tax (discussed below). In 2015, BHP Billiton revealed that between 2006 and 2014, it had only paid US$121,000 in taxes on its profits of US$5.7 billion earned by it through its marketing entity based in Singapore; BHP claimed that it also paid $945 million in Australia on these profits; however, the ATO was still

---

[16]   See further, P. Sandle, 'Britain to target global tax dodgers' *Australian Financial Review* (5 December 2014) 31.

[17]   Reported by P. Coorey and F. Anderson, 'Treasurer poised to impose "Google tax"' *Australian Financial Review* (9 December 2014) 1, 6. Also see, F. Anderson, 'Hockey backs law to wipe out tax avoidance' *Australian Financial Review* (4 December 2014) 3.

[18]   J. Hockey, 'Revenue system needs a refresh' *The Australian* (7 April 2015) 10.

[19]   P. Coorey, 'Labour eyes $2b tax evaded by multinationals' *Australian Financial Review* (2 March 2015).

[20]   S. Maher, 'Industry cans Labor's attack on tax loopholes' *The Australian* (3 March 2015) 4.

[21]   N. Chenoweth, 'ATO sees billions in multinationals' tax' *Australian Financial Review* (2 March 2015), 1, 6.

claiming that it was entitled to some $522 million in unpaid taxes from BHP Billiton.[22]

In 2015 BHP Billiton representatives resisted the efforts of an Australian Senate inquiry into the payment of taxes by multinational companies; the inquiry sought to obtain details of TNC tax payments, although much of that information was publicly available in Singapore.[23]

Although other mining companies, such as Rio Tinto, were more open than BHP Billiton, other multinationals appearing before the Senate multinational tax inquiry (such as Microsoft, Google and Apple) had also used offshore marketing hubs in places such as Singapore to minimize their taxes, but they resisted efforts to reveal how they paid tax on their Australian business operations.[24] Subsequently, ATO Tax Commissioner Chris Jordan reportedly told the Senate Committee that the claims by TNCs, such as BHP Billiton and Rio Tinto, that they are not engaged in profit shifting should not be taken at face value.[25]

Multinational mining companies in Australia now seem to have fallen silent on the subject of tax reform, despite concerns about the need for tax reform expressed by political leaders from both major Australian political parties, such as former Australian Treasurer Joe Hockey and Opposition Leader Bill Shorten,[26] as well as by the Senate Committee examining tax practices of multinational companies.

This chapter is organised as follows: section 2 discusses the review of Australia's future tax system undertaken by the Secretary of the Australian Treasury, Dr Ken Henry; section 3 discusses the Australian Mineral Resources Rent Tax; section 4 discusses the nature of the consultation process between the government and mining industry concerning the proposed new tax; section 5 examines various design faults in the proposed new mining tax; section 6 goes on to discuss the national campaign against

---

[22]    See further, A. Hepworth, 'BHP fights $522m in unpaid tax' *The Australian* (28 April 2015) 19, 20. Also see: N. Chenoweth, 'Singapore showdown hits moment of truth' *Australian Financial Review* (22 April 2015), 40.

[23]    B. Butler and R. Urban, 'Mining giant digs in at tax inquiry' *Weekend Australian* (11–12 April 2015) 1. See further, A. Saunders, 'BHP may now reveal zero tax Singapore deal' *Australian Financial Review* (16 April 2015) 7.

[24]    See generally, N. Chenoweth and P. Smith, 'What's a Double Irish? Microsoft, Google, Apple face Milne's wrath' *Australian Financial Review* (9 April 2015) 1.

[25]    N. Chenoweth, 'Tax Office chief unleashes on BHP, Rio Tinto, tech giants' *Australian Financial Review* (23 April 2015) 1, 10.

[26]    See for example, P. Coorey, 'Shorten backs mining tax but signals change' *Australian Financial Review* (13 March 2014) 4; E. Knight, 'Mining tax just offers more pain' *The Age* (14 October 2014) 28.

the new mining tax that was spearheaded by leading TNCs; section 7 examines the national government's efforts to resolve the crisis that had been created as a result of opposition from the mining industry; finally, section 8 offers some conclusions.

# THE HENRY REVIEW INTO AUSTRALIA'S FUTURE TAX SYSTEM

Australia's tax problems were reviewed in 2009 by a committee chaired by the then-Secretary of the Australian Treasury, Dr Ken Henry. In its report on Australia's future tax system, the Henry Review made a number of recommendations, including one that recommended that Australia enact a broad ranging resource rent tax:

> The current resource charging arrangements imposed on non-renewable resources by the Australian and State governments should be replaced by a uniform resources rent tax imposed and administered by the Australian government.[27]

Subsequently, the Revised Explanatory Memorandum to the Minerals Resource Rent Tax Bill 2011, considered by the Senate, explained that:

> Resource rent taxes are profit-based, cash flow, taxes. They differ from most royalties in that they take into account the profitability of a mining operation. A resource rent tax collects a percentage of the resource project's economic rent.[28]

Due to the finite supply of non-renewable natural resources, the Henry Review noted that large mining companies were able to earn profits that would be higher than normal from their exploitation of non-renewable mineral resources; in such circumstances the imposition of rents was appropriate. As the Henry Review explained:

> Rents exist where the proceeds from the sale of resources exceeds the cost of exploration and extraction, including a required rate of return to compensate factors of production (labour and capital) . . . However, economic rents can

---

[27] Henry Review, *Australia's Future Tax System – Report to the Treasurer* (Commonwealth of Australia, 2010) 231.

[28] Parliament of the Commonwealth of Australia, Senate, Revised Explanatory Memorandum to the Minerals Resource Rent Tax Bill 2011, at para 1.9, page 6 <http://parlinfo.aph.gov.au/parlInfo/download/legislation/ems/r4712_ems_2a f4ac24-ad50–42d7-b12f-27f8da034bb0/upload_pdf/362895rem.pdf;fileType=appli cation%2Fpdf>.

persist in the resources sector because of the future supply of non-renewable resources.[29]

Because onshore mineral resources in Australia belong to the Crown in right of State Governments, such resources are seen as a public asset, and it is accepted that the private sector should be charged for the right to exploit these mineral resources; mining companies therefore pay royalties to State governments. Some State governments, such as Western Australia and Queensland, have come to rely heavily upon such mining royalties.[30]

Some minerals, such as iron ore and coal, account for the bulk of royalties received by States; in New South Wales, for example, coal accounts for almost 96 per cent of the royalties received by that State.[31] The Henry Review argued that 'Australia should seek an appropriate return from these resources.'[32] A well-designed national resources rent tax was seen by the Review as a more effective means of achieving this goal than the payment of royalties; this was because such a tax was less likely to distort investment and production decisions.[33]

The Henry Review recommended that this new resource rent tax be levied by the national government at the rate of 40 per cent and that it should be applied to non-renewable resources such as petroleum and uranium, bulk commodities such as black coal and iron ore, base metals, diamonds and mineral sands; an exception to the tax would be provided in relation to some lower value minerals.[34] A number of options were presented regarding the future of existing State-based royalty regimes.[35]

---

[29]   (n 28) 218.

[30]   For a general assessment of the impact of mineral royalties see further: J. Otto et al., *Mining Royalties – A Global Study of Their Impact on Investors, Government, and Civil Society* (World Bank, 2006) <http://siteresources.worldbank.org/INTOGMC/Resources/336099–1156955107170/miningroyaltiespublic ation.pdf>.

[31]   NSW Parliamentary Research Service, Parliament of New South Wales, 'A history of mineral and petroleum ownership and royalties in NSW' *Issues Backgrounder* 5 (October 2012) 3.

[32]   (n 27) 220.

[33]   (n 27) 222.

[34]   The minerals that should be excluded from the resources rent tax are set out in Table C1–1 of the Henry review report (n 27) 238.

[35]   In 2014–2015 these State royalties were major sources of revenue for states such as Western Australia ($5.3 billion), Queensland ($3.7 billion) and New South Wales (2.3 billion); see further, S. Kompo-Harms and K. Sanyal, 'The Minerals Resources Rent Tax – selected concepts and issues' (24 November 2011) paper prepared by the Economics Section, Parliamentary Library, Parliament of Australia, Canberra, <http://www.aph.gov.au/About_Parliament/

In recommending the enactment of this resources rent tax, the Henry Review referred to earlier models for such a mining tax that had been proposed in an early paper by EC Brown in 1948 and again by Garnaut and Clunies Ross in their 1983 book, *Taxation of Mineral Rents*.[36] As a longstanding subject of interest among economists, the ideal of a resources rent tax was far from new, but implementing a theoretical model would prove to be politically very difficult.

However, the complexity of the scheme proposed to the Australian Government by the Henry Review, especially in regard to its compliance costs, led to considerable resistance from domestic and international mining companies in Australia, as well as from State Governments. The Henry Review controversially suggested that the proposed resources rent tax would in effect create a partnership between government and mining companies:

> Essentially, under a resource rent-based tax, the government is a silent partner whose share in the project is determined by the tax rate. However, each partner contributes something additional to the partnership – private firms contribute rents associated with their expertise and the government contributes rents associated with the right to the community's non-renewable resources. These rents are also shared according to the tax rate.[37]

As we will see below, the 'partnership' model would not be well received by local or global mining companies who were to be subject to this new tax. As Paul Kelly, a senior journalist working for *The Australian* newspaper observed, BHP Billiton 'had never conceived of the idea of government being a 40 per cent project partner.'[38]

Subsequently, the Australian Labor Government accepted the Henry Review's mining profits tax recommendations and hastily sought to enact a resources rent tax without obtaining agreement from the mining industry and State governments. Professor Garnaut noted that the Henry Review

---

Parliamentary_Departments/Parliamentary_Library/pubs/BN/2011–2012/MRRT>.

[36] E.C. Brown, 'Business-income taxation and investment incentives', in L.A. Metzler, H.S. Perloff and E.D. Domar (eds), *Income, Employment and Public Policy, Essays in Honor of Alvin H Hansen* (Norton, 1948); R. Garnaut and A. Clunies Ross, *Taxation of Mineral Rents* (Clarendon Press, 1983). Also see: C. Emerson and P. Lloyd, 'Improving mineral taxation policy in Australia' (Centre for Economic Policy Research ANU, Canberra, 1981). For a more recent assessment, see generally, B.C. Land, 'Resource rent taxes: a reappraisal' in P. Daniel, M. Keen and C. McPherson (eds), *The Taxation of Petroleum and Minerals: Principles, Problems and Practice* (Routledge, 2010) 241–262.

[37] (n 27) 222.

[38] Kelly (n 3) 306.

had laid out the policy framework that the Government relied upon in its proposal for a Resources Super Profits Tax:

> A Committee chaired by the Secretary of the Treasury has prepared an uncompromising statement of one conscientious perception of the national interest in an important area of policy. The Government has embraced the statement, and made it a central feature of an overall fiscal program that, if maintained, would have no near comparator in the developed world for rigour or suitability to the circumstances.[39]

Professor Garnaut added:

> [T]he Australian Government has taken a position on the basis of advice of people of knowledge and standing, that asserts some hard propositions about the national interest, at the expense of some private interests that exercise considerable influence in our polity . . . It is critically important to our future that we are able to discuss hard policy proposals on their merits, so that an informed perception of the public interest can emerge and eventually win broadly based support.[40]

However, in 2010 Garnaut also warned that the government was likely to encounter difficulties when it confronted powerful sectional interests in the form of multinational mining companies. It is therefore appropriate to closely examine the nature of the Australian resources rent tax and the obstacles to the passage and implementation of this law that were raised by Australian mining industry companies, led by TNCs such as BHP Billiton, Rio-Tinto and Xstrata, and exploited by opposition political parties.

## THE AUSTRALIAN GOVERNMENT'S MINERALS RESOURCES RENT TAX

In May 2010, the Australian Labor Government, under Prime Minister Kevin Rudd, floated the idea of the Minerals Resources Rent Tax after limited discussion within the government and limited consultation with the mining industry; in July 2010 amendments were made to the proposed new law. Thereafter, the Australian Senate Select Committee on New Taxes began an inquiry into the proposed mineral resources rent tax on 30 September 2010, and a report from this inquiry was published on 29 June 2011. Much happened between the announcement of the tax by the Rudd

---

[39]   R. Garnaut, 'The new Australian resources rent tax' *The Australian* (21 May 2010).
[40]   (n 39).

Labor Government in May 2010 and its eventual enactment by the Gillard Labor Government.

The Rudd Government's proposed Resources Super Profits Tax (RSPT) was reworked under the Gillard Government into a Minerals Resources Rent Tax (MRRT) and the Federal Treasurer introduced the MRRT into the House of Representatives on 2 November 2011; thereafter a package of bills relating to the proposed new tax was referred to the Australian House of Representatives' Standing Committee on Economics; the Committee reported back to the House on 21 November 2011.

The Senate, the upper house of the Australian Parliament, also considered the new MRRT[41] and then referred the Bill to the Senate's Economics Legislation Committee which reported back on 14 March 2012. In a minority report, the Opposition parties opposed passage of the new legislation, arguing that it was: 'divisive, complex, unfair, fiscally irresponsible and distorting, reduces our international competitiveness and was developed through a highly flawed and improper process.'[42]

In a submission to the Economics Legislation Committee regarding the provisions of the MRRT, the local mining company, the Fortescue Metals Group, and the Institute of Public Affairs argued that the legislation could even be unconstitutional.[43] These concerns were eventually to find their way into the High Court of Australia where the Court was to reject these constitutional law claims.[44]

The MRRT Bills were passed by both Houses of Parliament; the House of Representatives doing so on 23 November 2011 and the Senate narrowly passing the Bill on 19 March 2012, with the support of the Greens and Clive Palmer's Palmer United Party.[45] The Opposition parties, led by

---

[41]   (n 28).

[42]   Quoted by J. Tomaras, 'The Minerals Resources Rent Tax Bill 2011', *Law and Bills Digest* 124 (2011–12).

[43]   Arguably, the MRRT was in breach of s 51(ii) of the Australian Constitution, as the Bill would discriminate between the States; States imposed different Royalties upon companies within their jurisdictions. It was also arguable that the Bill was in breach of § 114 of the Constitution which prohibits the Commonwealth from imposing a tax on any property that belongs to a State. This was relevant as minerals in Australia are owned by the Crown in the right of the States.

[44]   *Fortescue Metals Group Limited v. The Commonwealth* (2013) HCA 34 (7 August 2013).

[45]   E. Griffiths, 'Mining tax repeal: Joe Hockey says $6.5 billion hit to budget bottom line is "damn good deal" for Australians' *ABC News* (3 September 2014) <http://www.abc.net.au/news/2014-09-02/government-strikes-mining-tax-deal-with-palmer-united-party/5713116>.

Tony Abbott, fought the 2013 federal elections with the intent of repealing the MRRT, and the tax law was eventually repealed on 2 September 2014. Many of the problems with the legislation could be attributed to inadequate consultation with the mining industry and state governments.

### Inadequate Consultation with the Mining Industry

The question has often been raised as to the manner in which the mining industry had been consulted before the new mineral resources rent tax was introduced into the Commonwealth Parliament. Whilst various models of a minerals resources rent tax had been circulating among economists in Australia for many years, and a previous Coalition federal Government had earlier enacted the much narrower 1986 Petroleum Resource Rent Tax[46] in the face of some industry opposition; the form of the new broader resources rent tax was not easy to sell. In a lecture in 2010, Professor Ross Garnaut observed that:

> We are all aware that the manner of public disclosure of such a new, large and complex policy was not world's best practice, taking industry by surprise with announcement of changes of immense financial consequences. Given the manner of the announcement, the immediate industry reaction was understandable.[47]

Initially, the Minerals Council of Australia (MCA) in its submission to the Henry Review panel stated that it was prepared to accept the principle of a profits-based tax. Also, the CEO of BHP-Billiton reportedly at first did not, in principle, oppose a resources rent tax, although it was believed that the tax was likely to affect Australia's competitiveness.[48] Subsequently, as Paul Kelly has noted, the MCA was prepared to make a deal; but, unfortunately, 'Labor did not want a deal' as they saw the tax as an electorally attractive vehicle for them.[49]

As Ken Henry said of this Labor attitude: 'They thought the resources

---

[46]   For the debate about this legislation in the House of Representatives on 23 March 1987, see further: <http://parlinfo.aph.gov.au/parlInfo/search/display/display.w3p;db=CHAMBER;id=chamber%2Fhansardr%2F1987-03-23%2F0053;query=(Dataset%3Aweblastweek,hansardr,noticer,webthisweek,dailyp,votes,journals,orderofbusiness,hansards,notices,websds)%20ParliamentNumber%3A%2234%22%20Electorate_Phrase%3A%22dawson%22%20Interjector_Phrase%3A%22mr%20tim%20fischer%22%20Party%3A%22np%22;rec=0>.

[47]   R. Garnaut, 'The new Australian resources rent tax' *The Australian* (21 May 2010) 4.

[48]   (n 3) 307.

[49]   (n 3) 298.

tax was a dead-set political winner for them.'[50] The new mining tax was given a provocative populist title (as the Resources Super Profits Tax) and became a key feature of the 2010 budget, as the government projected that it would raise $12 billion in its first two years.[51]

Mining companies were, however, concerned about the possibility of an even broader resources tax being imposed; this created anxiety in the mining industry. According to Wayne Swan, the Labor Treasurer at the time, the mining companies therefore assumed the worst:

> The mining companies knew the [Henry] report had been handed to the government just before Christmas [2009]. When, week after week, month after month, it was not released publicly they became increasingly anxious. This long period of silence caused the companies to assume the worst. It also allowed them much more time to prepare their campaign in opposition to the reforms.[52]

Swan argued that when the mining companies complained that they had not been consulted on the new tax, this was 'untrue' and was merely an attempt at 'rewriting of history'. He noted that:

> Companies met with the Henry panel and the government on numerous occasions throughout the review period. Indeed, the panel even discussed options for a resources rent tax with industry ahead of delivering its report to government.[53]

There was a delay in publicly circulating the mining tax recommendations of the Henry review as Prime Minister Rudd was slow to accept that such a tax was appropriate.

The situation was made more complex because of distrust between the Prime Minister and Mining Minister Martin Ferguson.[54] As Paul Kelly explained the problem, 'Rudd was disengaged and Ferguson was excluded from the policy decision.'[55] As a result of distrust of Ferguson, he was not briefed on the details of the new tax 'until very late in the process' although he was allegedly 'not caught unawares in relation to both the intent and the design of the policy approach' proposed by Henry.[56] Also excluded from Labor's policy making process was Dr Craig Emerson, a Labor Member

---

[50]   Quoted by Paul Kelly (n 3) at 300.
[51]   (n 3) 305.
[52]   Wayne Swan, *The Good Fight – Six years, two prime ministers and staring down the Great Recession* (Allen & Unwin, 2014) 198.
[53]   (n 52) 198.
[54]   (n 3) 298.
[55]   (n 3) 300.
[56]   Swan (n 52) 211.

of Parliament who had previously worked as an economist with Ross
Garnaut. As Maxine McKew noted:

> Emerson constantly tried to buy into discussions but was blocked. The ANU-
> trained economist could see the problems. As he says, the RSPT 'is theoretically
> elegant but practically useless' because it ropes in the government as a co-owner
> and joint risk partner in the development of the country's minerals wealth. The
> industry did not want a bar of it.[57]

Emerson had long argued that the inefficient system of State-based
mining royalties should be replaced by a more efficient tax on profits and
not a tax on the amount produced by miners.[58]

One of the reasons for this antagonism to the idea of a partnership
was suggested by Chris Richardson, a well-known economist from Access
Economics. In June 2010 Richardson noted that the imposition of a 40
percent tax by the RSPT taxed 'effort and entrepreneurial expertise (at 40
per cent) as well as mineral resources rents.'[59]

In his account of this period, Swan argued that Rudd distrusted
Ferguson 'because he was close to the mining industry and he represented
the sector's interests inside the government.'[60] The full details of the Henry
recommendations were not widely known before Prime Minister Rudd and
Mining Minister Ferguson announced a Resources Super Profits Tax on
2 May 2010; this was shortly before the federal government's budget was
handed down in May 2010 by Treasurer Swan.

### Legislative Design Faults and the Failure in Tax Law Making

The speed with which the tax was enacted after the release of the Henry
Review's recommendations meant that various major design flaws were
inevitable. Probably the most serious of these was the breadth of the reach
of the tax, as it applied to high-value mining activities (iron ore and coal) as
well as to low-value minerals (sand and gravel). Swan subsequently regret-
ted this over-reach of the proposed law.[61] Another design flaw concerned
the refunding of losses incurred by mining companies.

Unfortunately for Labor's proposals, Swan had failed to utilize all of the

---

[57]   M. McKew, *Tales from the Political Trenches* (Melbourne University
Press, 2013) 181.

[58]   C. Emerson, 'Déjà vu again on resources rent tax' *Australian Financial
Review* (25 November 2014) 42.

[59]   Quoted by McKew (n 57) 180.

[60]   (n 57) 211.

[61]   McKew (n 57) 209.

expertise that was available within the Party; this included Mining Minister Martin Ferguson, Craig Emerson (an MP who had completed a PhD on the taxation of petroleum resources) or Gary Gray, a Western Australian member of parliament who had been the Labor Party National Secretary and a corporate adviser of Woodside Petroleum. As McKew points out: '[t]he combined expertise of Gray, Ferguson and Emerson could have been harnessed earlier by Swan to work with industry, get the details right and arrive at a sensible middle ground position – one that industry could live with.'[62]

Although the mining industry had for some years called for a loss refundability provision in the tax system in regard to exploration expenses, in the context of the MRRT, Swan later acknowledged that 'in reality it was a red flag to the mining company bullies who argued publicly that they should bear the risk for their investments.'[63] In the end, these design flaws and a poor process of law-making, coupled with bitter industry opposition, dealt a death blow to the legislation. As Swan observed, '[g]ood policy, frustrated by insufficient process, had crashed head-on with powerful vested interests.'[64]

In commenting on the process involved in the passage of the minerals tax, Professor Garnaut noted that although the manner in which the RSPT had been introduced was not ideal, there was a need to balance public and private interests in this debate:

> We are all aware that the manner of public disclosure of such a new, large and complex policy was not world's best practice, taking industry by surprise with announcement of changes of immense financial consequence. Given the manner of the announcement, the immediate industry reaction was understandable ... Now, the future prospects of the resources industries and the living standards of the Australian people depend on the assertion of private interests soon being balanced by considered, independent and soundly based assessments of the public interest.[65]

The poor process was evident in the nature of the consultation phase. Limited efforts were made to brief the mining industry in late April; former Treasurer Swan noted that 'some of the major companies were brought into the Treasury and briefed thoroughly on its contents. This occurred on Thursday 29 April. They were required to sign confidentiality agreements

---

[62]   (n 57) 182.
[63]   (n 57) 209.
[64]   (n 57) 218.
[65]   R. Garnaut, 'The new Australian resources rent tax' *The Australian* (21 May 2010).

because they were presented with the entire details of the package.'[66] Numerous meetings with senior mining company officials also apparently took place immediately after the new tax package was announced.[67]

All of this activity was occurring just after the peak of the Global Financial Crisis and at a time that Australia was seen as having a 'two speed economy', the rich mining states (especially Western Australia which raised more than 50 per cent of state mining royalties) versus the other states that were suffering from an economic downturn. Constitutionally, the states had power to collect mining royalties, but the Commonwealth Government's new mining tax sought to bypass the States, so that state governments, such as that in Western Australia, were actively opposed to the new mining tax. As Paul Kelly noted,

> Labor never properly addressed the role of the states . . . There was no formal consultation with the states. This is because the problem would have required protracted dialogue with little prospect of agreement.[68]

Prime Minister Rudd was reportedly shocked when, at a Council of Australian Government (COAG) meeting[69] in April 2010, he heard from Colin Barnett, the Premier of Western Australia, that his State would not compromise its powers to collect mining royalties to facilitate the new RSPT.[70]

## THE NATIONAL ANTI-TAX CAMPAIGN: THE ROLE OF BHP BILLITON

Soon after the proposed new tax was announced, the mining industry commenced a national media campaign against the tax. There were concerns that the tax would significantly diminish the profits of multinational mining companies. The *Financial Times* even reported that:

> Analysts estimated that the new tax would cut earnings at BHP Billiton, the Melbourne-based mining group, 19 per cent. London-based Rio Tinto, which operates highly profitable iron ore mines in Western Australia, could suffer a fall of nearer 30 per cent.[71]

---

[66]   Swan (n 52) 211.
[67]   (n 57) 211–213.
[68]   Kelly (n 3) above at 310.
[69]   Council of Australian Governments.
[70]   (n 57) 179.
[71]   P. Smith, 'Australia plans 40% tax on mining sector' *Financial Times* (2 May 2010).

Marius Kloppers, the chief executive of BHP Billiton, was reported to have warned:

> If implemented, these proposals seriously threaten Australia's competitiveness, jeopardise future investments and will adversely impact the future wealth and standard of living of all Australians.[72]

When combined with the unpleasant notion of the tax being seen as a partnership between industry and government, this level of tax was seen as likely to have a significant impact on BHP Billiton's shareholder returns. The chief executive of the Minerals Council of Australia opined that the new tax would make the mining industry in Australia the most highly taxed mining industry in the world:

> Australia's hard-earned reputation as a stable investment environment will be dramatically undermined . . . If the government's new tax proposal goes ahead, A$108bn worth of future investment in the minerals industry will be under a cloud.[73]

Former Treasurer Swan described the industry campaign as involving 'blackmailing' scare tactics in which 'the big mining companies were deliberately, unnecessarily and selfishly fanning uncertainty.'[74] On the other hand, leading mining industry figures, such as the Rio Tinto managing director, reportedly 'believed the industry had been misled and ambushed.'[75]

The mining industry also argued that the tax created a sovereign risk for Australia.[76] The CEO of Rio-Tinto concluded that Australia was the main sovereign risk for his company.[77] A greater concern of the global mining industry was that the successful introduction of the Australian mining tax might create a precedent for other countries, especially in the developing world, that had expressed interest in such a tax.[78]

BHP Billiton reportedly believed that the RSPT would have global ramifications as other countries would be likely to follow Australia's example.[79]

---

[72]  (n 71).
[73]  Quoted in (n 71).
[74]  Swan (n 52) 207–208.
[75]  Kelly (n 3) 303.
[76]  Swan (n 52) 208.
[77]  Kelly (n 3) 307, 311.
[78]  Swan (n 52) 210.
[79]  Kelly (n 3) 308.

Although BHP has had a long association with Australia,[80] as a consequence of a number of mergers, only 24 per cent of the shareholders in BHP Billiton were domiciled in Australia; in the case of Rio-Tinto, only 16 per cent of its shareholders were Australian.[81]

One TNC played a leadership role in the attack on the proposed new mining tax. As Paul Kelly noted, BHP Billiton's CEO:

> Kloppers assumed the leadership role in the anti-tax campaign. The 'war room' was established at [its headquarters at] Lonsdale Street in Melbourne . . . BHP Billiton believed it had been 'set up.'[82]

Other groups were also brought together to support the attack on the tax. These included the Minerals Council of Australia, the Business Council of Australia, financial analysts, the media and the Opposition parties under Tony Abbott. As Kelly noted:

> The Minerals Council-paid advertising campaign began on Friday 7 May after the [Government's] announcement. The campaign was run from its Canberra HQ . . . Spanning fifty-four days, the campaign cost $25 million . . . It ranks . . . as the best special-interest campaign in recent decades.[83]

In addition:

> An early priority for Kloppers was to persuade the Business Council of Australia to line up against the tax. The miners put a priority on the financial analysts . . . In effect, the financial sector was recruited. Kloppers' aim was to dismantle the RSPT by a punitive assault, an extraordinary step for his company. It revealed the complete breakdown between the world's biggest mining company and the Rudd Government.[84]

In addition to these lobbying efforts to stop the tax, BHP Billiton organized a meeting with leading figures in the Opposition led by Abbott; this would provide the basis for the subsequent electoral defeat of the Labor Government. Abbott would 'enshrine the RSPT as an election winning issue,' according to Paul Kelly.[85] Similarly, Maxine McKew noted that following the announcement of the RSPT in the May 2010 Budget:

---

[80]    See, generally, P. Thompson and R. Macklin, *The Big Fella – The Rise and Rise of BHP Billiton* (William Heinemann Australia, 2010).

[81]    See further, D. Uren, *Takeover – Foreign Investment and the Australian psyche* (Black, 2015) 110.

[82]    Kelly (n 3) 307–308.

[83]    (n 3) 308.

[84]    Kelly (n 3) 308.

[85]    (n 3) 309.

The acrimony unleashed by the miners' campaign, along with Abbott's opportunistic rejection of any proposal for increased taxation, was the dramatic backdrop to the events that led directly to Rudd's removal as Prime Minister.[86]

Swan later observed that he did not think that the mining industry was serious about consultation and were instead preparing for a 'war' against the tax.[87] Swan argued that industry interest in consultation was 'somewhat disingenuous' and, in regard to one leading mining company officer,

> I have subsequently learned that at the time we were talking, his company was setting up a 'war room' in its headquarters, headed by a very senior public affairs practitioner, to coordinate the industry's campaign against the RSPT.[88]

It should also be noted that heads of leading domestic Australian mining companies, such as Andrew Forrest of the Fortescue Metals Group, Gina Rinehart of Hancock Prospecting and Clive Palmer also protested publicly against the RSPT. The former Labor Treasurer, Wayne Swan, was aghast at the reaction of billionaires who were 'protesting at having to pay more tax on the mineral resources they were ripping out of the ground.'[89]

Burrell's biography of Forrest notes that '[n]ever before had a protest against injustice been led by two of the richest people in the land [Forrest and Rinehart].'[90] Forrest later went so far as to launch a failed constitutional challenge against the Commonwealth Government's MMRT which by then had replaced the RSPT. Forrest was concerned that his iron ore mining company (Fortescue) 'would not exist under the RSPT.'[91]

Prime Minister Rudd sought to split the mining industry opposition to the RSPT by cutting a deal with Forrest and his company, Fortescue Metals Group (FMG), on 20 June 2010, three days before his resignation as Prime Minister.[92] But this deal fell far short of an agreement with the big three multinational mining companies.[93] The deal with Forrest would not, however, have stopped the advertising campaign against the government

---

86   McKew (n 57) 178.
87   Swan (n 52) 213.
88   (n 52).
89   Swan (n 52) 216.
90   A. Burrell, *Twiggy – The high-stakes life of Andrew Forrest*, Collingwood (Black, 2013) 199.
91   Quoted by Kelly (n 3) 307.
92   Kelly (n 3) 312.
93   Forrest's plan for reforming the RSPT proposed tax deductions for spending by miners that built open access mining infrastructure (like railways) and as such these would not benefit BHP or Rio. See further, Burrell (n 90) 201.

that was being driven by BHP, Rio and Xstrata.[94] Once Rudd was removed as Prime Minister, BHP, Rio and Xstrata no longer needed the assistance of Forrest as they were now able to organize their own deal with the new Prime Minister, Julia Gillard.[95]

In collaboration with the Federal Opposition parties, led by Tony Abbott, a massive media campaign against the resources rent tax arose; this involved television, print and radio advertisements. Abbott was reported to have said at this time that the mining tax would destroy the resources boom. He echoed industry warnings when he proclaimed that: '[p]utting a great big tax on the mining industry is like handicapping our most successful athletes. It's bound to drive investment and jobs overseas.[96]

The industry's advertising campaign against the new tax commenced in early May. *The Australian* newspaper was seen by Swan as launching an 'extraordinary' attack on the Government's new tax in May 2010. This campaign also mobilized 'numerous companies in the supply chain of the very large mining houses' which were advised that they, too, were at risk because of the mining tax and were urged to join the campaign against the tax. Some of these companies were reportedly even threatened that they would not receive further work if they did not join the campaign being led by the multinational mining companies.[97]

## GOVERNMENT EFFORTS TO SETTLE THE MINING DISPUTE

One effect of the mining industry campaign was to create popular concerns about Prime Minister Rudd, leading some within the Labor Government to create a leadership crisis which led to Julia Gillard replacing Rudd as Prime Minister. Gillard then saw the resolution of the mining tax campaign as one of her most pressing concerns as Prime Minister. The mining tax thus became the 'fatal blow' to the Rudd Labor Government.[98]

Kelly also noted that although the new mining tax 'was feasible and saleable', its formulation and implementation failed badly as 'Labor got the timing, design and politics wrong.'[99] This was because:

---

[94]    (n 90) 202.
[95]    (n 90) 206.
[96]    (n 78).
[97]    Swan (n 52) 217–218.
[98]    (n 3) 295.
[99]    (n 3) 295.

Every rule of established tax reform practice – consultation with stakeholders, ministerial assessment of bureaucratic advice, cultivation of the terrain
for reform – was breached. Yet this was the central tax reform of Rudd's first
term ... Rudd and Swan had taken the justified idea of a resources tax on
profits and botched it. They provoked the mining sector into a political war
and left much of the business community convinced they were untrustworthy.[100]

As a result, Prime Minister Gillard sought to rescue the situation that
the government had found itself in:

As one of her first acts as Prime Minister, she phoned Marius Kloppers, the
CEO of BHP. Her 'ceasefire' proposal to Kloppers and the mining companies –
getting them to agree to pull their TV ads as a condition of negotiation – was
her first big call as prime minister.[101]

Gillard called for a new discussion on the design of the RSPT, which was
to be rebranded as the Mineral Resources Rent Tax (MRRT). Paul Kelly
notes that 'Gillard would offer more than just peace; it became fiscal sur-
render' with the watered down MRRT principles being effectively drafted
by leading mining industry figures. This process of reviewing the tax commenced in late June with meetings between Treasurer Swan and Mining
Minister Ferguson, representing the government, and BHP's CEO Marius
Kloppers, accompanied by other mining industry representatives from Rio
Tinto and Xstrata.[102]

On 30 June senior BHP Billiton executive Gerard Bond sent a draft tax agreement to Swan's office. The main company was involved in drafting the deal.
The 'heads of agreement' dated 1 July was signed by the big three miners plus
Gillard, Swan and Ferguson. The new Minerals Resources Rent Tax (MRRT)
was no ordinary government decision, based on formal agreement with the 'big
three' it was a shared decision.[103]

Thus, on 2 July 2010 it was agreed to impose the mining tax on only two
commodities, iron and coal. It was also agreed to reduce the rate of tax on
profits from 40 per cent to 30 per cent. Furthermore, the tax would not
apply to smaller mining companies with profits of less than $50 million
per year. It was calculated that the new tax would collect $10.5 billion over
the forward estimates period, and $4.4 billion over four years. The actual
amount of revenue collected was projected to be around $200 million, in

---

[100]   (n 3) 295.
[101]   Swan (n 52) 246.
[102]   Swan (n 52) 247.
[103]   Kelly (n 3) 343.

large part due to fall in commodity prices and to the tax deductions available for new mining investment.[104] The MRRT was eventually abolished by the Abbott Government on 3 September 2014.

As Sarah-Jane Tasker observed at the time that the MRRT was repealed:

> The world's biggest miners, BHP Billiton, Rio Tinto and Xstrata, helped draft the MRRT with Wayne Swan and Julia Gillard, creating a watered-down version of Kevin Rudd's resources super profits tax. Australia's miners had spent $17.1m on a campaign against Mr Rudd's original proposal. The campaign, spearheaded by the Minerals Council of Australia, was one of the most expensive run by an industry against a government on a single policy issue.[105]

Following the repeal of the MRRT, the new Coalition government weakly called upon TNCs to pay more tax and eliminate situations in which TNCs avoided paying any taxes at all through the use of profit shifting to low tax jurisdictions.[106] This led to calls for further reduction of company tax rates in Australia, given that popular offshore jurisdictions such as Ireland imposed an attractive corporate tax of only 12.5 per cent.[107] There were also calls for greater transparency in tax practices of multinationals.

Some mining company leaders, such as Rio Tinto chair Jan du Plessis, later pointed out that the use of complex and artificial tax minimization schemes by TNCs should be avoided as their use 'impacts upon your reputation and if you are in the mining business, that impacts your ability to invest and I think is short sighted.'[108] However, the bitterness generated by both sides of the debate over the enactment and repeal of the MRRT was so extensive that, as the *Australian Financial Review* suggested, 'It has poisoned the ground against genuine reform.'[109]

---

[104]   Swan (n 52) 248–249. See also P. Ker, 'Mining tax revenue slumps' *Sydney Morning Herald* (14 May 2013) <http://www.smh.com.au/business/federal-budget/mining-tax-revenue-slumps-20130514–2jkm1.html#ixzz2TGVDRaYr>; P. Coorey, 'Swan admits MRRT revenue failure' *Australian Financial Review* (19 August 2014) 5l; P. Crowe, 'Super slug as mining tax buried' *The Australian* (3 September 2014) 1.

[105]   S.-J. Tasker, 'Miners escape with barely a tax scratch' *The Australian* (3 September 2014) 4.

[106]   F. Anderson, 'Hockey set to reveal tax plan' *Australian Financial Review* (4 September 2014) 7.

[107]   (n 106). See further, E. Byrne and J. O'Brien, 'No hiding from tax-have debate' *Independent* (26 May 2013) <http://www.independent.ie/opinion/analysis/dr-elaine-byrne-and-professor-justin-obrien-no-hiding-from-taxhaven-debate-29297279.html>.

[108]   Quoted by T. Boyd, 'Multinationals get away with murder' *Australian Financial Review* (25 November 2014) 8.

[109]   'Tax consensus a massive task' *Australian Financial Review* (9 November 2014) 50.

After the 2015 Senate hearings in Canberra into multinational taxation, Laura Tingle from the *Australian Financial Review* commented that:

> For Labor, the revelations are particularly bitter. They show that, even as the miners were campaigning to fight not just the contentious mining tax but the loss of any other tax concessions and trumpeting the huge amount of tax they were paying to keep our fine country going, they were busily establishing arrangements that have allowed them to drastically cut their Australian tax bill.

Tingle added:

> But the politics of these revelations are much more devastating for a business community in perpetual search of lower taxes. As we can see from the [Mineral Council of Australia's] approach to the tax discussion paper, the revelations that nobbled the industry's capacity to take part in the new tax debate. The miners have been in damage control, with the MCA releasing floods of figures to show how they pay lots of tax after all.[110]

The government's mining tax reform efforts had been roundly defeated by a mining industry led by three large TNCs. Further tax reform debates then had to take place in an environment of bitterness and mistrust poisoning the landscape for reform.

## CONCLUSIONS

Globalization has made TNCs some of the principal actors in markets. Although it can be argued that they are not always more powerful than governments,[111] TNCs have certainly been very powerful actors in tax reform discussions in Australia. In the case of the defeat of the Rudd Government's Resources Super Profits Tax, TNCs were overwhelmingly effective in mobilizing opposition and working to rewrite the draft legislation.

When a watered down version of the tax was passed by the Gillard Labor Government, it was a temporary outcome. The TNCs' campaign against the tax had provided support to the position of the opposition parties who were able to rely upon the ill-will created by the campaign against the poorly drafted tax to defeat the Gillard Government. This eventually led to

---

[110]   L. Tingle, 'Miners bury tax debate under tonne of selective truths' *Australian Financial Review* (1 May 2015) 39.

[111]   See, for example, the defense of multinationals against claims that countries have been cowed by corporations in Martin Wolf, *Why Globalization Works* (Yale UP, 2005) 220–248.

the repeal of the Mineral Resources Rent Tax in September 2014, bringing this episode to a close.

In the meantime, the government's serious problems of base tax erosion continued; these problems had contributed to government moves in 2010 to enact the mining tax. Subsequent revelations at Australian Senate hearings into the tax planning practices of large multinationals working in Australia served to illustrate that mining industry TNCs continued to resist efforts to ensure that they met their tax obligations. State governments have continued to have problems in collecting mining royalties from TNCs, and the Australian Taxation Office remains locked in dispute with large mining companies for unpaid taxes as a result of complex tax planning schemes.[112]

Despite some statements of verbal support for the introduction of more efficient mining tax laws, the collective power of mining industry TNCs in response to an unpopular mining tax was clearly sufficient to defeat government efforts to introduce such a tax in Australia. This will certainly send a message to other governments to rethink any ideas about seeking to impose unwelcome taxes upon powerful globally powerful TNCs.

---

[112] See further, B. Fitzgerald, 'BHP in $288m royalty rom with Queensland' *The Australian* (13 November 2015) 20; see also N. Chenoweth and L. Tingle, 'BHP reveals $522m Singapore tax bill' *Australian Financial Review* (28 April 2015) 10.

# 13. Risks and fiscal concerns in the extraction of natural resources: a study of transnational corporations in Papua New Guinea
*Diane Kraal*

## 1. INTRODUCTION

Transnational corporations (TNCs) dominate the extraction activities of high-value mineral resources in Papua New Guinea (PNG). Except for a brief period around the granting of independence from Australia in 1975, the ensuing discussion in the chapter will show how PNG's scarcity of technical expertise and capital has affected its negotiating leverage with extractive industry TNCs. These TNCs have generally been in stronger positions when negotiating the fiscal terms of their operations with the PNG Government.

Academic research concerned with extractive industries often considers issues around economic, social and environmental ramifications of relevant host country policies. Common economic enquiries ask questions about the real or spill-over benefits of mineral extraction to a local economy.[1] Socially orientated investigations into the impact of mining typically cover land rights, indentured labour, colonial class differences, displacement, dispossession and disempowerment of indigenous peoples.[2]

---

[1]  E.g., Michael C. Howard, *Mining, Politics and Development in the South Pacific* (Westview Press, 1991) 53; Ephraim Makis, 'Bougainville Copper and Local Businesses in Bougainville' (1975) Discussion paper No. 17, Department of Economics, University of PNG; John Tilton, John Millett and Richard Ward, 'Mineral and Mining Policy in Papua New Guinea' (1986) Discussion Paper No. 25, Institute of National Affairs; Suman Basu et al., *The Macroeconomic Effects of Natural Resource Extraction: Applications to Papua New Guinea* (International Monetary Fund, 2013).

[2]  E.g., Colin Newbury, 'Colour Bar and Conflict on the New Guinea Goldfields' (1957) 21 (3) *Australian Journal of Politics and History* 25; John Connell and Richard Howitt (eds), *Mining and Indigenous Peoples in Australia* (Sydney University Press, 1991); Paul Quodling, *Bougainville: The mine and the people* (Centre for Independent Studies, 1991).

The environmental discourse on mineral extraction overwhelmingly covers damage to land and its overall degradation.[3]

By contrast this chapter investigates the risks and the fiscal challenges for TNCs operating in the natural resource sector in the host country of PNG. It examines the importance of fiscal negotiations for formal agreements between a host country, which is endowed with natural resources, and extractive TNCs. The chapter contextualizes the extraction activities and taxation of a developing country and the impact of institutions, including agencies such as the International Monetary Fund and other global financial bodies on host country policies.

For background, the chapter reflects on the past mistakes of TNCs in the mining of copper and associated minerals around the Ok Tedi River in PNG's Western Province, and at the Panguna mine on Bougainville Island. The chapter then shifts to the latest TNC investment of major significance: the extraction of natural gas from fields in PNG's Southern Highlands and Western Provinces, and its processing into liquefied natural gas that is now being exported.

Given the PNG record of poor fiscal outcomes and operational disasters from copper and gold mining, a key question of the chapter is: Will the current and significant natural gas project improve PNG's tax revenues? Further, Do the recent and successful natural gas activities in PNG reflect any initiatives for social and environment issues or changes in regulatory controls? Finally, What are the wider lessons from this case study for other extractive industry TNCs?

The chapter proceeds as follows. Section 2 concerns the colonial past in PNG's mining and hydrocarbon (oil and gas) industries, with Section 3 considering the immediate post-World War II period, and from independence up to 1992. Section 4 is about lessons for TNCs arising from the Bougainville copper mining-related civil uprising, and the Ok Tedi mine's environmental damage. Sections 5, 6 and 7 look at institutional interest in PNG; the latest gas project in PNG, renewed TNC interest in the country; and whether PNG's current tax reforms will court sovereign risk. In conclusion, Section 8 summarises the overall risks and fiscal concerns for TNCs extracting natural resources in PNG and the wider lessons from the findings.

---

[3]   E.g., M.J.F. Brown, 'A Development Consequence: Disposal of Mining Waste on Bougainville, Papua New Guinea' (1974) 5 (2) *Geoforum* 19; John Gordon, 'Ok Tedi: The Law Sickens from a Poisoned Environment' (1995) 33 *Law Society Journal* 58; W.D. Scott, 'A Study of the Impact of the Bougainville Copper Project on the Economy and Society of Papua New Guinea' (1973) report by W.D. Scott and Co. Pty Ltd Management Consultants 3.2.

## 2. THE COLONIAL PAST

The colonial era shaped attitudes towards mining in PNG. In the wake of the late 19th century advance by European powers for territory in the Pacific region, the island of New Guinea was divided. The eastern part of the island of New Guinea was divided between Germany to the north (German New Guinea) and Britain (British Papua) to the south.[4] In 1902 Britain transferred British Papua to Australian administration and renamed it the Territory of Papua. German New Guinea formally came under Australian administration post-World War I and later the territories became the Territory of Papua–New Guinea.[5] In 1973 self-government was granted to the Territory, and in 1975 it was granted full independence as the Independent State of Papua New Guinea.

### 2.1 Gold

Gold mining prospectors moved into Port Moresby in British Papua as early as 1877, and from there moved westward and inland.[6] The colonial administration in Port Moresby failed to control these alluvial miners, who continued to mount prospecting expeditions. Conflicts with the indigenous people ensued, and the Administration gave tacit support to the miners by sending punitive expeditions. The result was an extension of administrative control to the miners, for courses of action were frequently decided by prospecting parties rather than by official regulation.[7] The appointment of Resident Magistrates stationed at goldfields was a further instance of the mining industry being given the opportunity to influence the pattern of administration. The colonial Administration financed the construction of public works, such as tracks, which were clearly for the benefit of the mining community, rather than the local indigenes.

Prison inmates provided cheap labour for colonial mining projects, and the general shortage of labour, indirectly forced the indigenous people to participate in the economy, 'both while preserving a façade of

---

[4]  H.C. Brookfield, *Colonialism, Development and Independence: The Case of the Melanesian Islands in the South Pacific* (Cambridge UP, 1972) xv.

[5]  (n 4) 60–61.

[6]  H.J. Gibbney, 'The New Guinea Gold Rush of 1878' (1972) 58 *Journal of the Royal Australian Historical Society* 284.

[7]  W.A. McGee and G.R. Henning, 'Investment in Lode Mining, Papua 1878 to 1920' (1990) 25 *Journal of Pacific History* 244, 255.

legality'.[8] The Administration's encouragement of the minerals industry in Papua was primarily designed to benefit the colonial power and its investors, whether resident in Papua or back home. Companies registered in Australia were the most active miners, and capital was drawn from investors in eastern Australia; however, the largest parcels of private funds invested in Australian-registered companies came from London.[9] There was an expectation that the mining sector could stimulate the Territories' overall economic activity, thus making the development of other local industries easier.

By 1910 high-grade alluvial mining at in Papua's Milne Bay Province was undertaken by large teams of Papuans led by Europeans in an employer and labour relationship. Many prospectors came from the Eastern Australian goldfields of the 1850s, where the prospecting experience was quite different, as sites were initially worked by individuals or small partnerships, with finds divided among the members.[10]

For a short time prior to 1914, both the Administration and private entrepreneurs invested in mining in the Territory of Papua. The Administrative policy provided subsidies for prospecting expeditions, and some infrastructure continued to be fully financed.[11]

The economic growth of the Territories of Papua and New Guinea mainly relied on grants from the Australian Government, supplemented with local revenues.[12] Beginning in 1920, Administrative policy and regulations levied taxes and required mining licences; some of these revenues were applied towards the required infrastructure. By the 1930s mining of alluvial gold transitioned to mechanised dredging in Papua's Morobe Province.[13] One constant through the decades, was the clash between employers and labour over wages and conditions in the Papua goldfields. Accounts of Gold Dredging Limited's treatment of its labourers in Bulolo detail violent encounters between miners and villagers.[14] By this stage it was the corporations, with their mechanised, capital-intensive techniques that mined in Papua territory. They were still mainly Australia-based, (such as BHP Ltd and British New Guinea Syndicate Ltd), but financed

---

[8]  (n 7) 255–256.
[9]  (n 7) 258–259.
[10]  H.N. Nelson, 'Miners, Laborers and Officials on the Lakekamu Goldfield of Papau' (1973) 25 *Labour History* 40.
[11]  (n 7) 256.
[12]  (n 7) 259.
[13]  Brookfield (n 4) 28.
[14]  E.g., Nelson (n 10) 41, fn 13.

by capital from London.[15] Burns Philp, an Australian wholesale merchant company operating in many Pacific countries, catered to the Papuan goldfields and amassed huge profits.[16]

## 2.2 Oil

In 1911 the first reports of oil seepage emerged from Upoia, near the Gulf of Papua. The Australian Government allocated limited funds for follow up oil exploration, to no avail.[17] After World War I the Australian Government undertook further exploration, this time sharing costs with the British Government. Together they financed the Anglo-Persian Oil Company Ltd (now BP Ltd), which was appointed as the operator, but the British soon withdrew, due to divergent views, with the seed funding spent.

The Australian Government saw the Papua oilfields as potentially being of inestimable value for both commercial and defence purposes, and had no intention of allowing such a prospect to pass into private hands.[18] At this time, distrust of oil companies was high. The Standard Oil monopoly in the United States had recently been broken up by judicial decree. In London, Churchill had attacked the Royal Dutch Shell Group over its attitude to pricing for Royal Navy contracts. A government monopoly was mandated for Papuan petroleum exploration, but by 1923 the Australian Government's rising exploration expenses led to it granting leases to companies such as the Papua Oil Exploratory Company Ltd, which failed to find viable prospects. In the late 1930s the Papua Oil Development Company, a subsidiary of Royal Dutch Shell, was granted prospecting rights. Then British Petroleum, Vacuum Oil, and Oil Search formed Island Exploration Company Pty Ltd to undertake exploration. Later Oil Search linked with D'Arcy Exploration Company and Vacuum Oil to form Australasian Petroleum Co. Pty Ltd.

---

[15]   For a list of early investor companies in the Papua territory, see McGee and Henning (n 7) 247, Table 2.

[16]   K. Buckley and K. Klugman, *The History of Burns Philp: The Australian Company in the South Pacific* (Burns Philip and Co. Ltd, 1981) 89.

[17]   'Search for Oil in Papua New Guinea, Part I: How Earliest Discoveries Were Made' (1937) *Pacific Islands Monthly* 49; 'Search for Oil in Papua New Guinea, Part II: The muddling of the Federal Government' (1937) *Pacific Islands Monthly* 40.

[18]   McGee and Henning (n 7) 257 fn 44 cites the 'Report from the Joint Committee of Public Accounts upon the Expenditure on Oil Exploration, Development, Refining, etc., in the Commonwealth and Papua', Pt 1, 1925, CPP Vol. II (1925), Paper no. 34, p. 6.

However by 1942 the Papua oilfields were found to lack prospectivity, and no alternative commercial hydrocarbon prospects had yet been found by the time the Pacific War interrupted the costly exploration activities.[19]

### 2.3    Commentary

Mining in the early colonial period of Papua New Guinea reflected the Administrative government's encouragement of the minerals industry in Papua to primarily benefit Australians and British rentiers. The Administration worked almost co-operatively with miners to facilitate the extraction of mineral wealth. With financing mainly through equity, risk factors for mining companies were infrastructure construction and extraction costs. Payments such as royalties and compensation for land use were paid to host country landowners. There were no labour policies, and impacts on the environment (such as from dredging) were not addressed by policy. As for oil exploration, the Administrative government mandated a monopoly for strategic and political reasons, but allocated leases for private exploration and test drilling to contain costs. The key risk factor for oil companies, some of which were the precursors of today's TNCs, were exploration costs.

## 3.    AFTER WORLD WAR II AND INDEPENDENCE

### 3.1    Oil and Gas

After World War II, oil exploration resumed, and in 1958 the Australasian Petroleum Company found a modest oil flow of 1,000 barrels a day at Puri in Western Papua. It is estimated that, up to 1958, costs for test drilling in the various parts of the Territory of Papua-New Guinea were a staggering £31 million, which reflected the costs associated with such ventures in the steep and difficult terrain of PNG.[20]

---

[19]    'Search for Oil in Papua New Guinea, Part III: Various Private Companies Fail' (1937) *Pacific Islands Monthly* 42; H.G. Raggatt, 'The Search for Oil in Australia and New Guinea' (1954) 1 *Australiasian Oil and Gas Journal* 5; W.D. Mott, 'An Australian Survey: A Review of Exploration Activity in Australia and Papua New Guinea in 1958' (1959) 5 *Australiasian Oil and Gas Journal* 5; '55 Holes – 31,000,000 pounds' (1958) 7 *Petroleum Gazette* 103. Other oil exploration companies included Oriomo Oil Ltd, the Australasian Petroleum Co. Pty Ltd, Papuan Apinaipi Petroleum Co. Ltd. Enterprise of New Guinea Gold and Petroleum Development NL.
[20]    *Petroleum Gazette* (n 19) 105.

In 1985 oil was discovered in the PNG's southern highlands. The prospect, known as the Kutubu project, was developed by a consortium led by a subsidiary of Chevron, a US company which had a 25 per cent holding; BP also had a 25 per cent share, with the balance of shares held by minor investors.[21] In 1992 commercial production commenced, peaking in 1993. As of 2014, oil is still produced but the reserves are in decline. The major TNC shareholder is now Oil Search Ltd.

Proven gas reserves in the southern highlands are now the focus of hydrocarbon activity in PNG. In 2008 the tax arrangements for what is known as the PNG-LNG project were settled, when the co-venturers formally signed a Resource Development Agreement with the PNG Government. A Resource Development Agreement is confidential and overrides income tax and regulatory legislation. It establishes the fiscal regime and legal framework by which the project is regulated, and sets the terms for the state's equity.[22] The PNG Government's equity share is at market value. In 2010 project construction commenced, with production starting on schedule in 2014.

### 3.2   Copper and Gold

Between 1972 and 1989 the bonanza prospect at the Panguna copper and gold mine on PNG's Bougainville Island was operated by Bougainville Copper Ltd, which today is a subsidiary of the TNC Rio Tinto. The Ok Tedi prospect of copper and gold, located in the Western Province of Papua, commenced production in 1984 under the operator Broken Hill Proprietary Ltd, a TNC which is now BHP Billiton. Both prospects are massive low-grade ore bodies that require highly mechanised, capital-intensive techniques.

There were a number of mining-agreement negotiation challenges for the TNCs over these copper and gold mining projects in the 21-month interval between PNG self-government in 1973 and its independence in 1975, as explained next.

---

[21]   Mary-Louise O'Callaghan, 'Trouble in Pipeline: Oil controversy further erodes confidence' (1990) 148 (24) *Far Eastern Economic Review* 55, 56. Other investors included the Ampolex Group (21.23%), BHP Petroleum (12.5%), Oil Search (10.2%) and Merlin Petroleum/Bond Energy (6.25%).

[22]   See <http://www.exxonmobil.com.au/Australia-English/PA/news_releases_20080522.aspx>. The Resource Development Agreement overrides provisions in the *Income Tax Act 1959* (PNG) and *Oil and Gas Act 1998* (PNG).

### 3.3 Bougainville

Bougainville Copper Ltd financed the capital requirements for its copper and gold project from debt and equity, reflecting a 2:1 debt equity ratio. Borrowings were from the United States, Europe and Japan.[23] In 1967 while copper exploration was still in progress, the Administration renegotiated the original Bougainville agreement, with its two objectives being to guarantee locally generated public revenue, and to stimulate the economy through export income.[24] For the company, the new 1967 agreement provided favourable tax concessions with a three-year tax holiday, after which a 100 per cent deduction for capital expenditure applied – effectively extending the tax holiday to six or seven years – and an exemption from company tax on 20 per cent of all income from copper sales. The agreement included social provisions to employ PNG locals, and requirements for local services and supplies.[25] To encourage the extraction of strategic metals, the agreement was not to be reviewed for another 42 years. However, just after the 1967 agreement, copper and gold prices rose, and the mine became highly profitable when production finally started in 1972. The poor tax take for PNG led to a UN report, which called for the Bougainville Copper Agreement's fiscal provisions to be reviewed.

Political pressure and further mineral price rises led to renegotiation, resulting in the 1974 Bougainville Copper Agreement. This 1974 Agreement heralded a new era of partnership between government and private business. It immediately applied company tax at 33.3 per cent, removed accelerated depreciation, as well as the exemption from company tax on 20 per cent of sales income. There was also a resource rent tax introduced in the form of a progressive profits tax – the extra tax applying once profits exceeded the prescribed threshold rate. It was a way of compensating the government for metal price rises above normal levels.[26] Other new fiscal innovations included a 15 per cent withholding tax on outward

---

[23] M.G. Treadgold, 'Bougainville Copper and Economic Development of Papua New Guinea' (1971) 47 (June) *Economic Record* 186, 187; M.L.O. Faber, 'Bougainville Renegotiated: An Analysis of the New Fiscal Terms' (1974) *Mining Magazine* 466, 448.

[24] Ciaran O'Faircheallaigh, *Host Countries and Multinationals: Case studies from Ireland, Papua New Guinea, Zambia of Negotiations with Mining Corporations* (Department of International Relations, Australian National University, 1982) 69.

[25] Scott (n 3).

[26] H.L. Davies et al., 'History of Ok Tedi Porphyry Copper Prospect, Papua New Guinea' (1978) 73 *Economic Geology* 796, 797–798; Faber (n 25). See Mining (Bougainville Copper Agreement) Act 1967 (PNG) as amended 1974.

dividends and a 1.25 per cent *ad valorem* royalty. The royalty was compensation paid by the company for the land occupied by the mine, destruction of livestock and gardens, destruction and detriment to fishing grounds, and the hardship created by enforced change, such as relocation of homes. However because of the indigenes' unproductive use of the funds, the compensation monies had no multiplier effect on the economy.[27] The PNG Government was allocated 20 per cent equity and paid at par value.

The Bougainville mine is potentially among the largest in the world; however troubles resulted from landowner dissatisfaction with environmental impacts and the lack of local benefits, which had been eclipsed by the government's pursuit of a national strategy.[28] All early negotiations had been between the Administration and the company, not the local indigenes. Indigene dissatisfaction over the miner's ravaging of the land arose from their local culture, which puts the highest importance on the land as the source of a material standard of life, security and the focus of religious attention. Disputes between Bougainville Copper and the villagers ensued. The land was the cornerstone of locals' lives.[29] Physical transformation of the land extended beyond the mining site to the Kawerong River valley where overburden and waste was dumped. Villages in the tailings area had to be relocated and fish life was disturbed.[30]

Ten years of civil war ended with military intervention in 1989 and the cessation of commercial operations. The mine is still idle. Thus for the TNC geological obstacles to the mining operations were minor compared with the environmental, political, social and cultural risks. Bougainville Copper sought to renew its production lease and reopen the mine, but in 2014 the PNG parliament passed legislation that withdrew the company's special lease for the Panguna mine.[31] The mine re-opening will be an underlying issue in the Bougainville islanders' vote on independence in 2019.

### 3.4 Ok Tedi

In 1968 geologists from Kennecott Copper Corporation, a US-holding company with transnational copper interests, discovered mineralised float

---

[27]  Scott (n 3) 3.7.
[28]  O'Faircheallaigh (n 24) 78.
[29]  Scott (n 3) 2.2.
[30]  (n 3) 3.2, 3.5.
[31]  The *Bougainville Mining (Transitional Arrangements) Act 2014* (PNG). See AGM Notice for 6 May 2014, Bougainville Copper Ltd <http://www.asx.com.au/asx/research/companyInfo.do?by=asxCode&asxCode=BOC#headlines> accessed 17 September 2014.

at the confluence of the Ok Tedi and Ok Menga rivers, and traced it back to a copper reserve in the Mount Fulbian region in the Western Province of Papua. The copper reserve was recognised as a potentially major project and drilling tests were carried out from 1969 to 1971. Over two years (from 1970 to 1972) discussions ensued, with the company wanting a Special Mining Lease, a government contribution to infrastructure and government equity participation. Kennecott sought an agreement along the lines of the 1967 Bougainville Copper Agreement.[32] Kennecott required a mining lease before more capital could be committed. From the Administrative-government perspective, the project was inadequately defined in terms of the test drilling and metallurgical reports and so, with a lack of data, it was reluctant to commit to infrastructure in such a remote area. By 1973 Kennecott placed the 'entire project on standby',[33] as it had failed to negotiate a mining lease, settle on likely government contributions to infrastructure, or a basis for government equity. It was also concerned about sovereign risk – as demonstrated by Chile's 1971 expropriation of mining activities – and PNG's shift towards self-government in 1973 meant there was pressure on the government not to overly concede fiscal concessions for Ok Tedi.

During the PNG self-government period, its parliament was required to articulate the principles that were to form the basis of a new minerals policy. These principles, reflecting strong nationalist sentiment, might be summarised as:

- Mineral exploitation is desirable not for any benefits that it might provide directly, but for the financial resources it could provide for the development in other sectors, and for the sake of greater independence from foreign aid;
- The mineral resources of PNG belong to the country's people, and the benefits of the exploitation of those resources must be made available to the people; and
- Foreign investors are needed to provide the management skills and risk capital to exploit mineral resources, and it is understood that they expect to receive a reasonable return on their investment, but any profits in excess of a reasonable return should accrue to PNG as taxation.[34]

---

[32]   Davies et al. (n 26) 798.

[33]   (n 26) 799.

[34]   Ross Garnaut and Anthony Clunies Ross, *Taxation of Mineral Rents* (Clarendon Press, 1983) 235.

The PNG Government converted these principles into policy, confirming that an Ok Tedi agreement would require private projects to be self-supporting with regard to infrastructure and to provide an option for the government to purchase equity. The 1974 draft agreement with Kennecott included a corporate tax at 33.3 per cent, 1.25 per cent *ad valorem* royalty; and a 15 per cent withholding tax on outward dividends. There was also an innovative resource rent tax, called an additional profits tax (APT), to apply over a threshold rate, but what constituted a 'reasonable rate of return' for the threshold could not be agreed upon.[35] Agreement over the choice of an independent party to adjudicate over disputes (for example, the Asian Development Bank) could not be resolved either, which foreshadowed a breakdown in contract negotiations.

Kennecott could not accede to the PNG Government's mineral policy, and in 1975 the company withdrew from the negotiations over Ok Tedi. Negotiations then commenced with several international companies, including BHP, which submitted a favourable proposal to the PNG Government, (after some persuasion by the Australian Government).[36] In 1976, after BHP finalized an acceptable full-scale feasibility study, it signed an agreement with the new Independent State of Papua New Guinea. The 1976 Ok Tedi Agreement represented a 'practical compromise between government and investor' that adhered to the host country's minerals policy.[37] The government could opt to provide facilities such as ports, roads, water and power, but the cost had to be borne by the TNC, allowing it to have priority use over such infrastructure. Third parties could have access to facilities on a user pays basis. As the host country, PNG could take over the infrastructure, but the TNC had the right to the depreciation.[38]

The tax concessions given to BHP included accelerated depreciation, no withholding tax on interest payments for external loans, and no export levies or excise. There were social provisions that required the company to employ PNG nationals, and requirements to use local services and supplies. There were provisions for an environmental management program and a 1.25 per cent *ad valorem* royalty. The PNG Government had the option of 20 per cent equity, either paid directly or through infrastructure;

---

[35]   Davies et al. (n 26) 800.
[36]   Colin Filer and Benedict Imbun, 'A Short Hisotry of Mineral Development Policies in Papua New Guinea, 1972–2002' in R.J. May (ed.), *Policy Making and Implementation: Studies from Papua New Guinea* (ANU E Press, 2009) 75–116.
[37]   Davies et al. (n 26) 806.
[38]   *Mining (Ok Tedi Agreement) Act of 1976* (PNG) clauses 14–22.

there was no provision for compulsory acquisition or carried interest.[39] An APT was designed and inserted into the agreement at an agreed threshold rate, and profits above it would trigger the APT. It is seen as a fair tax and meets the government's minerals policy principles.[40]

Ok Tedi is PNG's largest and longest operating mine and epitomises both the windfalls and challenges that mining brings to PNG. Social and environmental problems have plagued this mine and adversely affected PNG tax revenue. Tailings disposal by BHP during the 1980s and 1990s caused destruction of the Ok Tedi River ecology and thus impacted the livelihood of downstream villages.[41] In 2002, BHP, then the major shareholder and operator, divested its 63 per cent of Ok Tedi shares to a charitable trust, the PNG Sustainable Development Program (SDP) to help affected communities; the government owned 37 per cent of the shares. Remediation of the tailings-polluted land and ecosystem is ongoing and costly.[42] When BHP transferred its Ok Tedi shares to the SDP, the expectation was that the mine would close down within a relatively short time, but it has been kept in production.

After reviewing its fiscal regime, and in the wake of continuing low commodity prices, in 2003 the PNG Government introduced tax changes for the minerals sector, to encourage investment with minimal increases to taxes. Variations included changing income, royalty and withholding tax rates; introducing accelerated depreciation and double deductions for exploration; and abolishing the APT.[43] However it would seem the concessions were badly timed, for the mid-2000s progressed to a resource boom and high prices, which made Ok Tedi profitable again.

---

[39]   Davies et al. (n 26) 807. See also Mining (Ok Tedi Agreement) Act of 1976 (PNG).

[40]   Faber (n 25).

[41]   See e.g., 'Radio and Current Affairs Documentary: Ok Tedi', Radio National Australia, transcript <http://www.abc.net.au/radionational/programs/currentaffairs specials/ok-tedi/4434570>.

[42]   Craig Emerson and Diane Kraal, 'Papua New Guinea: Taxation Reform Options for the Petroleum, Gas and Mining Industries', paper presented at the National Taxation Research and Review Symposium, 29–31 May 2014, Port Moresby <http://www.nri.org.pg/research_divisions/economic_studies_division/ taxreview_symposium_index.htm>.

[43]   Benedict Imbun, 'Multinational Mining and Petroleum Companies Perceptions of the Policy Framework in Papua New Guinea' (2006) 21 *Pacific Economic Bulletin* 225, 238.

**3.5 Analysis**

In the immediate post-World War II period, exploration activities in PNG revealed proven and rich reserves of copper, along with its byproducts of gold and silver. At the time many developing countries, such as PNG, needed to attract external capital to build their infrastructure to extract minerals. Capital scarcity and a lack of local technical skills set the scene for competitive fiscal bidding, as was seen in the generous concessions in the 1967 Bougainville Copper Ltd Agreement. The Administration encouraged mining in pre-independence PNG. This met a strategic need for certain metals and resulted in a greater reliance on internally generated revenues and also created economic stimulation through export income.

As the various Southeast Asian and Pacific Island possessions gradually gained their independence, nationalistic sentiment peaked and affected fiscal negotiations by post-independence states, such as the adoption by Indonesia and Malaysia of oil production-sharing agreements. Likewise, in the hubris of Papua New Guinea's early independence days, its government displayed an ambivalent attitude toward foreign investment. The PNG Government's focused negotiations for the revised 1974 Bougainville Copper Agreement included provisions for an immediate imposition of income tax, a resource rent tax (the APT) – the first of its kind worldwide – and reduced tax concessions for capital expenditure. Government equity was introduced, along with the requirement for local employment and training, and an allowance for flexible provisions for changing circumstances.[44] The 1976 Ok Tedi Agreement was drafted using similar fiscal provisions.

After the first rush of nationalist sentiment following independence, the PNG Government's attitude changed, and it began to see foreign investment as a necessary part of the mix for a stable economy. The government's stance against foreign investment reversed after the Bougainville copper mine closure in 1989, for this venture had made a 20 per cent contribution to GDP.[45]

From a TNC perspective, the period from post-World War II to independence required changes in approach to the host country. Kennecott, the original Ok Tedi exploration company, was thwarted by its colonial mindset which intractably required a windfall return for its considerable risk, and it withdrew from the market. The successful replacement bidder, BHP, was more prepared to negotiate on fiscal issues. The BHP practical

---

[44] O'Faircheallaigh (n 24) 72.
[45] Filer and Imbun (n 36) 76.

compromise and final agreement came after a re-examination of the available geological data.[46] There was also a degree of acceptance that the old colonial order had changed and that this TNC was facing a strong and organised government negotiating team.[47]

Around the time of independence, sovereign risk became an issue for mining TNCs operating in PNG because of abrupt changes in the PNG government's fiscal and economic policy, as well as the new role of local landowner negotiations.[48] Other mining-related risks included debt servicing, Bougainville Copper, for instance, had an early A$250 million debt in 1972. The most significant operational risks were the environmental destruction caused by the BHP Ok Tedi tailings dam disaster of 1983–1984, and the violent civil uprising in Bougainville that led to the mine's closure in 1989.[49]

As for the oil industry in the post-war period, the risk of high exploration cost and low prospectivity continued. Security of operations became an issue, for example, in 1992 at the Kutubu oil project, central operations and infrastructure were enclosed in barbed wire compounds with 24-hour policing.

In 2013 the Fraser Institute petroleum industry survey ranked PNG at a lowly 125 out of 157 host jurisdictions.[50] It ranked PNG in the second-last quintile for regulatory risk (rule of law, environmental and labour regulations, transparency of legal system); and geopolitical risk (security of personnel and assets). However PNG was rated in the second quintile for industry's perceptions of its likelihood of 'transition to best practice.' Other TNC extractive industry risks of the time included fluctuating currency exchange rates; the future of Australian grants and aid to PNG; and the rate of domestic inflation in PNG.[51]

---

[46]    Davies et al., (n 26) 802, 805.
[47]    O'Faircheallaigh (n 24) 78–88.
[48]    As indicated by the Imbun (2006) study (n 43). The Additional Profits Tax (APT), as reintroduced in 2008, now only applies to designated gas projects.
[49]    Emma Gilberthorpe, 'Fasu Solidarity: A Case Study of Kin Networks, Land Tenure, and Oil Extraction in Kutubu, Papua New Guinea' (2007) 109 *American Anthropologist* 101; Bougainville Copper Pty Limited, *Kapa* (Bougainville Copper Pty Limited, 1972). See also <www.agsm.edu.au/bobm/teaching/BE/Cases_pdf/Ok_Tedi.pdf>.
[50]    Fraser Institute, *Global Survey of Petroleum 2013* (Fraser Institute, 2013).
[51]    Scott (n 3) 14.14.

*Table 13.1    PNG's Operating Mines and Leaseholders as of August 2014*

| Mineral Mine | Type | Leaseholder | TNC |
|---|---|---|---|
| Ok Tedi | Copper/gold/silver | PNG state | N |
| Lihir Newcrest | Gold/silver | Newcrest Mining | Y |
| Porgera | Gold/silver | Barrick Gold | Y |
| Tolukuma | Gold/silver | PNG state: Petromin PNG Holding | N |
| Morobe Mining Joint Ventures (MMJV) | Gold/silver | Newcrest (50%), Harmony Gold (50%) | Y |
| Simberi | Gold/silver | St. Barbara | N |
| Sinivit | Gold/silver | New Guinea Gold | Y |
| Ramu | Nickel/cobalt/chromium | (MCC) 70% + others | Y |

*Source:*   Emerson and Kraal (n 42).

## 4.   RECENT LESSONS

By mid-2014 PNG was host to eight large operating mines (extracting copper, gold and silver), mostly operated by TNCs, as shown in Table 13.1.

In 2012 PNG's Lihir mine, one of the world's largest known gold deposits, suspended operations briefly due to traditional landowner protests over inadequate benefits for Lihir Island indigenes. That same year, the Ramu nickel mine (in PNG's Madang province) faced ongoing court challenges by landowners over the practice of submarine tailings disposal.[52]

In 2013 Ok Tedi was nationalized when the PNG government cancelled the 63 per cent of Ok Tedi Mining shares that were previously owned by the SDP trust.[53] The PNG Government now owns all the Ok Tedi shares. The rushed passage of the legislation for the mine's nationalisation is seen as poor government minerals policy.[54] Nonetheless, as of 2014 Ok Tedi is PNG's largest mine and revenue earner.[55]

At Newcrest's Hidden Valley gold mine in Morobe province, social issues were raised again in March 2014, when workers' protests for better working

---

[52]   Mineral Resources Authority of Papua New Guinea (2012) *Mining and Exploration Bulletin* (July–December 1) 31; Emerson and Kraal (n 42).

[53]   *See, e.g.*, Liam Fox, 'PNG government Takes Control of OK Tedi Mine' ABC News (19 September 2013) <http://www.abc.net.au/news/2013-09-19/png-government-takes-control-of-png-ok-tedi-mine/4967004>.

[54]   *Mining (Ok Tedi Mine Continuation) (Ninth Supplement Agreement) (Amendment) Act 2013* (PNG).

[55]   See Fox (n 53).

conditions resulted in suspended production. It can be seen that – even after the civil uprising and military intervention in Bougainville, and the environmental concerns from the tailings pollution of the Ok Tedi river system – the same TNC mining risks, concerning landowner compensation, labour relations and environmental degradation, continue. The question of whether the 2014 commissioning of the liquefied natural gas venture (the LNG-PNG project) will reflect a reversal for TNCs' extraction activity risk in PNG, along with improved fiscal results for the host country, is covered in Section 6.

## 5.  INSTITUTIONAL INTEREST IN HOST COUNTRIES

Institutions such as the International Monetary Fund, international financial bodies, the global Extractive Industries Transparency Initiative and the Natural Resource Governance Institute exercise varying degree of influence in host countries that are classified as developing, as further discussed below.

### 5.1  International Monetary Fund

The International Monetary Fund (IMF) is a powerful institution which is enabled by wealthy subscriber governments to influence the economic policy of middle and low income countries. Its programs are about facilitating a liberal economic order in host countries. Criticisms of the IMF include promotion of subscriber governments' interests over those of targeted host countries; weak accountability within the IMF for its promoted programs; and inherent weaknesses in the discipline of economics and its methods for achieving improvements in host country governance.[56] Clements claims that IMF staff typically arrive at a host country 'with a standard template, insensitive to variations in economic conditions and political constraints'.[57] A country that joins the IMF must accept the principles and rules informed by free-market economics, which, according to Clements, are not varied enough to suit country-specific characteristics.

Commentary and key statistics from the IMF on PNG can be traced

---

[56]  Paul Clements, 'Multilateral Development Banks and the International Monetary Fund' in John Linarelli (ed.), *Research Handbook on Global Justice and International Economic Law* (Edward Elgar, 2013) 121–145.

[57]  Clements (n 56) 130.

back to at least 1989.[58] After the Bougainville mine closure, the late 1990s saw PNG's economy suffer large, adverse shocks related to a severe drought, the Asian economic crisis and falling export prices for copper and gold. Tax revenue fell by 4.5 per cent of GDP in 1998, led by large and natural declines in the petroleum sector. Despite cuts in capital spending and an increase in external grants, the PNG fiscal position shifted from near balance in 1997 to an overall deficit. The government deficit was financed mainly by recourse to central bank financing. The annual rate of inflation rose to around 20 per cent at the end of 1998 and early 1999. This fiscal deterioration in PNG prompted IMF intervention in March 2000 through the provision of a US$115 million standby credit facility.[59] The PNG government's associated letter of intent describes its economic policies for immediate implementation in the context of this financial support from the IMF.[60] Under Article IV of the IMF Articles of Agreement, each year bilateral discussions are required with members that receive financial assistance. PNG must submit a country report which covers key issues relating to economic stability; for example, policies and legislation for the sound fiscal management of resource extraction. This in turn impacts TNCs operating in PNG's extractive industry.

The IMF annual report includes commentary on the host country's general economic outlook and risks to economic growth, and the IMF's assessment of a host country's policies; for example resource revenue management, monetary and exchange rate macroeconomic policies, financial stability and associated structural reforms.[61] An adverse IMF report commentary can affect a host country's credit rating.

Scrutiny of PNG's economic policies by the IMF can be seen in the country reports from 2003 to the present.[62] Prior to these finance-triggered country reports, the IMF had been compiling background issues papers and statistics on PNG, most likely because of the country's strategic natural resources.

---

[58]   Christopher Browne and Douglas A. Scott, *Economic Development in Seven Pacific Island Countries* (International Monetary Fund, 1989).

[59]   Press Release No. 00/23, 29 March 2000, 'IMF Approves US$115 Million Stand-By Credit for Papua New Guinea' <http://www.imf.org/external/country/PNG/index.htm?pn=0>.

[60]   Letter of Intent from PNG Prime Minister M. Morauta and W. Kamit, Governor, Bank of Papua New Guinea, to S. Fischer IMF, 20 March 2000 <http://www.imf.org/external/country/PNG/index.htm?pn=0>.

[61]   E.g., *Papua New Guinea: Staff Report for the 2014 Article IV Consultation*, IMF Country Report December No. 14/325 (International Monetary Fund, 2014).

[62]   E.g., *Fiscal Regimes for Extractive Industries: Design and implementation* (International Monetary Fund, 2012).

## 5.2   International Financial Institutions

The World Bank is an institution allied with the objectives of the IMF. The World Bank is one of a range of international financial institutions (IFIs) that typically provide long-term development loans to host countries at terms lower than private market rates. In the 1960s, the World Bank recommended fiscal adjustments to promote PNG's agriculture and forestry exports, but it excluded consideration of the social consequences for the indigenes living in the local area.[63] Another class of international financial institution is the multilateral development bank (MDB) that is based on the World Bank model. The funds for MDB loans come from wealthy governments, which can influence lending policy. Whereas the IMF might provide interim funds, MDB loans to host countries may be long term, and normally provided because of a host county's lack of foreign exchange. Most MDB loans are for a specific project that fits long-term economic policy objectives. In some cases MDBs have requested host countries to introduce free market reforms, called structural adjustment programs.[64]

The Asian Development Bank (ADB) was established in 1964 and focuses on Asia and the Pacific. This MDB uses policy dialogue, loans, equity investments, grants and technical assistance to help developing host countries.[65] Papua New Guinea has been a member of the ADB since 1971 and has received loans on several occasions. For instance, it has sought funds for technical assistance to find new ways for the hydrocarbons sector to deal with landowner issues.[66] In 2010 PNG agreed on a new 'country partnership strategy' with the ADB. The strategy prioritises transport infrastructure and private sector development, which may affect TNCs in the petroleum and mining sectors. Under an ADB grant for PNG health and social protection initiatives, a TNC subsidiary, Oil Search (PNG) Ltd, was contracted for its expertise in its locale of operations.[67]

---

[63]   World Bank, *The Economic Development of Papua New Guinea* (Johns Hopkins Press, 1965); O'Faircheallaigh (n 24) 70. For some criticisms of World Bank and IMF programs see Clements (n 56) 123–127; Malcolm Fraser, *Dangerous Allies* (Melbourne University Press, 2014) 213–214.

[64]   Clements (n 56) 124–125.

[65]   Asian Development Bank, 'Asian Development Bank and Papua New Guinea: Fact Sheet', *Country Fact Sheets*, April 2014.

[66]   Filer and Imbun (n 36) 100, citing Talor and Wimp (1997).

[67]   PNG is the largest public-sector borrower in the Pacific region. ADB lending to PNG has increased substantially since 2007, and ADB is now PNG's second-largest development partner. ADB's active portfolio totals $1.1 billion, including 22 ongoing loans for 11 projects; eight grants, including one Asian Development Fund grant project; nine technical assistance projects; and two private sector loan

## 5.3   The Extractive Industries Transparency Initiative

From 2002 world mineral prices rapidly increased, driven by the demand for raw materials from China and other emerging economies. However many resource-rich but developing economies were still in poverty, despite the consistently strong demand for their natural resources. The Extractive Industries Transparency Initiative (EITI) was launched in 2002 to fight corruption, a primary cause of misallocation of tax revenue in host countries. One aim is to reduce opportunities for corruption by improving governance over company reporting of extractive industry revenues and government recording of tax expenditure. The EITI is a global coalition of governments, companies and civil society that work together to improve openness and accountable management of revenues from natural resources. All three sectors nominate representatives to a 'multi-stakeholder group' for a member country. The EITI's project finances come from donor countries that deposit monies into a trust fund managed by the World Bank. The trust monies are used for technical and financial assistance for EITI member countries.[68] There are currently 46 countries that are either EITI compliant or undertaking candidature.[69]

Papua New Guinea was admitted as an EITI candidate country in March 2014 and its multi-stakeholder group published its first activity report in 2015.[70] According to the EITI standard, which is the authoritative source on how countries might implement the initiative, the purpose of the first EITI Report is for citizens to trace the value of their country's natural resources from production all the way into the government's national accounts.[71] Validation of the PNG EITI Report will start within three years (2017) and requires an external, independent evaluation mechanism, undertaken by an accredited validator procured by the EITI International Secretariat.

---

and equity operations. See the ADB's PNG Fact Sheet <http://www.adb.org/publications/papua-new-guinea-fact-sheet April 2014>.

[68]   See World Bank and donor trust fund, <http://web.worldbank.org/WBSITE/EXTERNAL/TOPICS/EXTOGMC/EXTEXTINDTRAINI/0,contentMDK:21665712~menuPK:3634790~pagePK:64168445~piPK:64168309~theSitePK:3634715,00.html>. For current EITI supporting countries, see <http://eiti.org/supporters/countries>.

[69]   See EITI countries <http://eiti.org/countries>.

[70]   See EITI link for PNG <http://eiti.org/papua-new-guinea> and <http://www.treasury.gov.pg/html/misc/PNGEITI.htm>.

[71]   See EITI standard <http://eiti.org/document/standard>.

### 5.4    Natural Resource Governance Institute

The Natural Resource Governance Institute (NRGI) aims to facilitate the benefits of a country's endowments of oil, gas and minerals to a host country's constituents. Its work is funded by philanthropic organizations and wealthy national governments. The NRGI uses technical advice, advocacy, applied research, policy analysis, and capacity development to achieve its goals. The NRGI is underpinned by its Natural Resource Charter, which is concerned with applying initiatives such as the Resource Governance Index.

The Natural Resource Charter is a set of principles to guide governments and societies in their use of natural resources in achieving sustained returns for their country's citizens.[72] The Charter's 12 principles cover domestic foundations for resource governance, exploration and licence allocation, taxation, revenue volatility and distribution; sustainability for both government and the private sector; and the role of TNCs. Charter expectations of the TNC role go beyond profits and obligations to shareholders, to include economic, environmental and social standards. The Resource Governance Index measures the quality of governance in the oil, gas and mining sector for 58 countries.[73]

In the 2013 Resource Governance Index, PNG received a 'weak' score of 43, ranking 39th. A low score is interpreted as a reflection of critical gaps in government management across most aspects of the extractive industry sector, including its institutional and legal setting, reporting practices, safeguards and quality controls, and providing an enabling environment. The troubled history of the PNG mining industry, illustrated by the Ok Tedi and Bougainville mining operations and decades of poor management, has led to severe environmental damage and social upheaval. As a result of PNG's 2014 acceptance as an EITI candidate with its corresponding membership requirements, and its first report submitted in 2015, an improvement is expected in its Resource Governance Index score in the future.

### 5.5    Commentary

Developing countries quite rightly assert their sovereign status and may look upon the IMF, international financial institutions, the EITI and the

---

[72]    Natural Resource Governance Institute, *Natural Resource Charter* (Natural Resource Governance Institute, 2nd ed, 2013). See <http://www.naturalresourcecharter.org/>.

[73]    Revenue Watch Institute, *Resource Governance Index* (Natural Resource Governance Institute, 2013). See <http://www.resourcegovernance.org/rgi>.

NRGI initiatives as unwelcome interventions that cannot be uncoupled from financial aid. The lack of finesse in economic methodologies, and low institutional empathy – both perceived and real – for cultural and social differences between target countries have given rise to criticisms. Time will tell whether these institutions have raised the economic scorecard of PNG's new liquefied natural gas (LNG) project over its expected operational life of 20 years.[74]

## 6. THE LIQUEFIED NATURAL GAS PROJECT

The development of natural gas reserves in PNG's Southern Highlands and Western Province gas fields has captured the attention of the international petroleum and gas industry. There are now over 70 live petroleum prospecting licences covering most prospective areas in PNG.[75] Production of natural gas for the PNG-LNG project began in 2014. It involves the extraction and processing of gas through a conditioning plant, then transmission by pipeline to a liquefaction plant at Port Moresby for export as liquefied natural gas (LNG). The initial success to date of the PNG-LNG project encouraged further exploration for natural gas reserves.[76] However the rapid drop in prices since mid-2014, has impacted the profitability of the project. The project co-venture partners are Esso Highlands Ltd (a subsidiary of ExxonMobil), Oil Search Ltd, Santos Ltd and JX Nippon Oil and Gas Exploration. These entities, which are all TNCs, hold 80 per cent of the equity in the project.[77]

### 6.1 Risk Analysis

From a TNC risk perspective, PNG's natural gas sector has good resource prospectivity and acceptable debt-to-equity ratio legislation.[78] The inflow

---

[74]  See <http://www.resourcegovernance.org/countries/asia-pacific/papua-new-guinea/overview>.

[75]  PNG Chamber of Mines and Petroleum, 'Petroleum in PNG', 2014.

[76]  Emerson and Kraal (n 42).

[77]  Esso Highlands Ltd (33.2%) the operator, a subsidiary of ExxonMobil; Santos Ltd (13.5%), Oil Search Ltd (29%), Nippon Oil (4.7%); PNG State (16.6%) through state owned company, National Petroleum Company of PNG Limited; Mineral Resources Development Company Limited (2.8%) PNG landowners; and the state owned Petromin PNG Holdings Limited (0.2%). See <http://pngchamberminpet.com.pg/petroleum-in-png/>.

[78]  Where the debt to a taxpayer in relation to a research project exceeds 300% of the equity of the taxpayer, then the deduction for interest is limited.

from foreign investors has been strong, as evidenced by the application of US$20 billion to construction costs for the project.[79] The risk concerning clarity on rule of law, which is aligned with free markets and trade, is important to TNCs, and while a standard resource development agreement comes under PNG jurisdiction, it overrides legislation affecting natural resources – which may affect potential investor interest.[80] Questions also arise about whether the success of the PNG-LNG project reflects other risk mitigation initiatives, such as social and environment issues, or changes in regulatory controls. Current PNG social issues are unchanged and include those of indigene resettlement, claims for compensation and mineral royalties, and security of project personnel. Unemployment has grown due to redundancies linked to the completion of the PNG-LNG construction phase, compounding other social issues.[81] Hydrocarbon TNCs have some environmental programs that cover flora and fauna, reflecting the lower risk compared with the mining industry.[82] The Oil and Gas Act of 1998 (PNG), which regulates the industry, has not been amended since 2006; from a TNC perspective this stability is considered as 'low' regulatory risk.

In the period leading up to the 2014 export of LNG, there was an external institutional push on the PNG Government to apply the LNG project proceeds to a sovereign wealth fund (SWF) to stabilize the local currency and to pay for much-needed development infrastructure. However, and quite unexpectedly, the PNG Government made arrangements to apply its future receipts from the LNG project to repay a loan for the purchase of shares in Oil Search Ltd.[83] The SWF was finally established in July 2015, and the National Budget 2016 noted the expectation that revenues will be paid into the SWF in 2016.

PNG Government shareholding in extractive industry projects goes back to 1974 when the Bougainville Copper Agreement provided for government equity at 20 per cent par value. This gave the aspirant state a sense of participating in its mineral sector. In 2013 the PNG Government

---

[79]    Ibid.

[80]    See ExxonMobil statement on free markets, free trade and the rule of law: <http://corporate.exxonmobil.com/en/current-issues/energy-policy>. For further information on standard resource development agreements see Emerson and Kraal (n 42).

[81]    Emerson and Kraali (n 42). See also ExxonMobil PNG Limited 2013, 'Principles on Security and Human Rights'; and 'Resettlement Implementation Process' <http://pnglng.com/project/>.

[82]    See PNG-LNG environmental programs <http://pnglng.com/commitment/environment/case-studies>.

[83]    See <http://www.abc.net.au/news/2014-05-22/png-gas-gamble-as-the-lng-starts-to-flow/5471230>.

legislated for its 100 per cent equity interest the Ok Tedi copper mine, a rushed exercise that caused consternation. As for the PNG-LNG project, the PNG state venture partners borrowed funds to gain a direct interest of 19.6 per cent. The PNG wholly owned National Petroleum Company of PNG then borrowed AU$1.2 billion under a commercial arrangement to pay for 10 per cent of Oil Search shares.

There are a range of concerns about government equity in commercial projects generally. Such equity requires a diversion of public funds from social and public infrastructure, health and education projects. A developing host government may not possess the high level of technical expertise required for ongoing monitoring of the investment. Conflicts of interest arise with the government being both regulator and promoter of an industry. Equity holdings expose the government to risk, a vital issue for developing-country host governments with limited funds.

From the TNC perspective, the fact that a government can hold options for equity over a long period could be seen as an unfair advantage over potential private shareholders and can reduce the incentive to invest.[84] A PNG resource development agreement may include a government equity option to be exercised at full market value or at a discount. If the latter, then a TNC must look to negotiate tax concessions to cover the sunk costs of exploration, and the uncertainty of such an option poses yet another risk. The PNG Government has not contributed to exploration costs in the PNG-LNG project. TNCs have shown a preference for host country governments having equity participation on 'commercial terms' rather than a 'carried interest', as the latter negatively affects the attractiveness of a host country as an investment destination.

## 7.  TAX REFORM IN PNG

In any country, tax reform is generally claimed by investors to be a potential 'sovereign risk'. In 2013 the PNG Government announced its commitment to a fiscal review including petroleum, gas and mining taxation reform options. A Taxation Review Committee was established and its first initiative was a general public or 'Blue Sky' consultation process, whereby institutions, investors and community stakeholders were invited to formally submit their perspectives on broad directions for reform and key priority areas. Public forums included a National Research Institute of Papua

---

[84]  For a discussion on government equity see Tilton, Millett and Ward (n 1) 43–44.

New Guinea-sponsored 'Taxation Research and Review Symposium' in May 2014.[85] The second stage, also in 2014, involved the Taxation Review Committee's issuing papers on specific taxation areas to promote more targeted discussion and debate, such as their mining and petroleum studies.[86] For example, ExxonMobil submitted a response with a strong call for 'no change' to the existing PNG-LNG fiscal arrangements.[87]

The third tax reform stage included further debate in areas such as state equity participation in mining and petroleum projects, and property taxation. The Taxation Review Committee presented its Final Report in October 2015 to the PNG Government. The report drew on all stages of the review and under consideration by the Government for action in 2016. The Taxation Review's Final Report was noted in the National Budget 2016. The outcome of the PNG tax review was closely followed by stakeholders, with the consultation process seen to display all the elements of reasonable stakeholder engagement. Unless there are major retrospective changes in the fiscal regime, the issue of sovereign risk from a TNC perspective is unlikely. The unforeseen fall in prices is the key risk being addressed.

Given PNG's past record of poor fiscal outcomes and operational disasters from copper and gold mining,[88] the question arises about whether tax reform will improve PNG tax revenues – in the currently difficult time of low commodity prices. The commonly used measure of 'tax effort', the difference between predicted and actual tax take, should be given consideration.[89] In any country revenue performance can be improved by a few percentage points of GDP, and it would seem that sufficient institutional support for PNG is in place to progress tax reform and governance initiatives.[90]

---

[85]   See National Research Institute of PNG tax reform research papers <http://www.nri.org.pg/research_divisions/economic_studies_division/taxreview_symposium_index.htm>.

[86]   Taxation Review Committee, 'Papua New Guinea Taxation Review for 2013–2015. Issues Paper No. 1: Mining and petroleum taxation' (PNG Government, March 2014).

[87]   Submission by ExxonMobil PNG Pty Ltd to the PNG Taxation Review Committee, 30 May 2014, <http://taxreview.gov.pg/submissions/>.

[88]   IMF, *Papua New Guinea: Staff Report for the 2013 Article IV Consultation*, IMF Country Report December No. 13/339 (International Monetary Fund, 2013) 61, 68.

[89]   Mick Moore, 'Obstacles to Increasing Tax Revenues in Low Income Countries' (2013) 7, International Centre for Tax and Development Working Paper No. 15.

[90]   Basu et al. (n 1) 3.

# 8.   CONCLUSION

In colonial times, risk factors for mining companies included infrastructure construction and extraction costs, with financing mainly through equity. The key risk factor for oil companies, some of which were the precursors to today's TNCs, was the cost of exploration

In the post-World War II period, the mining industry required intensive extraction techniques, and capital scarcity set the scene for Southeast Asian and Pacific Island nations' competitive fiscal bidding, a consequence of which was the generous concessions for PNG copper mining made in 1967. Nationalistic sentiment peaked and affected fiscal negotiations by many post-independence states. In the hubris of PNG's early independence, the government displayed an ambivalent attitude toward foreign investment. For the new 1974 Bougainville Copper Agreement, the government's focused negotiations included provisions for an immediate imposition of income tax, a unique resource rent tax (the APT) and reduced tax concessions for capital expenditure. Government equity was introduced along with the requirement of local employment and training and for flexibility in provisions, to allow for changing circumstances. The 1976 Ok Tedi Agreement was cast with similar fiscal provisions. The PNG Government attitude changed after the 1989 events on Bougainville, and it began to be more accommodating toward foreign investment and to accept their presence as a necessary part of a stabilized economy.

From a TNC perspective, PNG independence required a new approach to the host country. The old colonial mindset demanded a high return for the miners' considerable risk. As illustrated in the finalization of the 1976 Ok Tedi agreement, the winning bidder had to be more prepared to negotiate on fiscal issues. Thus, around the independence period, as a consequence of abrupt and 'aggressive' changes in PNG governmental fiscal and economic policy, sovereign risk became an issue for mining TNCs operating in PNG. Other mining risks of the time included debt servicing, such as Bougainville Copper's early A$250 million debt. A most significant operational risk was the remediation required for the environmental destruction caused by BHP's Ok Tedi mining activities and the social backlash that led to the Bougainville mine closure in 1989.

As for the oil industry, the immediate post-World War II period saw continued risk in terms of high exploration cost and low prospectivity. In 1992 oil was finally produced from the Kutubu oil project, and security of operations became a key risk issue.

The newest LNG project indicates that PNG's natural gas has good resource prospectivity and acceptable debt-to-equity ratio legislative requirements. Risks connected to PNG social issues are unchanged and include those of indigene resettlement, claims for both compensation and mineral royalties, post-construction unemployment and the security of project personnel. Government equity in commercial projects remains controversial. TNCs tend to prefer government equity participation on 'commercial terms' rather than a 'carried interest'. For now, price has emerged as the key risk.

Developing countries quite rightly assert their sovereign status and may look upon the institutional initiatives from the IMF, MDBs, the EITI and the NRGI as unwelcome interventions. The lack of finesse in economic methodologies, and the low institutional empathy for cultural and social differences between target countries, have both given rise to criticism. These institutions share the common economic goal of improved revenue performance by target countries. PNG's tax reform process has had reasonably conservative aims and, as yet, no adverse reports of TNC concerns about sovereign risk.

The extractive industry is cyclical, with prices rising and falling according to demand and supply. Prospectivity for natural resources is generally uncertain, and exploration costs can be high, varying between the hydrocarbon and mining industries. There are many inherent risks for TNCs in the extractive industry, including price, fiscal regime, sovereign risk, concerns with legislated debt-to-equity ratios, security of operations, issues surrounding corruption, environmental and social concerns, infrastructure, rule of law and labour. Although this chapter focused upon the specific TNC experiences in PNG, it is also provides insights for TNCs operating in countries with a similar economic profile and lessons for other extractive industry TNCs, and developing-country host governments.

# Index